Brexit and the Digital Single Market

Brexit and the Digital Single Market

ALISON HARCOURT

OXFORD
UNIVERSITY PRESS

OXFORD
UNIVERSITY PRESS

Great Clarendon Street, Oxford, OX2 6DP,
United Kingdom

Oxford University Press is a department of the University of Oxford.
It furthers the University's objective of excellence in research, scholarship,
and education by publishing worldwide. Oxford is a registered trade mark of
Oxford University Press in the UK and in certain other countries

First Edition published in 2023

Published in the United States of America by Oxford University Press
198 Madison Avenue, New York, NY 10016, United States of America

British Library Cataloguing in Publication Data

Data available

Library of Congress Control Number: 2023932761

ISBN 978–0–19–289937–8

DOI: 10.1093/oso/9780192899378.001.0001

Printed and bound by
CPI Group (UK) Ltd, Croydon, CR0 4YY

Acknowledgements

I would like to thank the many colleagues, organisations, and institutions that facilitated the production of this book. First, I would like to thank Alex Flach at Oxford University Press for his encouragement and commitment to the monograph, my project editors Kezia Johnson and Matthew Williams, and also Rachel Mullaly, Fiona Blee, and Jo Dymond. I would also like to thank the external reviewers for their perceptive comments and recommendations.

Second, I thank the Economic and Social Research Council (ESRC) which funded my project, 'The UK Communications Industries: The Impact of a Proposed UK Brexit from the EU' under the 'UK in a Changing Europe' programme. I am thankful to all of those who participated in ESRC and subsequent conferences and seminars related to the book. I am grateful to Francesca Farmer at the University of Exeter for the organisation of events and technical support for online surveys. I acknowledge the administrative staff members at the University of Exeter for their support and Jane Tanner for maintaining the ESRC project and the Centre for European Governance website.

Third, I greatly appreciate the many discussions and insights from interviewees, policy experts, and representatives from government, the civil service, and civil society for their time and valuable expertise. I have also benefitted greatly over the years from my participation in the South West Data Protection and Privacy Network run by Nuria Pastor and Alison Gane. I would also like to thank Venice International University and the Department of Media and Communications at the London School of Economics and Political Science for hosting me as visiting professor in 2021 and 2022, respectively. Finally, I would like to thank my husband and daughters for their support.

Contents

Table of Cases

EU Legislation

Table of National Legislations

List of Abbreviations

ACE	Arts Council England
ACS	Artists' Collecting Society
ADR	alternative dispute resolution
ADSL	Asymmetric Digital Subscriber Line
AETN	Arts and Entertainment (A&E) Television Networks
AG	Aktiengesellschaft
AgID	Agenzia per l'Italia Digitale
AI	artificial intelligence
AIPCE	Alliance of Independent Press Councils of Europe
ALCS	Authors' Licensing and Collecting Society
ALMR	Association of Licensed Multiple Retailers
ALTAI	Assessment List for Trustworthy Artificial Intelligence
AMC	American Multi-Cinema
API	application programming interface
APPG	All-Party Parliamentary Group
ARCOM	Autorité de régulation de la communication audiovisuelle et numérique
ART	asset-referenced token
ASA	Advertising Standards Authority
AT&T	American Telephone and Telegraph
AU	African Union
AVMSD	Audiovisual Media Services Directive
AWS	Amazon Web Services
B2B	business-to-business sharing
B2C	business to consumer
BBC	British Broadcasting Corporation
BDB	British Digital Broadcasting
BECTU	Broadcasting, Entertainment, Communications and Theatre Union
BEIS	Department for Business, Energy and Industrial Strategy
BEPS	Base Erosion and Profit Shifting
BEREC	Body of European Regulators for Electronic Communications
BEUC	Bureau Européen des Unions de Consommateurs
BIC	Bank Identification Code
BLM	Bavarian media authority
BNPL	buy now pay later
BoE	Bank of England
BSG	Broadband Stakeholder Group
BSI	British Standards Institute
BT	British Telecommunications

BVerfG	Bundesverfassungsgericht
CAA	Civil Aviation Authority
CAT	Competition Appeal Tribunal
CBDC	central bank digital currency
CBI	Confederation of British Industry
CCPs	central counterparties
CDPA	Copyright, Designs and Patents Act
CE	Conformité Européene
CEC	Commission of the European Communities
CEF	Connecting Europe Facility
CEN	Comité Européen de Normalisation
CENELEC	European Committee for Electrotechnical Standardization
CEPT	Conférence Européenne des Administrations des Postes et des Télécommunications
CETA	EU–Canada Comprehensive Trade and Economic Agreement
CFIT	Centre for Finance, Innovation and Technology
CISAC	International Confederation of Societies of Authors and Composers
CISPE	Cloud Infrastructure Services Providers in Europe
CMA	Competition and Market Authority
CMO	Collective Management Organisation
CNBC	Consumer News and Business Channel
CNN	Cable News Network
COBA	Commercial Broadcasters Association
COO	Country of Origin
COREPER	Committee of Permanent Representatives in the European Union
CPTPP	Progressive Agreement for Trans-Pacific Partnership
CRA	Consumer Rights Act
CRD	Consumer Rights Directive
CRR	Capital Requirement Regulation
CSAM	child sexual abuse material
CSDs	central securities depositories
CTSI	Chartered Trading Standards Institute
DACS	Design and Artists Copyright Society
DCMS	Department for Digital, Culture, Media and Sport
DG	Directorate-General
DG Comm	Directorate-General for Communication
DG Competition	Directorate-General for Competition
DG Connect	Directorate-General for Communications Network, Content and Technology
DG INFSO	Directorate-General Information Society and Media
DiMA	Digital and Media Association
DIT	Department for International Trade
DIY	do it yourself
DLT	distributed ledger technology
DMU	Digital Markets Unit

DNS4EU	Domain Name System for the European Union
DORA	Digital Operational Resilience Act
DPA	Data Protection Authority
DPDI	Data Protection and Digital Information Bill
DPIA	Data Protection Impact Assessment
DP WP	Data Protection Working Party
DSA	Digital Services Act
DSIs	European Digital Service Infrastructures
DSM	Digital Single Market
DST	digital services tax
DT	digital television
DTAS	digital television additional services
DTPS	Digital Television Programme Services
DTT	digital terrestrial television
DVB-T	digital video broadcasting terrestrial
EAAA	European Association of Advertising Agencies
EAIB	European Artificial Intelligence Board
EAO	European Audiovisual Observatory
EAS	External Action Service
EASA	European Advertising Standards Alliance
EBA	European Banking Authority
EBDS	European Board for Digital Services
EBMS	European Board for Media Services
EBU	European Broadcasting Union
EC	European Commission
ECC	European Consumer Centre
ECHR	European Convention on Human Rights
ECJ	European Court of Justice
ECN	European Competition Network
ECNE	European Cooperation Network on Elections
ECTA	European Centre for Algorithmic Transparency
ECTT	European Convention on Transfrontier Television
EDAP	European Democracy Action Plan
EDiMA	European Digital and Media Association
EDMO	European Digital Media Observatory
EDPB	European Data Protection Board
EDPS	European Data Protection Supervisor
EEA	European Economic Area
EEAS	European External Action Service
EEC	European Economic Community
EFIP	European Forum for Innovation in Payments
EFTA	European Free Trade Association
eIDAS	Electronic Identification
EIU	Economist Intelligence Unit
ELU	Export Licensing Unit

EMC	electromagnetic compatibility
EMFA	European Media Freedom Act
EMI	Electric and Musical Industries
EMIR	European Market Infrastructure Regulation
EORI	Economic Operators Registration and Identification
EP	European Parliament
EPC	European Payment Council
EPG	Electronic Programme Guide
EPRA	European Platform of Regulatory Authorities
ERG	European Regulators Group
ERGA	European Regulators Group for Audiovisual Media Service
ERPB	Euro Retail Payments Board
ESA	European Supervisory Authority
ESDIS	Employment and Social Dimension of the Information Society
ESMA	European Securities and Markets Authority
ESO	European Standards Organisation
ESS	Export Support Service
ETSI	European Telecommunications Standards Institute
EU	European Union
EurID	European Registry for Internet Domains
EurOMo	Euromedia Ownership Monitor
EVP	executive vice-president
EWM	Edinburgh Woollen Mill
FAPL	Football Association Premier League
FATF	Financial Action Task Force
FCA	Financial Conduct Authority
FCCB	Foundation for Consumer Complaints Board
FIFA	Federation Internationale de Football Association
FMI	financial market infrastructure
FSM	financial services and markets
FTA	free-trade agreement
G20	Group of Twenty
GATS	General Agreement on Trade in Services
GATT	General Agreement on Tariffs and Trade
GBER	General Block Exemption Regulation
GCC	Gulf Cooperation Council
GDP	gross domestic product
GDPR	General Data Protection Regulation
GEMA	Gesellschaft für musikalische Aufführungs- und mechanische Vervielfältigungsrechte
GIF	Graphic Interchange Format
GmbH	Gesellschaft mit beschränkter Haftung
GSM	Global System for Mobile communication
GSP	Generalised Scheme of Preferences
HBO	Home Box Office

HLEG	High-Level Expert Group
HLG	High-Level Group
HMG	Holland Media Group
HMRC	His Majesty's Revenue & Customs
ICA	Institute of Contemporary Arts
ICE	International Copyright Enterprise
ICN	International Competition Network
ICO	Information Commissioner's Office
ICRT	International Communications Round Table
ICT	information communications technology
IDFA	identifier for advertisers
IDTA	International Data Transfer Agreement
IF	inclusive framework
IMRG	Interactive Media in Retail Group
IND	Network against Disinformation
IoT	Internet of Things
IP	intellectual property
IPCEI	Important Projects of Common European Interest
IPO	Intellectual Property Office
IPRED	Intellectual Property Rights Enforcement Directive
IPTV	internet protocol television
IRG	Independent Regulators Group
ISP	internet service provider
ITC	Independent Television Commission
ITU	International Telecommunication Union
ITV	Independent Television
JHA	Justice and Home Affairs
KCOM	Kingston Communications
KIDs	Key Information Documents
KO	Konsumentombudsmannen
KPMG	Klynveld Peat Marwick Goerdeler
LCH	London Clearing House
MCI	Microwave Communications Inc.
MCPS	Mechanical Copyright Protection Society
MEP	Member of the European Parliament
MFN	Most Favored Nation
MiCA	markets in crypto-assets
MiFID	Markets in Financial Instruments Directive
MiFIR	Markets in Financial Instruments Regulation
MNEs	multinational enterprises
MODINIS	monitoring of eEurope, dissemination of good practices and the improvement of network and information security
MoU	memorandum of understanding
MP	Member of Parliament
MS	multiple streams

NESTA	National Endowment for Science, Technology and the Arts
NetzDG	Netzwerkdurchsetzungsgesetz
NFC	near-field communication
NGA	next-generation access
NHS	National Health Service
NIS	Information Security Directive
NLF	New Legislative Framework
NMPA	National Music Publishers Association
NRA	national regulatory authority
NSI	National Security and Investment Act
OAI	Office for Artificial Intelligence
OAS	Organization of American States
OCA	online choice architecture
ODPS	On-Demand Programmes Service
ODR	Online Dispute Resolution network
OECD	Organisation for Economic Co-operation and Development
Ofcom	Office of Communications
Ofgem	Office of Gas and Electricity Markets
OFT	Office of Fair Trading
OFTEL	Office of Telecommunications
OIM	Office for the Internal Market
ONP	Open Network Provision
ONS	Office for National Statistics
OSCE	Organization for Security and Co-operation in Europe
OTC	over-the-counter
OTT	over-the-top
P2B	platform to business
PACT	Producers Alliance for Cinema and Television
PID	Price Indication Directive
PIIN	Public Interest Intervention Notice
PJCC	Police and Judicial Co-operation in Criminal Matters
POS	provision of services
PRIIPs	packaged retail and insurance-based investment products
PRS	Performing Rights Society
PSB	public service broadcaster
PSD	Payment Services Directive
QMV	Qualified Majority Voting
R&D	research and development
RAI	Radiotelevisione italiana
RAN	Radicalisation Awareness Network
RAS	Rapid Alert System
REFIT	Regulatory Fitness and Performance
REUL	Retained EU Law
RoO	rules on origin
ROPA	Record of Processing Activity

RPPD	Record of Processing of Personal Data
RSB	Regulatory Scrutiny Board
RSPG	Radio Spectrum Policy Group
RSPP	Radio Spectrum Policy Programme
RTÉ	Regulatory Fitness and Performance
RTI	Rete Televisiva Italiana
RTP	Rádio e Televisão de Portugal
RTVE	Radiotelevisión Española
SAAP	state aid action plan
SACEM	Société des Auteurs, Compositeurs et Éditeurs de Musique
SatCab	satellite and cable
SCBG	Satellite and Cable Broadcasters' Group
SCCs	standard contractual clauses
SCL	Strategic Communications Laboratories
SDNs	services digital networks
SEA	Single European Act
SEPA	Single Euro Payments Area
SGEI	Services of General Interest
SLAPP	strategic lawsuits against public participation
SME	small or medium-sized enterprise
SMP	significant market power
SMS	strategic market status
SOMA	Social Observatory for Disinformation and Social Media Analysis
SoS	Secretary of State
STIM	Svenska Tonsättares Internationella Musikbyrå
SUISA	SUISse Auteurs
TBE	telecommunications, broadcasting and electronic
TCA	Trade and Cooperation Agreement
TCM	Turner Classic Movies
TDM	text and data mining
TEC	Treaty establishing the European Community
TEU	Treaty on the European Union
TF1	Télévision Française 1
TFEU	Treaty on the Functioning of the European Union
TG4	Teilifís na Gaeilge
TIA	Transfer Impact Assessment
TNT	Turner Network Television
TRIPS	Trade-Related Aspects of Intellectual Property Rights
TWF	Television Without Frontiers
UAE	United Arab Emirates
UCPD	Unfair Commercial Practices Directive
UCTD	Unfair Contract Terms Directive
UEFA	Union of European Football Associations
UK	United Kingdom
UKCA	UK Conformity Assessed

UKie	UK Interactive Entertainment body
UNCTAD	United Nations Conference on Trade and Development
UNESCO	United Nations Educational, Scientific and Cultural Organization
UPS	United Parcel Service
USA	United States of America
VAT	value-added tax
VBER	Vertical Block Exemption Regulation
VGTR	video games tax relief
VLOPs	very large online platforms
VLOSEs	very large online search engines
VOD	video on demand
VoIP	Voice over Internet Protocol
VPRT	Verband Privater Rundfunk und Telekommunikation
VRT	Vlaamse Radio- en Televisieomroeporganisatie
VSP	video-sharing platforms
VTM	Vlaamse Televisie Maatschappij
VZBV	Verbraucherzentrale Bundesverband
WCT	WIPO Copyright Treaty
WIPO	World Intellectual Property Organization
WPPT	WIPO Performances and Phonograms Treaty
WRC	World Radiocommunication Conference
WTO	World Trade Organization
ZTE	Zhong Xing Telecommunication Equipment

1
Brexit and the Digital Single Market

Introduction

The Digital Single Market (DSM) 2014–19 comprised the largest component of the EU's Single Market programme. It contained a considerable number of Directives, Regulations, and instruments aimed at facilitating cross-border digital services. The DSM was important for the UK given that one-fifth of service exports stem from the digital sector and the EU continues to represent the UK's main export market. Accordingly, the UK played an important historic role in DSM development, having substantial input in policy formulation during its EU membership.

Involvement in the DSM was lucrative for the UK's digital economy. The UK, and London in particular, established itself as a European hub for digital entertainment services, online banking and shopping, gaming, FinTech, and Big Data services. The UK's digital economy was worth £268 billion in 2018 with an annual growth rate of 24.1 per cent, accounting for 14.6 per cent of the UK economy, according to the Department for Digital, Culture, Media and Sport (DCMS, 2021b). The DCMS estimated that the sector accounted for £62.9 billion of service exports, comprising 19.8 per cent of total UK service exports in 2019.[1] The UK had the leading audio-visual market in the EU with 21 per cent of overall revenue (Blázquez et al., 2018: 3). Film production counted for 16 per cent of all films produced within the EU, representing a trade surplus (EAO, 2018: 6). In 2018, the UK had the fifth largest videogame market globally after China, the USA, Japan, and Germany, with 45 per cent of turnover coming from international sales[2] (Creative Industries Council, 2021). The UK was the most popular country for cross-border online shoppers from Europe until 2022 (IMRG, 2021). Overall, the DCMS estimated that earnings in the digital sector saw the highest increases in 2019 to 2020 of 17.8 per cent and 14.6 per cent, respectively (DCMS, 2021). However, this dropped to only 5.3 per cent growth in 2021 (DCMS, 2022) and estimated 0.7 per cent growth to June 2022 after the end of the transition period. Overall, the UK economy fell by 0.1 per cent in the same period.[3]

[1] This estimate, which excludes tourism, was down from 21.0 per cent in 2018: www.gov.uk/government/statistics/dcms-sectors-economic-estimates-2019-trade-in-services/dcms-sectors-economic-estimates-2019-trade-in-services [last accessed 25.10.2022].

[2] www.thecreativeindustries.co.uk/site-content/industries-games-games-why-the-uk.

[3] www.gov.uk/government/statistics/dcms-sectors-economic-estimates-monthly-gva-to-june-2022 [last accessed 25.10.2022].

Brexit and the Digital Single Market. Alison Harcourt, Oxford University Press. © Alison Harcourt 2023.
DOI: 10.1093/oso/9780192899378.003.0001

Brexit has clearly presented substantial challenges to the sector. The UK left the EU on 31 January 2020. The transition period ended on 31 December 2020. From January 2021, UK-based providers were no longer able to provide services under the country of origin principle under DSM legislation such as the Audiovisual Media Services Directive (AVMSD), SatCab, and E-commerce Directive. UK companies could no longer benefit from freedom of movement and EU sector funding. They report problems in trade in goods and services, copyright, and VAT regimes, as well as complications with cross-border data transfer, over-complicated administrative procedures, and international taxes on digital products and services. In turn, citizens within the UK are receiving a large number of streaming and platform services from Europe which are unregulated in the UK.

This book examines the evolution of EU DSM policy and the UK's special role in its creation. It then analyses the consequences of Brexit for future UK and EU policy trajectories. The book is structured as follows: Chapters 2 to 7 cover DSM sector policies (audio-visual media services, creative industries, telecommunications, e-commerce, online platforms, and FinTech), followed by Chapters 8 to 11, which examine horizontal policies (competition law, state aid, data protection, and copyright) which cut across the sectors. The book finds that the UK continues to innovate in the digital sector but is constrained by external factors at both EU and global levels. It observes how EU policy is taking a new direction in its 2020 Digital Strategy, which leans towards greater protection of European champions and digital sovereignty, a tightening of its data protection regime, and greater regulatory intervention in digital markets.

Formulating the Digital Single Market

Built on four fundamental freedoms, the free movement of goods, services, people, and capital, the Single Market is the bedrock of European economic integration and trade liberalisation. It stretches beyond the EU, encompassing Iceland, Liechtenstein, and Norway, through the European Economic Area (EEA) and Switzerland, through a series of bilateral treaty agreements. As noted by the House of Lords European Union Committee 'the Single Market has always been championed by the United Kingdom, including the former Prime Minister, Baroness Thatcher, who played a key role in its formation'.[4]

The 1957 Treaty of Rome established the European Economic Community (EEC). A customs union facilitated the freedom of movement of goods under which the six original EEC members abolished tariffs and quotas. However, agreement on the freedom of services, people, and capital proved more difficult given

[4] https://publications.parliament.uk/pa/ld201011/ldselect/ldeucom/129/12905.htm [last accessed 25.10.2022].

that EEC decision-making required unanimity. A major advance in European integration took place when the UK appointed Arthur Cockfield to the Delors Commission as European Commissioner for Internal Market and Services in 1984. He authored the White Paper entitled 'Completing the Internal Market', which identified obstacles to trade under three categories—physical, technical, and fiscal—and comprised 300 proposals to remove trade barriers within the EEC. The paper was adopted at the Milan European Council[5] in 1985 and led to the enactment of the 1986 Single European Act (SEA).

Containing 283 proposals, the SEA introduced qualified majority voting (QMV) (currently Article 114 TFEU) and set a deadline of 1992 for completion of the Single Market. Technical standards and certification procedures were delegated to technical bodies, eliminating the need for time-consuming statutory legislative procedures. Importantly, the SEA introduced the country of origin principle based on the 1979 Cassis de Dijon case decision in the European Court of Justice (ECJ). The principle guaranteed that any good sold in one EEC state could be sold in another. This principle of mutual recognition was later applied to services initially in the 1989 Television Without Frontiers (TWF), the 2002 E-Commerce, and the 2006 Services Directives. This meant that companies could only be regulated by one member state rather than by multiple EU states. This broke down non-tariff barriers in the form of national regulatory restrictions, leading to an increase in cross-border service trade.

The 1992 Maastricht Treaty amended the Treaty of Rome and created the European Union (EU). It confirmed the free movement of capital as a Treaty freedom. During this period, the 1989 to 1995 Delors Commission assumed responsibility for Single Market programme implementation. The UK appointed Leon Brittan as European Commissioner for Competition between 1989 and 1993, who championed a pro-market agenda, particularly in telecommunications markets. A 1992 review of the telecommunications sector resulted in the 1996 Full Competition Directive, which set the goal of EU-wide liberalisation of public voice telephone services by 1998.

Maastricht was followed by the 1997 Amsterdam Treaty, which introduced a protocol recognising that 'the system of public broadcasting in the Member States is directly related to the democratic, social and cultural needs of each society and to the need to preserve media pluralism', and Article 7d relating to services of general economic interest. Article 7d, which specified that 'services operate on the basis of principles and conditions which enable them to fulfil their missions', was later interpreted in the 2003 Altmark case relating to state aid. The protocol and Article 7D enabled the European Commission (EC) to formulate a policy on state

[5] www.consilium.europa.eu/media/20646/1985_june_-_milan__eng_.pdf [last accessed 25.10.2022].

aid for on public service broadcasting which incorporated aspects of the UK public value test.

Although the bulk of the Single Market focused on legislative instruments, self-regulation and soft governance were used in policy areas which had weak Treaty basis, often to encompass public interest issues. The 1995 Data Protection Directive and the 2000 Electronic Commerce Directive contained 'soft' codes of conduct. The Annex of the 1998 Council Recommendation on the protection of minors and human dignity included 'indicative guidelines for the implementation, at national level, of a self-regulation framework for the protection of minors and human dignity in on-line audio-visual and information services'. The Guidelines contained recommendations, codes of conduct, and monitoring mechanisms. The EC advanced these forms of soft governance through regular reviews and progress reports.

Soft governance was formally embraced in 2000, marking the initiation of the Lisbon Strategy, which ran until 2010. The 2001 Treaty of Nice changed the institutional decision-making structure to cope with enlargement. In parallel, the 2001 White Paper on European Governance provided political legitimacy to the expansion of soft governance to cope with an expected corresponding stagnation in decision-making (Senden, 2005: 9). It focused on legitimisation of self-regulatory bodies based upon national models. This greatly facilitated agreement on EU approaches to regulating digital markets.

In preparation for its 1999 Internet Action Plan, the EC commissioned a University of Oxford study to identify 'self-regulatory codes of conduct across national, EU and international boundaries covering a wide range of media from Internet, film, video (games), (digital) television to mobile communications'.[6] These self-regulatory practices were encouraged by the Commission for use at the European level. For example, the European Advertising Standards Alliance (EASA) adopted an agreement for cross-border advertising complaints in 2004 based upon its 2002 paper, 'Self-Regulation—A Statement of Common Principles and Operating Standards of Best Practice'.[7] This was based on the UK Advertising Standards Authority's (ASA's) self-regulatory approach to advertising. The UK continues to participate in the agreement post-Brexit.[8]

The Lisbon Strategy introduced the soft governance in the Open Method of Coordination (OMC). The OMC established agreement on policy guidelines through the exchange of information, benchmarking, emulation of best practice, target-setting, monitoring, and peer review (De La Porte, 2002). It innovated EU policy

[6] https://eur-lex.europa.eu/EN/legal-content/summary/action-plan-for-a-safer-internet-1999-2004.html [last accessed 25.10.2022].

[7] www.easa-alliance.org/wp-content/uploads/2022/03/EASA-Best-Practice-Self-Regulatory-Model.pdf [last accessed 25.10.2022].

[8] www.asa.org.uk/static/47eb51e7-028d-4509-ab3c0f4822c9a3c4/4869041b-06d3-4745-b209d2a5c37500b3/The-Cap-code.pdf [last accessed 25.10.2022].

formation as OMCs were initiated by the European Council, not the Commission. Under Lisbon I (2000–5), the information society was one of six policy areas designated for the OMC as outlined in the presidency conclusions following the Lisbon Special European Council of 23–24 March 2000.

The 2000 Summit established the 'Information Society Project', which aimed at a 'knowledge-based economy with more and better employment and social cohesion' by 2005. It established OMCs in the areas of e-government, e-democracy, e-voting, e-learning, e-culture, e-health, e-banking, e-education, e-media, e-security, e-banking, e-business, and e-commerce based on recommendations in the Commission's e-Europe initiative. The High-Level Group (HLG) on the Employment and Social Dimension of the Information Society (ESDIS) executed OMC objectives through the 2005 e-Europe Action Plan: 'An Information Society for All', adopted at the 2002 Seville Council Summit. Labelled 'e-Europe 2005', the Action Plan promoted the growth of the internet and e-commerce as a part of the strategy.

Implementation was achieved through the monitoring of e-Europe, dissemination of good practices and the improvement of network and information security (MODINIS) programme, which established two e-Europe steering groups in 2003, the first made up of member state representatives with the EC as chair and the second made up of 37 independent experts. Lisbon II (2005 to 2010) was launched by the EC's HLG 2004 paper, 'Facing the Challenge: The Lisbon Strategy for Growth and Employment under the "i2010 strategy"'. It outlined three goals to develop the Single Market: a Single European Information Space which promotes an open and competitive internal market for information society and media; strengthening innovation and investment in ICT research; and achieving an inclusive European information society.

The Single Market was strengthened further in the mid-2000s. In 2007, freedom of capital was enshrined in Article 63 of the Treaty of Lisbon, establishing the Treaty on the Functioning of the European Union (TFEU). It was used to ban restrictions on the movement of payments between member states, resulting in the Payment Services Directive. In summary, the four freedoms are now found in Articles 34–35 TFEU (goods), Articles 56–57 TFEU (services), Articles 45 and 49 TFEU (people), and Article 63 TFEU (capital). In parallel, the New Legislative Framework clarified the Conformité Europèene (CE) mark and accreditation of conformity assessment bodies in 2008. The Framework strengthened conformity assessment of products across the EU and improved its market surveillance system.

Soft governance began in earnest when the Regulatory Framework for Electronic Communications and Services was updated in 2009. A 2009 Regulation recommended that national regulatory authorities (NRAs) 'develop and disseminate among NRAs regulatory best practice, such as common approaches, methodologies or guidelines on the implementation of the EU regulatory framework'. The Body of European Regulators for Electronic Communications (BEREC) was established under the Regulation as a European-level platform for NRAs 'for enforcing the relevant provisions and for monitoring developments in whole-sale and retail charges'. A second forum, the European Regulators Group for Audiovisual Media Service (ERGA), was established under Article 30 of the 2010 Audiovisual Services Directive. It was modelled on BEREC for the exchange of best practice and cooperation on implementation of audio-visual media policy.

The 2000 Lisbon Strategy was succeeded by the Europe 2020 strategy which ran from 2010 to 2020. Under the strategy, the Single Market was forwarded through Commissioner Monti's 2010 report, 'The Future of the Single Market', which culminated in the Single Market Act I (2011) and Single Market Act II (2012), largely in response to the 2008 financial crisis. The Digital Agenda for Europe was launched in 2010 as one of the seven flagships of the Europe 2020 Strategy. It focused on the creation of a Single Market for content, improving internet connectivity, addressing roaming charges, net neutrality, and broadband rollout. The agenda was implemented through two five-year strategies, the Digital Single Market (2015–20) and Shaping Europe's Digital Future (2020–5).

The Digital Single Market Strategy for Europe was initiated in a May 2015 Communication.[9] Under the agenda, the legislation train greatly accelerated with a large number of Directives and Regulations for digital markets. It outlined 16 targeted actions and three key pillars: better access for consumers and businesses to digital goods and services across Europe; creating the right conditions and a level playing field for digital networks and innovative services to flourish; and maximising the growth potential of the digital economy. Key outputs were the 2016 General Data Protection Regulation (GDPR), the 2018 Regulation on the free flow of non-personal data, the 2018 Open Data Directive, the 2018 AVMSD, the 2018 Regulation on geo-blocking, the 2019 Directive on Copyright in the Digital Single Market, and the 2019 Cybersecurity Act.

Digital technical solutions and new tools for large data, including artificial intelligence (AI), were introduced under the framework. Related to this, the Europeana Data Model was established and supported by the EC's Digital Cultural Heritage and Europeana Expert Group, set up in 2017 and funded through the Connecting European Facility. Under the Facility, the EU worked on best practice solutions for the collection of metadata via national partner institutions, resulting in the 2020 Data Exchange Agreement.[10] This included the adoption of a Creative Commons Universal Public Domain Dedication which has been viewed as a major success in the international community.

Several forms of soft governance can be found under the Commission's Digital Single Market agenda, particularly in the regulation of online platforms. The EC addressed disinformation online with a Code of Conduct on Countering Illegal

[9] 2015 Communication of 6 May 2015, 'A Digital Single Market Strategy for Europe'.
[10] https://pro.europeana.eu/page/the-data-exchange-agreement [last accessed 25.10.2022].

Hate Speech. This was firstly implemented with commitments to address hate speech online from Facebook, Microsoft, Twitter, and YouTube in 2016. It was followed by the establishment of a High-Level Expert Group (HLEG) to address disinformation online in 2018. The HLEG published a report identifying best practice, requesting that online platforms adopt a wide range of measures.

In 2018, the EC published its Communication on Tackling online disinformation: 'A European Approach', followed by an updated Code of Practice on Disinformation in September. The Code was signed in October 2018 by several social media platforms, namely Facebook, Twitter, Mozilla, and Google, and industry associations, namely the European Association of Communication Agencies, the Interactive Advertising Bureau, and the World Federation of Advertisers. The Communication was initially designed to reduce disinformation prior to the May 2019 European Parliament election through fact-checking. But it committed signatories over a longer period to the transparency of political advertisers, policies against misrepresentation, the closure of fake accounts, and investment and implementation of technologies to promote accurate information. By January 2019, signatories were asked, on a voluntary basis, to submit monthly reports on Code implementation to the EC.[11] This was updated in 2022 with a revised Code of Practice on Disinformation.[12]

In parallel, a number of soft initiatives resulted from the EC HLG on Media Freedom and Pluralism. Originally established by Neelie Kroes, European Commissioner for the Digital Agenda in 2011, the HLG was a response to the European Parliament's 2011 Resolution on media law in Hungary. The European Parliament had long been lobbying for a Directive on media freedom, pluralism, and independent governance, but the Commission was hampered by the Treaty basis. In response to the 2011 Resolution, the HLG made several recommendations in its 2013 report entitled 'A Free and Pluralistic Media to Sustain European Democracy'. It did not recommend any legislative measures.

Accordingly, several projects were funded by the EC from 2014 onwards. These were: Strengthening Journalism in Europe; Mapping Journalism; Strengthening Journalists' Rights, Protections and Skills; Index on Censorship; Safety Net for European Journalists; and the Media Pluralism Monitor. The projects were aimed at providing training courses to journalists and tracking legislation and states' actions that could threaten journalistic freedom. Under continued pressure from the European Parliament, the Media Pluralism Monitor was established in 2014 and produced annual reports until 2022 with a specialist report on Hungary in 2019. In 2020, it established a tool to assess media pluralism risks across Europe.[13] This

[11] https://ec.europa.eu/digital-single-market/en/news/first-results-eu-code-practice-against-disinformation [last accessed 25.10.2022].

[12] https://digital-strategy.ec.europa.eu/en/policies/code-practice-disinformation [last accessed 25.10.2022].

[13] https://cmpf.eui.eu/media-pluralism-monitor/mpm-2020 [last accessed 25.10.2022].

legislative train eventually culminated in a 2022 proposal for a European Media Freedom Act.

Post-Brexit, the 2019 elected European Parliament appointed the von der Leyen Commission. Three executive vice-presidents (EVPs) were appointed, one of whom, EVP Vestager, assumed the title Executive Vice-President of the European Commission for A Europe Fit for the Digital Age, which was one of the six core priority areas for the Commission. Vestager initiated the next five-year digital strategy of the Digital Agenda, entitled 'Shaping Europe's Digital Future: The Communication Shaping Europe's Digital Future', centred around three objectives: technology that works for the people, a fair and competitive digital economy, and an open, democratic, and sustainable society. It was flanked by a 10-year (2020–30) plan delineated in the 2021 Communication 2030 Digital Compass: 'The European Way for the Digital Decade'.

The digital compass outlined four targets to be achieved by 2030: (for businesses) that 75 per cent of European enterprises will have cloud computing services, Big Data, and AI; that 90 per cent of European small or medium-sized enterprises (SMEs) will reach a basic level of digital intensity, and to double the number of unicorns; (for public services) to facilitate the online provision of key public services and citizen access to electronic medical records and to introduce digital IDs and a European digital identity with 80 per cent of citizens using an electronic ID by 2030; (for infrastructure) to cover all European households with a gigabit network and populated areas with 5G, and that Europe would house 20 per cent of global semiconductors and secure edge nodes and its first quantum computer; and (for skills) that 80 per cent of adults would have basic digital skills and Europe would have 20 million ICT specialists. These targets were underpinned by the Digital Europe funding programme which committed 7.5 billion Euros to the period 2021 to 2027 and a Regulation obligating member states to pledge 20 per cent of recovery funds to digitalisation.[14]

Since the UK left the EU, the legislative programme has accelerated. Key legislative actions resulting from Shaping Europe's Digital Future included a 2020 competition sector inquiry; 2020 Digital Strategy White Paper on Artificial Intelligence; 2021 adoption of the EuroHPC JU Regulation with investment of 7 billion Euros to build super and quantum computers; Action Plans on 5G and 6G; 2021 Radio Spectrum Policy Programme; the establishment of a joint Cybersecurity Unit;[15] 2021 Global Digital Cooperation Strategy; 2021 proposal for an Artificial Intelligence Act; 2022 Data Governance Act; 2022 Digital Services Act; 2022 Digital Markets Act; 2022 Chips Act; 2022 Media and Audio-Visual Action Plan;[16]

[14] Regulation of 29 April 2021 establishing the Digital Europe Programme and repealing Decision (EU) 2015/2240.

[15] https://digital-strategy.ec.europa.eu/en/policies/joint-cyber-unit [last accessed 25.10.2022].

[16] https://digital-strategy.ec.europa.eu/en/policies/media-and-audiovisual-action-plan [last accessed 25.10.2022].

2022 European Democracy Action Plan; and the 2022 proposal for a European Media Freedom Act. In addition to this, there are initiatives on digital sovereignty and blockchain technology. The UK will not adopt or participate in any of these measures.

Overview of the chapters

This section outlines the structure, argument, and logic of the book. Its analytical approach is to identify conditions under which the UK was able to bring about EU policy change through application of the multiple-streams (MS) approach (Kingdon, 1995, 2011; Zahariadis 2007; Ackrill et al., 2013). Kingdon (1994) observed that agendas were often changed through focusing events which created policy windows. Technological advance in digital markets led to multiple cross-border issues, creating a situation of ambiguity under which many different policy proposals were suggested at the EU level.

The UK is shown to have pressed for a liberal market agenda at the EU level in most DSM policy areas. In this respect, each chapter shows how the UK exploited temporal events which determined the direction of EU policy formation. Windows of opportunity were created by focusing events which enabled entrepreneurship by UK actors. The chapters of this book shed light on the role of institutions and importance of decision timing and entrepreneurship in opening policy windows. It innovates by outlining the important role of the state. The UK, acting as a policy entrepreneur, was able to exploit events and couple policy and politics streams with problems streams. Hence, causal mechanisms were temporal against a background of successive EU governance architectures, identified in the book as the Lisbon Agenda, the Convergence Initiative, the Better Regulation Agenda, and the DSM Agenda, which provided the political opportunity structure for policy-making. The EU institutions, particularly the EC and ECJ, acted as fixed external constraints on policy action.

UK governments were proactive. Kingdon (1994: 179) observed that a salient role of policy entrepreneurs is advocacy. They act as 'advocates who are willing to invest their resources—time, energy, reputation, money—to promote a position in return for anticipated future gain'. Princen (2011) perceived agenda-setters to be forwarding agendas through four strategies: mobilising support, arousing interest, claiming authority, and building capacity. Each chapter details how UK governments engaged with these four strategies in DSM policy areas. They also expand the analysis beyond the role of the state to include the actions of private companies, consultants, and law firms among consideration of policy entrepreneurs.

Hence, each chapter of the book firstly analyses the history of EU policy-making in the sector, then the UK's role in EU decision-making and the mechanisms which impacted on the direction of policy development. The chapters in turn assess the

UK's digital economy strategy in each policy area following the 2020 Trade and Cooperation Agreement (TCA), then the implications of Brexit for policy areas going forward. The book also explores the reaction of markets and stakeholders to Brexit at the domestic level.

Chapter 2, 'Audio-Visual Media Services: The New Regulatory Environment', details the rise and fall of the UK as a major hub for cross-border streaming and satellite television services and the new regulatory environment for audio-visual services. During its membership, the UK attracted broadcasting companies to London by influencing the trajectory of EU legislation. In this respect, it acted as a policy entrepreneur by putting together active coalitions to forward its proposals in Brussels. The revision of the TWF Directive finalised in 1997 set the stage for conflict over definition of regulatory alternatives when a number of different proposals came to the fore. Most significantly, there was member state discrepancy over the definition of the EC's 'country of origin' principle, which originated in the 1979 Cassis de Dijon case. Based on this principle, a product provided in one country, but received in another, must be regulated in the state from which it originates. TWF was one of the first Directives which applied the principle to services along with the E-commerce Directive and banking and insurance Directives.

Under TWF's 'country of origin' principle, the regulation of content and advertising was governed by the state where the signal was broadcast from, not by the state where it was received. The UK's first act of entrepreneurship was to actively attract foreign investment by encouraging satellite companies to locate in the UK. The UK regarded 'origin' to mean where a company operated from. Other member states defined 'origin' as the physical origin of signals, namely where satellite transmitters were located. This created a situation of ambiguity wherein states challenged the UK's jurisdiction for satellite broadcasting. European court decisions functioned as focusing events.

For example, when the Swedish consumer ombudsman challenged UK-based channels for broadcasting children's advertising to Sweden, the ECJ rules in favour of the UK. The ECJ rulings acted as mechanisms which triggered a window of opportunity for a change to the governance structure under which EU policy was made. The formal legal change to the definition of the country of origin under the 1997 TWF was prompted by an alliance between UK government representatives and national stakeholders. The new definition fit well with the EC's agenda, which was for a one-stop shop for regulation of satellite broadcasting in Europe.

The chapter tracks these and other historic developments in the TWF, Audiovisual Media Services, and SatCab Directives. For example, when the 2007 Audiovisual Media Service Directive was negotiated, a UK-led stakeholder coalition pushed for deregulation in advertising, flexibility in the European works requirement, and the stemming of extensions of the scope of the Directive to social media and online streaming services. This stakeholder coalition included ministers, the secretary of state, Ofcom, the DCMS, and industry associations.

However, the 'country of origin' principle, so heavily promoted by the UK, worked against its own interests post-Brexit. Audio-visual services were excluded from non-discriminatory treatment and commercial considerations in the TCA. UK licences for broadcasting and on-demand services to EU member states applied only until 31 December 2020. Prior to Brexit, no fewer than 1,523 UK-based television channels and 515 on-demand services targeted other EU states, which represented a 65 per cent and 20 per cent share of the EU market, respectively (EAO, 2018). However, by the end of 2020, UK-based channels only represented 10 per cent of the European market[17] as most cross-border channels relocated to the EU before the 2020 deadline in order to continue their operation in Europe.

This left the UK with the receipt of a large number of cross-border online streaming and music services such as Amazon Prime Video, Netflix, Disney+, Apple Music, Amazon Music, SoundCloud Spotify, and Tidal, which are not subject to UK legislation. The chapter details current proposals under the UK 2022 White Paper 'Up Next: The Government's Vision for the Broadcasting Sector', which aims to regulate streaming services at the UK level with high fines for non-compliance. The chapter concludes that Brexit may affect the UK's historical regulation of domestic content regulation with a lighter-touch approach expected towards traditional broadcasters. Lastly, the chapter analyses the market status quo with consideration of cross-border dispute mechanisms.

Chapter 3, 'UK Policy towards the Creative Industries Sector Post-Brexit', examines the promotion and protection of creative works, freedom of movement, changes to the domestic market, and the UK's changed position under the World Trade Organization. Historically, the influx of US-imported films and programming was seen to undermine the growth of domestic media in Europe (Katsirea, 2014: 301). For this reason, the policy goals of protecting language, culture, and identity were pursued by EU states in the form of 'cultural toolboxes' (Gibbons and Humphreys, 2011). Cultural toolboxes consist of national support measures in the form of financial incentives, tax measures, subsidies, quotas for national content, and the subsidy of public service broadcasting. These measures received state aid exemptions at the European level.

As a component of the cultural toolkit, quotas for domestic content were inserted into the AVMSD. A key issue post-Brexit was whether UK-produced content could continue to count as 'European works' or not. If not, UK-produced content could be excluded from national quotas in favour of EU-produced content in catalogues and channels. In January 2021 the DCMS stated that the 'EU's "Notice to Stakeholders" for audio-visual media services confirmed that works originating in the UK continued to be classed as European Works'.[18] This was in reference only to

[17] www.broadbandtvnews.com/2021/06/17/brexit-brings-huge-channel-licence-migration [last accessed 25.10.2022].

[18] www.gov.uk/guidance/broadcasting-and-video-on-demand-services-between-the-uk-and-eu [last accessed 25.10.2022].

states which signed the Council of Europe's European Convention on Transfrontier Television (ECTT) which permitted the freedom of reception of audio-visual services from the UK. However, it does not apply to video on-demand (VOD) services. Under the AVMSD, there is a mandate for on-demand services to reserve at least 30 per cent of their catalogues for European works and to make these works prominent. This means that, for example, Netflix, licensed in the Netherlands, which is required to have 30 per cent of its catalogue devoted to European content, is not obliged to include UK content as part of its European quota. The EU is discussing, particularly under pressure from France, excluding UK content from its European works requirement.

The EU gained exemptions for its cultural measures at the international level under WTO (General Agreement on Tariffs and Trade (GATT), GATS (General Agreement on Trade in Services), UNESCO) agreements coupled with 'cultural protocols' in bilateral treaty agreements between the EU and third countries to which the UK is no longer party. On 31 December 2020, the UK exited all international agreements agreed by the EU, which includes the EU's negotiated l'exception culturelle exemptions under Article IV of GATT[19] for national treatment of screen quotas for cinematographic film and Most Favored Nation (MFN) exemptions for audio-visual services under GATS[20] within the WTO. The chapter examines how the UK is renegotiating these exemptions[21] with the WTO post-Brexit and how it could be subject to future pressure to open commitments in audio-visual services under GATS.[22] Furthermore, negotiated exemptions in bilateral treaty agreements[23] for 'culture' between the EU and third states no longer apply to the UK. Exemptions under these agreements included screen quotas, subsidies, duties, deposits and taxes for film, the transmission of radio and television, and VOD packages (linear and non-linear). Accordingly, the chapter also scrutinises UK free-trade agreements (FTAs) with Australia, Comoros, the European Free Trade Association (EFTA—Iceland, Liechtenstein, and Norway), the European Supervisory Authority (ESA—Mauritius, Seychelles, and Zimbabwe), Japan, Madagascar, Turkey, and New Zealand and economic partnership agreements

[19] www.wto.org/english/docs_e/legal_e/gatt47_e.pdf [last accessed 25.10.2022].

[20] www.wto.org/english/tratop_E/serv_e/audiovisual_e/audiovisual_e.htm [last accessed 25.10.2022].

[21] https://assets.publishing.service.gov.uk/government/uploads/system/uploads/attachment_data/file/762809/SCW381_-_UK_MFN_list_FINAL_03_12_2018.pdf [last accessed 25.10.2022].

[22] www.google.com/url?sa=t&rct=j&q=&esrc=s&source=web&cd=&ved=2ahUKEwja6ZbZ2_fsAhWHUcAKHRo_DlUQFjAAegQIBRAC&url=https%3A%2F%2Fassets.publishing.service.gov.uk%2Fgovernment%2Fuploads%2Fsystem%2Fuploads%2Fattachment_data%2Ffile%2F862656%2F200131_GC_statement.odt&usg=AOvVaw1XYtc7Jb7MYMFnmyp0rHD8 [last accessed 25.10.2022].

[23] www.europarl.europa.eu/RegData/etudes/STUD/2016/535013/EXPO_STU(2016)535013_EN.pdf [last accessed 25.10.2022].

with Japan and Singapore. They are found to contain audio-visual market sector exemptions but not cultural protocols, marking a divergence from the EU.

The chapter then turns to funding of the creative sector. The UK government replaced public funding under the EU's Creative Europe programme in some areas but investment in the UK sector is increasingly dominated by large platforms such as Amazon, Netflix, and Disney. However, the obligation for companies to use independent production companies under the AVMSD was lost under Brexit. This has led to a sharp decline in commissions to UK production companies by foreign investors and streaming services. The result is an increase in funding for streaming content, a decrease in funding for independent content, and sizeable cuts to the arts sector and public service broadcasting. There has been a simultaneous 'battle for staff' between UK companies and the large US streaming giants and mounting problems with licensing.

A further policy investigated within the chapter is that of free movement for creative sector workers. In 2020, the UK signed the Council of Europe Convention on Cinematographic Co-Production,[24] which permits creative sector employees to work on co-productions in European signatory states. 'High-skilled' workers can seek work within the UK, but movement is more difficult for lower-skilled and temporary workers. The chapter makes some conclusions about the UK's agreements with the EU concerning current rules on the freedom of movement, the views of stakeholders, and the potential for domestic policy change.

In Chapter 4, 'The UK's Role in EU Telecommunications Policy, Brexit and Beyond', the role of the UK in policy sector formation is explored. The UK pushed for deregulation and privatisation of markets over a period of four decades in a sector which had long been restricted at national levels. It pressed for the break-up of monopolies, privatisation, and flexibility in spectrum use. The UK simultaneously chaired negotiations for liberalisation of basic telecommunications services in the WTO at the international level and supported the EU's Regulatory Framework for Electronic Communications and Services, leading to a major overhaul and removal of national restrictions in the telecommunications sector. The chapter also analyses the UK's positions on roaming charges, net neutrality, spectrum trading, and the use of white space.

It then turns to the UK's post-Brexit position with a focus on policy divergence. For example, the UK initially announced that it would retain net neutrality post-Brexit.[25] However, the UK's position on net neutrality is complex given that it permitted traffic management policies prior to 2015. Currently, under the UK's 2016 Open Internet Access Regulations,[26] net neutrality implementation refers to

[24] www.gov.uk/government/publications/council-of-europe-convention-on-cinematographic-co-production-revised-ms-no22020 [last accessed 25.10.2022].

[25] www.seenit.co.uk/ministers-publish-post-brexit-changes-to-uks-net-neutrality-laws [last accessed 25.10.2022].

[26] www.legislation.gov.uk/uksi/2016/607/contents/made [last accessed 25.10.2022].

BEREC guidelines. However, the UK is no longer bound to commit to the EU's 2015 Open Internet Regulation post-Brexit. Domestic policy is constantly under review[27] and subject to substantial lobbying by domestic internet service providers (ISPs).[28]

The chapter scrutinises the UK's position in international fora, namely the International Telecommunication Union (ITU), World Radiocommunication Conference (WRC), and Conférence Européenne des Administrations des Postes et des Télécommunications (CEPT). Here there is little regulatory divergence from the EU. The UK remains a member of the CEPT, which feeds into the EU's Council position, and is a full member of the European Telecommunications Standards Institute (ETSI), which develops standards for the EC. However, policy divergence can be observed in the newer EU policy areas of AI and digital sovereignty.

Chapter 5, 'The Regulation of E-commerce Post-Brexit', explores the UK's continued role in the sector as the EU's largest trading partner for e-commerce[29] and the second most popular country for European online shoppers from Europe (IMRG, 2021). The EU has agreed a large number of Directives and Regulations governing e-commerce, including data protection and privacy, consumer rights, and cross-border dispute resolution legislation. Historically, most UK e-commerce legislation contained strong soft governance components. The chapter takes into consideration past opposition voiced by the UK to EC proposals to introduce greater statutory regulation for platforms.[30] In alliance with Nordic and Central and Eastern European states, the UK was opposed to the expansion of EU statutory instruments. The chapter contrasts the UK approach to more rigid instruments preferred by other EU member states. The UK preferred a light-touch approach coupled with soft governance and self-regulatory trust schemes. It endorsed this through its Better Regulation Agenda, which acted as a governance architecture for forwarding UK interests within the EU.

Post-Brexit, the EU increased the number of legislative initiatives in the area of e-commerce, beginning with a 2017 competition sector inquiry, the introduction in 2018 of cross-border parcel rules, a 2019 consumer protection rules Directive, a 2019 Directive for the supply of digital content and digital services, a 2019 Platform to Business Regulation, 2021 VAT rules for online sales of goods and services, and its 2022 Digital Services Act. This has created a new governance structure which has constrained UK preferences. As a third country, UK-based companies offering cross-border digital services in the EU have met with a whole host of new

[27] www.ofcom.org.uk/__data/assets/pdf_file/0019/234334/Statement-Plan-of-Work-2022_23.pdf [last accessed 25.10.2022].

[28] www.ispreview.co.uk/index.php/2021/09/ofcom-begin-new-review-of-uk-net-neutrality-rules-post-brexit.html [last accessed 25.10.2022].

[29] https://researchbriefings.files.parliament.uk/documents/CBP-7851/CBP-7851.pdf [last accessed 25.10.2022].

[30] www.europarl.europa.eu/RegData/etudes/BRIE/2017/607323/IPOL_BRI(2017)607323_EN.pdf [last accessed 25.10.2022].

rules. Chapter 5 examines arrangements for trade in e-commerce between the UK and EU post-Brexit. In view of services, the chapter discusses post-Brexit EU legislation, along with changes to '.eu' domain names, the legal framework for e-signatures, and international cooperation on judicial recognition and a digital services tax.

The chapter finds that, although there are no tariffs or quotas on goods under the TCA, the delivery of goods cross-border has become increasingly complex. Supply chains have changed. The costs of hiring staff and shipping have increased. UK exports to the EU require customs declarations, Economic Operators Registration and Identification (EORI) numbers, and rules on origin (RoO) to be met. EU imports are subject to UK VAT and will need a future UK Conformity Assessed (UKCA) mark. Delivery companies such as TNT, DHL, and UPS have introduced surcharges for UK imports post-Brexit. The increase in regulations and longer delivery times have caused many companies to cease selling cross-border, including UK flagships such as John Lewis and Fortnum & Mason. However, the greater impact has been on SMEs and new market entrants. Services trade has also fallen both to the EU and to non-EU states.

Lastly, the chapter covers online dispute mechanisms. UK buyers and companies no longer have access to the EU's Online Dispute Resolution platform. The UK applied to accede to the 2007 Lugano Convention in 2020, governing jurisdiction for court judgments in civil and commercial matters. However, its application was rejected by the EC and UK contracts are now governed under the Hague Conference, which constitutes a complex arrangement for cross-border e-commerce. This demonstrates that the EU has substantially changed the political architecture under which agreement is made. It prefers to deal with the UK within international fora as opposed to a more 'Swiss'-style approach with multiple sector agreements.

The growth in online and social media platforms has led to greater rules in Europe around protecting users from harmful content. Chapter 6, 'Platform Regulation and the Liability of Intermediaries', investigates EU and UK policy development. It firstly details the history of the EU's disinformation policy, beginning with European Parliament proposals in 2000 leading to the 2022 Code of Practice on Disinformation. Then it examines the 2022 Digital Services Act (DSA) with comparison to the UK's 2022 proposals for an Online Safety Act.

Until 2021, the EC's self-regulatory approach to platform content was very similar to the UK's. This could be found in a 2018 Action Plan culminating in the aforementioned 2018 and 2022 Codes of Practice on Disinformation, where corporations voluntarily adopt codes. Indeed, the UK continues to participate in the Code of Disinformation post-Brexit. However, the 2022 DSA sees a much stricter approach, reflecting Germany's 2017 Netzwerkdurchsetzungsgesetz law and France's 2018 Loi relative à la lutte contre la manipulation de l'information. The 2022 Act marks a significant change in the EU's approach. It places the EC firmly in the driver's seat, providing it with full authority and introducing hefty fines for contravention. The introduction of a Regulation rather than a Directive makes the Act directly applicable with no room for national deviation.

The UK-proposed Online Safety Bill resemblances the DSA in terms of transparency reporting requirements, legal representation, NRA cooperation, fines, and advertising transparency. However, it is much more self-regulatory in nature, proposing a framework under which companies take responsibility for user safety. The UK Bill is accompanied by codes of conduct on child sexual exploitation and abuse, terrorist content and activity online (enforceable by Ofcom), and traceability of traders (enforceable by the Digital Markets Unit). The chapter assesses the similarities and differences between UK and EU approaches to regulating online platforms and draws conclusions about the significance for operators, taking into consideration stakeholder views. It concludes that most companies level up by adopting stricter rules rather than UK measures in the name of efficiency.

Financial services remain a growth area for the UK. However, between 2019 and 2021, the UK experienced a decline in exports to the EU and a 5 per cent rise to non-EU countries.[31] The UK did not receive the equivalence decisions it had expected from the EU in the financial services sector and there is increasing policy divergence. The proposed UK 2022 Financial Services and Markets Bill aims to remove remaining EU legislation relating to financial services. Chapter 7, 'FinTech: The UK as a Global Model', shows how these factors have led the UK to concentrate on emerging FinTech (financial technology) markets in its trade with third countries.

As the world moves towards paperless money and online transactions, London established itself as a world hub for FinTech. The UK's FinTech market was worth £7 billion in 2019 and grew by 70 per cent since 2015, according to HM Treasury (2020). In its 2021 FinTech Strategic Review, the UK Treasury stated, 'the UK has more than 10 per cent of the global market share in FinTech and the sector is now worth more than £11 billion a year to the UK economy'.[32] The review proposed a five-pronged approach to maintain this status on the global stage. Regulatory responses have been strategic, involving processes of both regulatory competition and cooperation. The chapter details the UK's sandbox approach to FinTech innovation and the use of FinTech in UK trade negotiations. The 2022 legislative proposals aim to remove 30 EU Regulations retained in the Withdrawal Act and 25 national laws implementing EU Directives and including the Markets in Financial Instruments Regulation (MiFIR). The chapter also assesses the effect of Brexit on London's FinTech industry as a large number of companies have re-established in the EU, creating new FinTech hubs such as in Lithuania.

[31] www.ons.gov.uk/economy/nationalaccounts/balanceofpayments/articles/theimpactsofeuexitandcoronaviruscovid19onuktradeinservices/july2021#exports-and-imports-of-services [last accessed 25.10.2022].

[32] www.gov.uk/government/news/uks-global-FinTech-leadership-bolstered-by-new-review [last accessed 25.10.2022].

In turn, the chapter details the EU's growing focus on FinTech in the context of its relationship with the UK. It is clear that the EU views the UK as a competitor on its doorstop and has taken action accordingly. The chapter examines EU policy in its 2018 FinTech Action Plan, 2020 digital finance package, and 2022 electronic retail payments strategy. A large number of Regulations and Directives revising rules on financial services have been proposed, including a Regulation on crypto-assets, a Directive on EU financial services, and a Regulation for digital operational resilience.

Chapter 8, 'Competition Law: Decision-Making in the Digital Sector', analyses the progression of EU competition policy with attention to how the UK influenced EU competition policy historically with support of subsidiarity in the protection of the public interest, security, and media plurality. The chapter then details the UK 2019 Competition Regulations and establishment of the Office for the Internal Market (OIM) within the Competition and Market Authority (CMA). It discusses the rise in digital market cases in the UK and assesses the CMA's capacity to deal with large platforms post-Brexit.

The chapter provides analysis of the EU 2021 Digital Markets Act (DMA) which sets out new classifications for online platforms that can be identified as 'gatekeepers'. The Act endorses third-party access to platforms, regulates digital advertising and transparency, and has enlisted publishers to verify advertisers. The EU DMA is contrasted with UK proposals for a Digital Markets Unit (DMU) to be situated in the CMA. The UK approach is based upon a self-regulatory code of conduct for online platforms with strategic market status (SMS). Lastly, the chapter assesses the end to UK participation in EU competition cooperation agreements and EU memoranda of understandings with third countries. However, continued cooperation between the CMA and the EC is expected in digital markets.

Related to Chapter 8 on competition policy, Chapter 9, 'State Aid and Exclusive Rights Agreements', follows the development of exemptions to competition law in digital markets. It details UK input into EU rules governing public service broadcasting with consideration of public value tests. The chapter then assesses growing exemptions from state aid rules for broadband markets and cultural subsidies. The TCA still commits the UK to a subsidy control agreement and an effective mechanism of recovery. However, the UK is no longer subject to Directorate-General for Competition scrutiny of state aid post-Brexit. This provides it with an opportunity to expand public funding to the digital sector.

The chapter concludes with examination of policy divergence with scrutiny of the UK Subsidy Act 2022. The chapter also explores the expiry of block exemptions post-Brexit. Whereas the Commission has widened the scope of block exemptions to include broadband, mobile phone networks, and digital connectivity projects, the UK is found to be reining in state aid. In its 2021 Communication on State Aid Rules for Important Projects of Common European Interest, the EU has addressed the importance of state aid in innovation in technology and infrastructure. Lastly, the chapter assesses the UK's state aid regime status under the WTO.

The UK represents an attractive and stable regulatory environment for data handling in Europe as the Information Commissioner's Office is recognised as being well resourced in terms of regulatory expertise. This can be seen as a claiming authority strategy (Princen, 2011). However, there is a great difference in opinion between the UK and many EU states on approaches to regulation of metadata, deep packet capture, and the harvesting of location data. Chapter 10, 'Data Protection and Privacy post-Brexit', examines the development of EU data protection policy which has taken its lead from continental European states. It then turns to possible divergence in policy post-Brexit.

The GDPR was retained in UK law through amendment of the Data Protection Act 2018[33] referred to as the 'UK GDPR'. The UK received two adequacy decisions from the EC in June 2021 which means that cross-border data transfer between the UK and EU can continue post-Brexit. However, adequacy decisions only last four years and can be withdrawn at any time. The UK proposal for a 2022 Data Protection and Digital Information Bill, which the Queen's Speech announced would be a 'less burdensome data rights regime compared to the EU's GDPR', is being closely watched by the EU.

At the same time, companies are experiencing serious issues with the implementation of Data Protection Impact Assessment (DPIA) required under the UK GDPR which came into force in March 2022, particularly in relation to risk assessments under Schrems for transfer outside the EU. Exporters can utilise either the international data transfer agreement (IDTA) or the UK addendum when making restricted transfers, which replaced standard contractual clauses for international transfers post-Schrems II. Article 35 states that a DPIA must consider 'risks to the rights and freedoms of natural persons', which comprises risks to both privacy and data protection and wider fundamental rights and interests.

If data is transferred to a country without an adequacy decision, which includes important trading partners for the UK such as the US, India and Singapore, the data controller must complete a Transfer Impact Assessment (TIA) which makes an assessment as to whether the laws of the states to which the data is being transferred present surveillance risks. This has greatly increased the workload for companies which report greater internal staff costs and often the necessity to hire external lawyers. In many cases, the additional costs incurred have stemmed trade to third countries.

The EU has agreed a large number of copyright measures to enable cross-border commerce in the creative industries sector. This includes the 1993 SatCab Directive, 1996 Database Directive, 2012 Orphan Works Directive, 2014 Collective

[33] www.legislation.gov.uk/ukpga/2018/12/contents/enacted [last accessed 25.10.2022].

Rights Management Directive, 2017 Regulation on cross-border portability of on-line content services, and 2017 Marrakesh Directive and Regulation. In 2019, the EU agreed a number of copyright Directives, including the Copyright in the Digital Single Market Directive. Although the 'creative industries' were named in the 2017 UK Green Paper, 'Building Our Industrial Strategy',[34] as one of the five key sectors which the UK government aimed to support post-Brexit, the sector has since suffered ostensibly from the dual impact of Brexit and COVID-19. Chapter 11, 'Brexit and Copyright', analyses the how copyright legislation has presented challenges to the creatives industries post-Brexit.

The EU 1993 SatCab Directive allowed linear content (satellite channels, cable, and digital terrestrial packages) to be broadcast from one member state to another without restrictions. The 2019 television and radio programmes Directive extended this to non-linear services, allowing VOD services, online games, and music streaming. These Directives are flanked by the 2018 geo-blocking Regulation,[35] the 2018 Digital Content and Digital Services Directive[36] governing online contracts, and the 2019 Copyright Regulation which includes a mechanism to facilitate negotiations of licensing agreements for European-produced films, television, and radio programmes to promote their availability across borders; for example, on VOD platforms. This is coupled with an extension to online services for European content quotas under the AVMSD, which also has requirements for visibility of European content in film and programming catalogues. The 2017 Regulation on cross-border portability also permits consumers to view packages such as Sky Cinema or Spotify subscribed to in one country while travelling abroad.

The 2019 Copyright Directive ostensibly targets content-sharing platforms such as YouTube and Twitter[37] which are obliged to seek licensing agreements with rights holders for use of their content under Article 17. Article 16 provides publishers with the right to be 'entitled to a share of the compensation for the use of the work'. Although the UK showed support and voted in favour of its ratification in the Council of Ministers, the UK did not implement the Directive.

The 2019 Intellectual Property (Copyright and Related Rights) (Amendment) (EU Exit) Regulations made amendments to relevant UK regulation. Under the UK's Withdrawal Act, four notices covering intellectual property relate to copyright Directives and Regulations. The notices state that operators when 'broadcasting into the EEA may need to clear copyright in each member state to which they broadcast' post-Brexit, in addition to which the AVMSD has supplementary

[34] https://assets.publishing.service.gov.uk/government/uploads/system/uploads/attachment_data/file/611705/building-our-industrial-strategy-green-paper.pdf [last accessed 25.10.2022].

[35] Regulation 2018/302 of 28 February 2018 on addressing unjustified geo-blocking.

[36] https://data.consilium.europa.eu/doc/document/PE-26-2019-INIT/en/pdf [last accessed 25.10.2022].

[37] Content platforms which have more than three years of existence in the EU, a turnover of more than 10 million Euros, and more than 5 million monthly users.

requirements.[38] Notably, under the 1996 Database Directive on the legal protection of databases, there will be 'no obligation for EEA states to provide database rights to UK nationals, residents, and businesses. UK owners of UK database rights may find that their rights are unenforceable in the EEA.' In reference to the 2014 Collective Rights Management Directive for multi-territorial licensing of rights in musical works for online use, 'UK Collective Management Organisations will not be able to mandate EEA Collective Management Organisations to provide multi-territorial licensing of the online rights in their musical works.' However, operators broadcasting to the UK 'will not need specific right holder permission for the UK, except where: the broadcast is commissioned or uplinked to a satellite in the UK or it originates from a country that provides lower levels of copyright protection.'[39]

Although the 2017 Portability Regulation was operative in the UK, the Regulation ceased to apply to UK nationals when they travel to the EU post-Brexit. This means that UK citizens might not be able to access their streaming services such as Disney+ or Amazon Prime when travelling abroad to Europe. Much of this depends upon whether copyright has been cleared for the states visited. The geo-blocking Regulation no longer applies to the UK post-Brexit,[40] meaning that UK citizens might be subject to differential pricing when searching for services abroad such as car rental or hotel pricing. The 2017 Marrakesh Directive for the benefit of persons who are blind, visually impaired, or otherwise print-disabled was implemented by the UK in 2018 but updated in 2021 after a two-year review. Markedly, the UK removed the compensation mechanism in the 2021 amendment. Chapter 11 analyses the UK's historical position to EU copyright legislation, then assesses UK divergence post-Brexit and consequences for the sector.

Chapter 12, 'Conclusion: The UK's New Place in the Global Digital World', analyses how the UK historically steered policy agendas within the EU. It is clear that this would not have occurred if the EU institutions, the EC and ECJ in particular, had not facilitated the opening of policy windows by creating environments conducive to policy change. The chapter confirms work by Ackrill and Kay (2011: 878) who view policy-makers as proactive agenda-setters who construct policies from changes in the environment. The first half of the chapter explains how the UK and EC were working in tandem in pushing forward a liberal agenda for the digital market and received substantial support from the ECJ.

In this respect, a key explanatory cause for UK influence is temporal as the ECJ Decisions acted as focusing events. Court cases opened up windows of opportunity which allowed the UK to forward its policy preferences and couple streams at key moments in the legislative timeline. An important observation in this respect is

[38] http://data.parliament.uk/DepositedPapers/Files/DEP2018-0944/Copyright_UPDATE_Jan_2019.docx [last accessed 25.10.2022].

[39] www.gov.uk/guidance/copyright-clearance-for-uk-satellite-broadcasting [last accessed 25.10.2022].

[40] www.gov.uk/guidance/geo-blocking-from-1-january-2021 [last accessed 25.10.2022].

that agreements would not have been made if the UK had not found support from the European institutions. This confirms Ackrill and Kay's (2011: 874) observation that the separation of policy entrepreneurs and decision-makers is overly stark.

The second half of the chapter analyses the effect of Brexit on both the trajectories of future UK policy formation and EU DSM policy. Post-Brexit, the UK no longer participates in EU policy-making. The chapter analyses how the UK's loss of influence could affect the future trajectory of EU policy-making in key areas of importance for the UK: broadcasting, creative content production, data protection and privacy, copyright, e-commerce, and FinTech. This could mark a change in the provision of a wide range of cross-border services from mobile phone companies to broadcasters, to content providers such as the BBC and the Premier League, to UK-domiciled online games companies and financial services.

The UK and UK-based companies could continue to participate in certain aspects of the Single Market under future bilateral agreements (the 'Swiss' model), and UK regulatory authorities may participate in soft fora under MoUs or association status. There is a potential role for the UK (similar to Norway's 'association status') in EU-coordinated self-regulatory fora such as BEREC and ERGA. However, the political situation at the time of writing is constraining the potential for both informal participation in EU fora and formal bilateral agreement. In any case, as the book demonstrates, a number of companies have already left in either anticipation or implementation of Brexit. Broadcasters, platforms providing on-demand content, internet sales, online financial services, and online gaming companies were unwilling to risk losing passports to EU markets. This is because companies are required to have an EU base (i.e. to be headquartered in the EU) to access service markets under Directives and Regulations.

2

Audio-Visual Media Services

The New Regulatory Environment

Introduction

Audio-visual policy is one of the cornerstones of the Single European Market as initiated in the 1987 Single European Act (SEA). Prior to Brexit, the UK established itself as a major European hub for cross-border streaming and satellite television services. It acted as a policy entrepreneur by forwarding key developments in Single Market policies for audio-visual services by putting together active coalitions to influence the trajectory of EU legislation. However, audio-visual services were excluded from non-discriminatory treatment and commercial considerations in the EU–UK Trade and Cooperation Agreement (TCA, 2020: 74). Therefore, Ofcom licences for broadcasting and on-demand services from the UK to EU member states were only valid until 31 December 2020.

After this time, the UK Withdrawal Act notices and Department for Culture, Media and Sport (DCMS) recommended that broadcasters continue broadcasting to Europe under the 1989 Convention on Transfrontier Television (ECTT) which was agreed by the Council of Europe.[1] However, options for broadcasting from the UK to Europe were limited as several states had not signed the ECTT,[2] it did not cover video on-demand (VOD) services, and the EU considers Audiovisual Media Services Directive (AVMSD) to take precedence over the ECTT.[3] As a result, dozens of channels relocated to the EU before the 2020 deadline in order to continue operation in Europe. This chapter details the rise and fall of the UK as a major European hub for cross-border audio-visual media services and evaluates the new and changing UK regulatory environment.

[1] www.gov.uk/guidance/broadcasting-and-video-on-demand-services-between-the-uk-and-eu and https://assets.publishing.service.gov.uk/media/601965568fa8f53fbe1a0795/_Proposed_Negative_SI__-_Audiovisual_Media_Services__Amendment__Regulations_2021_SI.pdf [both last accessed 25.10.2022].

[2] The following states are signatories to the ECTT: Albania, Austria, Bosnia and Herzegovina, Bulgaria, Croatia, Cyprus, Czech Republic, Estonia, Finland, France, Germany, Hungary, Italy, Latvia, Liechtenstein, Lithuania, Malta, Montenegro, North Macedonia, Norway, Poland, Portugal, Republic of Moldova, Romania, San Marino, Serbia, Slovakia, Slovenia, Spain, Switzerland, Turkey, Ukraine, and United Kingdom. The following EU member states are not signatories to the ECTT: Belgium, Denmark, Greece, Ireland, Luxembourg, the Netherlands, and Sweden.

[3] https://rm.coe.int/1680707a83 [last accessed 25.10.2022].

Brexit and the Digital Single Market. Alison Harcourt, Oxford University Press. © Alison Harcourt 2023.
DOI: 10.1093/oso/9780192899378.003.0002

History of EU policy-making

The EU has long grappled with balancing the democratic goals of audio-visual media markets with their liberalisation.[4] The European institutions were constrained from protecting the democratic functioning of the media due to a lack of Treaty basis. The seeds of EU legislation therefore began with market liberalisation in a series of European Court of Justice (ECJ) cases beginning with the 1974 Sacchi case, when the court declared that broadcasting should be considered a service under the Treaty of Rome. This was followed some years later by the 1980 Debauve case which extended the principle of non-discrimination for cross-border broadcasting services to cable television signals.

As explained in Chapter 11, the liberalisation of cross-border broadcasting in the early days of European Economic Community (EEC) policy formation was constrained by copyright agreements as established in the 1982 Coditel cases. Initial proposals for harmonisation centred around the policy goals of greater European integration. These were most explicit in the European Parliament's 1982 Hahn report, which recommended that the EEC should fund a pan-European broadcaster which would televise news from the activities of the European institutions in 'close cooperation with the EBU and Eurovision' (Hahn, 1982). It was envisioned that this would increase citizens' interest in European-level decision-making.

The European Commission (EC) responded positively to the Hahn report but, in reaction to the pan-European broadcaster proposal, raised issues of cost in its 1983 Communication, Realities and Tendencies in European Television: Perspectives and Options. Instead, the Commission put forward its own approach to developing a European broadcasting market based upon internal market logic. This was three-pronged: to facilitate the trans-border transmission of national and international programmes within Europe, to harmonise technical standards for television, and to provide support measures for content production. The resulting 1984 Green Paper, Television Without Frontiers (TWF), was constructed on this reasoning which had received considerable input from large media groups and the advertising industry, as Palmer and Tunstall (1991: 95) point out:

> In the pre-1986, as in the 1986–9 phase, the advertising industries proved skilled not only in presentation and lobbying, but also in the provision of the data central to an 'informed' debate. For instance: the green paper contains seventeen appendices, intended to provide a statistical overview of the funding, organization, technologies and availability of broadcasting in Europe. Six of these appendices came from a study conducted by Alastair Tempest of the EAAA, 'New Communication

[4] This was recognised, for example, in the 2001 EC Communication on certain legal aspects relating to cinematographic and other audio-visual works.

Developments' (November 1983). At least two others were taken from studies compiled for advertising groups (including J. Walter Thompson).

The 1983 European Association of Advertising Agencies (EAAA) study, 'New Communication Developments', argued that the foundation for the Single Market should be built on the 1979 Cassis de Dijon ECJ decision which could provide a basis for the country of origin principle. At the time, there was limited sector liberalisation across Europe with public service broadcasters dominating television viewing in most states. Only the UK and Italy had private channels with enough market share to be important for the advertising industry, which is why governments and national stakeholders from these states were the most vocal in the European-level debate.

The 1985 White Paper 'Completing the Internal Market' laid the groundwork for sector liberalisation, noting that 'broadcasting is an important part of the communications industry which is expected to develop very rapidly into a key sector of the Community economy and will have a decisive impact on the future competitiveness of Community industries in the internal market'. Therewith, broadcasting was earmarked as internal market policy with responsibility for the initiative allocated to Directorate-General (DG) III (for industrial and internal market policies).

The proposed TWF Directive adopted in 1989 established a legal framework for the cross-border transmission of broadcasting (radio and television) with the aim of creating a single audio-visual market. The European content rules were supported by France and opposed by Germany (Humphreys, 2005). The UK was opposed to the European content component of the Directive in alliance with the US and advertising associations. As explained by many authors, the European works requirement was weakened during the concluding stages of the 1989 Directive. As detailed by Williams (2007: 31):

> Jack Valenti, President of the Motion Picture Association of America (MPAA), lobbied President Ronald Reagan over the proposed quotas. Reagan in turn contacted Margaret Thatcher and the two words 'where practicable' were added to the directive as a result of the intervention of the then Foreign Secretary, John Major, at a Council of Ministers meeting (Cole 1995, 347). During negotiations on the draft directive the MPAA also used the services of a Dutch Westminster Papers in Communication and Culture 4(3) lobbyist, who influenced the decisions of Denmark, the Netherlands and Germany to vote against the French position for strengthening the Directive (Jacek 1995, 205).

Accordingly, a majority proportion of transmission time was reserved for European works and 10 per cent of transmission time or 10 per cent of the programming budget for European works created by independent producers. But the words 'where applicable' were added to the final version of the Directive, as per UK preferences.

A number of minimum standards were included in the Directive aimed at harmonising rules on advertising and content production. Specifically, advertising during films was limited to once every 45 minutes and prohibited during news, current affairs, religious and children's programmes, and documentaries. The advertising of cigarettes, prescription medicines, and medical treatment was prohibited. There was a limit of advertising time to 20 per cent of the daily transmission time and 20 per cent within a given clock hour. The Directive also included measures related to the protection of minors and incitement to hatred on grounds of race, sex, religion, or nationality.

Based upon the Cassis de Dijon ruling, a broadcasting company would fall under the jurisdiction of the state it was transmitting from, not the state of reception. As explained by Krebber (2001: 117), the Directive was agreed under the French presidency which moved it away from the Internal Market Council to the General Affairs Council in an unsuccessful attempt to increase the time reserved for European works. Under the General Affairs Council, TWF was ratified by national ministers for trade under qualified majority voting.

UK entrepreneurship and policy mechanisms

The UK's first act of entrepreneurship was to actively attract investment from satellite companies. In TWF implementation, the UK applied a different regulatory regime to non-domestic satellite services to domestic satellite services under Section 43 of the 1990 Broadcasting Act. Non-domestic satellite licences were exempt from rules applied to national broadcasting and benefited from relaxed advertising restrictions. Companies began to license themselves in the UK to broadcast programming across Europe. This included a number of large operators with multi-channel packages such as BskyB, Disney, Polsat, SBS, Turner, Viacom, and Viasat. Channels broadcasting from the UK with non-domestic satellite licences began to overtly bypass national broadcasting rules particularly in France, Germany, Sweden, and Norway (Nikoltchev, 2015). The UK's non-domestic licensing policy became highly controversial.

The biggest discrepancy between member states was over the implementation of the EC's country of origin principle. The country of origin principle, which originated in 1979 Cassis de Dijon case, determined where a company is regulated. Based on this principle, a service provided in one country, but received in another, must be regulated in the state where it originates. The discrepancy revolved around what constituted origin. Under the 1989 TWF Directive, 'origin' was understood to be the member state where the satellite up-link was located. Many satellite packages broadcast from the Luxembourg registered satellite, Astra, even though companies were located in different member states. This meant that the Commission determined Luxembourg to be the regulatory base. The UK regarded 'origin' to mean where companies operating the satellite services were located. Other member states viewed origin to be where signals were received (via television sets).

In 1994, the EC brought an action against the UK in the ECJ Case C-222/94 for failure to fulfil its obligations under the TWF Directive in 1994 for 'applying to non-domestic satellite services a different regime from that applicable to domestic satellite services'. It also questioned UK jurisdiction over channels using satellites registered abroad. The UK was exercising control over BSkyB which was, at the time, using the Astra satellite in Luxembourg. According to the EC, jurisdiction of BSkyB belonged to Luxembourg. The ECJ ruling recommended a rewording of the 1990 Broadcasting Act accordingly.

The UK's non-domestic licensing scheme was also subject to a Belgian decision prohibiting the TNT/Cartoon Network broadcasting from the UK. Belgium took issue with the fact that the UK 1990 Broadcasting Act did not stipulate a European works requirement for non-domestic satellite broadcasters. This was challenged by the ECJ in Case C-14/96. The ECJ ruled against the UK which subsequently repealed the non-domestic satellite provision in its Satellite Television Service Regulations 1997. Even though the UK lost both cases, the ECJ clarified that the origin principle meant that companies should fall under the jurisdiction of the state in which they were established. In the first case, the court expanded its interpretation of jurisdiction to be not only based upon the country of establishment but also Where a broadcaster has the centre of its activities, in particular the place where decisions concerning programme policy are taken and the programmes to be broadcast are finally put together'.

Subsequent ECJ cases addressed the fact that UK-based companies were broadcasting abroad, but not to the UK. In the 1997 VT4 Ltd v Vlaamse Gemeenschap case, the Flemish media authority refused to permit the UK-based channel VT4 to broadcast on Flemish cable networks. VT4 was licensed in London even though it solely broadcast in Flemish and was aimed exclusively at Flemish audiences. At the time, another provider, Vlaamse Televisie Maatschappij NV (VTM), was the only channel licensed in Belgium to broadcast in Flemish and carry advertising. This had been consolidated in the 'Codex' degree of 1995 which reflected not only Belgian's policy protecting Flemish content but also the promotion of domestic companies. Specifically, the 'Codex' degree stipulated that Dutch-language newspapers and magazines should own 51 per cent of the capital of the licensed broadcaster, VTM. The Flemish media authority did not consider the UK-based VT4 to be adhering to Belgian broadcasting law.

The court countered this argument with the statement, 'the Treaty does not prohibit an undertaking from exercising the freedom to provide services if it does not offer services in the Member State in which it is established', meaning that VT4 could broadcast to Belgium, even if it did not provide services in the UK. The same conclusion was established in the joined cases, Konsumentombudsmannen (KO) v De Agostini and TVShop. The Swedish consumer Ombudsman challenged TV3 and TV4 channels broadcasting from the UK to Sweden for contravening Swedish advertising law which prohibited advertising to children under the age of 12. The ECJ ruled in favour of TV3 and TV4, upholding the UK's jurisdictional rights.

Kingdon (1994) observes that agendas are often changed through focusing events which create policy windows. The ECJ decisions functioned as focusing events. They triggered a window of opportunity enabling the UK to lobby for a change to the definition of the principle of origin. A number of different proposals came to the fore. The Nordic states proposed that states retain jurisdiction over children's programming. Denmark, Sweden, and Norway opposed teleshopping. This was because the UK-licensed channels TV3 (Homeshopping Channel) and TV4 were broadcasting teleshopping to Denmark, Sweden, and Norway, bypassing national bans.

The proposals from France and Germany banning tobacco and restricting alcohol advertising were adopted under Article 13 and Article 15. However, the Nordic states' proposals to ban advertising to minors and teleshopping were not taken on board. Instead, Article 22 on the protection of minors was added to TWF 1997, stating that programming which could 'seriously impair the physical, mental or moral development of minors' or 'contain any incitement to hatred race, sex, religion or nationality' could not be broadcast. In place of a change in jurisdiction, a UK proposal to introduce infringement procedures and undergo consultation in the case of complaints was adopted. Article 22 permitted technical solutions (namely, encryption) to block certain types of content according to user preferences. This was founded in a 1999 EC Communication, Study on Parental Control of Television Broadcasting, based on a study commissioned at the University of Oxford.

Princen (2011) conceives agenda-setters to be forwarding agendas through four strategies: mobilising support, arousing interest, claiming authority, and building capacity. A change to the definition of the country of origin was promoted by mobilising an alliance between UK government representatives and the Satellite and Cable Broadcasters' Group (SCBG) members, which included Discovery Networks Europe, MTV Networks Europe, Turner Broadcasting System Europe, and Disney Channel UK, and the International Communications Round Table (ICRT) representing '25 leading media, computer and communications companies, including Time Warner, Walt Disney, News International/News Corporation, Reed Elsevier, Sony Entertainment, Bertelsmann, Philips, Siemens and Microsoft' (Williams, 2007: 31). This new definition fit well with the EC's agenda which was for a one-stop shop for regulation of satellite broadcasting in Europe. Article 2 of the 1997 TWF Act was amended to include paragraph 3 (a), which stated that a member state has jurisdiction over a broadcaster under the following conditions:

(a) the broadcaster has its head office in that Member State and the editorial decisions about programme schedules are taken in that Member State;
(b) if a broadcaster has its head office in one Member State but editorial decisions on programme schedules are taken in another Member State, it shall be deemed to be established in the Member State where a significant part of the workforce involved in the pursuit of the television broadcasting activity operates; if a significant part of the workforce involved in the pursuit of the television broadcasting activity operates in each of those Member States, the broadcaster shall be deemed to be established in the Member State where it has its head office; if a significant part of the workforce involved in the pursuit of the television broadcasting activity operates in neither of those Member States, the broadcaster shall be deemed to be established in the Member State where it first began broadcasting in accordance with the system of law of that Member State, provided that it maintains a stable and effective link with the economy of that Member State;
(c) if a broadcaster has its head office in a Member State but decisions on programme schedules are taken in a third country, or vice-versa, it shall be deemed to be established in the Member State concerned, provided that a significant part of the workforce involved in the pursuit of the television broadcasting activity operates in that Member State.

The revision of paragraph 3 (a), which redefined the country of origin to mean a company's place of operation (based on the number of staff, satellite up-link, and other criteria outlined above), was highly beneficial to the UK. This allowed the UK to continue jurisdiction of BskyB but also enabled regulatory arbitrage whereby companies geographically relocated their headquarters to the UK to license broadcast services. The UK therefore claimed an authority strategy. The Independent Television Commission (ITC) and, from 2003, Ofcom established themselves as trusted regulatory bodies with high levels of expertise, seen as providing stable operating environments for companies broadcasting across Europe, thereby building capacity.

The 1997 TWF significantly loosened advertising restrictions. Article 11 was revised to permit the insertion of a sponsor's name during television programming. Advertising during films and television series was extended to interruption once every 45 minutes. Further interruption was allowed if the duration was 20 minutes longer than two or more periods of 45 minutes. Article 18 relaxed daily and hourly limits for advertising time to 20 per cent of daily broadcasting time and 20 per cent of any given clock hour. Teleshopping was added under Article 18a. Right of reply was introduced under Article 23 (1) which had been supported by most member states, but not by the UK. The inclusion of right of reply set precedence for the UK's objection to extending TWF provisions to new services.

The 1997 TWF Directive was agreed under the co-decision process established under the 1992 Maastricht Treaty. This involved greater scrutiny by the European Parliament. The Parliament added 44 amendments to the EC's proposals in February 1996, all of which were rejected by the Council in its summer sitting. These related to extending the Directive to new services, programming content, strengthening protection for minors, and restricting advertising. The UK opposed extension of the Directive to new services, a position backed by the International Communications Round Table (ICRT). The UK also supported flexibility in implementation of the European works requirement and the further lifting of limits on advertising.

Negotiations between the European Parliament and the Council lasted one year. The European Parliament needed 314 votes to overturn the Council Decision in its second reading in November 1996. Only 291 votes were achieved and TWF was ratified without the European Parliament amendments at the conciliation stage. In the resulting 1997 Directive, the hourly and daily time permitted for advertising doubled. Forms of advertising 'other than advertising spots and teleshopping spots' were exempted from the hourly ceiling of 20 per cent. Counter to the Nordic states' proposals, this included 'teleshopping windows' and 'telepromotions' based on an ECJ Decision in its 1996 Rete Televisiva Italiana case which opened a window for policy change. Greater flexibility was provided to the European works requirement (Krebber, 2001: 152). By the end of 2000, 325 non-domestic satellite licences had been issued by the ITC (Harcourt, 2003).

The next version of the TWF Directive would embrace the Convergence initiative which presented a change in the EU governance architecture. Convergence was high on the global agenda in the mid-1990s. Pressure for sector liberalisation came chiefly from large European corporations following the enactment of the 1996 US Telecommunications Act. In 1997, the Commission published a paper on the Convergence of the Telecommunications, Media and Information Technology Sectors, and the Implications for Regulation. Consultation took place between 1998 and 1999, resulting in a proposal for a new regulatory framework for communications in a 1999 Communication, 'Towards a New Framework for Electronic Communications Infrastructure and Associated Services'. As discussed in Chapter 4, this culminated in the 2002 Regulatory Framework for Electronic Communications and Services.

Consultation for TWF revision began in 2003 based around six themes: access to events of major significance for society; the promotion of cultural diversity and competitiveness in the European programming industry; the protection of general interest of television advertising; sponsorship, teleshopping, and promotion; protection of minors and public order; and the right to reply (Craufurd-Smith, 2003). The UK supported the loosening of advertising rules, including the introduction of product placement. It was, however, opposed to other proposals such as extending existing restrictions on broadcasting, like the right to reply, to 'non-linear' audio-visual services, including the internet (House of Lords, 2007: 9).

Significantly, in the context of its policy on the information society, the Commission's 2005 EC Communication on the EU's i2010—A European Information Society for growth and employment recommended a change to TWF. As its basis, the Communication cited the 1998 Green Paper on the convergence of the telecommunications, media, and information technology sectors, and the implications for Regulation—Towards an Information Society Approach (Convergence Green Paper). The 1998 Convergence Green Paper had been the product of a Council of Ministers Higher Level Group (HLG) initially established in 1994 which focused on European competitiveness in the information society.[5]

The UK used the Convergence initiative to support its more liberal approach to regulatory audio-visual markets. As Kingdon (1994: 179) observes, a salient role of policy entrepreneurs is advocacy. They act as 'advocates who are willing to invest their resources—time, energy, reputation, money—to promote a position in return for anticipated future gain'. The UK engaged in advocacy as a policy entrepreneur by putting together an active coalition to forward its position. The UK's opposition to the proposal to extend TWF to new services began from an isolated position within the Council of Ministries where it initially only received support from Slovakia. As Williams (2007: 26) explains, a 'UK-based coalition of the government, the media regulator Ofcom, and industry groups organised a sustained lobbying campaign to challenge the proposal'.

The Westminster eForum arranged a seminar in July 2005 to discuss the six options. Ofcom—in alliance at the UK level with Intellect, the UK trade association for the information technology industry, the Satellite and Cable Broadcasters' Group (SCBG), and the Broadband Stakeholder Group (BSG), a UK government advisory group—voiced opposition to application of TWF to information society services (Edgecliffe-Johnson, 2006). The UK position was supported by the European Digital and Media Association (EDiMA), a group which served the dual purpose of representing digital technology companies at the European level and coordinating licensing for online content. As Williams (2007: 30) notes, the EDiMa was 'the European offshoot of the US Washington-based trade association, DiMa'. The UK alliance opposed seven other member states' calls to weaken the country of origin principle.

Shortly after the eForum, an impact assessment commissioned by Ofcom entitled 'the Extension of the Television Without Frontiers Directive' was published in September 2005 (Indepen, Ovum, and Gathom, 2005). In its assessment, Ofcom supported the deregulation of advertising and product placement but maintained

[5] The HLG published the paper 'Europe and the Global Information Society', which was referred to as the 'Bangemann I report'. The 1998 Convergence Green Paper was referred to as the 'Bangemann II' report.

that extending existing content provisions in TWF to all audio-visual media services 'would be premature at this stage and ... would risk hindering the development of new services' (cited in Petley, 2014: 263). This stance was reiterated at the Liverpool audio-visual conference, Between Culture and Commerce, in September 2005 during the UK presidency of the EU where Ofcom presented its formal response to the EC proposals.

This coordinated UK response was repeated by the secretary of state for culture, media and sport, Tessa Jowell, at the Oxford Media Conference; James Purnell, minister for the creative industries at the Department for Digital, Culture, Media and Sport (DCMS), at the Foreign Policy Centre in January 2006; and by the DCMS minister Shaun Woodward in a second Westminster Media Forum seminar entitled 'From Television Without Frontiers to the Audiovisual Media Services Directive' in July 2006 (Williams, 2007: 35–36). As Williams details, Ofcom also promoted the UK's position in the European Regulator's Group (ERG) and the European Parliament was intensively lobbied, notably in a Media Declaration 'signed by 53 European media companies and interest groups spanning advertising, print and broadcast media, telecommunications, satellite and cable' (2007: 40).

The resulting 2007 AVMSD did extend existing TWF provisions to on-demand audio-visual media services: at that time, the downloading of films and music files over satellite and the internet. The term 'audio-visual media services' now applied to both 'traditional television broadcasting and on-demand' or 'non-linear' services (Apa and Gangemi, 2021: 327). However, the UK position was reflected in a weakening of the definition of audio-visual services to 'TV-like' programmes, namely VOD, and the scope of the Directive did not cover new services on the internet such as streaming. UK implementation was also light touch regarding Ofcom's interpretation of 'TV-like' (Mac Sithigh, 2017).

The AVMSD did not cover audio-visual content on newspaper websites based upon an ECJ ruling in the 2015 News Media Online case (Katsirea, 2017). This court decision is also of relevance in the context of the 2022 Digital Services Act (as discussed in Chapter 6) which, agreed by the EU post-Brexit, did extend to newspaper websites. The 2007 AVMSD Directive also introduced further deregulation on television advertising and product placement. Bans on product placement were limited to news, children's programming, and documentaries with national flexibility for further programming. The European works quota was retained in the 2007 Directive along with protection for events of major importance.

Under the 2010 version of the AVMSD, there was a softening of rules on advertising, particularly in relation to product placement, and the maximum daily transmission time for advertising was removed. Broadcasters were permitted to access events of high interest to the public for short news reporting for the first time. There was no change to the country of origin definition. However, the Directive also permitted member states to restrict on-demand services in cases of protection of minors, incitement to hatred, the protection of public health, public security, and consumer protection, based on legitimate interest, which had been a key lobbying point for the UK. The Directive was implemented in the UK in the Audiovisual Media Services Regulations 2014 which updated the Communications Act 2003 with extension to on-demand services.

Under Article 4 of the AVMSD, any disputes must seek a 'mutually satisfactory solution'. Accordingly, Ofcom issued guidelines for dealing with regulators of other EU member states (Ofcom, 2012). In 2014, the European Regulators Group for Audiovisual Media Service (ERGA) was formalised in an EC Decision based on the 2010 Directive. It ran in parallel to the pre-existing European Platform of Regulatory Authorities (EPRA), a national regulatory authority (NRA) network which was independent of the Commission. ERGA was set up to 'serve as an advisory body to the Commission in its implementation activities concerning areas coordinated by the Directive 2010/13/EU', acting as a soft governance body.

In the last 2018 revision of the AVMSD, the UK drew heavily on the EU's Better Regulation Agenda. The 2001 White Paper on Governance and the 2003 Interinstitutional Agreement on Better Law Making both recommended a scaling down of the amount and removal of the duplication of regulation produced by the EU institutions. The Better Regulation Agenda, which was aimed at the removal of red tape and cost-effectiveness, originated in the UK Better Regulation Task Force established in 1997 (Haskins, 1999). As Golberg explains, 'Better Regulation' was at the heart of the EU policy agenda in the UK under successive Labour and Conservative Governments as 'a largely business-driven exercise, the UK effort focused domestically on cost reduction and quantitative offsetting (regulatory budgeting) and the UK lobbied for the application of similar approaches at EU level' (Golberg 2018: 15). The lobbying power of the Better Regulation Agenda was recognised by the House of Lords as 'bargaining tools at the EU level', suggesting that the UK 'push harder for new, sweeping improvements of the EU's Better Regulation Agenda, possibly by using its contribution to the EU budget as negotiation leverage'.[6]

The Better Regulation Agenda promoted the use of soft governance and self-regulatory measures to introduce flexibility in regulatory oversight. As the EU was curtailed under the Better Regulation Agenda to limit the number of Directives and Regulations produced annually, this increased reliance on self- and co-regulation to meet EU policy goals. These 'new' or 'softer' forms of governance were embedded into audio-visual policy with an increasing number of committees within the Commission working in close cooperation with external actors, particularly national regulatory authorities. It introduced a self-regulatory framework for minors and food advertising in line with the 2006 Regulation on nutrition and health claims made on foods. In the Commission's 2007 White Paper for Europe on

[6] https://publications.parliament.uk/pa/ld200910/ldselect/ldeucom/61/61we06.htm [last accessed 25.10.2022].

Nutrition, Overweight and Obesity, member states and the Commission were to encourage media service providers to:

> develop codes of conduct regarding inappropriate audiovisual commercial communication, accompanying or included in children's programmes, of foods and beverages containing nutrients and substances with a nutritional or physiological effect, in particular those such as fat, trans-fatty acids, salt/sodium and sugars, excessive intakes of which in the overall diet are not recommended.

In 2010, the EC published its Communication on Smart Regulation and introduced 'fitness checks'. These checks were designed to check whether existing legislation continued to be fit for purpose and that additional legislation should only be value added. Fitness checks focused on policy sectors in their entirety. In 2013, the Commission listed the AVMSD in its REFIT mapping exercise. The REFIT Evaluation and Impact Assessment of the EU AVMSD was conducted in 2016.[7] The REFIT exercise found the AVMSD to be still fit for purpose, but in need of update mainly due to the differentiated regulation of on-demand service providers and traditional broadcasters (Micklitz and Villanueva, 2019: 54).

In its 2015 consultation, the Commission asked for six main areas to be considered in the AVMSD revision: to ensure a level playing field for audio-visual media services; to provide an optimal level of consumer protection; to protect against and prohibit hate speech; to promote European audio-visual content; to strengthen the Single Market, media freedom and pluralism, and access to information and accessibility; and to broaden the scope of the Directive to include online services. In its 2016 response, the UK expressed that there remained a 'tangible difference between the concepts of broadcasting regulation and internet regulation'.[8] It also supported the country of origin principle which it considered to be 'a fundamental and critical precondition for the generation of a Digital Single Market in content; it is the core of the directive and must not be lost or eroded'.

UK strategy post-Brexit

However, the country of origin principle, so heavily promoted by the UK, worked against its interests post-Brexit. As a result of the UK's proactive stance in attracting foreign investment, in 2018 no fewer than 1,523 UK-based television channels targeted other EU countries (65 per cent of the EU market) and 515 on-demand

[7] https://ec.europa.eu/smart-regulation/roadmaps/docs/2015_cnect_006_cwp_review_avmsd_iia_en.pdf [last accessed 25.10.2022].

[8] https://assets.publishing.service.gov.uk/government/uploads/system/uploads/attachment_data/file/489539/bis-16-15-audiovisual-media-eu-consultation-response.pdf [last accessed 25.10.2022].

services such as video and catch-up services over digital terrestrial television (DTT), cable, satellite, internet protocol television (IPTV) channels, online, and mobile phones (20 per cent share of the EU market) by 2018 (EAO, 2018). In 2018, there were 4,106 broadcasting channels licensed in the UK, 1,340 of which solely targeted other member states, including AMC Networks, AETN Disney Discovery, the Modern Times Group, Sony, Time Warner, 21st Century Fox, Universal Studios, and Viacom. The UK was also home to international channels such as CNN International, Al Jazeera, CNBC Europe, Bloomberg TV Europe, and (the recently banned) Russia Today. But, by the end of 2020, UK-based channels only represented 10 per cent of the European market (Dziadul, 2021).

By 2022, most cross-border broadcasters had left the UK for licences abroad. AMC, BBC Studios, Discovery, Disney, Sony, and Viacom relinquished their Ofcom licences in April 2018. Viacom International Media Networks obtained licences in the Netherlands and MTV, MTV Hits, the Paramount Channel, BET, Nickelodeon, Nickelodeon Junior, Nickelodeon Teen, and Paramount Channel in France. VIMN channels for Denmark have been operating under a Dutch licence since 2018. In November 2018, Turner obtained licences in Munich for the television channels TCM Ireland/Malta, TCM Greece, TCM France, WBTV France, TNT Poland, and TNT Romania. WarnerMedia's Turner also applied for Munich licences for all of its channels including CNN in November 2018. In December 2018, NBCUniversal procured licences for Munich licences for its DIVA, Entertainment Television (E!), Entertainment (2x), 13th Street, and Syfy channels.

Regarding on-demand services, in 2019 Discovery moved its operations to Netherlands. Amazon moved jurisdiction for its Amazon Prime Video service to Germany in 2020, registering with the Bavarian media authority, BLM. To continue operating across Europe, the BBC secured licences in the Netherlands for BBC First, BBC Entertainment, BBC Brit and BBC Earth; Luxembourg for BBC Global News, BBC One, BBC Two, BBC Four, CBBC, and CBeebies for distribution in the Netherlands and Belgium from 2021. The last operator to relocate licences away from the UK was Stingray, which relocated to Germany at the end of 2021. According to Schneeberger (2021: 12), the number of channels 'originating from the Netherlands more than doubled (+104%) . . . channels coming from Spain increased by +38%'. Overall, this presented a loss for the UK not only in terms of company exodus but also in jurisdictional oversight given that UK citizens are receiving content from a large number of Europe-based broadcasting and platform services which are not regulated in the UK, including news services such as CNN.

The 2018 AVSMD widened its scope to include online platforms and 'video-sharing platforms' (VSP) services. The Directive was agreed under the Maltese presidency in 2017. The Directive was flanked by a 2019 Directive on the supply of digital content and digital services and the 2017 Portability Regulation which required providers of online content services, such as Netflix, to ensure that customers could access services purchased in their member state of residence while visiting other EU member states abroad. Neither the 2017 nor 2019 Directives were continued in the UK post-Brexit but the 2018 AVMSD was retained.

The Directive introduced greater flexibility in times for advertising with the maximum limit of 12 minutes replaced by a daily limit of 20 per cent for linear services. For linear services, no sponsorship was permitted during news or current affairs programmes and member states were permitted to prohibit advertising during children's programmes, documentaries and religious services. As in the 2010 version of the Directive, the 2018 AVMSD excluded 'video clips embedded in the editorial content of electronic versions of newspapers and magazines and animated images such as GIFs', a precedent confirmed in the ECJ 2015 News Media Online case.

The requirement to promote European works was extended to online platforms (such as Netflix) which should devote 30 per cent of their catalogue to European content. Member states could also oblige online platforms to financially contribute to the production of European works, a measure which was promoted and taken on board by France, Germany, Belgium, Italy, and Spain (Kostovskak, Raats, and Donders, 2020; Leiva and Albornoz, 2021). The UK voted against the text along with the Czech Republic, Denmark, Finland, Ireland, Luxembourg, the Netherlands, and Sweden in objection to the rules on financial contributions to European works (Apa and Gangemi, 2021: 340).

There was a greater focus on consumer issues. The Directive encouraged states to 'ensur[e] freedom of information, diversity of opinion and media pluralism'. The Directive also requires independence of NRAs from government and that 'objectives of media pluralism, cultural diversity, consumer protection, the proper functioning of the internal market and the promotion of fair competition' are respected. The requirement for NRA independence is markedly strengthened compared to former versions of the AVMSD given that greater legal and functional separation from industry and government is required and that NRAs must have 'adequate financial and human resources and enforcement powers to carry out their functions effectively' (Mutu, 2021: 354).

Media service providers are also required to use 'appropriate measures' to protect minors such as age verification and parental control software. Codes of conduct are encouraged for foods high in fat, salt, and sugar content. The provisions on the protection of minors, incitement to violence or hatred, and the exposure of children to fat, trans-fatty acids, salt, or sodium and sugars were applied to VSP services (such as YouTube) which are also required to have flagging mechanisms, age verification systems, and parental controls.

The Directive steers states to co-regulation for dispute mechanisms, recommending that 'Member States should, in accordance with their different legal traditions, recognise the role which effective self-regulation can play as a complement to the legislative and judicial and/or administrative mechanisms in place and its useful contribution to the achievement of the objectives of this Directive'.

Accordingly, ERGA developed a memorandum of understanding (MoU) which included a dispute mechanism for cross-border mediation.[9]

Implementation of dispute mechanisms has been carried out by nine national regulatory authorities[10] and four further states have published proposals for implementation[11] including Ireland, which hosts Europe's largest online platforms, notably Apple, Facebook, Google, and YouTube. However, seven states have chosen to deal with disputes with alternative fora.[12] In the Netherlands, which licenses Discovery, Netflix, VIMN, and Viacom channels, consumer complaints need to be made either to the Dutch Media Authority[13] or the Foundation for Consumer Complaints Board (FCCB).[14] EU citizens not based in the Netherlands are required to contact the European Consumer Centre (ECC) in their own member state.

The transposition of the 2018 AVMSD was required under the terms of the EU Withdrawal Agreement.[15] The 2018 Directive was implemented in the UK with the Audiovisual Media Services Regulations 2020, the Audiovisual Media Services (Amendment) Regulations 2020, the Audiovisual Media Services (Amendment) Regulations 2021, and Section 8 of the European Union (Withdrawal) Act 2018. Ofcom was nominated as the co-regulator for advertising on video-sharing platforms.[16] The European works requirements apply to on-demand services. Accordingly, Ofcom published guidance on on-demand programmes service (ODPS) providers in September 2022 relating to European works.[17]

It sits alongside Ofcom guidance on jurisdictional issues[18] and the ODPS Rules and Guidance document[19] published in 2021. The ODPS document stipulates under Section 368CB(1) and (2) that on-demand services will ensure that at least 30 per cent of their programmes are European works and ensuring the prominence of such content. This includes both European works originating from the EU and ECTT signature states. Even though the UK is enforcing the European works

[9] https://erga-online.eu/wp-content/uploads/2020/12/ERGA_Memorandum_of_Understanding_adopted_03-12-2020_l.pdf [last accessed 25.10.2022].

[10] Belgium, Denmark, Estonia, Finland, France, Germany, Malta, Slovenia, and Sweden (European Audiovisual Observatory, 2022: 76).

[11] Cyprus, Hungary, Ireland, and Luxembourg.

[12] Austria, Bulgaria, the Czech Republic, Greece, the Netherlands, and Portugal.

[13] www.cvdm.nl/en/contact/questions-or-complaints [last accessed 01.04.2022].

[14] The Board stipulates 'in case you are a citizen of the Netherlands, who does not speak Dutch and you want to file a complaint with one of the complaints boards, you could ask a friend or relative, who is able to speak and write in the Dutch language, to assist you with filing a complaint at the complaints board'. www.degeschillencommissie.nl/english [last accessed 01.04.2022].

[15] www.ofcom.org.uk/consultations-and-statements/category-2/odps-obligations-european-works [last accessed 25.10.2022].

[16] www.ofcom.org.uk/consultations-and-statements/category-1/regulation-of-advertising-on-vsp [last accessed 25.10.2022].

[17] www.ofcom.org.uk/__data/assets/pdf_file/0031/243769/ODPS-European-works-guidance.pdf [last accessed 25.10.2022].

[18] www.ofcom.org.uk/__data/assets/pdf_file/0024/215457/statement-video-sharing-platforms-who-needs-to-notify.pdf [last accessed 25.10.2022].

[19] www.ofcom.org.uk/__data/assets/pdf_file/0029/229358/ODPS-Rules-and-Guidance.pdf [last accessed 25.10.2022].

quota, the EU has indicated that it may cut the amount of British television shown on European screens post-Brexit (Boffey, 2021).

The UK plans to remove the Charter of Fundamental Rights from its broadcasting law. The 2022 publication, *The Benefits of Brexit: How the UK Is Taking Advantage of Leaving the EU*, states, 'following the implementation of the Audiovisual and Media Services Directive, UK legislation currently references the Charter of EU Fundamental Rights. It is the Government's intention to replace the EU definition in the Communications Act 2003 with a UK specific measure over the coming months due to our concerns about the chilling effect it has on free speech'.[20]

At the time of writing, UK-based services operate under a complex licensing system wherein multiple satellite licences are needed: both for domestic Ofcom broadcasting services and licences from the respective regulatory bodies across Europe in the 22 states receiving broadcasts from the UK who have signed the ECTT.[21] On 23 October 2009, Commissioner Viviane Reding, the former European Commissioner for Information Society and Media, sent a letter to EU member states which reminded ECTT signatories 'of their dual obligation not to enter into international commitments that conflict in substance with Community Law and to respect the case law of the European Court of Justice with regard to the external powers of the Community'. As a consequence, the Committee of Ministers

> stopped its work on the adoption and opening for signature of the draft protocol since then. This is highly regrettable. Having transposed the new European Union Directive into their national law, European Union member States party to the European Convention on Transfrontier Television have a vital legal interest in completing the revision of this Convention in order to align it with the European Union Directive and avoid any legal conflicts with the current non-revised Convention. At present, all parties to the Convention are de facto blocked from amending the Convention.[22]

This means that VOD services are not covered under the ECTT, so companies providing services must be headquartered within an EU state and comply with the AVMSD.

Digital Television Programme Services (DTPS) and Digital Television Additional Services (DTAS) received from ECTT states operating in the UK

[20] https://assets.publishing.service.gov.uk/government/uploads/system/uploads/attachment_data/file/1054643/benefits-of-brexit.pdf [last accessed 25.10.2022].

[21] Austria, Bulgaria, Croatia, Cyprus, the Czech Republic, Estonia, Finland, France, Germany, Hungary, Italy, Latvia, Liechtenstein, Lithuania, Malta, Norway, Poland, Portugal, Romania, Slovakia, Slovenia, and Spain. www.coe.int/en/web/conventions/full-list/-/conventions/treaty/132/signatures?p_auth=Vkx [last accessed 25.10.2022].

[22] https://rm.coe.int/1680707a83 [last accessed 25.10.2022].

need only apply for Ofcom licences if services are included in electronic programme guides (EPGs). Companies operating in states which have not signed the ECTT (Belgium, Denmark, Greece, Ireland, Luxembourg, the Netherlands, and Sweden) need licences for all digital television services. VOD services from non-ECTT signatory states, however, do not need to obtain an Ofcom licence. This includes streaming services such as Netflix (based in the Netherlands) and Amazon (Germany). In a 2021 communication,[23] Ofcom stated that it 'will only regulate a service if both its head office and editorial decision-making capacity are based in the UK'.

The Dutch Commissariaat voor de Media came under scrutiny from the House of Commons in 2019 when it claimed that it had never received a complaint from the UK about Netflix (McDonald, 2019). As the European Audiovisual Observatory (2018) explains, complaints about Netflix need to be made in reference to provisions under the 2020 Dutch Media Act which is only available in the Dutch language.[24] There are also no transparency requirements compelling operators to publish the number of complaints or their outcomes.

Accordingly, the White Paper 'Up Next—The Government's Vision for the Broadcasting Sector'[25] published by DCMS in April 2022 following consultation[26] proposes that online streaming services such as Amazon Prime Video, Netflix, and Disney+ be brought under Ofcom jurisdiction and subject to the Broadcasting Code. The White Paper proposes fines of up to £250,000, or an amount up to 5 per cent of an organisation's revenue, for non-compliance. The consultation[27] leading to the proposal recognised that streaming services with large audience shares 'including Netflix and Apple TV+, are not regulated in the UK at all', even though 75 per cent of UK households subscribe to at least one provider. However, the majority of respondents to the consultation[28] leading to the proposal submissions did not support the proposals for Broadcasting Code compliance.

A new Broadcasting Code is expected specifically designed for on-demand services which will run in parallel to the traditional media code. The on-demand services code is expected to be lighter touch than the existing code for traditional

[23] www.ofcom.org.uk/__data/assets/pdf_file/0019/190342/faq-television-on-demand-services-after-brexit.pdf [last accessed 25.10.2022].

[24] Belgium, Denmark, Estonia, Finland, France, Germany, Malta, Slovenia, and Sweden (EAO, 2018: 76).

[25] https://assets.publishing.service.gov.uk/government/uploads/system/uploads/attachment_data/file/1071939/E02740713_CP_671_Broadcasting_White_Paper_Accessible__1_.pdf [last accessed 25.10.2022].

[26] www.gov.uk/government/consultations/audience-protection-standards-on-video-on-demand-services/audience-protection-standards-on-video-on-demand-services [last accessed 25.10.2022].

[27] www.gov.uk/government/consultations/audience-protection-standards-on-video-on-demand-services [last accessed 25.10.2022].

[28] www.gov.uk/government/consultations/audience-protection-standards-on-video-on-demand-services/outcome/government-response-to-the-consultation-on-audience-protection-standards-on-video-on-demand-services#consultation-on-audience-protection-standards-on-video-on-demand-services [last accessed 25.10.2022].

broadcasters. What is unclear is the future for the regulation of cross-border advertising. In October 2022, Netflix announced a new tier system for the provision of its online streaming programmes. A cheaper subscription will be provided with advertising (Cain, 2022). As Netflix and other platforms established abroad are not yet regulated in the UK, Ofcom has accordingly recommended the lifting of advertising restrictions on traditional broadcasters to compete with online streaming services.[29]

EU policy divergence

Post-Brexit policy divergence can not only be seen in the extension of AVMSD provisions to online services, against UK preferences, but also with increased EU focus on media plurality, an issue long protected by subsidiarity at the EU level. Although the European Parliament has been campaigning for EU legislation on media ownership and plurality for decades, the EU has been restricted from legislating in this area by a lack of Treaty basis. Article 11.2 of the Charter of Fundamental Rights of the European Union introduced in the 2007 Lisbon Treaty states that 'the freedom and pluralism of the media shall be respected'. However, unlike a Treaty Article, a Charter cannot be a basis for legislation; as explained by the ECJ, it 'does not extend the field of application of EU law beyond the powers of the Union or establish any new power or task for the Union, or modify powers and tasks as defined in the Treaties'.[30] It only needs to be adhered to by member states.

European Parliament campaigns on media pluralism began in the 1980s, when it published three Resolutions[31] requesting a provision to be included in the 1989 TWF Directive. It followed with more Motions for Resolutions, European Parliament Resolutions, and five Reports in the 1990s.[32] In the mid-1990s, the pressure came from Members of the European Parliament (MEPs) from Italy in particular as shown in the 1996 Barzanti Report, as Italy at the time was dealing with high levels of media concentration and the involvement of the media owner

[29] www.gov.uk/government/consultations/audience-protection-standards-on-video-on-demand-services/audience-protection-standards-on-video-on-demand-services [last accessed 25.10.2022].

[30] https://curia.europa.eu/jcms/upload/docs/application/pdf/2018-05/fiche_thematique_-_charte_-_en.pdf [last accessed 25.10.2022].

[31] 1985 Resolution on the Economic Aspects of the Common Market for Broadcasting; 1986 Resolution on the Fifteenth Report of the CEC on Competition Policy; 1987 Resolution on the Sixteenth Report of the CEC on Competition Policy.

[32] 1990 Resolution on Media Takeovers and Mergers; 1990 Ortega Motion for Resolution on Local Television in Europe; 1991 Titley and others Motion for Resolution on Importance of Diversity in the Media; 1991 Titley and others Motion for Resolution on Tendency Towards the Concentration of Ownership in the Media Industry; 1992 Resolution on Media Concentration and Diversity of Opinions; 1992 Resolution on Media Concentration and Pluralism of Information; 1990 Albor Motion for Resolution on Concentration of Information; 1990 Ferri Motion for Resolution on Anti-trust Legislation for the Media; Resolution of 20 November 2002 on media concentration.

Berlusconi in the political sphere with his founding and leadership of Forza Italia. The EC responded by drafting a Directive on media ownership in the 1990s. However, it was based upon internal market logic and the harmonisation of national ownership rules, and never came to fruition due to political infeasibility.

Under continued European Parliament pressure, a European Charter on the Freedom of the Press was adopted in 2009.[33] It had been engineered by Commissioner Viviane Reding and the Commission's Media Task Force. However, the Charter was not supported by any piece of EU legislation but was a separate agreement signed by 48 editors-in-chief and journalists from 19 European states. Notably, none of the UK press representatives signed the Charter. This was followed by two more European Parliament Resolutions in 2010.[34] The European Parliament continued to pressure the EC but no action was taken until 2011 when the European Parliament published its Resolution on media law in Hungary.

The Resolution called for a Directive on media freedom, pluralism, and independent governance. It condemned Hungarian 'media law and constitutional changes enacted in Hungary between June and December 2010' for not 'respect[ing] the fundamental right to freedom of expression and information enshrined in Article 11 of the Charter of Fundamental Rights' and lack of 'compliance with the principles governing public-service broadcasting'. It referred to Hungary's 'extreme penalties imposed for debatable and undefined reasons' and also cited an Organization for Security and Co-operation in Europe (OSCE) report which criticised Hungary for 'disproportionate and extreme penalties imposed for debatable and undefined reasons', 'violation of the principle of the confidentiality of journalistic sources', and 'the exertion of pervasive and centralised governmental and political control over all media'.[35]

The EC responded to the European Parliament by establishing the High-Level Group on Media Freedom and Pluralism in 2011. It was set up by the vice-president of the European Commission, Neelie Kroes. The HLG ran a public consultation[36] and established the Media Task Force,[37] after which it published the report 'A Free and Pluralistic Media to Sustain European Democracy' in 2013.[38] The report made 30 recommendations, including the establishment of an independent centre to monitor media freedom and pluralism; European-wide standards for media councils; media pluralism to be a requirement for EU accession; state aid decisions

[33] www.pressfreedom.eu [last accessed 25.10.2022].

[34] 2010 Resolution on Public Service Broadcasting in the Digital Era: The Future of the Dual System; and 2010 Resolution on Journalism and New Media—Creating a Public Sphere in Europe.

[35] www.osce.org/fom/71218?download=true [last accessed 25.10.2022].

[36] http://ec.europa.eu/digital-agenda/en/public-consultations-media-issues [last accessed 25.10.2022].

[37] http://ec.europa.eu/information_society/media_taskforce/doc/pluralism/forum/report.pdf [last accessed 25.10.2022].

[38] https://ec.europa.eu/digital-agenda/sites/digital-agenda/files/HLG%20Final%20Report.pdf [last accessed 25.10.2022].

to be restricted to organisations with codes of conduct; increased funding for journalists; and to introduce EU-level libel restrictions which would also cover the internet. The HLG did not recommend any legislative measures.

However, under continued pressure from the European Parliament,[39] a number of projects were funded by the EC from 2014 onwards to promote media pluralism and freedom, namely: Strengthening Journalism in Europe; Mapping Journalism; Strengthening Journalists' Rights, Protections and Skills; Index on Censorship; Safety Net for European Journalists; and the Media Pluralism Monitor. The projects were aimed at providing training courses to journalists and tracking legislation and states' actions that could threaten journalistic freedom.

The Media Pluralism Monitor was established in 2014 and produced annual reports until 2022 with a specialist report on Hungary in 2019. In 2020, it introduced a tool to assess media pluralism risks across Europe.[40] These activities led to a 2021 Recommendation on the protection, safety, and empowerment of journalists,[41] a 2022 Recommendation to protect journalists and rights defenders from abusive litigation (SLAPP),[42] a proposal for a Regulation on the transparency and targeting of political advertising, and eventually a 2022 proposal for a European Media Freedom Act (EMFA). The EMFA proposal was purposely released on the same day as the 2022 publication of the Study on Media Plurality and Diversity Online led by the Centre of Media Pluralism and Media Freedom for maximum impact.[43]

The September 2022 proposal for an EMFA put forward a number of measures to protect media pluralism and media independence. It also recommended that ERGA be made into a European Board for Media Services (EBMS) with a wider remit. Organised into eight categories, the proposal covers: the protection of editorial independence; a ban on spyware use on media, journalists, and their families; ensuring the stability of independent public service media; media pluralism tests; the transparency of state advertising; the protection of media content online; and the right for users to set their own preferences for the use of online media. It introduces a right to know about the ownership of media companies under Article 6[44]. As criticised by the European Federation of Journalists (Killeen, 2022), micro

[39] Resolution of 21 May 2013 on the EU Charter: standard settings for media freedom across the EU; Resolution of 25 October 2016 with recommendations to the Commission on the establishment of an EU mechanism on democracy, the rule of law and fundamental rights; Resolution of 14 February 2017 on the role of whistleblowers in the protection of EU's financial interests; Resolution of 24 October 2017 on legitimate measures to protect whistleblowers acting in the public interest when disclosing the confidential information of companies and public bodies; Resolution of 3 May 2018 on media pluralism and media freedom in the European Union.

[40] https://cmpf.eui.eu/media-pluralism-monitor/mpm-2020 [last accessed 25.10.2022].

[41] https://digital-strategy.ec.europa.eu/en/library/recommendation-protection-safety-and-empowerment-journalists-factsheet [last accessed 25.10.2022].

[42] https://ec.europa.eu/commission/presscorner/detail/en/ip_22_2652 [last accessed 25.10.2022].

[43] www.eui.eu/news-hub?id=new-study-on-media-pluralism-and-diversity-online-published [last accessed 25.10.2022].

[44] The European Democracy Action Plan established the Euromedia Ownership Monitor (EurOMo) as a pilot project to monitor media ownership transparency in Europe https://media-ownership.eu/ [last accessed 25.10.2022].

enterprises are exempt from the right-to-know provision and also from guaranteeing the independence of individual editorial decisions.[45] However, as Tambini (2022) points out, the Regulation is being proposed under Article 114 of the TFEU based upon Single Market logic.

Conclusion

This chapter has shown how the UK promoted state interests through alliance and mobilisation of stakeholders at key stages of EU policy-making. It was supported by the EC and ECJ which utilised the UK position in turn to promote greater sector harmonisation in audio-visual media services. The Convergence and Better Regulation agendas acted as governance architectures limiting the quantity of statutory measures taken at the EU level, reflecting UK interests. This in turn brought the Commission to increasingly rely on soft governance and self-regulation to extend its agenda, particularly in collaboration with self-regulatory networks such as ERGA. Post-Brexit, the EU is shown to have significantly expanded its agenda in areas such as media pluralism and the protection of journalistic freedom, areas the UK historically objected to on the grounds of subsidiarity.

Brexit brought significant challenges to the UK. It lost market share in audio-visual services. But, at the same time, it is bound by the TCA to continue implementation of EU provisions relating to the AVMSD, including the European works quota. At the time of writing, audio-visual services from the EU are not subject to UK content or advertising rules. Although proposals have been made to impose rules on cross-border operators, the most likely effect will be a loosening of restrictions on domestic providers.

[45] Micro enterprises are understood to be SMEs earning under 350,000 Euros. Micro enterprises are defined under Directive 2013/34/EU of the European Parliament and of the Council of 26 June 2013 on the annual financial statements, consolidated financial statements and related reports of certain types of undertakings, amending Directive 2006/43/EC of the European Parliament and of the Council and repealing Council Directives 78/660/EEC and 83/349/EEC (OJ L 182, 29.6.2013, p. 19-76). The EMMA-ENPA is lobbying to include family enterprises under the meaning of microenterprises.

3
UK Policy towards the Creative Industries Sector Post-Brexit

Introduction

The UK's position on promotion of the creative industries sector has changed little post-Brexit both in terms of aid to the sector and its protection at the international level. The Department for Digital, Culture, Media and Sport (DCMS) defines the creative industries[1] as those 'which have their origin in individual creativity, skill and talent and which have a potential for wealth and job creation through the generation and exploitation of intellectual property'.[2] The largest subsector is 'film, tv and music' which represents approximately 60 per cent of income followed by 'arts'.

Although UK growth dipped by 2.7 per cent in 2019 due to the COVID-19 crisis, previously the sector had been developing continuously with 9.5 per cent growth reported between 2017 and 2018 and overall 27 per cent growth since 2010. The sector is showing signs of recovery with the combined subsectors contributing £2.5 billion to the UK economy in 2020, representing an annual increase of 2.4 per cent.[3] In 2020, the sector employed 2.2 million people with a 43.5 per cent increase in jobs since 2011.[4] The UK is a leading European producer of film and television programming with £1.4 billion in exports in 2021.[5] In terms of production hours, the European Audiovisual Observatory (EAO) finds 'the UK at the top of the ranking, both in terms of titles and hours, with 124 titles and 550 hours produced in 2020' (2022: 5). The bulk of export income is derived from BBC Studios which generated £800 million in 2021–2.[6]

[1] The Standard Industrial Classification for the creative industries lists: advertising, architecture, design, fashion, film, television, radio, photography, IT, book, newspaper, and journal publishing, library and museum activities, and performing arts.

[2] https://lordslibrary.parliament.uk/impact-of-government-policy-on-the-creative-sector [last accessed 25.10.2022].

[3] www.gov.uk/government/statistics/dcms-sectors-economic-estimates-monthly-gva-to-september-2021 [last accessed 25.10.2022].

[4] https://lordslibrary.parliament.uk/impact-of-government-policy-on-the-creative-sector [last accessed 25.10.2022].

[5] www.pact.co.uk/members-hub/resourcelibrary.html?q=UK+TV+Exports+Report+2020-2021 [last accessed 25.10.2022].

[6] https://committees.parliament.uk/publications/23091/documents/169130/default [last accessed 25.10.2022].

Brexit and the Digital Single Market. Alison Harcourt, Oxford University Press. © Alison Harcourt 2023.
DOI: 10.1093/oso/9780192899378.003.0003

The key point of concern over Brexit voiced by the creative industries is the end to freedom of movement of people within Europe, which has had a pronounced effect on a wide range of activities from film production to restrictions on travel for musicians, visual artists, and other cultural performers. The situation was exacerbated by the COVID-19 crisis which greatly impacted mobility in the sector with lasting repercussions. The second main concern was the loss of EU funding. Faucher (2022: 1) reports that 'between 2007 and 2016, 1,385 projects related to the arts, museums, and the creative industries in England received £345 million in EU funding (approximately £40 million per year)'. Creative Europe UK reported that the EU's Creative Europe programme had invested 111 million Euros into the UK's creative sector between 2014 and 2020 out of an overall budget of 1.46 billion Euros, representing 10 per cent of the overall funding awarded to 28 EU member states.[7] The UK was also the largest recipient of the 3.4 million Euro videogames fund under the latest Creative Europe programme which went, for example, towards funding the Broken Sword developer, Revolution Software.[8]

This chapter explains the UK's approach towards the creative industries post-Brexit. It examines the UK's positions on the promotion and protection of the sector. This includes the retention of cultural toolkits containing measures to promote content production including subsidies, tax relief, quotas, and the support of public service broadcasting. The chapter then analyses the market effect of Brexit on foreign investment, independent production, and employment. It then observes the UK's position post-Brexit under the General Agreement on Tariffs and Trade (GATT), General Agreement on Trade in Services (GATS), and free-trade agreements (FTAs). The chapter concludes that the main consequence of Brexit has been constraint to the freedom of movement in a sector which requires a high level of staff mobility.

UK policy trajectories

The 'creative industries' was identified in the 2017 paper 'Building Our Industrial Strategy'[9] as one of the five key sectors which the government pledged to support post-Brexit. The industrial strategy was published following a period of consultation, notably the Culture, Media and Sport Committee inquiry into the impact of Brexit on the creative industries, tourism, and the Digital Single Market.[10]

[7] www.bfi.org.uk/get-funding-support/funding-support-international-activity/creative-europe-desk-uk [last accessed 25.10.2022].

[8] https://ukie.org.uk/news/member-view-what-will-brexit-mean-for-european-funding-of-the-games-industry [last accessed 25.10.2022].

[9] www.gov.uk/government/uploads/system/uploads/attachment_data/file/586626/building-our-industrial-strategy-green-paper.pdf [last accessed 25.10.2022].

[10] www.parliament.uk/business/committees/committees-a-z/commons-select/culture-media-and-sport-committee/inquiries/parliament-2015/impact-of-brexit-16-17 [last accessed 25.10.2022].

According to the DCMS,[11] exports in digital services accounted for 8.7 per cent of total exports of services for the UK at the time. The EU represented its largest export market.

Of the 126 submissions to the Culture, Media and Sport committee consultation, 35 were from the film and television sector. Of the remaining submissions, 17 were from design/fashion/architecture representatives, 15 from the tourist industry, 14 performing arts and arts, 12 from cultural heritage and museum representatives, 8 copyright/intellectual property associations, 7 from telecommunications, computing, and gaming, 6 from music and radio, 4 from publishing, 2 from advertising, and 7 individual.[12] All but three (Airbnb, Electrolight, and Rare Corporate Design) expressed concern that Brexit would be harmful for the sector.

Three key issues were highlighted: the loss of Single Market access, the loss of EU sector funding, and the loss of freedom of movement. Most responses from content producers (comprising broadcasting and film associations and companies) pointed to the loss of access to EU markets post-Brexit. As detailed in Chapter 2, this concerned company access to provide services under the country of origin principle set out under the Audiovisual Media Services Directive (AVMSD), SatCab, e-commerce, copyright legislation, and other Digital Single Market legislation.

Regarding the loss of Single Market access, problems with VAT regimes were highlighted in the trade in goods. RWAP Services stated, 'UK businesses [could be] subject to other over-complicated and expensive administration regimes for remittance of international taxes on digital products' outside of the EU. The Crafts Council stated, 'nearly half of respondents (45.8%) thought Brexit would have an adverse effect on their own business. The majority (53.9%) of respondents felt Britain's position as a global leader in craft and innovation would be weakened'.[13] Copyright/intellectual property regimes were seen to be under threat by eight associations. The Incorporated Society of Musicians stated that '81% of respondents believed leaving the EU would have a harmful or very harmful impact on the music profession'.

Regarding loss of EU funding, the British documentary association BRITDOC (renamed the Doc Society in 2018) pointed out that the EU's Creative Europe programme had contributed a Gross Value Added of £10,807 billion to the UK in 2016. The Royal Institute of British Architects similarly illustrated that, although the UK contribution to the EU was '€5.4 billion over the period 2007–2013, during the

[11] www.gov.uk/government/uploads/system/uploads/attachment_data/file/523024/Creative_Industries_Economic_Estimates_January_2016_Updated_201605.pdf [last accessed 25.10.2022].

[12] One government department, one higher education institute funding body, one university campus, one academic, two consultancies, and one law association.

[13] The Crafts Council (2019) Written evidence FUU0009 submitted to the Culture, Media and Sport Committee inquiry into the impact of Brexit on the creative industries, tourism, and the Digital Single Market. https://committees.parliament.uk/writtenevidence/22401/default/ [last accessed 25.10.2022].

same period, the UK had received €8.8 billion in direct EU funding for research, development and innovation activities', representing a net gain.

Almost all submissions stressed the need to maintain free movement for sector workers. Most expressed concern over the loss of access to high-skilled workers. For example, UK Interactive Entertainment (2019), ie trade body for the UK's games and interactive entertainment industry, stated in its submission to the Lords EU Internal Market Sub-Committee on the inquiry Brexit: future trade between the UK and the EU, 'the most detrimental aspects of the referendum result are perceived to be the new difficulties this would bring in sourcing high-skilled EU workers—such as software engineers—who play a big part the UK's game and tech sectors'. The Publishers' Association (2019) stated, 'a third of publishing houses [said] that retaining freedom of movement is their top priority post-Brexit. A number of others said that securing the status of EU nationals living the UK was their primary concern'. Digital Catapult (2019) responded, '1 in 5 directors of technology start-ups are foreign nationals, and a high percentage are EU nationals that are attracted to London, leaving the EU would potentially make the UK less appealing for entrepreneurs'. The Association of Licensed Multiple Retailers (ALMR, 2019) wrote, '12% of all workers in the industry, are non-UK EU nationals. This includes 37% of all skilled roles and 28% of all managerial positions'. The tourism industry requested that tourist workers be considered for Tier 2 visas and that visa-free travel between the UK and EU countries be continued.

A number of association studies expressed concern about the potential loss of EU workers. The Creative Industries Federation's Global Talent reported that 75 per cent respondents from 250 of their members employed EU nationals. Arts Professional reported that '8% of the classical music workforce and 20% of the dance workforce are from the EU',[14] an estimate put together by the Musicians Union, One Dance UK, and the Association of British Orchestras. The Arts Council England submission to the House of Lords EU Committee stated that EU employees accounted for 15 per cent of employees in large national museums.[15] The Museums Association reported that 'EU nationals account for approximately 15% (150) of staff' working at the British Museum and 11 per cent of staff at the Science Museum.[16] This reflected education and skills gaps which could not be filled at the national level. The Royal Opera House testified that it was 'rarely able to secure cover from the UK and are therefore dependent on the ability of EU nationals to

[14] www.artsprofessional.co.uk/news/current-music-education-system-disaster-post-brexit-uk [last accessed 25.10.2022].

[15] www.theartnewspaper.com/2018/07/26/house-of-lords-warns-brexit-may-starve-uk-museums-of-skilled-workers [last accessed 25.10.2022].

[16] www.museumsassociation.org/museums-journal/news/2017/02/08022017-fears-of-brexit-brain-drain-national-museums [last accessed 25.10.2022].

immediately board a plane'.[17] Arts Council England expressed the importance for UK visual artists and musicians to be able to travel to Europe to perform.[18]

Following the 2017 consultation, commitments were made to the sector at public meetings and in Parliament. When Baroness Bonham-Carter of Yarnbury asked in Parliament whether Her Majesty's Government would 'match current levels of European Union funding for the creative industries following the United Kingdom's exit from the European Union',[19] the reply from Lord Ashton, under-secretary of state at the DCMS, was 'the Treasury will provide a guarantee for all new structural investment fund projects signed after the Autumn Statement and before we leave the EU where they provide value for money and support domestic strategic priorities'. He added that 'leaving the EU means that we want to take our own decisions about how to deliver the policy objectives previously targeted by EU funding'. The latter statement is of particular interest in respect of funding delivery given that the UK no longer needs to follow EU rules on the distribution of state aid. However, this chapter finds that the parameters for the delivery of aid have changed little since Brexit.

Creative sector funding

Historically, the policy goals of protecting supporting the creative industries have been pursued by European states through the use of 'cultural toolboxes' (Gibbons and Humphreys, 2011). Cultural toolboxes consist of support measures in the form of financial incentives, tax relief, subsidies, content quotas, and the support of public service broadcasting. A variety of exemptions exist for subsidies, quotas, and state aid for public service broadcasting in international trade agreements.

Between 1995 and 2001, film production received direct subsidies from the Arts Council and the British Screen Finance Group. Subsidies were subsequently administered by the UK Film Council between 2000 and 2011 underpinned by National Lottery funding. From this time onwards, funding has been managed by the British Film Institute (BFI) with the BFI production fund[20] and BFI network.[21] However, tax relief has been a preferred method of sector support in the UK, particularly in comparison to EU member states which have favoured direct subsidies.

[17] http://data.parliament.uk/writtenevidence/committeeevidence.svc/evidencedocument/culture-media-and-sport-committee/impact-of-brexit/written/42186.pdf [last accessed 25.10.2022].

[18] www.artscouncil.org.uk/sites/default/files/download-file/Arts%20Council_Brexit%20Research%202017_Report_FINAL.pdf [last accessed 25.10.2022].

[19] https://hansard.parliament.uk/Lords/2016-10-27/debates/FB242047-BA8C-416D-8216-AA8DDBFAEE10/BrexitCreativeIndustries#contribution-9969EC23-199E-48B1-8785-E7C3F38310E4 [last accessed 25.10.2022].

[20] www.bfi.org.uk/get-funding-support/create-films-tv-or-new-formats-storytelling/production-fund [last accessed 25.10.2022].

[21] www.gov.uk/government/news/7-million-global-screen-fund-launched [last accessed 25.10.2022].

Tax relief rules were originally brought in under Section 42 of the 1992 Finance (No. 2) Act[22] and Section 48 of the Finance (No. 2) Act 1997. Films needed to be certified as British under Schedule 1 of the Films Act 1985 to qualify. In practice, however, 'the reliefs for qualifying films were rarely accessed directly by film producers themselves, but were usually claimed by financial intermediaries (for example, banks or partnerships of wealthy individuals) using sale and lease back or production and licence schemes'.[23] Essentially, they were viewed as enabling tax relief for third-party financiers. However, an Oxford Economics study (2007: 2) estimated that 'UK film production would [have been] 75% smaller, at a cost of around £1.3 billion of lost GDP a year' without the tax relief measures.

Subsidies for film and other audio-visual works and tax relief schemes needed to be exempt from state aid rules by the European Commission. Exemptions were granted as long as they did not significantly affect competition within the EU. As explained in more detail in Chapter 9, member states were required to request prior notification for film subsidies from the Directorate-General for Competition (DG Competition) from 2001 onwards under the EU Cinema Communication. This required a number of specific conditions including: that aid be allocated to a nationally defined cultural product; that production must spend 20 per cent of film budgets in other member states; and that aid was limited to 50 per cent of production budgets. Aid to post-production services was not permitted under EU state aid. These rules no longer apply post-Brexit, providing the UK with some flexibility for state spending in the sector.

The UK film tax incentive scheme introduced in 2006 was approved under the 2006 Cinema Communication by DG Competition until 2012.[24] Section 42 of the 1992 Act and Section 48 of the 1997 Act were replaced under the UK Finance Act 2006 with a cash rebate of up to 25 per cent on UK-qualifying expenditure for production companies. Under EU rules, subsidies needed to undergo a 'cultural test'. The UK film tax incentive scheme was aimed at encouraging film producers to make culturally British films. Aid was provided to production companies up to 80 per cent tax relief on core expenditure (but with no cap on total expenditure).

The 2001 Cinema Communication was extended in 2006 to 2009 and then again until 2012. In 2012, the UK introduced its Creative Sector Tax relief which included a package of measures aimed at supported a wider bracket of industries. Notably, the public consultation for the measures included a number of influential US groups, namely Discovery, HBO, Nickelodeon, Turner, and the Walt Disney Company.

[22] www.legislation.gov.uk/ukpga/1992/48/contents [last accessed 25.10.2022].

[23] www.gov.uk/hmrc-internal-manuals/business-income-manual/bim56010 [last accessed 25.10.2022].

[24] https://ec.europa.eu/competition/state_aid/cases/201489/201489_629015_97_2.pdf.

From this time onwards, subsidies and tax relief schemes were either approved under the 2013 EU Cinema Communication[25] for film or on the basis of Article 107(3)d of the Treaty on the Functioning of the European Union (TFEU).[26] Corporation tax relief was granted in the UK Finance Bill 2013 to companies producing animation, high-end television, and videogames to encourage UK investment. Subsequently, Animation Tax Relief, High-End TV Production Tax Relief, and Video Games Tax Relief (VGTR) were introduced in 2014. As under the Film Tax Relief, companies needed to undergo cultural tests to demonstrate that they were culturally British. The cultural tests were published under the Finance Bill 2013 and conducted by the BFI. The policy was extended to Theatre Tax Relief in 2015, Childrens Television Tax Relief in 2016, Orchestra Tax Relief in 2017, and the Museums and Galleries Exhibition Tax Relief in 2018.[27] Many similar measures have been adopted at the EU level as discussed in Chapter 9.

Post-Brexit, the UK cultural test and limitation to 80 per cent of core expenditure remain in place. Neither requirement has been changed. To meet the requirements, films must qualify as British by the BFI on behalf of the DCMS.[28] The cultural test requires that 'to qualify for creative industry tax reliefs, all films must be certified as British. The film must pass a cultural test or qualify through an internationally agreed co-production treaty'. The Treaty referred to by the DCMS, under which films must qualify as British, is the Council of Europe's European Convention on Cinematic Co-Production.

Although the UK had received a disproportionate amount of funding from the programme historically compared to other EU member states, it declined to participate in the EU's Creative Europe Programme (2021 to 2027) post-Brexit as a third country.[29] Existing projects under the previous existing funding scheme which ran from 2014 to 2020 were permitted to continue past January 2021. Creative Europe UK reported that 81 films had received distribution support from the EU's Creative Europe programme in 2020, 39 of which were British.[30]

The replacement funding provided has changed the incentive structure for UK production. For example, in 2020, the UK film *Supernova*, starring Colin Firth and Stanley Tucci, was awarded circa 1 million Euros for distribution within Europe through the EU Selective Distribution scheme, supporting its release in 27 countries. The current UK Global Screen Fund limits by contrast funding up to £500,000 for a single eligible film including distribution and £25,000 under its International

[25] https://eur-lex.europa.eu/LexUriServ/LexUriServ.do?uri=OJ:C:2013:332:0001:0011:EN:PDF [last accessed 25.10.2022].

[26] https://competition-policy.ec.europa.eu/system/files/2022-06/stateaid_decisions_audiovisual_0.pdf [last accessed 25.10.2022].

[27] www.gov.uk/guidance/corporation-tax-creative-industry-tax-reliefs [last accessed 25.10.2022].

[28] www.gov.uk/guidance/claiming-film-tax-relief-for-corporation-tax [last accessed 25.10.2022].

[29] https://ec.europa.eu/culture/creative-europe.

[30] www.bfi.org.uk/get-funding-support/funding-support-international-activity/creative-europe-desk-uk [last accessed 25.10.2022].

Distribution Film Sales Support and £15,000 for film festivals.[31] Distribution support is therefore more globally focused and is no longer concentrated on Europe. The lower funding thresholds put pressure on the competitiveness of British independent production.

The UK can no longer apply for Structural Funds in the cultural field under EU regional policy, which houses several actions including the Music Moves Europe Awards. This also means that the UK will not be able to host European Capitals of Culture going forward. The UK agreed under the Trade and Cooperation Agreement (TCA) to contribute to and partake in the EU's Horizon Europe programme. Under the 2021–7 programme, there is a call under 'Culture, Creativity and Inclusive Society'. However, at the time of writing, the UK has been temporarily excluded from Horizon Europe due to the Northern Ireland protocol dispute.

In place of EU funding, the government committed £150 million under the Creative Industries Sector deal in 2018, including £39 million to industry–academic partnerships[32] and £33 million to immersive technologies. In parallel, the DCMS funded a Digital Culture Network to assist with digital skills in the sector.[33] In July 2020, a one-off £1.57 billion Culture Recovery Fund was introduced to help mitigate losses from the COVID-19 pandemic.[34] In November 2020, the UK government committed £7 million to support independent film and screen content in 2021 with its Global Screen Fund which is distributed by the BFI network.[35] It was notably less than the BFI's proposal of £17 million. UK film and television production support is mainly fuelled by tax relief.[36] In addition to this, in 2022, six English regions received £17.5 million to help support creative businesses.[37] The Department for International Trade (DIT) is also funding international collaboration particularly via the British Film Commission, including investment with European states.[38]

A large package of measures was provided to the creative industry during the COVID-19 recovery period in the form of direct aid[39] and tax relief in 2020.[40] Most

[31] www.bfi.org.uk/get-funding-support/funding-support-international-activity/film-export-fund [last accessed 25.10.2022].

[32] www.gov.uk/government/publications/creative-industries-sector-deal [last accessed 25.10.2022].

[33] www.artscouncil.org.uk/developing-digital-culture/digital-culture-network [last accessed 25.10.2022].

[34] www.gov.uk/government/news/157-billion-investment-to-protect-britains-world-class-cultural-arts-and-heritage-institutions [last accessed 25.10.2022].

[35] https://network.bfi.org.uk [last accessed 25.10.2022].

[36] www.bfi.org.uk/industry-data-insights/reports/uk-screen-sector-economy [last accessed 25.10.2022].

[37] www.gov.uk/government/news/creative-businesses-across-the-uk-receive-funding-boost-and-government-backing-to-spur-future-growth [last accessed 25.10.2022].

[38] https://britishfilmcommission.org.uk/wp-content/uploads/2022/02/BFC-ITT-UK-European-Hub-Research-FINAL.pdf [last accessed 25.10.2022].

[39] https://ec.europa.eu/competition/state_aid/cases1/202042/288220_2197202_88_3.pdf [last accessed 25.10.2022].

[40] https://ec.europa.eu/competition/elojade/isef/case_details.cfm?proc_code=3_SA_56047 [last accessed 25.10.2022].

funding went to support the restart of film and audio-visual productions which needed to halt under the pandemic period. The cultural sector suffered greatly during lockdown. Music and festivals were cancelled, as were 15,000 theatre performances, resulting in a loss of £303 million.[41] In July 2020, a £1.57 billion Culture Recovery Fund was introduced to help mitigate losses from the COVID-19 pandemic. This was followed by the DCMS Cultural and Heritage Capital Framework in 2021 to assess the value of the culture and heritage sector.[42] A Four Nations International Fund was established as a pilot in 2021 which supports creative projects involving at least two UK nations and another partner 'in Europe and beyond', with grants of up to £5,000. This is flanked by regional and city programmes (e.g. London's £2.3 million Culture at Risk Business Support fund).

In preparation for Brexit, the UK signed the Council of Europe Convention on Cinematographic Co-Production in 2020 to maintain co-production with European partners post-Brexit.[43] Under the Convention, films qualify for tax relief if a UK production company is responsible for all UK parts of a production. Co-production films also qualify for relief under co-production agreements with Australia, Brazil, Canada, China, France, India, Israel, Jamaica, Morocco, New Zealand, the Occupied Palestinian Territories, and South Africa (Blázquez et al., 2018). Television programmes also qualify under the Australia, Canada, New Zealand, Israel, and the Occupied Palestinian Territories agreements.

Although the UK opted out of the EU's Creative Europe programme, UK institutions such as the British Library continue to contribute to the Europeana portal.[44] Europeana began as an EU project to preserve books, at first as a counter to the Google Books project. Today, it serves as a single web portal which digitally preserves cultural artefacts including books, films, music, and paintings from cultural institutions across Europe. The Europeana Network at the time of writing includes over 4,000 cultural institutions (libraries, archives, and museums) with over 50 million digital objects (Plank, Ogunyemi, and Blok, 2020).

Lastly, in 2022, the UK government proposed a new digital licensing scheme for cultural goods (art and antiquities). Licences are issued by the UK Arts Council online on behalf of the secretary of state.[45] This replaces the EU's Export Licensing Unit (ELU) which is paper based.[46] UK export licences no longer need to be physically validated by Border Force officers and it is envisioned that this new digital system could be a blueprint for other states. New rules have been introduced to

41 https://committees.parliament.uk/writtenevidence/3564/html [last accessed 25.10.2022].

42 www.gov.uk/guidance/culture-and-heritage-capital-portal [last accessed 25.10.2022].

43 www.gov.uk/government/publications/council-of-europe-convention-on-cinematographic-co-production-revised-ms-no22020 [last accessed 25.10.2022].

44 www.europeana.eu/en [last accessed 25.10.2022].

45 www.artscouncil.org.uk/supporting-arts-museums-and-libraries/export-licensing [last accessed 25.10.2022].

46 https://assets.publishing.service.gov.uk/government/uploads/system/uploads/attachment_data/file/1054643/benefits-of-brexit.pdf [last accessed 25.10.2022].

'provide an opportunity for the UK to retain cultural goods judged to be of outstanding national importance that would otherwise be exported'. These rules encompass goods that have reached a certain age and financial value.

DSM legislation affecting the creative sector

The BFI reported an overall record investment in film and high-end television of £4.713 billion in 2021, an 86 per cent increase on 2020. However, the bulk of this income comes from US platform investment. There is no longer an obligation for companies to use UK independent production companies, which was a requirement under the AVMSD. Although public service broadcasters are required under Section 285 of the 2003 Communications Act[47] to commission independent producers approved by Ofcom, there is no requirement for large streaming platforms to do the same.

Domestically, the large streaming services such as Amazon, Netflix, and Disney provided ample investment to UK production post-Brexit, accounting for £356 million in national income in 2020, three times the 2016 income (Gray, 2022). Most of these large platforms commission non-domestic production companies. As explained by the Producers Alliance for Cinema and Television (PACT), although revenue from the large platform providers such as Netflix and Amazon Prime has grown year on year, investment growth in the UK independent production sector has slowed in the UK.[48]

Ofcom details that 'commissions to UK production companies by foreign broadcasters and streaming services as well as licensing of finished programmes ... declined by 13% in 2021, to £952m', at its lowest level since 2011. At the same time, the UK has become the third largest production base globally for Netflix, which holds long-term leases with Shepperton Studies and Longcross Film Studios, neither of which are available for hire by third-party productions.[49] There has been a 'battle for staff' between UK independent production companies and the large US streaming services, with US players outbidding on production staff salaries, studio space, and equipment and engaging in last-minute gazumping practices (Gray, 2022).

By contrast, flexibility under the 2018 AVMSD has allowed EU states to oblige large platform providers to invest in domestic content production. This option has been taken up by France, Germany, Belgium, Italy, and Spain (Kostovskak, Raats, and Donders, 2020; Leiva and Albornoz, 2021). For example, France requires large

[47] www.legislation.gov.uk/ukpga/2003/21/section/285 [last accessed 25.10.2022].
[48] www.pact.co.uk/latest-updates/news/detail.html?id=revenues-fall-as-pandemic-hits-tv-production-sector [last accessed 25.10.2022].
[49] www.screendaily.com/news/netflix-to-lease-longcross-film-studios-in-second-long-term-uk-facility-deal/5163454.article [last accessed 25.10.2022].

platform providers to invest 20 per cent of their French turnover in French content production, 85 per cent of which must be of French-language origin and the majority of which retain rights for producers. Accordingly, Amazon, Disney, and Netflix committed to invest 250 million Euros annually in French production from 2022 (Barker and Abboud, 2022). Italy has a similar obligation, with large platforms investing up to 20 per cent of Italian turnover in independent works.

Under the AVMSD, there is a mandate for a majority proportion of transmission time to be reserved for European works for linear services. On-demand services are required to reserve at least 30 per cent of their catalogues for European works and to make these works prominent. This means that, for example, Netflix, which is licensed in the Netherlands, is required to have 30 per cent of its catalogue devoted to European content. Although the requirement is not obligatory 'where practical', according to market reports the main video on-demand (VOD) service providers have greatly increased European content provision, with Netflix and Amazon exceeding the 30 per cent quota in most markets.[50]

A key issue post-Brexit was whether UK-produced content could continue to qualify as 'European works' under Articles 13, 16, and 17 of the AVMSD. Although the 2021 DCMS 'Notice to Stakeholders' for audio-visual media services confirmed that works originating in the UK continue to be classed as European works,[51] this was only in reference to states which signed the European Convention on Transfrontier Television (ECTT), which permitted the freedom of reception of audio-visual services from the UK. As explained in Chapter 3, the ECTT does not apply to VOD (streaming) services.

Of more concern for the UK was discussion in the Council of the European Union's Audiovisual Working Party of 'the disproportionate presence of UK content in the European VOD quota and the effects on the circulation and promotion of diverse European works' in 2021.[52] Reportedly, France is proposing that UK content be excluded from the European works category (Boffey, 2021). This would mean that UK-produced content could be excluded from national quotas in favour of EU-produced content in catalogues and channels in the next revision of the AVMSD.

Gaming remains highly profitable for the UK. Similar to film, it has been supported by tax relief schemes and investment by large US groups. As the Creative Industries report, 'international investments in the UK's games industry include the acquisition of Codemasters by Take Two Interactive and the purchase by Warner Bros. of Traveller's Tales, makers of titles such as LEGO Batman, LEGO

[50] www.ampereanalysis.com/press/release/dl/netflix-now-at-or-above-30-european-content-in-almost-all-major-european-markets [last accessed 25.10.2022].

[51] www.gov.uk/guidance/broadcasting-and-video-on-demand-services-between-the-uk-and-eu [last accessed 25.10.2022].

[52] https://data.consilium.europa.eu/doc/document/CM-3322-2021-INIT/en/pdf [last accessed 25.10.2022].

Star Wars and LEGO Harry Potter. The UK hosts the European headquarters of overseas games companies such as Microsoft, Sony, and Konami'.[53] Currently the top three export markets for UK gaming are the USA, China, and Japan, followed by Europe.

Free movement of workers

The greatest impact on the creative industries is undoubtedly the removal of free movement for sector workers. Domestically, retaining staff post-Brexit has presented additional costs for the creative industries. As one company, Framestore, explained in the *Financial Times*, 'We have about 1,200 people in London and about 30 per cent of them are from the 27 member states so I'm going to be paying for more than 300 visas' (Garrahan, 2018). By 2022, the BFI pointed to a severe skills shortage in its 2022 Skills Review. Screenskills estimated between 15,130 and 20,770 additional staff were needed in the film industry in 2022.[54]

Similarly, the House of Commons DCMS Committee found in its 2022 'Reimagining Where We Live: Cultural Place Making and the Levelling Up Agenda' report[55] that the 'creative industries are experiencing a significant, ongoing national shortage in skilled labour'. In its consultation, the Commercial Broadcasters Association (COBA), the trade association for commercial broadcasters and on-demand services, claimed skilled labour shortages were responsible for one of the largest obstacles to growth in the sector. PACT, along with a University of Exeter study,[56] reported that most skills shortages comprised camera operators, line producers, and production coordinators.

The National Youth Theatre found shortages in visual effects, 2- and 3D animation, and videogame skills. The Broadcasting, Entertainment, Communications and Theatre Union (BECTU) reported in its consultation document that backstage workers had suffered a 50 per cent decline with over half of freelance professionals not having returned to post-pandemic full-time work. The music industry has lost schoolteachers, particularly for orchestral instruments. The heritage sector, which historically employed large numbers of EU nationals, noted a steep decline in staff.

From January 2021, those seeking permanent employment in the UK had to have offers in 'high-skilled' professions with a salary over £20,480 and be able to speak English. Companies need to pay immigration and NHS costs. But the situation

[53] www.thecreativeindustries.co.uk/site-content/industries-games-games-why-the-uk [last accessed 25.10.2022].

[54] www.screenskills.com/news/new-forecast-of-skills-and-training-needs-to-support-uk-film-and-high-end-tv-production-boom [last accessed 25.10.2022].

[55] https://committees.parliament.uk/publications/31429/documents/176244/default [last accessed 25.10.2022].

[56] https://committees.parliament.uk/writtenevidence/106450/html [last accessed 25.10.2022].

was more difficult for temporary workers. The UK only permits foreign (including EU nationals) to stay for up to 30 days for paid engagements and only if they can validate their profession and are invited by established UK businesses.[57] Longer stays require T5 temporary work visas[58] which require performers to have 'proof the applicant is known internationally, or they have demonstrable international box-office appeal'.[59] Exemptions include a number of creative industry sector employees[60] but not musicians. The global talent visa which covers academia or research, arts and culture, and digital technology only covers exceptional talent.[61]

Under the 2020 Council of Europe Convention on Cinematographic Co-Production, performers taking part in co-productions under the Treaty and other bilateral co-production treaties who provide certification from the UK Film Council can travel abroad to work. The UK government sought visa-free travel for musicians within the EU but this was rejected by the European Commission because the UK refused to provide European musicians reciprocal days of visa-free travel. Without an EU-wide agreement, musicians needed to comply with the rules of each individual state they are visiting. Some states permit cultural activity work, whereas others do not.[62]

The loss of freedom of movement has meant that UK nationals have faced obstacles in performing in Europe. This includes visa bureaucracy and cost and the transportation of musical instruments and theatre props. In 2021, the House of Lords received a petition for the negotiation of visa-free work permits for touring professionals and artists with over 282,000 signatures. The Petitions Committee survey found that 81 per cent of respondents stated they were likely to cease touring in Europe post-Brexit.

Subsequently, the UK updated the rules for those travelling to the UK.[63] At the time of writing, musicians, entertainers, and artists from 'non-visa national countries' which include EU states and the US can work in the UK for one month without a visa if they are invited and explicitly paid by a UK organisation. They can come to the UK for three months visa free if they have been granted a certificate of sponsorship by a 'licensed sponsor' under the Temporary Work—Creative Worker visa concession.[64] Staff can work up to six months without a visa if they perform

[57] www.gov.uk/permitted-paid-engagement-visa [last accessed 25.10.2022].

[58] www.gov.uk/temporary-worker-creative-and-sporting-visa [last accessed 25.10.2022].

[59] www.gov.uk/guidance/immigration-rules/immigration-rules-appendix-t5-creative-workers-codes-of-practice [last accessed 25.10.2022].

[60] These are producers, directors, directors of photography (cinematographer), production designers, costumer designers, hair/make-up supervisors, editors, composers, visual effects supervisors, sound designers, and script writers.

[61] www.gov.uk/global-talent-arts-culture [last accessed 25.10.2022].

[62] https://ec.europa.eu/home-affairs/sites/homeaffairs/files/e-library/documents/policies/borders-and-visas/visa-policy/22122020_information_december_2020.xlsx [last accessed 25.10.2022].

[63] www.gov.uk/guidance/visiting-the-uk-as-a-creative-professional-from-a-non-visa-national-country#full-publication-update-history [last accessed 25.10.2022].

[64] www.gov.uk/creative-worker-visa/creative-worker-concession [last accessed 25.10.2022].

at a permit-free festival which is published under the Immigration Rules. If they attain a visa, and a certificate of sponsorship, they can work up to 12 months on under the Temporary Work—Creative Worker route.

However, there were no reciprocal arrangements in the EU. The DCMS therefore sought bilateral arrangements with a number of EU countries.[65] From October 2021, short-term visas were permitted in 20 EU and three European Free Trade Association (EFTA) countries for UK musicians and performers. The 20 EU states are Austria, Belgium, Czech Republic, Denmark, Estonia, Finland, France, Germany, Hungary, Ireland, Italy, Latvia, Lithuania, Luxembourg, Netherlands, Poland, Romania, Slovakia, Slovenia, and Sweden. The DCMS is at the time of writing negotiating further agreements with Bulgaria, Croatia, Cyprus, Greece, Malta, Portugal, and Spain. The arrangements with the three EFTA states were made under the UK–EFTA FTA in 2021 with Iceland, Liechtenstein, and Norway.[66]

Lastly, it should be noted that, although the UK never joined the Schengen Area even while an EU member, opting out under the Amsterdam Treaty, it does continue to participate in the Common Travel Area[67] with Ireland, Jersey, Guernsey, and the Isle of Man. The agreement, which has its roots in previous agreements that took place prior to EU membership, guarantees freedom of moment with minimum checks, the right to work, access to social welfare benefits and health services, studying, and voting in certain elections. This allows some flexibility for creative sector workers to travel but also encouraged collaboration with the establishment of the British-Irish Council Creative Industries work sector.[68]

International trade fora

The EU gained 'l'exception culturelle' under GATT for goods and Most Favored Nation (MFN) exemptions for services under GATS at the World Trade Organization (WTO). Cultural exemptions have made up the majority of all MFN exemptions since the establishment of the WTO. The Council of Ministers lobbied for an exemption for cultural services within the GATS for the European Communities during Uruguay Round negotiations (1986–94). This was not achieved, and audio-visual services (including motion picture, radio, television, videotape production, and distribution services) were introduced to the WTO along with telecommunication, postal, and other communication services. GATS requires that specific commitments are made between states.

[65] www.gov.uk/government/news/visa-free-short-term-touring-allowed-in-20-member-states [last accessed 25.10.2022].

[66] www.efta.int/Free-Trade/news/EEA-EFTA-States-sign-free-trade-agreement-UK-524641 [last accessed 25.10.2022].

[67] www.gov.uk/government/publications/common-travel-area-guidance [last accessed 25.10.2022].

[68] www.britishirishcouncil.org/areas-work/creative-industries [last accessed 25.10.2022].

Thus far, no commitments have been made by the UK or any EU member state. Instead, the Council of Ministers negotiated a cultural exemption to the MFN agreement for production and distribution of audio-visual works, cinematographic works, television radio programmes, and broadcasting services. This protects film and television subsidy schemes, linguistic quotas, ownership legislation, market access, levies on non-European content, and subsidisation of endeavours such as digital switchover at national and European levels within Europe. The Council of the European Union confirmed that it 'shall not agree to rules or commitments for audio-visual services' in the current Doha round.[69] As Dongchul and Kimm (2020: 14) note, it is 'a common practice that the audio-visual sector is put aside from mainstream negotiations; not only was it excluded from the General Agreement on Trade in Services (GATS) negotiations but it is often left out of the scope of regional trade talks'.

On 31 December 2020, the UK exited all international agreements it was party to as a member of the EU, which included the EU's negotiated l'exception culturelle exemptions under Article IV of GATT[70] for national treatment of screen quotas for cinematographic film and MFN exemptions for audio-visual services under GATS.[71] The UK's position on exemptions did not change post-Brexit and needed to be renegotiated by the UK[72] on an individual basis.[73] As Bickel (2021: 226) explains, the UK's status within the WTO has changed. European states do not have separate goods and services schedules at the WTO but operate under EU schedules. For this reason, the UK needed to submit new goods and services schedules post-Brexit. These have not diverged from the EU schedules. In July 2018, the UK's draft schedule of concessions and commitments for goods, draft Schedule XIX—United Kingdom,[74] was disseminated for certification under WTO Procedures for Modification and Rectification of Schedules of Tariff Concessions. In December 2018, the UK schedule of concessions and specific commitments in services and list of Article II GATS (MFN) exemptions were disseminated for certification.[75]

On 26 June 2019, the UK sent a communication to the WTO Secretariat with a request to circulate to WTO members. It outlined that the UK would remain a

[69] www.consilium.europa.eu/media/39505/st08993-ad01-en19.pdf [last accessed 25.10.2022].

[70] www.wto.org/english/docs_e/legal_e/gatt47_e.pdf [last accessed 25.10.2022].

[71] www.wto.org/english/tratop_E/serv_e/audiovisual_e/audiovisual_e.htm [last accessed 25.10.2022].

[72] https://assets.publishing.service.gov.uk/government/uploads/system/uploads/attachment_data/file/762809/SCW381_-_UK_MFN_list_FINAL_03_12_2018.pdf [last accessed 25.10.2022].

[73] https://assets.publishing.service.gov.uk/government/uploads/system/uploads/attachment_data/file/862657/200131_GC_statement_pdf.pdf [last accessed 25.10.2022].

[74] https://goods-schedules.wto.org/member/united-kingdom [last accessed 25.10.2022].

[75] The United Kingdom's list of Article II GATS (MFN) exemptions were circulated for certification under the Procedures for the Certification of Terminations, Reductions and Rectifications of Article II (MFN) exemptions in documents S/C/W/380 and S/C/W/381. https://assets.publishing.service.gov.uk/government/uploads/system/uploads/attachment_data/file/949410/201231_General_Council_Statement_FINAL.pdf [last accessed 25.10.2022].

part of the EU's customs union and Single Market during the transition period until 31 December 2020, for which reason 'the United Kingdom is treated as a Member State of the European Union for the purpose of international agreements entered into by the European Union'. This meant that the UK applied the EU's Generalised Scheme of Preferences up until this time. This position was supported by a 27 January 2020 note verbale sent by the EU to the Director-General of the WTO and third countries, notifying them that for the duration of the transition period, 'the United Kingdom is to be treated as a Member State of the European Union for the purpose of international agreements and arrangements'.[76] A second UK communication was circulated to WTO members in January 2021,[77] detailing its negotiations to date and indicating its tariff regime and Generalised Scheme of Preferences (GSP), stating, 'the United Kingdom GSP will provide the same level of access as the current European Union trade preference scheme'.

Clearly, at the time of writing, the UK's position within the WTO remains unchanged to that prior to Brexit. It should, however, be considered that, now the UK has left the EU, it could face pressure, particularly from the US, to take on new commitments in the sector. Under Doha, the US is targeting the liberalisation of cross-border streaming services with a proposal to include it under the category of 'E. Information Services (Value-added services)' introduced in 2005 (Dongchul and Kimm, 2020: 18). Indeed, it proposed that the WTO delete the subgroup of 'Enhanced Telecommunications Services' under the heading 'C. Telecommunications Services' and transfer the list of subcategories to E. Information Services (Value-added services).

The EU also played a salient role in negotiation of the 2005 UNESCO Convention on the Protection and Promotion of the Diversity of Cultural Expressions. The Committee of Permanent Representatives in the European Union (COREPER) presented a common position of all EU member states within UNESCO. The Convention supports a number of measures aimed at promoting cultural expression. Article 6 supports subsidisation of content and public service broadcasting. Article 7 supports dissemination and distribution rights.

The EU supported implementation of the 2005 Convention in a number of ways. Firstly, it inserted 'cultural protocols' into bilateral treaty agreements between the EU and third countries. Protocols on cultural cooperation in Economic Partnership Agreements that referenced the UNESCO Convention include the 2008 EU–Cariforum, the 2009 EU–South Korea FTA, 2010 EU—Central America, 2011 EU—Andean countries, and the 2014 EU–Canada Comprehensive Trade

[76] https://docs.wto.org/dol2fe/Pages/SS/directdoc.aspx?filename=q:/WT/LET/1462.pdf [last accessed 25.10.2022].

[77] WT/GC/226 4 January 2021 (21-0057) Page: ¼ General Council End of the UK-EU Transition Period Communication from the United Kingdom. https://assets.publishing.service.gov.uk/government/uploads/system/uploads/attachment_data/file/949410/201231_General_Council_Statement_FINAL.pdf [last accessed 25.10.2022].

and Economic Agreement (CETA). These protocols are updated every five years. For example, the 2015 Protocol on Cultural Cooperation with Korea was updated in 2020.[78] All of the protocols reference the Convention and define terms such as cultural diversity, cultural expression, and cultural goods and services (Vlassis, 2016: 449). Secondly, the EU funded the UNESCO Convention's international Expert Facility under the Strengthening the EU's System of Governance for Culture in Developing Countries projects (2001–15, 2015–18, and 2019–22).

The negotiated exemptions in bilateral treaty agreements[79] for 'culture' between the EU and third states no longer apply to the UK. Exemptions under these agreements included screen quotas, subsidies, duties, deposits and taxes for film, the transmission of radio and television, and VOD packages (linear and non-linear). Post-Brexit, the UK is inserting sector exemptions into most of its FTAs. The UK has thus far signed agreements with Japan (2020),[80] Australia (2021),[81] Comoros (2022), EFTA (2021),[82] the European Supervisory Authority (ESA) (Mauritius, Seychelles, and Zimbabwe),[83] Madagascar (2021), Singapore (2022),[84] Turkey (2021),[85] Switzerland (2021),[86] and New Zealand (2022).[87] It should be noted that only the EU TCA, EFTA, Japanese Comprehensive Economic Partnership Agreement, and Single Digital Economic Agreement have been enacted at the time of writing. The UK is also negotiating agreements with Canada, Mexico, the Gulf Cooperation Council (GCC), and Israel, and applying to join the Progressive Agreement for Trans-Pacific Partnership (CPTPP).[88]

Under the FTA with Australia, which is undergoing ratification at the time of writing, chapter 8 on the cross-border trade in services exempts audio-visual services. Chapter 12 on telecommunications does not apply to:

[78] https://eur-lex.europa.eu/legal-content/EN/TXT/?qid=1585963382194&uri=CELEX:32020D0470 [last accessed 25.10.2022].

[79] www.europarl.europa.eu/RegData/etudes/STUD/2016/535013/EXPO_STU(2016)535013_EN.pdf [last accessed 25.10.2022].

[80] For exemptions under UK–Japan trade agreement, see pp. 138 and 246 at https://assets.publishing.service.gov.uk/government/uploads/system/uploads/attachment_data/file/929181/CS_Japan_1.2020_UK_Japan_Agreement_Comprehensive_Economic_Partnership__v1.pdf [last accessed 25.10.2022].

[81] https://assets.publishing.service.gov.uk/government/uploads/system/uploads/attachment_data/file/1099438/CS_Australia_1.2022_Free_Trade_vol5.pdf [last accessed 25.10.2022].

[82] www.efta.int/free-trade/free-trade-agreements/uk [last accessed 25.10.2022].

[83] www.gov.uk/government/collections/esa-uk-economic-partnership-agreement-epa--2 [last accessed 25.10.2022].

[84] https://assets.publishing.service.gov.uk/government/uploads/system/uploads/attachment_data/file/1060050/CS_Singapore_1.2002_UK_Singapore_Digital_Economy_Agreement.pdf [last accessed 25.10.2022].

[85] https://assets.publishing.service.gov.uk/government/uploads/system/uploads/attachment_data/file/963851/CS_Turkey_1.2021_UK_Turkey_Free_Trade_Agreement.pdf [last accessed 25.10.2022].

[86] www.seco.admin.ch/seco/en/home/Aussenwirtschaftspolitik_Wirtschaftliche_Zusammenarbeit/Wirtschaftsbeziehungen/brexit.html [last accessed 25.10.2022].

[87] www.gov.uk/government/collections/uk-new-zealand-free-trade-agreement [last accessed 25.10.2022].

[88] www.gov.uk/government/collections/the-uks-trade-agreements [last accessed 25.10.2022].

(a) audio-visual services;
(b) any measure affecting services providing, or exercising editorial control over, content transmitted using telecommunications networks or services; or
(c) any measure affecting broadcast or cable distribution of radio or television programming, except that:
    (i) Article 12.4 (Access and Use) applies with respect to a cable or broadcast services supplier's access to and use of public telecommunications services; and(ii) Article 12.21 (Transparency) applies to any measure affecting broadcast or cable distribution of radio or television programming, to the extent that the measure also affects public telecommunications networks or services.

Chapter 13 of the proposed FTA on investment under Senior Management and Boards of Directors has an exemption for audio-visual services. Chapter 14 on digital trade contains exemptions for audio-visual services and government procurement. Chapter 18 on state-owned enterprises and designated monopolies also does not apply to audio-visual services. Similar exemptions were inserted into the other FTAs depending on their trade focus. For example, the Digital Economy Agreement with Singapore has opt-outs for audio-visual services under Article 8.58 for open and connected digital markets. However, the UK has not negotiated cultural protocols in FTAs as the EU has done.

Conclusion

This chapter has shown that the creative industries are weathering the post-Brexit period despite substantial challenges to the market. The sector continues to be a growth sector for the UK as a whole, although this has slowed with a 2.4 per cent growth in 2021 compared to near 10 per cent annual growth in the pre-Brexit years. The UK can react more quickly in the administration of state aid post-Brexit, as exemplified by its response to the COVID-19 crisis. It no longer has to adhere to EU state aid rules which provide substantial flexibility in the administration of funding. Related to this, the UK is also not bound by the parameters established in the Next Generation EU recovery package. At the same time, it is preserving protection for national subsidies and quotas in FTAs and on world trade platforms.

However, the sector has lost European market access, notably under the country of origin principle as shown in Chapter 2. Performers and artists are experiencing European visa difficulties. UK cities can also no longer apply to be European Capitals of Culture under EU structural funding and researchers have been closed out of the EU's Horizon Europe programme. The loss of funding from the EU's Creative Europe Programme has been replaced under a number of schemes and UK funding schemes for film and gaming have not changed substantially post-Brexit, with the 'cultural test' and limits for tax relief remaining in place for British content production.

However, the initial Brexit period has witnessed an increased push from governments for a more global focus for British content with greater reliance on market incentives, particularly private sector funding and tax relief schemes. Clearly, the initial direction of government policy was to steer the industry towards the global level away from Europe. This has resulted in increased investment at the domestic level from large US platforms but has been coupled in turn with a decrease in British independent production, which continues to be mainly fuelled by the BBC and has seen a major cut to funding.

Direct funding to the arts has seen major cuts post-Brexit. The government's aim to spread funding more evenly across the UK is in line with its policy of levelling up. In the 2023–6 Arts Council England (ACE) budget, announced in November 2022, cuts were made to theatres, museums, and arts organisations in London in particular, which suffered £50 million in government cuts, one-third of its former budget. The theatre sector has seen the most cuts, with the English National Opera receiving no regular funding. For example, annual cuts of £319,673 were made to Camden Arts Centre, £280,964 to the Crafts Council, £184,131 to the Institute of Contemporary Arts (ICA), and £485,725 to the Serpentine Galleries.[89] Other organisations have seen their funding maintained or increased, including the Jewish Museum London and Autograph ABP.

The EU remains the UK's largest export market for the creative industries and the UK continues to benefit from the European works requirement within the Council of Europe Convention on Cinematographic Co-Production. More recently, there has been a recognition of the UK's European role in content production which can most clearly be seen through the actions of the DIT, which is funding a number of European schemes through the British Film Commission (BFC). The BFC has engineered a number of MoUs with other states. In October 2021, the BFC signed an MoU with the Spain Film commission and in May 2022 with Italian Film Commissions. In November 2022, it signed an MoU with Norway for collaboration between the UK and Norwegian screen industries, film, and high-end TV production.[90] Faucher (2022) points to the initiation of similar bilateral arrangements with European states in the arts sector. Cultural partnerships are encouraged through British Council collaboration grants which include Europe but have more of a global reach.[91] It remains to be seen whether this renewed focus on Europe is sustainable given France's reluctance to maintain UK content under the AVMSD European works quota and potential US pressure for the opening of UK markets to over-the-top services at the WTO level.

[89] www.theartnewspaper.com/2022/11/04/brutal-cuts-to-london-arts-organisations-as-national-funds-are-moved-away-from-capital [last accessed 25.10.2022].

[90] https://britishfilmcommission.org.uk/about [last accessed 25.10.2022].

[91] www.britishcouncil.org/arts/international-collaboration-grants [last accessed 25.10.2022].

4
The UK's Role in EU Telecommunications Policy
Brexit and Beyond

Introduction

The UK has exerted considerable influence on the direction of EU telecommunications policy. Successive UK governments in cooperation with private actors pushed for privatisation and deregulation of telecommunications markets over a period of four decades. Before the 1980s, the telecommunications sector had long been restricted at national levels, particularly in the provision of telephony and spectrum use, areas heavily guarded by member states. EU sector liberalisation began with a series of Directives in the late 1980s and 1990s which opened markets for telecommunications services and networks across Europe. Based upon the UK's lead, the EU framework was proactive in breaking up monopolies in telecommunications and mobile phone provision.

The sector has experienced substantial privatisation and competition since this time. This chapter will discuss the history of the UK's role in EU telecommunications policy up to the present day. It examines a number of UK-led initiatives adopted at the European level, including the introduction of competition to incumbent services, flexible rules for spectrum trading, and the use of white space in spectrum. The chapter then turns to the UK's role in agreements at international levels among coordination bodies: the International Telecommunication Union (ITU), World Radiocommunication Conference (WRC), and Conférence Européenne des Administrations des Postes et des Télécommunications (CEPT). Lastly, the chapter examines the position of UK policy post-Brexit with a focus on EU policy divergence.

The UK's role in EU policy development

Telecommunications deregulation was one of the first policies anchoring the European Commission's Single Market programme established by the 1986 Single European Act. It was influenced by liberalisation in the UK, which introduced competition to the national market in the early 1980s. UK market liberalisation, flanked

Brexit and the Digital Single Market. Alison Harcourt, Oxford University Press. © Alison Harcourt 2023.
DOI: 10.1093/oso/9780192899378.003.0004

by the break-up of AT&T into the 'baby bells' in the United States, induced pressure from industry for Europe-wide liberalisation (Dyson and Humphreys, 1990).

UK market liberalisation began in 1981 with the separation of BT from the Post Office under the British Telecommunications Act. In 1982, a competitor, Mercury Communications, was granted a licence to compete with BT in fixed-line networks. At the time, the European Commission took a competition Decision against BT and found it to be abusing its dominant position as a state monopoly in the provision of telephone and facilities. In 1984, 51 per cent of BT was sold in a public auction and the Telecommunications Act established the independent regulatory body, Oftel. Mobile phone licences were issued to Cellnet and Racal-Vodafone in 1985. Sandholtz noted that 'the United Kingdom was the only European country with a major degree of liberalization' at that time (1993: 245).

Based upon this model, the Commission introduced a 1983 Communication entitled 'Telecommunications' urging the European Economic Community (EEC) to develop a European-wide telecommunications policy. However, the European Commission's ambition to open national markets to private competition met with opposition from the key member states of France, Germany, Italy, and Spain (Natalicchi, 2001: 13). A key catalyst for EU telecommunications liberalisation was the 1985 European Court of Justice (ECJ) ruling on BT in Case 41/83. The case began in 1982 when BT's pricing schemes were judged by the Directorate-General (DG) Competition in its 1982 Decision to be contravening Article 86 of the Treaty of Rome. The UK supported the decision. However, Italy contested it in the ECJ, fearing a challenge to its national telecommunications incumbent. The Court rejected Italy's challenge, confirming that public-owned companies were subject to Article 86 and could potentially abuse their dominant positions. Importantly, it confirmed the Commission's power to apply competition law to the telecommunications sector (Michalis 2007: 144).

This paved the way for EU legislative action. Significantly, following the ECJ ruling, the Commission DG Information Market and Innovation was renamed DG Telecommunications, Information Industry and Innovation (DG XIII) in 1986 to provide greater political focus on the telecommunications sector. This began gradually with a common market for telecommunications equipment (Natalicchi, 2001: 41). In 1986, Council Directive 86/361/EEC was agreed. This introduced common conformity specifications for a pan-European cellular digital mobile communications system (the Global System for Mobile communication (GSM) Directive).

By 1987, the Commission had produced its Green Paper, 'Towards a Dynamic European Economy on the Development of the Communication Market for Telecommunications Services and Equipment'. The paper recommended liberalisation of the provision of terminal equipment and the 'free provision of all services other than basic services'. Basic services referred to incumbents' monopolies on voice telephony. The paper called for the establishment of independent regulatory bodies for telecommunications at national levels, clearly based on the Oftel model, the opening of the market for non-discrimination against providers from other member states, and a common European position in the General Agreement on Tariffs and Trade (GATT) and the ITU. It further recommended that 'consensus must be achieved on standards, frequencies and tariff principles'.

The Green Paper was followed by agreement on the 1990 Open Network Provision (ONP) Directive that introduced conditions for the harmonisation of public telecommunications networks and public telecommunications services. All conditions needed to be 'based on objective criteria, non-discriminatory, transparent and public; tariffs had to be cost-oriented; restrictions on access were to be minimized' (Thatcher, 2001: 564). The ONP also recommended that the European Telecommunications Standards Institute (ETSI) draw up European standards for EU harmonisation in coordination with the Joint European Standards Institution Comité Européen de Normalisation/European Committee for Electrotechnical Standardization (CEN/CENELEC). The ONP Framework Directive enabled the Commission to establish guidelines for telecommunications services, namely leased lines, public packet-switched data services, integrated services digital networks (SDNs), and voice telephony. Each guideline outlined a set of standards for interoperability which were to be developed by ETSI.

The ONP was flanked by a number of Directives, namely the 1988 Directive on competition in the markets in telecommunications terminal equipment and the 1989 Directive on review procedures to the award of public supply and public works contracts, which withdrew exclusive rights for incumbents for the supply of terminal equipment and stipulated procedures to the award of public supply and public works contracts. This was followed by the 1990 Services Directive on competition in the markets for telecommunications services, which banned monopoly over services such as email, fax, and data processing, and the 1990 Public Procurement Directive opening supply contracts to public tender (Thatcher, 2001: 564). The Directives stipulated the establishment of independent regulators that would license and approve equipment, allocate frequencies, and set usage conditions in the market. The terminal Directive was challenged in court by France, a case supported by Italy, Belgium, Germany, and Greece. However, the ECJ upheld the decision in 1991 in C-202/88.

The approval of the Directives in the Council was greatly facilitated by the introduction of the Single European Act (SEA) (Natalicchi 2001: 41). The SEA had introduced qualified majority voting, making it easier for legislative proposals to pass in the Council, as well as introducing freedom of movement for capital and the removal of legal obstacles to investment. This framework lay the groundwork for a number of Directives and Regulations in telecommunications and e-commerce, leading up to full liberalisation of telecommunications markets by 1998 outlined in the 1996 Full Competition Directive.

The UK proactively pursued its pro-market agenda with the appointment of Don Cruickshank as Director-General of the UK telecoms regulator, Oftel, from 1993 to 1998. As Walden explained, because Cruickshank came from the airline Virgin Atlantic, he 'was perceived as being pro-new entrant and naturally untrusting towards BT as the incumbent' (Walden, 2018: 19). From 1993, Oftel started to issue public telecommunications operator (PTO) licences and cable licences to provide competition to BT. Oftel granted 140 PTOs to provide domestic and international services between 1990 and 2000 for domestic and international services (Walden, Kemmit, and Angel, 2018: 109).

This approach found support within the 1989–95 Delors Commission, which was responsible for the implementation of the Single Market programme. Margaret Thatcher appointed Sir Leon Brittan as European Commissioner for Competition between 1989 and 1993. Brittan championed a pro-market agenda while in office, introducing the Green Paper, 'Review of the Telecommunications Sector', in 1992 which recommended that the competition policy instrument Article 90 be used for breaking up monopolies in telecommunications and mobile phone provision Europe-wide (Claveloux, 1993; Brittan, 2000). The Green Paper was the basis for the 1996 Full Competition Directive amending the ONP, which was actively supported by the UK (Sandholtz, 1993: 265; Brittan, 1995). This called for the liberalisation of all public voice telephone services by January 1998.

By the mid-1990s, digital technology had enabled the compression of terrestrial television signals, freeing up spectrum for other services such as mobile phones, wireless mobile communications, and mobile broadband. It also facilitated two-way communication, making interactive television, advertising, and online gaming possible. It was envisioned that separate markets (terrestrial, satellite, cable, voice telephone, internet service providers (ISPs)) were to converge and compete in a single market. The potential of convergence for new services, particularly on-demand, was recognised by the EU early on, which devised a policy framework to encompass all communication technologies.

In 1994, the Commissioner for Internal Market and Industrial Affairs Martin Bangemann established a high-level group on the information society. It published an influential 'Europe and the Global Information Society' report in 1994 which became known as the 'Bangemann Report'. Based upon the policy framework set out in the report, DG XIII began work on its convergence initiative. It drew upon a much wider definition of the communications market. The framework was launched by the Bangemann Group II (the 'High-Level Group of Experts') report, 'Building the European Information Society for Us All', in 1997.

In parallel, within the UK, the Information Society Initiative was launched in February 1996 which aimed to create a favourable market environment for encouraging the use of information and communication technologies. At the time, the UK was chairing World Trade Organization (WTO) negotiations on the opening of telecommunications networks where 69 governments made commitments in

General Agreements on Trade in Services (GATs).[1] In 2000, the UK published a Communications White Paper[2] which focused on the convergence of telecommunications and broadcasting industries and globalisation of communications systems.

DG XIII was renamed DG Information Society in 1999. Following an EU Review of telecommunications in 1999 and a joint initiative in 2001 between Erkki Liikanen, European Commissioner for Enterprise and Information Society and Mario Monti, European Commissioner for Competition, new guidelines on market analysis and the calculation of significant market power were drafted for a new regulatory framework for electronic communications services and networks. The key focus was unbundling the local loop, shortening delivery times, cost orientation for leased lines concerning the rollout of broadband and e-commerce, and removing tariff distortions.

In 2000, the Commission ran a sector inquiry on local loop unbundling under which it proposed a Regulation requiring unbundling of the local loop (the 'last mile'), which was approved by the end of the year. As broadband was using the same lines for the same services as telephony, they were reliant on monopoly providers for the provision of high-speed internet services. Incumbents were sent investigation letters by DG Competition, then five cases were opened in Belgium, Greece, Italy, Portugal, and Spain on the competitive use of leased lines.

This set the stage for the introduction of the 2002 Regulatory Framework for Electronic Communications and Services (also referred to as the 'Convergence' framework or the 'Telecomms Package'), which comprised five Directives (the Framework Directive, Authorisation Directive, Access Directive, Universal Service Directive, and Privacy and Electronic Communications Directive) and the Radio Spectrum Decision. The framework dealt with the harmonisation of telecommunications provision across Europe. It recommended 18 product and service markets at the wholesale and retail level for ex-ante regulation by national regulatory authorities (NRAs).

The Framework Directive allocated the responsibility for number allocation schemes to NRAs, which assigned number plans on a non-discriminatory basis. The Authorisation Directive outlined conditions NRAs can attach to licences including charges, interoperability, and must-carry obligations. The Universal Service Directive mandated that operators provide access to telephone services at fixed locations, comprehensive directories and a directory enquiry service, adequate public pay telephones, and for users to be able to call emergency services and the single European emergency call number (112) free of charge from any telephone.

[1] www.wto.org/english/news_e/pres97_e/summary.htm [last accessed 25.10.2022].

[2] https://api.parliament.uk/historic-hansard/commons/2000/dec/12/communications-white-paper [last accessed 25.10.2022].

It also governed contractual terms in that customers needed to be guaranteed contracts of at least 12 months but no longer than 24 months. Contracts needed to contain a stipulated list of information including the identity and address of suppliers, services provided, service quality levels offered, time of initial connection, maintenance offered, prices and tariffs, duration of the contract, and compensation measures. The Directive took into consideration a 2001 ruling of the Court of Justice on France's mechanism for financing the universal service which was found to be disproportional and lacking in transparency.

The Radio Spectrum Decision outlined coordination of the efficient use of radio spectrum. It set up the Radio Spectrum Policy Group (RSPG), which comprises high-level experts seconded from NRAs and national ministries. The implementation of spectrum policy was overseen by the European Regulators Group (ERG), established in 2002, which worked together with the Independent Regulators Group (IRG),[3] an independent network which operated externally to the Commission. Both groups were made up of national regulatory authorities. The deadline for the transposition of the new regulatory framework was July 2003. The UK was the only large member state to implement the framework by the deadline. The Commission began infringement proceedings against Belgium, France, Germany, Greece, Luxembourg, the Netherlands, Portugal, and Spain regarding all five Directives, and Sweden regarding the Framework Directive.

In parallel, the Commission opened a sector inquiry into roaming prices in 2000. Most national markets were operating at the time with two incumbent operators. Nine mobile telephone operators came under investigation in Germany and the UK by DG Competition in 2003.[4] In the UK, the Commission found that Vodafone had charged unfair and excessive prices between 1997 and 2003 and O_2 between 1998 and 2003. In Germany, T-Mobile International AG & Co. KG (T-Mobile) and Vodafone D2 GmbH (Vodafone) were found to be charging excessively for roaming charges between 1997 and 2003.

Based upon these decisions, the European Commission brought in a Regulation on roaming on public mobile telephone networks (the Roaming Regulation) in 2007 which addressed excessive roaming charges under Article 95 (formerly Article 100a). Mobile operators in member states were obliged to apply a roaming Eurotariff, setting a retail price cap for calls customers made while abroad. The tariff entered into force on 30 September 2007 for three years. The Regulation also set a price cap for wholesale roaming charges and an obligation to keep customers informed about changes.

The UK had actively worked with France to promote the 2007 Regulation and recommended the use of Article 95 for harmonisation. This was based upon an

[3] www.irg.eu [last accessed 25.10.2022].

[4] Case COMP/38.097 Follow-up International Roaming UK and Case COMP/38.098 Follow-up International Roaming Germany.

ECJ ruling in its 2000 Tobacco Advertising case which recommended the use of Article 95 'to prevent the emergence of future obstacles to trade resulting from heterogeneous development of national laws'. As detailed in a Select Committee on European Scrutiny report, European compromise was brokered by the UK Minister for Industry and the Regions at the Department of Trade and Industry Margaret Hodge.[5]

The 2007 Roaming Regulation was followed by the 2009 EU Regulation on intra-community roaming. It reduced price caps for mobile roaming calls to .19 Euros per minute (not including VAT) for calls received abroad and .43 Euros for calls made abroad. Texts were limited to a .11-Euro charge while abroad (compared to the previous .28 Euros). Costs on downloaded data were capped to 1 Euro per megabyte downloaded, which was to be reduced annually. Post-Brexit, at the end of the transition period (1 January 2021), there is no longer an obligation on UK mobile operators to provide surcharge-free roaming in the EU.[6] The daily limit costs expired at the end of June 2022. Currently UK consumers need to check the roaming policies of individual providers before travel to Europe.

Hence, the roaming policy that the UK had campaigned so strongly for no longer applies to the UK. However, post-Brexit, the Trade and Cooperation Agreement (TCA) requires under Article 181 that:

1. The Parties shall endeavour to cooperate on promoting transparent and reasonable rates for international mobile roaming services in ways that can help promote the growth of trade among the Parties and enhance consumer welfare.
2. Parties may choose to take steps to enhance transparency and competition with respect to international mobile roaming rates and technological alternatives to roaming services, such as:
   (a) ensuring that information regarding retail rates is easily accessible to end users; and
   (b) minimising impediments to the use of technological alternatives to roaming, whereby end users visiting the territory of a Party from the territory of the other Party can access telecommunications services using the device of their choice.
3. Each Party shall encourage suppliers of public telecommunications services in its territory to make publicly available information on retail rates for international mobile roaming services for voice, data and text messages offered to their end users when visiting the territory of the other Party.

[5] https://publications.parliament.uk/pa/cm200607/cmselect/cmeuleg/41-xxiv/4103.htm [last accessed 25.10.2022].

[6] https://commonslibrary.parliament.uk/research-briefings/cbp-8649 [last accessed 25.10.2022].

Hence, EU customers visiting the UK will still have access to their home services when travelling in the UK, showing an imbalance in requirements.

In the mid-2000s, the UK also pioneered spectrum liberalisation in Europe. The 2002 Regulatory Framework for Electronic Communications and Services stipulates the neutral allocation of spectrum. The UK introduced spectrum trading from 2004 where rights to frequencies could be transferred or leased to other providers. Related to this, as Ofcom reported, 'the UK was the first country within Europe to identify a digital dividend'.[7] As detailed in an Ofcom report, in 2003 the government decided to release parts of the 112-MHz band when digital switchover had been completed.

The Directorate General Information Society and Media (DG INFSO) (as DG Information Society was renamed in 2005) followed the UK's lead, beginning with an Opinion of the RSPG on a Wireless Access Policy for Electronic Communications Services (WAPECS) in 2005 to allow more flexible use of spectrum. The Commission pushed for spectrum liberalisation with the support of the European Parliament in its 2007 Resolution Toward a European Policy on Spectrum. Policy action began with a proposal in 2007 to repeal the 1987 GSM Directive to open frequencies to new 3G services including internet, streaming, and other uses. The resulting EU 2009 Directive, for the coordinated introduction of public pan-European cellular digital land-based mobile communications, removed the requirement for GSM technology to operate in the 900-MHz and 1800-MHz bands.

The Commission invested €1 billion during 2009 and 2010 to areas under-served by broadband. In 2009, a Regulation on Cooperation between DG Competition and DG Information Society worked together on the 2010 Recommendation on regulated access to Next Generation Access Networks (NGA), which addressed the transition to NGA based on electronic communication networks. It was flanked by a Communication on broadband and a Proposal for a European radio spectrum policy programme, which was adopted in 2012, establishing a multiannual radio spectrum policy programme. These focused on the regulatory treatment of fixed and mobile rates and lowering harmonisations of rates. This was coupled with a Commission Recommendation on the regulatory treatment of fixed and mobile termination rates in the EU which addressed priced regulation by NRAs of termination rates.

The telecoms package was updated in 2009. The 2009 package was aimed at simplifying access to infrastructure sharing, promoting flexible spectrum management, strengthening the security of networks, and creating a single European e-communications market. Much of it was aimed at reducing red tape based on the Better Regulation agenda. The 2009 Better Regulation Directive, which was

[7] www.ofcom.org.uk/__data/assets/pdf_file/0007/33001/800mhz.pdf [last accessed 25.10.2022].

agreed under the co-decision procedure, amended the Framework, Access, and Authorisation Directives. It was accompanied by the 2009 Citizens Rights Directive amending the Universal Service and Data Protection Directives. As detailed in Chapter 1, the 2009 package drew heavily on self and co-regulation as introduced at the 2001 Lisbon Summit.

The package included two Regulations. The first established a Body of European Regulators for Electronic Communications (BEREC) as a successor to the European Regulators Group (ERG). The 2009 Regulation recommended that NRAs 'develop and disseminate among NRAs regulatory best practice, such as common approaches, methodologies or guidelines on the implementation of the EU regulatory framework'. The second governed roaming on public mobile communications networks.[8]

The 2009 Better Regulation Directive outlined a policy framework for e-commerce, powers to be allocated to national regulatory authorities, and significant market power (SMP). Amendments to the Framework Directive encouraged NRAs to promote net neutrality. Significantly, the amendment to the Access Directive required functional separation between a provider's network and service activities. This was only to be imposed on providers with SMP or vertically integrated operators if other ex-ante regulatory obligations were unsuccessful.

The UK was one of only five EU member states which implemented the 2009 Regulatory Framework by the deadline of May 2011 and the only large member state to do so.[9] It did so through the enactment of the Privacy and Electronic Communications (EC Directive) (Amendment) 2011; Electronic Communications (Universal Services) Amendment (Order 2011); and Electronic Communications and Wireless Telegraphy (Mobile Spectrum Trading) Regulations. The UK introduced 'white space' use from 2013 which permitted access to unused parts of the spectrum in the 470- to 790-MHz frequency band. This rapid implementation indicated a 'goodness of fit' between EU and UK policy but also pointed to broader institutional settings and cultural traditions of the UK. The UK did not have to change much to be compliant with Europe as most of the policies, particularly those on spectrum flexibility and better regulation, had already been introduced at the domestic level and had indeed been promoted at the EU level by the UK.

President of the European Commission José Manuel Barroso launched the Digital Agenda for Europe in a 2010 Communication as one of the seven flagships of the Europe 2020 Strategy. Its focus was on broadband rollout and improving internet connectivity, net neutrality, and roaming charges. The broadband objective of the strategy was to ensure that by 2020 '(i) all Europeans have access to much

[8] The roaming Regulation was later updated by the 2012 Regulation on public mobile communications networks and the 2015 Regulation on open internet access.

[9] https://assets.publishing.service.gov.uk/government/uploads/system/uploads/attachment_data/file/610586/PIR_EU_Electronic_Communications_Regulatory_Framework_2009.pdf [last accessed 25.10.2022].

higher internet speeds of above 30 Mbps and (ii) 50% or more of European households subscribe to internet connections above 100 Mbps'. September 2013 saw publication of the legislative package 'Connected Continent: Building a Telecoms Single Market' with a Recommendation on consistent non-discrimination obligations and costing methods, a Communication on the Telecommunications Single Market, a proposal for a European Single Market for electronic communications, and measures to achieve a 'Connected Continent'. This culminated in a 2014 Directive Council on measures to reduce the cost of deploying high-speed electronic communications networks.

The 2009 Better Regulation Directive had included a 'Commission declaration on Net Neutrality'. Net neutrality is the non-discrimination of web traffic based upon universal service obligations. The Declaration aimed 'to enshrine net neutrality as a policy objective and regulatory principle to be promoted by national regulatory authorities'. Up until April 2011, the European Commission was arguably sitting on the fence on net neutrality (Marsden, 2013). However, after the UK introduced guidelines on net neutrality and the Netherlands adopted a law on net neutrality in June 2011, the European Data Protection Supervisor (EDPS) published a statement in October 2011 in favour.

After the EDPS published its October 2011 statement, the European Parliament published a November 2011 European Parliament Resolution supporting net neutrality. A March 2012 Body of European Regulators for Electronic Communications (BEREC) study also supported net neutrality, but the European Commission remained undecided. At the time, the European Commission was being heavily lobbied by ISPs in favour of traffic management, particularly from the UK, namely BT, Sky, and Virgin, who introduced the practice under (BT) Content Connect and (Sky, Virgin) 'codes of practice'. The BBC by contrast lobbied strongly for net neutrality as it feared additional fees for use of its iPlayer. Overall, Ofcom was in favour of net neutrality and supported recommendations within BEREC but was hampered on the domestic front by intense lobbying by ISPs introducing instead a self-regulatory framework for traffic management. Net neutrality therefore was not formally introduced in the UK until the introduction of the EU's 2015 Open Internet Regulation.

The 2015 EU Open Internet Regulation enshrined net neutrality and amended the Universal Service Directive. It guaranteed fair price standards with remedies to be imposed by NRAs on operators with SMP and ended roaming charges from 15 June 2017. Telecommunications operators were obliged under the Directive not to 'treat all traffic equally, when providing internet access services, without discrimination, restriction or interference, and irrespective of the sender and receiver, the content accessed or distributed, the applications or services used or provided, or the terminal equipment used'. BEREC published Net Neutrality Guidelines for NRAs to implement net neutrality by August 2016. It prohibited traffic management by ISPs. ISPs were, however, not prohibited from implementing traffic management measures as long as they were 'transparent, non-discriminatory and proportionate, and shall not be based on commercial considerations'.

Prior to 2015, the UK tolerated a policy of traffic management in that it allowed ISPs to create 'walled gardens' which gave preference to some content providers over others and permitted the demand of payment for this. Examples of this were the blocking of Voice over Internet Protocol (VoIP) providers such as Skype by mobile phone operators or allowing content providers such as Google to pay for their content to be 'backboned' by ISPs, for example BT's Content Connect service (Marsden, 2010). This changed when the 2015 Directive was enacted into UK law under the 2016 Open Internet Access Regulations.[10] The problem with the UK regulations is that they referred to BEREC guidelines on net neutrality, meaning that the provisions on net neutrality would no longer apply post-Brexit. Ofcom announced in 2020 that it would, however, continue to implement net neutrality and to send annual reports to BEREC.[11]

However, the UK is no longer bound to commit to the EU's 2015 Open Internet Regulation post-Brexit. Domestic policy is constantly under review[12] and subject to substantial lobbying by domestic ISPs.[13] In 2021, Ofcom ran a consultation on net neutrality and published a review in October 2022.[14] The proposals look towards advising government to reintroduce traffic management. Proposals include permitting ISPs to offer premium-quality and low-latency packages and 'specialised services' (e.g. virtual reality or driverless vehicles) and to allow 'ISPs [to] use "traffic management" measures to manage their networks'.

Meanwhile, BEREC ran a review and updated its guidelines[15] in the same period in response to the outcome of ECJ cases C-854/19, C-5/20, and C-34/20. The new guidelines stipulate that any differentiated pricing practices are inadmissible, including zero rating options defined by the ECJ as 'a commercial practice whereby an internet access provider applies a "zero tariff", or a tariff that is more advantageous, to all or part of the data traffic associated with an application or category of specific applications, offered by partners of that access provider'. This points to a possible future UK–EU divergence in net neutrality policies.

[10] www.legislation.gov.uk/uksi/2016/607/contents/made [last accessed 25.10.2022].

[11] www.ofcom.org.uk/research-and-data/internet-and-on-demand-research/net-neutrality [last accessed 25.10.2022].

[12] www.ofcom.org.uk/__data/assets/pdf_file/0019/234334/Statement-Plan-of-Work-2022_23.pdf [last accessed 25.10.2022].

[13] www.ispreview.co.uk/index.php/2021/09/ofcom-begin-new-review-of-uk-net-neutrality-rules-post-brexit.html [last accessed 25.10.2022].

[14] www.ofcom.org.uk/__data/assets/pdf_file/0028/245926/net-neutrality-review.pdf [last accessed 25.10.2022].

[15] www.berec.europa.eu/sites/default/files/files/document_register_store/2022/6/BoR_%2822%29_81_Update_to_the_BEREC_Guidelines_on_the_Implementation_of_the_Open_Internet_Regulation.pdf [last accessed 25.10.2022].

Policy divergence post-Brexit

The review of the telecoms framework took place under the second pillar of the Digital Single Market strategy in 2016. The Commission introduced a proposal for a Directive for a new European Electronic Communications Code, an Action Plan to deploy 5G in the EU, and a 2017 Regulation to introduce free Wi-Fi internet connectivity in local communities (WIFI4EU) and an update to the BEREC Regulation. The Commission also updated its Guidelines on Significant Market Power as part of the telecoms framework, replacing the 2002 Guidelines. This was proposed by DG Connect (the Directorate General for Communications Network, Content and Technology) which had replaced DG INFSO in 2012.

The resulting 2018 Directive establishing the European Electronic Communications Code reconfirmed BEREC, set up the Agency for Support for BEREC (BEREC Office), and established the European Electronic Communications Code. The key aim of the 2018 Directive is to 'create an internal market for electronic communications within the Union'. It is aimed at increasing market competition, encouraging investment particularly in very high-capacity networks, reducing regulation, and improving spectrum coordination. The Directive repealed the Framework, Authorisation, Access, and Universal Service Directives.

The Code aims to move away from legacy infrastructure; that is, from copper networks to next-generation networks. It replaced the term 'publicly available telephone service' in Directive 2002/22/EC with 'voice communications service', thereby removing the requirement for the universal supply of public telephone boxes. The Code adds additional consumer protection requirements including the provision of information in contracts; transparency, comparison tools, and publication of information; quality of service; contract duration and termination; switching and porting; and bundled offers. As de Streel and Hocepied (2021: 123) point out, member states need to take into account 'that radio spectrum is a public good that has an important social, cultural and economic value' under the Electronic Communications Code. The Commission, upon the advice of BEREC, is to provide a template for contract summaries. The Code was implemented in the UK in the Electronic Communications and Wireless Telegraphy (Amendment) (European Electronic Communications Code and EU Exit) Regulations 2020.

In its guidelines for implementation, in reply to BT's request for interpretation of 'Internet Access Service', Ofcom refers to BEREC's definition in its guidelines accompanying the Open Internet Regulation.[16] The Commission also established a new definition for the term 'electronic communications service' with three categories: internet access service, interpersonal communications service, and 'services consisting wholly or mainly in the conveyance of signals such

[16] www.ofcom.org.uk/__data/assets/pdf_file/0020/209504/eecc-statement-dec-20.pdf [last accessed 25.10.2022].

as transmission services used for the provision of machine-to-machine services and for broadcasting'. 'Over-the-top' services (OTTs) such as Skype and WhatsApp came within the scope of the new Code under the new heading 'interpersonal communications service'. The universal service definition was updated to state 'Universal service is a safety net to ensure that a set of at least the minimum services is available to all end-users and at an affordable price to consumers, where a risk of social exclusion arising from the lack of such access prevents citizens from full social and economic participation in society'. In the UK, Ofcom designated BT and Kingston Communications (KCOM) as universal service broadband providers.[17]

In continuation of principles outlined in the Authorisation Directive, the 2018 Directive stipulates conditions which member states can attach to authorisation of services including fees, interoperability standards, accessibility, and must-carry obligations. Individual rights for radio frequencies are to be mandated by NRAs to prevent interference. Spectrum sharing and tradability is encouraged but greater coordination powers have been allocated to BEREC under Articles 4.3 and 35. Regarding spectrum, NRAs agreed upon a minimum licence duration of least 20 years, timely availability of spectrum, and greater European-level coordination. Agreements on spectrum caps, spectrum reservation for new entrants, and wholesale access obligations were also made. The rules on the tradability of spectrum licences have changed to prevent rights refusal, unless there is a clear risk that conditions will not be met. The UK's position on spectrum has not changed post-Brexit and it is largely following the EU lead.

The 2018 Directive also updates the Universal Service Directive with a set of new services, including adequate broadband internet access and voice communications services at fixed locations and an obligation to offer lower tariffs to those on a low income or with special needs. Number portability, which is required under the Directive, applies to both fixed and mobile networks and to geographic and non-geographic numbers. Specifically, 'in order to effectively support the free movement of goods, services and persons within the Union, it should be possible to use certain national numbering resources, in particular certain non-geographic numbers, in an extraterritorial manner, that is to say outside the territory of the assigning Member State'. Contractual obligations in the Universal Service Directive remain in place and have been extended to include detailed lists of end-to-end user requirements. The contractual requirements were enshrined in the EU's 2019 Implementing Regulation for providers of publicly available electronic communications services. In 2020, BEREC also updated its guidelines on the Implementation of the Open Internet Access Regulation (referring to Regulation 2015/2120).[18]

[17] www.ofcom.org.uk/about-ofcom/latest/features-and-news/broadband-uso-advice [last accessed 25.10.2022].

[18] https://digital-strategy.ec.europa.eu/en/policies/open-internet [last accessed 25.10.2022].

The UK has not participated in newer policy areas formulated by the European Commission since the end of the transition period. It is not implementing the Commission's Connectivity package which aimed to meet a number of targets by 2025 as set out in its 2016 'EU 2025 Gigabit Society', 2020 'Shaping Europe's Digital Future' and 2021 '2030 Digital Compass' Communications. A key aim of the EU is that all European households should have a download speed of at least 100 Mbps, there should be uninterrupted 5G coverage for urban areas, major roads, and railways, and there should be gigabit connectivity for schools, universities, public service providers, and companies reliant on digital technology. It has proposed under the package a Broadband Cost Reduction Directive, an update to the Action Plan on 5G and 6G, and a revision to the 2014 Radio Spectrum Policy Programme (RSPP). The Commission committed €27.5 million in funding for cross-border European Digital Service Infrastructures (DSIs) under the Connecting Europe Facility (CEF).

There is UK policy divergence in the regulation of artificial intelligence (AI). Following the formation of a High-Level Expert Group on AI (AI HLEG) in 2018, the European Commission published a proposal for an Artificial Intelligence Act in April 2021. As with the 2022 Digital Services Act (DSA) and 2018 and 2022 Codes of Practice on Disinformation, the AI proposal is built upon 'ethical codes and principles developed by many private and public organisations in Europe and beyond, that AI development and use should be guided by certain essential value-oriented principles'. This follows a self-regulatory approach. The Regulation establishes harmonisation for 'high-risk AI systems' on standards for traceability, transparency, accuracy, the provision of information, and human oversight. However, 'non-high-risk AI systems', which make up most operators in the sector, will follow self-regulatory code of conducts on a voluntary basis. High-risk systems will be registered in an EU database and need to acquire a Conformité Européene (CE) mark.

Member states will delegate representatives from NRAs for implementation of the Act following the model established in other communications sectors. This will take the form of a European Artificial Intelligence Board (EAIB) made up of NRA representatives collaborating to implement provisions in the Act with powers to impose penalties for infringement. The Board coordinates with the DSA's European Board for Digital Services and the General Data Protection Regulation's (GDPR's) European Data Protection Supervisor. In laying the groundwork for the Act, the AI HLEG piloted a self-assessment list for trustworthy AI (ALTAI) with 350 organisations in 2020 on a self-assessment basis.

AI 'regulatory sandboxes' are to be established to eliminate regulatory restrictions on a case-by-case basis to encourage innovation. This includes the introduction of flexible rules for chosen new entrants and self-regulatory trust schemes. The combination of self-regulation of AI with the removal of existing restrictions at national levels marks the proposal as a highly deregulatory initiative firmly placing policing again in the hands of private-sector providers (Veale and Zuiderveen Borgesius, 2021: 101). Companies require only an approved declaration of conformity in order to operate on the market.

The UK proposed its own approach to AI.[19] Following two reports published by the House of Lords Liaison Committee entitled 'AI in the UK: Ready, Willing and Able?' in 2018 and 'AI in the UK: No Room for Complacency' in 2020, the UK government published its AI strategy in 2021. This was followed by publications of an AI policy paper and Action Plan by the Department for Digital, Culture, Media and Sport (DCMS), the Department for Business, Energy and Industrial Strategy (BEIS), and the Office for Artificial Intelligence (OAI) in 2022. Unlike the EU proposals, there is no recommendation for legislation or a single regulator. Rather, the UK has adopted a decentralised approach. There is no categorisation of high-risk-use cases but a recommendation of assessment by respective sector regulators. Instead, recommendations centre around safety, fairness, transparency, and designing a set of common principles. Consultation is taking place at the time of writing.

Regarding spectrum, there is little change in UK policy post-Brexit. The ITU governs the use of frequency ranges and coordinates cross-border services. It may allocate a part of spectrum for specific use such as 5G and 6G. The EU is not a full member of the ITU in its own right. As a 'sector member' of the ITU, it cannot vote. However, as it holds competence for spectrum policy, it negotiates a common EU position which is negotiated on behalf of the EU by its member states at the World Radiocommunication Conference (WRC). The WRC meets circa every four years. For example, in 2023 the Radio Regulations treaty-level document is being updated.

Since 2015, a common EU position has been taken by a Council Decision which is binding on all member states. The policy is determined by the Commission in consultation with the RSPG which advises it on spectrum policies. The UK is no longer involved in preparation of the European position at the WRC within the Council. It is also no longer a member of the Radio Spectrum Committee or the RSPG. However, it is still a member of Conférence Européenne des Administrations des Postes et des Télécommunications (CEPT), which is an association of telecommunications bodies in Europe. Normally, the EU Council Decision is the same as that taken by CEPT. CEPT also develops standards and band plans for spectrum use in consultation with industry. The British Standards Institute (BSI) also continued its membership of CENELEC following a General Assemblies vote in June 2021.[20]

[19] www.gov.uk/government/news/uk-sets-out-proposals-for-new-ai-rulebook-to-unleash-innovation-and-boost-public-trust-in-the-technology [last accessed 25.10.2022].

[20] www.bsigroup.com/en-GB/about-bsi/uk-national-standards-body/standards-and-eu-exit [last accessed 25.10.2022].

Spectrum is governed under the 2014 New Legislative Framework (NLF) of the European Commission which issued the 2014 Radio Equipment,[21] Electromagnetic Compatibility (EMC), and Low Voltage Directives. The UK Withdrawal Act 2018 retained the Directives. The UK Radio Equipment Regulations 2017 implemented Directive 2014/53/EU on radio equipment. ETSI, which was established by CEPT in 1988 upon recommendation of the Commission, develops standards harmonised under the Directives. The UK has continued full membership under ETSI. The UK Radio Equipment Regulations 2017 stipulates that the manufacturer draw up a declaration of conformity and affix an additional UK Conformity Assessed (UKCA) marking.

Ofcom updated its 10-year spectrum management strategy in 2021,[22] which aims at providing increased flexibility in spectrum use and licensing to 'enable types of use, to evolve where possible, without the need to request a technical licence variation from Ofcom'. This could be through auctions, spectrum trading, or leasing agreements between licensees. Ofcom stated in the strategy that it 'remains committed to working within international organisations and to taking a leading role in decisions about the future use of radio spectrum. We are already working with other European administrations to examine the use of airborne equipment on mobile networks. However, we note there may be circumstances where UK-specific approaches – including through the use of UK Approved Body (GB) process 11 – may provide opportunities for developers, where practical and where international agreements allow', denoting possible policy divergence from the EU.

Two 5G auctions took place in 2018 and 2021. In 2018, spectrum was awarded to (BT-owned) EE in the 40-Mhz frequency, Three EE in the 20-Mhz frequency, (Telefónica-owned) O_2 EE in the 40-MHz frequency, and Vodafone EE in the 3.4-GHz frequency. Reserved slots were awarded to Hutchinson 3G in the 20-Mhz frequency. In 2021, EE, Hutchinson, Telefonica, and Vodafone acquired 80 MHz of spectrum in the low band at 700 MHz and 120 MHz of spectrum in 3.6–3.8-GHz mid-band frequencies. The government has set 2033 for the switch-off of all public 2G and 3G networks in the UK.

Conclusion

This chapter has shown that UK telecommunications regulation has not diverged substantially to date post-Brexit, with maintenance of EU regulation in most areas. Historically, the UK played a key role in EU policy development. It promoted sector liberalisation in key policy areas, notably fixed- and mobile-line deregulation,

[21] Directive 2014/53/EU on radio equipment.
[22] www.ofcom.org.uk/__data/assets/pdf_file/0017/222173/spectrum-strategy-statement.pdf [last accessed 25.10.2022].

spectrum liberalisation and trading, convergence, and roaming. However, UK customers no longer benefit from set roaming charges under EU regulation. Indeed, EE reintroduced charges from June 2021.[23] The UK is also more prone to ISP lobbying to deregulate net neutrality now that it is no longer committed to the EU's regulatory framework going forward.

The UK has notably influenced the EU in its move towards self- and co-regulation after the 2001 Lisbon Summit. Under this model, regulatory best practice, guidelines, methodologies, and benchmarking exercises are implemented through established NRA co-regulatory bodies in conjunction with the Commission, as exemplified by BEREC. Indeed, NRA bodies have been shown to be effective in forwarding EU-level policy consensus in the digital sector. Subsequent NRA co-regulatory boards such as the European Regulators Group for Audiovisual Media Service (ERGA) for audio-visual services, the European Artificial Intelligence Board for AI, the European Board for Digital Services for the DSA, and the European Data Protection Board (EDPB) for GDPR have been based upon the BEREC model.

This is very much a UK approach pioneered by Ofcom in the UK. Duly, NRA fora have operated on a market-based approach. It remains to be seen whether the EU will continue to apply a light-touch co-regulatory approach promoted by the UK. Initial proposals following the UK's exit from Europe indicate that the EU is continuing to follow a self-regulatory framework. However, this may be due to reasons of forging policy consensus and forwarding the EU agenda. Certainly, there is appetite for more hands-on direct oversight of markets by the EU in telecoms markets. This has arguably been mimicked in other policy areas such as the regulation of online platforms as shown in Chapter 5.

[23] www.bbc.co.uk/news/technology-57595913 [last accessed 25.10.2022].

5

The Regulation of E-commerce Post-Brexit

Introduction

In 2021, 74 per cent of EU internet users shopped online.[1] In 2020, the UK had the highest European GDP income from e-commerce[2] and was the most popular country for cross-border online shoppers from Europe (IMRG, 2021).[3] However, it lost this position to Germany in 2022 according to a Cross-Border Commerce Europe study. The study reported that 'UK cross-border sales dropped to a historically low level (-12%) resulting in €29bn cross-border B2C sales online',[4] with a 35 per cent loss in UK consumer confidence in cross-border commerce between 2021 and 2022. Brexit has been identified as the main cause for UK e-commerce market loss due to cost rises, delivery delays, and the bureaucracy involved in non-EU membership.

E-commerce refers mainly to the sale of goods over the internet but can also include the sale of certain kinds of services such as the downloading of films, music, or games.[5] The EU facilitates online shopping via its e-commerce, Services, and GDPR Directives which are underpinned by Consumer Rights Directives and Regulations, an Online Dispute Resolution (ODR) network,[6] and a European Consumer Centres Network.[7] This e-commerce framework is flanked by EU Regulations on Unjustified Geo-blocking Regulation and ePrivacy (including rules on data localisation), the Payment Services II Directive, and rules on product liability. Post the Brexit referendum, the EU updated its e-commerce framework with a number of initiatives including a 2017 Competition sector inquiry into e-commerce, 2018 Regulation on cross-border parcel delivery services,

[1] https://ec.europa.eu/eurostat/web/products-eurostat-news/-/ddn-20220202-1 [last accessed 25.10.2022].

[2] https://e-Commercece-europe.eu/wp-content/uploads/2021/09/2021-European-E-commerce-Report-LIGHT-VERSION.pdf, page 10 [last accessed 25.10.2022].

[3] Online shopping represents 10 per cent of UK GDP: www.statista.com/statistics/1113005/market-size-of-e-commerce-in-europe-by-country [last accessed 25.10.2022].

[4] www.cbcommerce.eu/press-releases/fourth-edition-of-the-top-16-countries-cross-border-europe-an-annual-ranking-of-the-best-16-european-countries-in-cross-border-online-shopping [last accessed 25.10.2022].

[5] https://ec.europa.eu/eurostat/statistics-explained/index.php?title=E-commerce_statistics [last accessed 25.10.2022].

[6] https://ec.europa.eu/consumers/odr/main/?event=main.home2.show [last accessed 25.10.2022].

[7] https://ec.europa.eu/info/live-work-travel-eu/consumer-rights-and-complaints/resolve-your-consumer-complaint/european-consumer-centres-network-ecc-net_en [last accessed 25.10.2022].

Brexit and the Digital Single Market. Alison Harcourt, Oxford University Press. © Alison Harcourt 2023.
DOI: 10.1093/oso/9780192899378.003.0005

2019 Directive on contracts for the supply of digital content and digital services, 2019 better enforcement and modernisation of Union consumer protection rules Directive, 2019 Platform to Business Regulation, and 2021 VAT rules for online sales of goods and services.[8]

These legislative measures were followed by the EU's Digital Services package[9] comprising a Digital Services Act which reforms e-commerce rules and Digital Markets Act which addresses gatekeepers. Both Acts were agreed in 2022 under the French presidency. Adjoining these legislative measures, the EU introduced initiatives on digital sovereignty,[10] a 2018 Regulation on the free flow of data,[11] and an e-Government Action Plan including a piloted 'Once-Only' principle[12] and an initiative on building up the interconnection of business registers.[13] A number of these initiatives integrate self-regulatory trust schemes based upon UK models. But there is an increasing move towards the use of statutory instruments and less reliance on self-regulatory models in the post-Brexit period. This chapter will discuss the policy trajectories of the UK and EU post-Brexit in e-commerce by explaining the history of EU legislation and the UK's role therein and what has happened because of Brexit.

The EU's e-commerce framework

The most important component of the EU's e-commerce framework was the EU's 2000 Directive on electronic commerce. The UK implemented the 2000 Directive in its Electronic Commerce (EC Directive) Regulations 2002 which outlined obligations for online sellers, particularly in relation to the provision of information about operators and services provided. One of the three pillars of the 2015 Digital Single Market strategy was to ensure 'better access for consumers and businesses to online goods and services across Europe'. Accordingly, a substantial overhaul of

[8] https://ec.europa.eu/taxation_customs/business/vat/modernising-vat-cross-border-e-Commercece_en [last accessed 25.10.2022].

[9] https://ec.europa.eu/info/law/better-regulation/have-your-say/initiatives/12418-Digital-Services-Act-package-ex-ante-regulatory-instrument-of-very-large-online-platforms-acting-as-gatekeepers [last accessed 25.10.2022].

[10] https://ec.europa.eu/info/strategy/priorities-2019-2024/europe-fit-digital-age_en [last accessed 25.10.2022].

[11] https://eur-lex.europa.eu/legal-content/EN/TXT/?uri=CELEX%3A32018R1807 [last accessed 25.10.2022].

[12] Under the 'once-only' principle, businesses and citizens only have to communicate data once to public administrations. This aims to reducing regulatory burden. https://digital-strategy.ec.europa.eu/en/policies/egovernment-action-plan [last accessed 25.10.2022].

[13] The basis for Business Registers Interconnection System (BRIS) can found in Directives 2009/101/EC and 2012/17/EU and the Implementing Regulation 2015/884. The BRIS is at https://ec.europa.eu/cefdigital/wiki/display/CEFDIGITAL/Business+Registers+Interconnection+System [last accessed 25.10.2022].

the framework began with the Commission's e-commerce sector inquiry in 2016.[14] This resulted in many measures, some of which the UK implemented before it exited the EU, and greater scrutiny of the sector under competition law, as covered in Chapter 8.

The 2016 inquiry showed an increase in the use of contractual restrictions to control product distribution.[15] Based upon 1,800 responses and the collection of 8,000 distribution contracts, price transparency was identified in a 2017 final report as the most salient factor affecting market behaviour.[16] It argued that resale-price related restrictions were prevalent in e-commerce markets. The report also highlighted an increase in the use of automatic software use by retailers for price monitoring and price setting. As Kramler (2017: 81) argues, this has led to increased vertical constraints with producers opening their own webshops along with 'pricing restrictions/recommendations, online sale restrictions, and territorial restrictions'.

The inquiry also pointed to the widespread practice of geo-blocking which is defined as when 'retailers refuse to sell to customers abroad, for example by blocking access to websites, re-routing customers to websites targeting other Member States or by simply refusing to deliver cross-border or to accept cross-border payments'. Although some content was legally justified on copyright grounds for digital content services, geo-blocking practices which prevented cross-border shopping for goods were identified by the EU as counter to the objectives of the Single Market. The inquiry found that 38 per cent of online retailers collected data for the purpose of geo-blocking in order to refuse cross-border delivery and payments. In parallel, the Directorate-General for Competition (DG Competition) was taking an increasing number of decisions on geo-blocking. For example, in 2018, the Commission fined the clothing company Guess 40 million Euros for blocking cross-border sales, guaranteeing it higher prices, particularly in Central and Eastern European states.[17]

Accordingly, the Commission recognised that territorial restrictions in the form of cross-border geo-blocking were highly problematic. Based upon this recognition, the 2018 Unjustified Geo-blocking Regulation, which makes it illegal to discriminate trade in goods and services on the basis of customers' nationality,

[14] The e-sector inquiry focused on goods rather than services. It identified that the most goods sold online were: clothing; shoes; consumer electronics; electrical household appliances; computer games and software; toys and childcare articles; media (books, CDs, DVDs, and Blu-ray discs); cosmetics and healthcare products; sports and outdoor equipment; and house and garden products. Respondents could comment on any 'other' product categories.

[15] https://ec.europa.eu/competition/antitrust/e-Commercece_swd_en.pdf [last accessed 25.10.2022].

[16] http://ec.europa.eu/competition/antitrust/ sector_inquiry_final_report_en.pdf [last accessed 25.10.2022].

[17] Commission decision of 17 December 2018: antitrust case AT.40428 Guess, available at http://ec.europa.eu/competition/elojade/isef/case_details. cfm?proc_code=1_40428 [last accessed 25.10.2022].

place of residence, or establishment, was introduced. The UK implemented the EU Regulation in the Geo-blocking (Enforcement) Regulations 2018 which came into force on 3 December 2018. Post-Brexit, UK sellers must continue to adhere to the Geo-Blocking Regulation to sell goods and services to the EU after 1 January 2021 and cannot 'discriminate between customers in different EU countries, for example between a customer in France and a customer in Germany'. However, by contrast, 'EU businesses will not have to follow the EU Geo-Blocking Regulation when they sell to the UK'.[18] This represents an imbalance in requirements for UK- and EU-based companies.

The Unjustified Geo-blocking Regulation was followed by a second Regulation in 2019 on promoting fairness and transparency for business users of online intermediation services (P2B Regulation). It aims to promote transparency and fairness for small or medium-sized enterprises (SMEs) and traders on online platforms and established an EU Observatory on the Online Platform Economy.[19] The UK retained the Regulation in its Online Intermediation Services for Business Users (Enforcement) Regulations 2020 (Enforcement Regulations) and stipulated that enforcement of the platform-to-business Regulation will be through the courts.[20] It does not participate in Observatory activities. The 2019 Regulation was accompanied by a set of guidelines for ranking transparency. Although not legally binding, the guidelines stipulate transparency of algorithms and online ranking.

Implementation is monitored by the EU Observatory on the Online Platform Economy, established in 2019 by a Decision, in which the UK no longer participates.[21] The UK also no longer participates in the Single Digital Gateway[22] established in 2018 under which the European Commission and national regulatory authorities (NRAs) are setting up 'Your Europe' national portals for cross-border digital users. These aim to replace paperwork procedures such as 'registering a car or claiming a pension' with digital registration. This is flanked by the European Interoperability Framework which supports interoperability between national public administrations.

As a part of its Review of EU consumer law,[23] seven Directives were amended and introduced as a part of the Commission's 2018 New Deal for Consumers: the Unfair Commercial Practices Directive (UCPD), the Unfair Contract Terms Directive (UCTD), the Price Indication Directive (PID), the Consumer Sales Directive, Consumer Rights Directive (CRD), the Misleading and Comparative Advertising

[18] www.gov.uk/guidance/geo-blocking-from-1-january-2021 [last accessed 25.10.2022].
[19] https://platformobservatory.eu [last accessed 25.10.2022].
[20] www.gov.uk/eu-withdrawal-act-2018-statutory-instruments/the-online-intermediation-services-for-business-users-amendment-eu-exit-regulations-2020 [last accessed 25.10.2022].
[21] https://digital-strategy.ec.europa.eu/en/policies/eu-observatory-online-platform-economy [last accessed 25.10.2022].
[22] www.legislation.gov.uk/uksi/2020/793/contents/made [last accessed 25.10.2022].
[23] https://ec.europa.eu/info/law/law-topic/consumer-protection-law/review-eu-consumer-law_en [last accessed 25.10.2022].

Directive, the Injunctions Directive, and the Directive on representative actions for the protection of the collective interests of consumers.[24] As explained by Merdi (2017: 127), the UCPD, CRD, UCTD, and PID were updated to fit with the digital age. The Review was intended by the Juncker Commission to 'fully unleash the potential of e-commerce in the Digital Single Market' and was announced in the 2015 Digital Single Market as '(i) covering harmonised EU rules for online purchases of digital content, and (ii) allowing traders to rely on their national laws based on a focused set of key mandatory EU contractual rights for domestic and cross-border online sales of tangible goods' (Merdi, 2017: 127).

Accordingly, the CRD and UCPD were amended with the 2019 EU Directive on the better enforcement and modernisation of Union consumer protection rules (the 'Omnibus Directive') which came into force in May 2022. As Howells et al. (2017: 47) explain, the UCPD in particular:

> removed the scope for the Member States to adopt or retain domestic legislation offering a higher level of consumer protection. In particular, as the UCPD contains a list of commercial practices prohibited outright, the ability of the Member States to prohibit other commercial practices has been pre-empted by the Directive. Non-prohibited practices need to be challenged under the general standards in the UCPD instead.

This notwithstanding, the UCPD is comprehensive in its approach and introduced an extensive number of requirements for online sellers. Non-compliance could result in a high fine of at least 4 per cent of the businesses' annual turnover or 2,000,000 Euros. Although the UK did not adopt the Omnibus Directive, UK companies selling products and services to the EU need to abide by the rules including those on consumer redress. Guidance was released in December 2021 for the UCPD, CRD, and PID and outlined the changes introduced by the Omnibus Directive.[25] In terms of online selling, there needs to be transparency for paid ads ranked higher up in webpage search results. Sellers are prohibited from placing fake consumer reviews on their websites and must inform customers whether website reviews are from customers who have actually purchased their products.

Section 3.8 of the guidance on prizes was based on a landmark European Court of Justice (ECJ) ruling, the Office of Fair Trading (OFT) v Purely Creative Industries case, stemming from the UK. Section 3.8 prohibits prizes when the false impression is created that a customer 'has already won, will win, or will on doing a particular act'. The ECJ ruled against the company Purely Creative which had

[24] https://ec.europa.eu/smart-regulation/roadmaps/docs/2016_just_023_evaluation_consumer_law_en.pdf [last accessed 25.10.2022].
[25] https://eur-lex.europa.eu/legal-content/EN/TXT/?uri=CELEX%3A52021XC1229%2805%29&qid=1640961745514 [last accessed 25.10.2022].

sent out millions of scratch cards inviting people to call a premium rate number to find out what they had won. Under the Paragraph 31 of Annex I of the 2005 UCPD it stated that it was illegal to create the 'false impression that the consumer has already won, will win, or will on doing a particular act win, a prize or other equivalent benefit, when in fact either there is no prize or other equivalent benefit; or (b) taking any action in relation to claiming the prize or the equivalent benefit is subject to the consumer paying money or incurring a cost'. The UK Court of Appeal referred an appeal to the ECJ, seeking interpretation of paragraph 31. The court found that it was unfair practice if the claim of the prize required the consumer to bear cost, even if it is low.

The 2019 guidance introduces Section 4.2.6 on influencer marketing on social networks. If a commercial practice is not declared by an influencer, it could be considered a misleading action under Article 6 or a misleading omission under Article 7 of the UCPD. Section 4.2.7 is on data-driven practices and dark patterns. A 'dark pattern' is recognised as unfair practice and refers to 'a type of malicious nudging, generally incorporated into digital design interfaces'. These could be 'data-driven and personalised, or implemented on a more general basis, tapping into heuristics and behavioural biases, such as default effects or scarcity biases'. This was flanked by European Data Protection Board (EDPB) Guidelines on dark patterns in social media platform interfaces.[26] Under Section 4.2.9 gaming, hidden in-game marketing is prohibited. A definition of a dark pattern was included in the 2022 Digital Services Act (DSA) to provide support to the UCDP with the European Data Protection Board drafting guidance on dark patterns on social media.

The December 2021 Commission Notice on the interpretation and application of Article 6a of the Price Indication Directive explains how the Omnibus Directive amends the Price Indication Directive (PID) by adding rules on price reduction announcements under Article 6a. The price reduction announcement must include an indication of the 'prior' price of a good. The Guidance also provides interpretation of the interplay with the UCPD. In 2022, the Commission followed these amendments with a Fitness Check of EU consumer law on digital fairness.[27]

The year 2019 also saw the passage of two Directives: the Directive concerning contracts for the supply of digital content and digital services and the Directive concerning contracts for the sale of goods. Both address harmonisation of business-to-consumer (B2C) consumer contract laws. Importantly, consumers in receipt of faulty digital goods or digital services are entitled to the same rights as receiving tangible goods or services. The Directives also include requirements for security updates 'in order to keep the digital content or digital service in conformity

[26] https://edpb.europa.eu/our-work-tools/documents/public-consultations/2022/guidelines-32022-dark-patterns-social-media_en [last accessed 25.10.2022].

[27] https://ec.europa.eu/info/law/better-regulation/have-your-say/initiatives/13413-Digital-fairness-fitness-check-on-EU-consumer-law_en [last accessed 25.10.2022].

and secure'. Both Directives came into force in January 2022. Again, the UK has not adopted these Directives but companies selling in Europe will need to abide by them.

In 2020, the European Commission introduced its New Consumer Agenda which will run from 2020 to 2025. Five key goals were outlined in a Communication: a green transition, digital transformation, redressing and effective enforcement of consumer rights, specific needs of certain consumer groups, and international co-operation. There is a focus on providing access to products and services for low-income citizens, older people, and those with disabilities based upon the European Social Policy Network and Commission Recommendation on Energy Poverty. Accordingly, there are increased requirements for accessibility. Third countries are under greater scrutiny for product safety particularly for goods originally produced in China.

Lastly, the EU 2000 E-commerce Directive was updated in 2022 with the EU Digital Services Act, post-Brexit, although the 2002 Electronic Commerce Directive was retained in the 2019 Electronic Commerce Regulations. The UK 2019 Regulations retained most of the original 2002 provisions, only removing the Country of Origin (COO) requirement as 'UK based information society services [must] adhere to the rules governing online activities within each EEA state in which they operate'.[28] The 2022 DSA was not adopted in the UK. UK e-commerce legislation is therefore outdated as EU legislation has moved on and is expected to be updated with the Online Safety Bill.

The 2022 DSA retains limited legal liability for intermediary services and the COO principle for jurisdiction is not waived. But there is a marked change in the EU's approach in that there are no exemptions under subsidiarity as there were under the 2000 e-Commerce Directive,[29] as 'a targeted set of uniform, effective and proportionate mandatory rules should be established at Union level' (DSA, 2022: 2). This represents a more direct top-down regime which greatly strengthens the European Commission's role as the primary regulator for large online platforms, delegating authority for smaller platforms to member states.

As a third country under the DSA, UK-based companies offering digital services within the EU must appoint a legal representative in the EU based on 'where a substantial connection to the Union should be considered to exist where the service provider has an establishment in the Union or, in the absence of such

[28] The UK government also announced that its existing commitments under the PSD II, under which certain powers were delegated to the European Banking Authority (EBA), will continue post-Brexit. However, when the UK became a third country, its forward-going relationship with the EBA became uncertain.

[29] The UK subsidiarity exemptions to the COO principle under the 2000 E-commerce Directive wherein member state consumer laws apply to all e-commerce transactions under subsidiarity were included under the UK: 'derogations from Regulation 4': public policy; protection of public health; public security, including the safeguarding of national security and defence; and protection of consumers, including investors.

an establishment, where the number of recipients of the service in one or more Member States is significant in relation to the population thereof, or on the basis of the targeting of activities towards one or more Member States' (DSA, 2022: 22).

This will be determined based upon several factors including language, the use of a top-level domain, and the currency used for transactions (DSA, 2022: 33). The member state where the legal representative is located will retain jurisdiction for the service provider which will be regulated by a nominated NRA 'Digital Services Coordinator'.

EU policy on online platforms has largely been led by France. In line with its dirigiste approach to digital markets, France introduced a number of initiatives in the latter half of the 2000s to promote growth and protect national champions, an approach it promotes at the European level. In his 2017 Sorbonne speech on Europe, the French president Emmanuel Macron stated, 'we must create European champions, we must invent in this global upheaval fair securities and efficient regulations ... Major digital platforms and data protection are at the core of our sovereignty in that regard'.[30] This logic was reflected in a 2017 Communication which supports the European 'fight for digital sovereignty' (Floridi, 2020).

The UK, France, the Netherlands, Germany, Spain, and Italy serve as bases for the highest number of platforms in Europe (Ramella and Manzo, 2020: 62). Many of these states have taken a proactive approach to promoting online platforms. France regulates platforms through several Acts. Its 2016 Digital Republic Act ('Projet de loi pour une République numérique'[31]) introduced a definition for online platforms which includes whether they rank goods and services according to algorithms (for example, search engines) and enable online selling. It imposes transparency rules on ranking, customer rights, and consumer contracts.

France has witnessed the birth of a number of online platforms such as Ankorstore for independent wholesalers, Back Market for mobile phones, BlaBlaCar for car-pooling, Deezer for music streaming, Doctolib for medical professionals, iad for real estate, ManoMano for DIY labour, OVHcloud for cloud computing, and Spendesk for SME accounting. Many of these were underpinned by a government programme which first started in 2013, La French Tech,[32] which provided accelerator funding to cities. In 2019, Macron aimed to have 25 French unicorns[33] by 2025, a goal which was reached in 2022. The new goal is to achieve 10 large tech companies within Europe by 2030.

Italy imported a number of online platforms from France such as BlaBlaCar and ManoMano and has since created two unicorn companies, Yoox and MutuiOnline.

[30] Macron, Emmanuel's Sorbonne speech. Ouest France. 26 September 2017. http://international.blogs.ouest-france.fr/archive/2017/09/29/macron-sorbonne-verbatim-europe-18583.html [last accessed 25.10.2022].

[31] www.legifrance.gouv.fr/loda/id/JORFTEXT000033202746 [last accessed 25.10.2022].

[32] https://lafrenchtech.com/en [last accessed 25.10.2022].

[33] Unicorns are companies valued at $1 billion.

Proposals for online platform regulation such as the proposed sharing economy law[34] have largely not come to fruition (Wei, Nehf, and Marques, 2020: 44). Decrees are common in Italy which enables governments to bypass political deadlock.[35] The Italian Constitution provides the two chambers with symmetrical legislative power. As both chambers have to approve all legislative acts, it makes it very difficult to get regulation passed in Italy. Accordingly, laws No. 218/2017 and No. 36/2020 which implemented the Payment Services Directive (PSD2) were implemented with Legislative Decrees. Oversight of platforms is undertaken by the Agency for Digital Italy (Agenzia per l'Italia Digitale) (AgID).

In July 2021, the UK updated its Plan for Digital Regulation in the paper 'Digital Regulation: Driving Growth and Unlocking Innovation'.[36] The publication was accompanied by an online consultation, Reforming the Framework for Better Regulation,[37] and the policy paper, 'UK Innovation Strategy: Leading the Future by Creating It'.[38] The revised 2022 Digital Regulation policy paper recommends a combination of soft and hard regulatory tools to legislate the sector but there is a clear emphasis is on co-regulation integrating codes of conduct, transparency for algorithms,[39] and regulatory sandboxes. Increased cooperation is envisioned between the ICO, FCA, Ofcom, and CMA which collaborate through the Digital Regulation Cooperation Forum.[40]

The UK's approach to e-commerce post-Brexit

The UK was opposed to increased platform regulation while still a member of the EU. In 2016, it coordinated a letter sent by the then Department of Business, Innovation and Skills to European Commission vice-president Andrus Ansip.[41] Signed by 11 states, the United Kingdom, the Czech Republic, Poland, Luxembourg, Finland, Sweden, Denmark, Estonia, Latvia, Lithuania, and Bulgaria, it argued:

[34] Proposta di legge No. 3564: Disciplina delle piattaforme digitali per la condivisione di beni e servizi e disposizioni per la promozione dell'economia della condivisione.

[35] Powers of decree are granted under Articles 76 and Article 77 of the Italian Constitution. The latter promotes 'urgent and necessary decrees'.

[36] Last updated June 2022: www.gov.uk/government/publications/digital-regulation-driving-growth-and-unlocking-innovation/digital-regulation-driving-growth-and-unlocking-innovation [last accessed 25.10.2022].

[37] www.gov.uk/government/consultations/reforming-the-framework-for-better-regulation [last accessed 25.10.2022].

[38] www.gov.uk/government/publications/uk-innovation-strategy-leading-the-future-by-creating-it [last accessed 25.10.2022].

[39] https://assets.publishing.service.gov.uk/government/uploads/system/uploads/attachment_data/file/954331/Algorithms_++.pdf [last accessed 25.10.2022].

[40] www.gov.uk/government/collections/the-digital-regulation-cooperation-forum [last accessed 25.10.2022].

[41] www.gov.uk/government/uploads/system/uploads/attachment_data/file/513402/platforms-letter.pdf [last accessed 18.07.2022].

> Existing legislative and non-legislative instruments, including data protection law, competition law and consumer law, already apply to platforms and can be used to regulate them. In addition, we should make sure that we have explored the role of industry self-regulation fully as this may often be more appropriate and effective than government regulation in the fast pace of the digital world.

The UK viewed platform regulation as stemming development and innovation in the sector. As an alternative, it had recommended lifting regulatory burdens for SMEs through the EU Capital Markets Union package which was proposed in 2020.[42] This was in line with the UK's preference for soft governance and self-regulatory trust schemes as opposed to 'traditional' regulation which it promoted during its EU membership, particularly in circumstances of emerging or fast-moving markets.[43] This approach was promoted under the UK's Better Regulation Agenda.[44] As explained in a Department for Business, Energy and Industrial Strategy (BEIS) research paper in 2019, self-regulation works best when it is:

> backed by statutory powers[;] financial sanctions also play an important role in encouraging compliance, similar to traditional regulation. For example, Muela-Molina and Perelló-Oliver (2014) find that the self-regulation of advertising in the UK can attribute part of its success to the ASA's sanctioning powers and its ability to refer cases or issues to Ofcom, who can then take further action. Attempts to enact self-regulation without sanctions have been shown in the literature to be ineffective (see for example King and Lenox (2000) in relation to Responsible Care). In the case of SROs with sanctioning abilities, however, there is a risk that SROs may not actually make use of sanctioning powers, which can also work to undermine their effectiveness. This is evident in the example of the Independent Press Standards Organisation (IPSO).

Accordingly, e-commerce is governed in the UK by several national Acts with strong soft governance components. The Consumer Protection from Unfair Trading Regulations 2008 (implementing the CPR) outlines unfair practices and introduced a blacklist of banned operators. The Provision of Services Regulations 2009 (POS Regulations) stipulates transparency requirements for online operators and standards for complaints procedures. The Consumer Rights (Payment Surcharges) Regulations 2012 and Consumer Contracts (Information, Cancellation and Additional Charges) Regulations 2013 (Consumer Contract

[42] https://ec.europa.eu/commission/presscorner/detail/en/ip_21_6251 [last accessed 25.10.2022].
[43] https://assets.publishing.service.gov.uk/government/uploads/system/uploads/attachment_data/file/840564/designing-self-co-regulation-initiatives.pdf [last accessed 25.10.2022].
[44] https://assets.publishing.service.gov.uk/government/uploads/system/uploads/attachment_data/file/1005119/reforming-the-framework-for-better-regulation.pdf [last accessed 25.10.2022].

Regulations) have obligations for B2C online sellers and introduced cancellation rights.

The Consumer Rights Act 2015 (CRA), which combined preceding UK consumer rights regulations, provides consumers with statutory contractual obligations and remedies for breach of contract. It was flanked by the Alternative Dispute Resolution for Consumer Disputes (Competent Authorities and Information) Regulations 2015. The UK retained EU consumer law in the 2018 Consumer Protection (Amendment etc.) (EU Exit) Regulations 2018/1326 (the 'Protection Regulations') and the 2019 Consumer Protection (Enforcement) (Amendment etc.) (EU Exit) Regulations 2019/203 (the 'Enforcement Regulations') which came into effect on 1 January 2021 with minimal changes.[45]

The biggest challenge for UK businesses post-Brexit is the loss of cross-border dispute mechanisms, particularly as the EU remains the UK's largest trading partner for e-commerce.[46] In 2016, the European Commission set up an ODR platform[47] available under its 2013 Online Dispute Resolution Regulation. This allows customers and businesses with disputes about products or services to submit an online complaint form to sellers based within another EU state. The Regulation was annulled in the UK by the Consumer Protection (Enforcement) (EU Exit) Regulations 2018. UK consumers and businesses are no longer permitted to use the ODR platform from January 2021.

The European Commission also requires regulatory bodies to publish a list of alternative dispute resolution (ADR) bodies for relevant sectors. This requirement has been replaced in the UK by lists published by the Financial Conduct Authority (FCA) and, for all other sectors apart from Ofgem and the Civil Aviation Authority (CAA), the Chartered Trading Standards Institute (CTSI) on behalf of the UK secretary of state. Sellers are obliged to publish the name and website of the relevant ADR on its website, the general terms and conditions of sale, or service contracts. However, UK-based ADR bodies are not obliged to offer services to consumers in the EU.

Post-Brexit, the UK Online Intermediation Services for Business Users (Enforcement) Regulations 2020 (P2B Regulations)[48] was introduced to retain the 2019 EU Regulation 2019/1150 on promoting fairness and transparency for business users of online intermediation services. Known as the Online Intermediation Services Regulation (or the P2B Regulation), the 2019 EU Regulation governs online platforms or search engines.[49] The P2B Regulation guarantees transparency

[45] https://researchbriefings.files.parliament.uk/documents/CBP-9126/CBP-9126.pdf [last accessed 25.10.2022].
[46] https://researchbriefings.files.parliament.uk/documents/CBP-7851/CBP-7851.pdf [last accessed 19.07.2022].
[47] https://webgate.ec.europa.eu/odr [last accessed 25.10.2022].
[48] www.legislation.gov.uk/uksi/2020/609/made/data.pdf [last accessed 25.10.2022].
[49] www.gov.uk/eu-withdrawal-act-2018-statutory-instruments/the-online-intermediation-services-for-business-users-amendment-eu-exit-regulations-2020 [last accessed 25.10.2022].

and conditions for companies using online platforms for service provision including redress mechanisms. In addition to this, there are rules on website accessibility under the UK Equality Act 2010 and Public Sector Bodies (Websites and Mobile Applications) (No. 2) Accessibility Regulations 2018.

Regarding foreign court decision recognition, court cases submitted before the end of the transition period came under the Brussels (Recast) Regulation ('Brussels Ibis') which recognises and enforces judgments in civil and commercial matters. The Brussels Ibis Regulation was retained in UK law in Civil Jurisdiction and Judgments (Amendment) (EU Exit) Regulations 2019 (amended by the Civil, Criminal and Family Justice (Amendment) (EU Exit) Regulations (SI 2020/1493)) but only until the end of the transition period under Article 67 of the Trade and Cooperation Agreement (TCA).

Post-Brexit, UK private contracts continue to be bound by the earlier 2008 Rome I Regulation and Rome II Regulations. Under the Rome I Regulation, the law in the country where the seller is located applies if there is a contractual obligation. Rome II applies for non-contractual obligations where the dispute is decided in the state where the damage occurred. The UK implemented both earlier Rome Regulations in its 2019 Law Applicable to Contractual Obligations and Non-Contractual Obligations (UK Regulations) post-Brexit. However, the arrangements are not reciprocal and are dependent on the interpretation by each individual European Union state.[50] Indeed, Hörnle (2021: 286) identified this as 'one of the highly problematic areas of Brexit, as it means that the automatic cross-border recognition and enforcement of judgments in civil and commercial matters is in jeopardy'.

To mitigate this, the UK applied to accede to the 2007 Lugano Convention in 2020. The Convention is an international agreement between EU member states and the European Free Trade Association (other than Liechtenstein) on the jurisdiction and enforcement of court judgments in civil and commercial matters. The 2007 agreement superseded the 1988 agreement originally signed between the members of the European Communities, the Republic of Iceland, the Kingdom of Norway, and the Swiss Confederation. The UK adopted the Lugano Convention into law in its Civil Jurisdiction and Judgments Regulations 2009.[51] This was replaced by the Civil Jurisdiction and Judgments (Amendment) (EU Exit) Regulations 2019 (SI 2019/479) and subsequently the Jurisdiction, Judgments and Applicable Law (Amendment) (EU Exit) Regulations (SI 2020/1574), which effectively withdrew the UK from the Convention.

However, the European Commission vetoed the UK's application to re-join the 2007 Lugano Convention. In a 2021 Communication,[52] the Commission reasoned

[50] https://researchbriefings.files.parliament.uk/documents/CBP-9126/CBP-9126.pdf [last accessed 25.10.2022].
[51] www.legislation.gov.uk/uksi/2009/3131/contents/made [last accessed 25.10.2022].
[52] https://ec.europa.eu/info/sites/default/files/1_en_act_en.pdf [last accessed 25.10.2022].

that the Lugano Convention is preserved as a 'flanking measure for the EU's economic relations with the EFTA/EEA countries', for 'EU's relationship with third countries which have a particularly close regulatory integration with the EU'. Given this logic, the Commission concluded that the Convention was not the appropriate legal framework for judicial cooperation with the UK and indeed pointed out that no third country had joined the Convention except for Poland before accession.

The Commission recommended instead that the UK join the Hague Conference regime for its private law relationship with the EU. It also referenced the 2019 'Political declaration setting out the framework for the future relationship between the European Union and the United Kingdom', which also referred to the Hague regime and made no mention of Lugano.[53] Accordingly, the UK did apply to the Hague Convention of Convention on Choice of Court Agreements.[54] However, discrepancy remains on when the UK officially began its membership of the Convention as it considers itself to have joined in 2015 where the EU considers the Convention to apply to the UK from 1 January 2021 only.[55]

In addition, as the European Parliament points out, 'the degree of legal integration provided for by the Hague Convention is far lower than the quasi-automatic system of recognition provided for by the Lugano Convention or the automatic one of the Brussels Ibis Regulation'.[56] It is clear, however, that, in future, the EU intends to liaise with the UK through international treaty platforms rather than bilateral agreements in a stark rejection of the 'Swiss model'. The EU announced in July 2022 its intention to accede to the 2019 Hague Convention on the Recognition and Enforcement of Foreign Judgments in Civil or Commercial Matters.[57] Thus far, only Costa Rica, Israel, Russia, Ukraine, the United States, and Uruguay have signed the Convention, and they have not yet ratified it. However, the Commission stated in its 2021 Communication that the Convention 'has the potential to improve the current system of the circulation of foreign judgments', denoting its preference for international level agreements.

Under the TCA, there are no tariffs or quotas on goods moving between the UK and EU.[58] However, the UK ceased to be a member of the EU Customs and VAT territory (with the exception of Northern Ireland for goods) from January 2021. This has complicated the delivery of goods cross-border post-Brexit. From January

[53] https://eur-lex.europa.eu/legal-content/EN/TXT/?uri=CELEX%3A12019W%2FDCL%2801%29 [last accessed 25.10.2022].

[54] www.hcch.net/en/instruments/conventions/full-text/?cid=98 [last accessed 25.10.2022].

[55] www.hcch.net/en/instruments/conventions/status-table/notifications/?csid=1318&disp=resdn [last accessed 25.10.2022].

[56] www.europarl.europa.eu/RegData/etudes/BRIE/2021/698797/EPRS_BRI(2021)698797_EN.pdf [last accessed 25.10.2022].

[57] www.consilium.europa.eu/en/press/press-releases/2022/07/12/convention-on-the-recognition-of-judgements-council-adopts-decision-on-eu-accession [last accessed 25.10.2022].

[58] https://commonslibrary.parliament.uk/new-customs-rules-for-trade-with-the-eu [last accessed 25.10.2022].

2022, imported goods need a valid declaration and customs clearance.[59] The EU's Conformité Européene (CE) marking will also be replaced by the UK Conformity Assessed (UKCA) mark.[60] This means that companies exporting goods from the UK and those EU companies importing to the UK will need to provide both markings even though, as pointed out by the Confederation of British Industry (CBI), the standards are virtually identical.

Because of lobbying pressure, the introduction of the UKCA was postponed until 2025. Industry argues that it will cause an excessive amount of red tape for businesses. The introduction of the UKCA mark was postponed three times. Initially, it was postponed in August 2021, then in June 2022, when the UK government introduced 'easements to the procedure for procuring UKCA marks' and an extension on the deadline for goods imported to the UK with a CE mark until 2023. The British Chambers of Commerce contended that 'it does not change the underlying fact that businesses will still face major cost pressures to obtain UKCA marks from 2023 onwards'.[61] The date of introduction was delayed further until 2025 in November 2022. Make UK was quoted as stating 'we need to ask why the government is still ploughing ahead with the plans which are only adding costs and extra bureaucracy'.[62] The CBI, Make UK, and other associations propose that the UK simply drop UKCA entirely and accept the CE as equivalent in the UK.

For UK-based companies, under the TCA, all goods imported into the EU need an accompanying customs declaration and an Economic Operators Registration and Identification (EORI) number and to meet rules of origin (RoO).[63] The proof of origin must come in the form of 'a statement on origin—this must be made out by the exporter to confirm that the product originates in the UK or EU' or 'the importer's knowledge—this option allows the importer to claim tariff preference based on their own knowledge of where the goods they're importing originate from'. In addition, a supplier declaration may be needed. Member states may have additional requirements. Because of these complexities, several UK brands have ceased selling to the EU, including John Lewis and Fortnum & Mason.[64]

From July 2021, the EU introduced new VAT rules on e-commerce sales for online sellers.[65] Both EU and non-EU sellers with over 10,000 Euros per year annual income are required to register for an electronic portal, the 'One-Stop Shop',[66] where VAT is registered for sales across the EU where sellers obtain an Import One

[59] www.gov.uk/government/news/less-than-a-month-until-full-customs-controls-are-introduced [last accessed 25.10.2022].
[60] www.gov.uk/guidance/using-the-ukca-marking [last accessed 25.10.2022].
[61] https://committees.parliament.uk/publications/23011/documents/168574/default [last accessed 25.10.2022].
[62] www.ft.com/content/aa5ad4fc-342f-475a-90fa-bba46d4c6197 [last accessed 25.10.2022].
[63] https://trade.ec.europa.eu/access-to-markets/en/content/customs-clearance-documents-and-procedures [last accessed 25.10.2022].
[64] www.bbc.co.uk/news/business-55576571 [last accessed 25.10.2022].
[65] https://ec.europa.eu/commission/presscorner/detail/en/ip_21_3098 [last accessed 25.10.2022].
[66] https://vat-one-stop-shop.ec.europa.eu/index_en [last accessed 25.10.2022].

Stop Shop (IOSS) number. This is viewed to have greatly simplified EU VAT rules and compliance (Papis-Almansa, 2019). Third countries do not need to register unless they are providing services. Below the 10,000-Euro threshold, 'supplies of TBE (telecommunications, broadcasting and electronic) services and distance sales of goods within the EU may remain subject to VAT in the Member State where the taxable person is established'.

The VAT exemption for goods sold with a value under 22 Euros has been removed. For goods imports into the EU, customs declarations forms must include the IOSS number and an EU code F48[67] for low-value items (under 150 Euros). Monthly VAT returns need to be submitted to the relevant EU tax national office. Online sellers in the UK need to register EU goods sales with HMRC if sales exceed £85,000 (until April 2024). For importation into the UK, EU online sellers needed to register for UK VAT and report to HMRC if the sales are less than 150 Euros from January 2021. Sales of goods up to £135 are subject to UK VAT rates.[68] Above £135, importers need to register companies with the HMRC via the Government Gateway[69] and file VAT returns.[70] Many EU retailers withdrew delivery to the UK at least temporarily as a result[71].

As a consequence of these changes, delivery times have become longer. The Interactive Media in Retail Group (IMRG), which specialises in e-commerce market data, stated in a 2022 report that 'supply chain issues became prevalent ... The cost of hiring warehouse staff, and obtaining shipping containers skyrocketed, and cross-border commerce became tricky, with changes in regulations and the process of importing stock'.[72] As customers expect goods to arrive quickly, this has arguably made UK goods sold online less competitive compared to European counterparts. The import of products has also become much more expensive due to the low value of the pound, and the rise in costs of staff, shipping, and storage and transport. TNT, DHL, and UPS have also introduced surcharges for UK imports.

Regarding e-signatures, Article 206 of the TCA, although not a mutual recognition instrument as such, prohibits discrimination of electronic signatures; namely, 'a Party shall not deny the legal effect and admissibility as evidence in legal proceedings of an electronic document, an electronic signature, an electronic seal or an electronic time stamp, or of data sent and received using an electronic registered

[67] https://taxation-customs.ec.europa.eu/system/files/2020-12/guidance_on_import_and_export_of_low_value_consignments_final.pdf [last accessed 25.10.2022].
[68] www.gov.uk/vat-rates [last accessed 25.10.2022].
[69] www.gov.uk/vat-registration/how-to-register [last accessed 25.10.2022].
[70] www.gov.uk/government/publications/changes-to-vat-treatment-of-overseas-goods-sold-to-customers-from-1-january-2021/changes-to-vat-treatment-of-overseas-goods-sold-to-customers-from-1-january-2021 [last accessed 25.10.2022].
[71] www.bbc.co.uk/news/business-55530721 [last accessed 25.10.2022].
[72] www.imrg.org/blog/two-years-since-the-first-lockdown-whats-changed-for-online-retail [last accessed 25.10.2022].

delivery service, solely on the ground that it is in electronic form'. Accordingly, the UK legal framework for e-signatures was updated with the Electronic Identification and Trust Services for Electronic Transactions (Amendment etc.) (EU Exit) Regulations 2019 in the UK. It amended the Electronic Identification and Trust Services for Electronic Transactions Regulations 2016 which had implemented the EU 2014 Electronic Identification Regulation (eIDAS). The 2019 Regulations remove reference to mutual recognition within the EU. However, they continue to recognise e-signature platforms based in the EU so UK consumers can continue to use these.

Regarding domain names, UK citizens and entities can no longer register .eu names post-Brexit. In 2018, there were 240,000.eu domain names registered in the UK. By 2019, this had dropped to 190,000, then, in 2021, 81,000 remaining .eu domains were suspended by EurID.[73] If UK registrants did not meet the eligibility criteria by July 2021, they were revoked. The criteria mandates that a company established in the UK and not in the EU/EEA cannot hold an .eu domain name. UK citizens not residing in the EU/EEA who do not hold EU citizenship cannot hold an .eu domain name. The eligibility requirements are set out in the 2019 Regulation (EU) 2019/517 amending 2002 Regulation (EC) No 733/2002. EU citizens and entities are by contrast still permitted to register .uk addresses post-Brexit.[74] Interestingly, the impact of the UK's withdrawal meant that there was a negative growth of .eu registrations in 2019–20 but this recovered with the impact of COVID-19.

International cooperation and the digital services tax

In March 2018, the European Commission proposed two Directives for an EU-wide digital services tax (DSTD). The first Directive, on the common system of a digital services tax on revenues resulting from the provision of certain digital services, proposed a national corporation tax of 3 per cent on companies which had a global revenue exceeding 750,000,000 Euros and EU tax revenue exceeding 50,000,000 Euros within a given tax year. It stipulated that tax profits would be registered where corporations had significant interaction with users. The second Directive laid out rules for corporate taxation of a significant 'digital footprint' in a member state based upon revenues in a jurisdiction exceeding 7,000,000 Euros, if the number of users exceeds 100,000 Euros and the number of business contracts

73 https://eur-lex.europa.eu/legal-content/EN/TXT/PDF/?uri=CELEX:52022DC0001 [last accessed 25.10.2022].

74 www.gov.uk/guidance/registering-and-renewing-eu-domain-names-in-the-uk [last accessed 25.10.2022].

exceeds 3,000 Euros in a given tax year. This extensively targeted large US technology companies.

The EU proposal was strongly supported by France, Italy, and Spain and initially the UK.[75] But it met with backlash from several key EU states, principally Ireland as it moved the tax base to where users were located rather than where the company's headquarters are located. This would have meant that Ireland, in particular, would have lost considerable tax revenue, but the proposal would also have presented a serious challenge to the COO principle. The tax was also opposed by Denmark, Finland, Luxembourg, and Sweden (Lips, 2020). Germany, although initially ambiguous, announced that it preferred action at the G20/OECD level.[76] At the November 2018 EU finance ministers' meeting, a presidency compromise was reached, introducing an interim tax from January 2022 for taxation of digital services for companies which were not sufficiently paying tax within the EU.[77]

Several states had enacted legislation to introduce DSTDs early on. Hungary introduced an advertising tax on advertising revenue tax its 2014 Advertisement Tax Act which was amended to 5.3 per cent on corporations earning over HUF 100 million after a DG Competition ruling.[78] France has long taxed audio-visual media services. It began with a tax on the distribution of audio-visual content and expanded this to a tax of 2 per cent on free but advertising funded video on-demand (VOD) services in 2016. Following the European Commission's 2018 Directive proposals, the French government passed legislation in 2019 for a 3 per cent on gross revenues digital interface services and targeted advertising services generating 25 million Euros in France by corporations with a global profit of over 750 million Euros. This experienced delay when the Trump administration commenced an investigation under Section 301 of the 1974 US Trade Act[79] and threatened tariffs on the import of French goods.[80]

Austria was also subject to investigation by the US Trade Representative under Section 301[81] when it enacted its Digital Tax Act of 2020 which levies a 5 per cent tax on digital advertising services with a profit of over 25 million Euros. The Trump administration objected to the targeting of large US multinationals. Spain enacted

[75] www.europarl.europa.eu/RegData/etudes/BRIE/2018/625132/EPRS_BRI(2018)625132_EN.pdf [last accessed 25.10.2022].

[76] www.oecd.org/tax/beps/statement-on-a-two-pillar-solution-to-address-the-tax-challenges-arising-from-the-digitalisation-of-the-economy-october-2021.pdf [last accessed 25.10.2022].

[77] https://data.consilium.europa.eu/doc/document/ST-14886-2018-INIT/en/pdf [last accessed 25.10.2022].

[78] The European Commission found in 2022 that the 2014 Hungarian tax was incompatible with EU State aid rules (case number SA.39235). Hungary had originally taxed advertising including on websites progressively ranging from 1 per cent to 50 per cent.

[79] https://ustr.gov/sites/default/files/Report_On_France%27s_Digital_Services_Tax.pdf [last accessed 25.10.2022].

[80] www.nytimes.com/2019/12/02/business/trump-tariff-france.html [last accessed 25.10.2022].

[81] https://ustr.gov/sites/default/files/files/Press/Releases/AustriaDSTSection301Report.pdf [last accessed 25.10.2022].

legislation in 2020 for 3 per cent tax on revenue over 3 million Euros. Italy introduced a 3 per cent tax on digital interface advertising revenue generated from users of over 5.5 million Euros from 2020. The Czech Republic, Latvia, Norway, Slovakia, and Slovenia are considering measures at the time of writing.

In parallel, several states imposed taxes on audio-visual media services. Poland introduced a 1.5 per cent on audio-visual media services and audio-visual commercial communications in 2020. Portugal introduced a 4 per cent advertising tax on video-sharing platform services such as Amazon Prime and YouTube and a 1 per cent tax on audio-visual on-demand service operators (such as HBO and Netflix) in 2021, which aims to support Portuguese cinema and audio-visual production. In the UK, Philip Hammond, the British chancellor of the exchequer, introduced a digital services tax of 2 per cent from April 2020 under Theresa May's government. This is levied on social media platforms, internet search engines, and online marketplaces.

At the international level, an OECD proposal for a digital tax arose out of a counter-movement to the G20/OECD Base Erosion and Profit Shifting (BEPS) project under which profits should be taxed in states where businesses create value (Carlini, 2021: 251; Lips, 2020: 984). As digital corporations can easily evade national taxation as they are reliant on intangibles, arguments arose that the international corporate tax system is being challenged by business models wherein value creation is reliant on user participation (HMRC, 2018). The Trump administration was opposed to an OECD-level solution. However, following the inauguration of Biden, the US position softened.

Accordingly, the OECD/G20 was able to progress its Inclusive Framework (IF) on Base Erosion and Profit Shifting which agreed on a two-pillar solution in October 2021.[82] Pillar One, which opened for signature in 2022, introduced a special purpose nexus rule which means that multinational enterprises (MNEs) with a global turnover above 20 billion Euros and profitability above 10 per cent can be taxed in a jurisdiction where an MNE derives over 1 million Euros in revenue. For small states, with GDPs less than 40 billion Euros, the nexus is set at a lower 250,000-Euro threshold. Pillar two proposes a minimum tax rate of 15 per cent for Income Inclusion Rule (IIR) and an Undertaxed Payment Rule (UTPR).

The introduction of a minimum global corporate tax level was aimed at tax avoidance in low-tax states. This received support from the US which introduced a rise in corporate taxation from 21 per cent to 28 per cent and a minimum tax of 15 per cent on book income for large corporations flanking the OECD proposals. In 2021, a compromise was reached between the EU and US. European states agreed to remove existing Digital Services Taxes and not to introduce new ones.

[82] www.oecd.org/tax/beps/statement-on-a-two-pillar-solution-to-address-the-tax-challenges-arising-from-the-digitalisation-of-the-economy-october-2021.pdf [last accessed 25.10.2022]. Four members abstained: Kenya, Nigeria, Pakistan, and Sri Lanka.

Accordingly, in a Joint Statement,[83] Austria, France, Italy, Spain, and the United Kingdom agreed to phase out DSTD taxes from 2024 when Pillar I of the OECD/G20 agreement comes into force. This was accompanying by proposed rules on how digital platforms report to tax authorities.[84]

Conclusion

This chapter demonstrated that, although the UK continues to be the EU's largest trading partner for e-commerce, there is increasing divergence in legislation between the UK and EU. This is due to the rapid advance of EU legislation in the field following the Brexit period. The EU is pursuing a more consumer-based approach to online selling with an increasing number of statutory measures to protect customers online, as demonstrated by the update to its e-commerce and consumer law frameworks. This is flanked by increasing cooperation between NRAs and the Commission with several European-level portals established at the EU level, such as the European Consumer Centres Network, the European Interoperability Framework, the ODR network, One Stop Shop, and Your Europe, which support customers and businesses across Europe as well as seeking interoperability between digital systems. The EU is also showing a preference for dealing with the UK through international fora such as the WTO, OECD, and the Hague Convention rather than future bilateral trade deals, as shown by its vetoing the UK from joining the Lugano Convention.

The UK has not changed the national regulatory environment substantially with maintenance of pre-Brexit EU legislation in most areas. However, the delivery of goods to the EU has become difficult, with UK businesses reporting problems of increased red tape and having to adhere to both EU and UK requirements on conformity assessment, taxation, and rules of origin. Costs for staff, transport, and storage have increased for the UK and delivery times have lengthened. The UK government set up an Export Support Service (ESS) to assist companies with the sale of goods and services abroad.[85] It is considering accepting the CE mark as equivalent to the UKCA for imports. This shows that the UK has followed the EU lead in e-commerce with little divergence thus far post-Brexit.

[83] https://home.treasury.gov/news/press-releases/jy0419 [last accessed 25.10.2022].
[84] www.gov.uk/government/consultations/reporting-rules-for-digital-platforms/reporting-rules-for-digital-platforms-consultation [last accessed 25.10.2022].
[85] www.gov.uk/ask-export-support-team [last accessed 25.10.2022].

6
Platform Regulation and the Liability of Intermediaries

Introduction

Recent legislation at national and EU levels has shifted the primary responsibility for user-generated content to online platforms. Self-regulatory measures stipulated under the EU's 2018 and 2022 Codes of Disinformation have been adopted by several social media platforms, including Google, Facebook, Twitter, Microsoft, Mozilla, and TikTok, and advertising associations, such as the European Association of Communication Agencies, the Interactive Advertising Bureau, and the World Federation of Advertisers. The EU's 2022 Digital Services Act (DSA) updates obligations of online platforms as intermediaries which are responsible for actions to flag illegal content online, safeguard users, and mitigate against risks such as disinformation, electoral manipulation, violence against women, and harmful content to minors.

The UK decided to participate in the Codes post-Brexit as the former minister for Digital, Culture, Media and Sport, Margot James, decided that it was non-legislative and did not require implementation of EU law. As such, the UK is 'broadly supportive of the EU's actions in this area, and do[es] not believe that such action will prevent the UK taking action in this area'.[1] The UK's 2022 Online Safety Bill has proposed a similar self-regulatory framework for content under which social media firms and online platforms should take responsibility for user safety under the duty of care. However, it does not go as far as the EU's DSA in committing online platforms to statutory measures. The UK commenced work on the Bill after a UK Commons committee investigation by the Digital, Culture, Media and Sport Committee (2019) concluded that Facebook's founder Mark Zuckerberg failed to show 'leadership or personal responsibility' over fake news. Since this time, it has undergone many changes, reflecting different government approaches. The Bill needs to pass by April 2023, otherwise it will expire under House of Commons procedures and will need to be carried over to the next parliamentary session.

[1] Explanatory Memorandum from the Government (tackling online disinformation) (21 May 2018): http://europeanmemoranda.cabinetoffice.gov.uk/files/2018/07/Scan_Les_Saunders_20180709-141252_0465_001.pdf [last accessed 25.10.2022].

Brexit and the Digital Single Market. Alison Harcourt, Oxford University Press. © Alison Harcourt 2023.
DOI: 10.1093/oso/9780192899378.003.0006

Post-Brexit, the EU is experiencing greater coordination in the regulation of online platforms now that the UK has been removed from the equation, given the bigger appetite for more interventionist measures by France and Germany. European states are now requiring greater cooperation between public and private European news outlets as well as involvement of press councils, European-level associations, and the Alliance of Independent Press Councils of Europe (AIPCE). This combined effort is considerably different from the UK's stance, which has maintained its hands-off approach to the regulation of press markets. This chapter compares different national- and European-level approaches and draws some conclusions about the future trajectory of UK and EU policies post-Brexit. It takes into consideration the opposition voiced by the UK[2] to earlier European Commission proposals to introduce stricter platform regulation in 2017[3] as discussed in Chapter 5 and contrasts the UK approach with those of large EU member states.

History of EU legislation

Disinformation and misinformation have grown substantially over the last decade with social media accounting for a sizeable proportion of its distribution (Marchal et al., 2019). This has been propagated with the use of bots to create astroturfing on social media which is particularly prevalent during national election periods (Marsden and Meyer, 2019; García-Orosa et al., 2021). Disinformation presented as news reporting has witnessed extraordinary growth with the arrival of COVID-19 (Cuan-Baltazar et al., 2020), causing the World Health Organization to declare the pandemic to be accompanied by a parallel 'infodemic'.[4] Government social media manipulation is also on the rise (Bradshaw and Howard, 2019). This is coupled with continued lack of accountability and transparency (particularly of ownership) in the traditional media, problems of journalism sustainability, and declining trust in both traditional and online media.[5]

Germany and France were the first two states in Europe to produce laws to tackle online harm. Germany introduced its Netzwerkdurchsetzungsgesetz in 2017, updated with the Gesetz zur Änderung des Netzwerkdurchsetzungsgesetzes in 2021. The laws mandate that online platforms take down online content when

[2] www.europarl.europa.eu/RegData/etudes/BRIE/2017/607323/IPOL_BRI(2017)607323_EN.pdf [last accessed 25.10.2022].

[3] https://assets.publishing.service.gov.uk/government/uploads/system/uploads/attachment_data/file/513402/platforms-letter.pdf [last accessed 25.10.2022].

[4] www.who.int/health-topics/infodemic and www.who.int/news-room/spotlight/let-s-flatten-the-infodemic-curve [last accessed 25.10.2022].

[5] See also findings in European Parliament Resolution 2017, Online Platforms and the Digital Single Market; 2018 Resolution on the use of Facebook users' data by Cambridge Analytica and the impact on data protection; and 2019 Resolution on foreign electoral interference and disinformation in national and European democratic processes.

notified. France passed its 2018 Loi relative à la lutte contre la manipulation de l'information, under which candidates and political parties can appeal to a judge to stem the spread of 'false information' during elections.

The EU's approach to tackling disinformation online arose out of security policy in the 1990s. Following the adoption of the 1992 Maastricht Treaty and its creation of the Justice and Home Affairs (JHA) pillar II (renamed Police and Judicial Co-operation in Criminal Matters (PJCC) under the 1997 Amsterdam Treaty), the EU initiated several measures to fight crime. This began in the Council as pillar II provided an opportunity to address crime based upon intergovernmental cooperation. In 1996, a Council Joint action to combat racism and xenophobia identified difficulties in judicial cooperation between international organisations, particularly the EU and Council of Europe. It was followed by a 1998 Action Plan of the Council and the Commission on how best to implement the provisions of the Treaty of Amsterdam in the areas of freedom, security, and justice.

The early stage of the EU's online platform policy had its roots in the 2000 European Parliament Resolution on the EU's position at the World Conference Against Racism and the current situation in the Union. This was followed by a European Commission call for action in its 2000 Communication, suggesting the creation of a Scoreboard for an area of 'freedom, security and justice'. In response, the Council proposed a Framework Decision in 2001 to combat illegal hate speech online, which eventually culminated in the 2008 Framework Decision on combating certain forms and expressions of racism and xenophobia by means of criminal law.[6] It was aimed at curtailing illegal online hate speech through judicial cooperation. This focus on hate speech was based upon the German approach.

Work grounded in the Framework Decision began in the Directorate-General for Home with the establishment of the Centre of Excellence at the Radicalisation Awareness Network (RAN network)[7] in 2011. This was followed, in 2015, by the European Agenda on Security[8] launched by the European Commissioner for Migration, Home Affairs and Citizenship, Dimitris Avramopoulos, together with the Commissioner for Justice, Consumers and Gender Equality, Věra Jourová. The European Commission simultaneously established the EU Internet Forum in December 2015 based upon the findings of its first high-level conference on the criminal justice response to radicalisation.[9] The Forum set up regular meetings between home and justice ministers, high-level representatives of large internet corporations, Europol, European Parliament representatives, and the EU Counter

[6] Framework Decision 2008/913/JHA of 28 November 2008 on combating certain forms and expressions of racism and xenophobia.

[7] https://ec.europa.eu/home-affairs/networks/radicalisation-awareness-network-ran_en [last accessed 25.10.2022].

[8] http://ec.europa.eu/dgs/home-affairs/e-library/documents/basic-documents/docs/eu_agenda_on_security_en.pdf [last accessed 25.10.2022].

[9] http://europa.eu/rapid/press-release_IP-15-5861_en.htm [last accessed 25.10.2022].

Terrorism Co-ordinator. The aim was to develop a self-regulatory approach to tacking online harmful content, namely hate speech, cybercrime, organised online crime, and terrorism. This incremental self-regulatory approach based on Council initiatives and national cooperation reflected a lack of Treaty basis for Commission action.

The EU Internet Forum efforts were flanked by the launch of the East Stratcom Task Force[10] by the European External Action Service, which worked on countering disinformation originating from 'foreign sources'. In 2015, the EUvsDiSiNFO website was established to raise awareness about disinformation with a focus on Russian misinformation in particular.[11] Within two years of its establishment, the East Stratcom Task Force had identified '4000 individual disinformation cases' from Russia which were aimed at Europe.[12] Two further task forces were subsequently established, the Task Force for the Western Balkans and the Task Force South for the Arab-speaking world.

Following the March 2016 suicide bombing attacks in Brussels, a Joint Statement[13] was issued by the High-Level Group on Combating Racism, Xenophobia, and all forms of intolerance and an extraordinary JHA Council stating that 'the Commission will intensify work with IT companies, notably in the EU Internet Forum, to counter terrorist propaganda and to develop by June 2016 a code of conduct against hate speech online'. The Code of Conduct on Countering Illegal Hate Speech online was agreed in May 2016 between IT companies and the European Commission.[14]

The 2016 Code requested companies to put in place community guidelines which prevent incitement to violence and hatred. It asked that processes be adopted to enable users to alert others to hate speech so that online platforms could respond and take down content within 24 hours of notice. Signatories to the 2016 Code included Facebook, Microsoft, Twitter, and YouTube. The Code encouraged platforms to utilise civil society organisations as 'trusted reporters', but this did not take place. Notably, there was a shift at this point on the basis of EU measures. The 2016 Code was based not on police and judicial cooperation policy (pillar II), but on Article 16 of the 2000 Directive on electronic commerce, placing it firmly in the realm of the internal market and placing it under the jurisdiction of the European Commission.

[10] www.eeas.europa.eu/eeas/questions-and-answers-about-east-stratcom-task-force_en [last accessed 25.10.2022].

[11] https://euvsdisinfo.eu [last accessed 25.10.2022].

[12] 2014 Joint Communication on increasing resilience and bolstering capabilities to address hybrid threats.

[13] www.consilium.europa.eu/en/press/press-releases/2016/03/24-statement-on-terrorist-attacks-in-brussels-on-22-march [last accessed 25.10.2022].

[14] https://ec.europa.eu/info/files/code-conduct-countering-illegal-hate-speech-online_en [last accessed 25.10.2022].

In 2018, a High-Level Expert Group (HLEG) was established to address disinformation online which published a report in March identifying best practice. The report requested that the European Commission draw up a Code of Practice on disinformation. It was the first that time 'disinformation' and 'fake' were mentioned as part of the EU's strategy as opposed to 'illegal content' and 'hate speech'. Disinformation was defined by the HLEG as 'all forms of false, inaccurate, or misleading information designed, presented and promoted to intentionally cause public harm or for profit'.[15] It reflected similar definitions adopted by the United Nations, Organization for Security and Co-operation in Europe (OSCE), Organization of American States (OAS), African Union (AU) (OSCE, 2017), and the Council of Europe (Council of Europe, 2017). The term 'disinformation' was chosen rather than 'fake news' to disassociate it from the meaning of news. This was because 'disinformation' cannot be legally defined as 'news'.

Recommended requirements for online platforms were expansive and reflected wider EU policy goals, particularly relating to the promotion of the internal market and national champions; namely, in this case, news publishers and press agencies reflecting French dirigisme. It should be considered that these same companies (news and press) were at the time at odds with online platforms over the loss of advertising revenue, as explained in Chapter 11. In this respect, the Code can be understood as addressing two issues at once: online harmful content and transparency in payment and fairness for online advertising.

The report asked that a Coalition be established 'representing relevant actors, including online platforms, news media organisations (namely press and broadcasters), journalists, publishers, independent content creators, the advertising industry fact checkers and other practitioners' to agree on key performance indicators to be included in the Code. The Coalition should seek to: enhance the transparency of online news; introduce transparency in data sharing; promote media and information literacy; develop tools for empowering users and journalists; safeguard diversity and the sustainability of the 'European news media ecosystem'; promote research on disinformation; adapt social media advertising policies to a 'follow-the-money' principle based on clear, transparent, and non-discriminatory criteria; ensure transparency in the processing of users' data for advertisement placements; and distinguish sponsored content, including political advertising, from other content. Voluntary fact-checking recommendations included 'cooperation with public and private European news outlets', steering users towards recommended news and fact-checking sites.

The European Commission aimed to provide a greater role to press councils and the European-level association, the AIPCE. The report was followed by a

[15] A multi-dimensional approach to disinformation. Report of the independent high-level group on fake news and online disinformation: https://digital-strategy.ec.europa.eu/en/library/final-report-high-level-expert-group-fake-news-and-online-disinformation [last accessed 25.10.2022].

Communication on 'Tackling Online Disinformation: A European Approach' in April 2018. Based upon this Communication, the European Commission created an internal Network against Disinformation (IND) which was made up of national representatives, the European External Action Service (EEAS), and representatives of other EU institutions coordinated by the Directorate-General for Communication (DG Comm). Initially the IND coordinated national online repositories to detect and counter disinformation online and produce positive messaging.

In June 2018, the European Commission published its Code of Practice on Disinformation.[16] Reflecting external lobbying by online platforms, it removed any reference to voluntary obligations to cooperate with European press councils or promote European publisher content as recommended in the HLEG report. Instead, it focused on fact checking and disinformation. Without referring directly to news publishers, it did, however, point signatories to 'the new independent network of fact checkers facilitated by the European Commission' (namely, the IND).

The Code commits signatories to 'improve the scrutiny of advertisement placements to reduce revenues of the purveyors of disinformation'; 'ensure transparency about political and issue-based advertising'; 'implement and promote reasonable policies against misrepresentation'; 'close fake accounts and establish clear marking systems and rules for bots to ensure their activities cannot be confused with human interactions'; 'communicate on the effectiveness of efforts'; 'invest in technological means to prioritize relevant, authentic, and accurate and authoritative information where appropriate in search, feeds, or other automatically ranked distribution channels'; 'not be compelled by governments ... to delete or prevent access to otherwise lawful content'; enable 'users to understand why they have been targeted by a given political or issue-based advertisement'; 'dilute ... disinformation by improving the findability of trustworthy content'; empower 'users with tools ... to facilitate content discovery and access to different news sources representing alternative viewpoints'; provide 'tools to report Disinformation' by users; and enable 'factchecking and research activities ... including data for independent investigation by academic researchers and general information on algorithms'.

From January 2019, signatories to the 2018 Code were requested to submit monthly reports to the European Commission.[17] By 2020, there were 16 signatories to the Code: Facebook, Google, Microsoft, Mozilla, TikTok, Twitter, eight advertising associations,[18] Goldbach Audience (Switzerland) AG, and Dot Europe.[19]

[16] https://ec.europa.eu/newsroom/dae/document.cfm?doc_id=54454 [last accessed 25.10.2022].

[17] https://ec.europa.eu/digital-single-market/en/news/first-results-eu-code-practice-against-disinformation [last accessed 25.10.2022].

[18] The eight advertising associations were the Association des agences conseils en communication (AACC), the European Association of Communications Agencies (EACA), IAB Europe, the SAR Marketing Communication Association, Union of Belgian Advertisers (UBA), World Federation of Advertisers (WFA), AKA, and Kreativitet & Kommunikation.

[19] Dot Europe, founded as the European Digital Media Association (EdimA) in 2000 and renamed in 2020, represents the online platforms Airbnb, Allegro, Amazon, Apple, Dropbox, Etsy, Expedia group,

The European Digital Media Observatory (EDMO) was founded in June 2020 at the European University Institute to link up academics, journalists, and large platforms representatives to draw upon in its implementation.[20] The Code was referred to in the 2020 proposal for a Digital Services Act as a basis for co-regulation.[21]

In parallel, the European Commission published its Action Plan on disinformation: Commission as a contribution to the European Council in December 2018.[22] This had been requested by a Joint Communication from the High Representative and the Commission on bolstering resilience against hybrid threats[23] in a reaction to the March 2018 Salisbury chemical attack in the UK. The Action Plan proposed a more coordinated response to challenges of disinformation with a request for sufficient resources to 'protect the Union's democratic systems and combat disinformation, including in the context of the upcoming European elections'. It outlined actions to be taken by the Commission in coordination with the High Representative and the European External Action Service, member states, and the European Parliament under four pillars and actions.

Pillar 1 of the Action Plan called for additional funding and staff for East Stratcom Task Force, a review of the Task Force South, and Task Force Western Balkans mandates. Pillar 3 recommended employing the European Regulators Group for Audiovisual Media Service (ERGA) to monitor implementation of the Code of Practice on Disinformation by its signatories. Pillar 4 called on member states to deal with fact checking with the promotion of media literacy, identifying a number of projects and measures of best practice. In particular, the Social Observatory for Disinformation and Social Media Analysis (SOMA)[24] and the European Platform on Disinformation[25] were supported under the Action.

Under Pillar 2, a Rapid Alert System (RAS) was set up by the EEAS in March 2019 ahead of the European Parliament elections. RAS connected national 'Points of Contact' across EU member states and EU institutions, among whom 'alerts' on substantial disinformation campaigns were shared. RAS later linked up with the European Cooperation Network on Elections (ECNE) and the internal Network Against Disinformation of the Commission with regular meetings.

Google, King, Meta, Microsoft, Mozilla, Nextdoor, OLX, Shopify, Snap Inc, Spotify, TikTok, Twitter, Yahoo, and Yelp.

[20] https://digital-strategy.ec.europa.eu/en/news/hubs-european-digital-media-observatory-now-extend-whole-eu27 [last accessed 25.10.2022].

[21] Specifically, the proposal stated 'the rules on codes of conduct established in this Regulation could serve as a basis and be complemented by a revised and strengthened Code of practice on disinformation, building on the guidance of the Commission'.

[22] https://ec.europa.eu/info/publications/action-plan-disinformation-commission-contribution-european-council-13-14-december-2018_en [last accessed 25.10.2022].

[23] www.eeas.europa.eu/sites/default/files/joint_communication_increasing_resilience_and_bolstering_capabilities_to_address_hybrid_threats.pdf [last accessed 25.10.2022].

[24] www.disinfobservatory.org [last accessed 25.10.2022].

[25] www.disinfo.eu [last accessed 25.10.2022].

In parallel, the Commission also founded a working group with the European Parliament and the European External Action Service to tackle disinformation during the European elections. The December 2019 Council[26] reiterated that the 2018 EU action plan 'remains at the heart of the EU's efforts' to fight disinformation. In June 2020, the Commission and the High Representative published a further Communication, 'Tackling COVID-19 Disinformation: Getting the Facts Right',[27] which specifically addressed COVID-19 disinformation.

The DSA recommends the transparency of algorithms and filtering technologies for the automatic take-down of illegal content.[28] The 2020 EU Regulation on the Prevention of Dissemination of Terrorist Content Online and Article 13 of the Copyright in the Digital Single Market Directive also promoted the use of artificial intelligence for removing illegal content in the original proposals. However, as Marsden, Meyer, and Brown (2020: 7) have argued, 'Automated technologies such as AI are not a silver bullet for identifying illegal or "harmful" content. They are limited in their accuracy, especially for expression where cultural or contextual cues are necessary'.

Large platforms and social media companies are also being called on to improve quality journalism and media literacy. Meta (formerly Facebook) and Google became the largest funders of journalism globally from 2018.[29] Google began funding news in 2015 with News Lab. It introduced a fact-checking tool from 2017.[30] In 2017, the Digital News Initiative (DNI) began operating in Europe as a partnership between Google and news publishers. The Google News Initiative funded publishers to counter disinformation during the COVID-19 pandemic.[31] Facebook launched its News Project in 2017, now called the Meta Journalism Project.[32] Academic assessments of the projects, however, point to a lack of transparency in funding allocation (Fanta and Dachwitz, 2020; González-Tosat and Sádaba-Chalezquer, 2021).

Academic studies have also indicated that definitions of online political advertising need to be better addressed (Dobber et al., 2019; Jaursch, 2020; Nelson and Jaursch, 2020). A New York University (NYU) Ad Observatory project pointed to how the line between ads on social issues and political issues is blurred identifying advertising categorisations in a study of Facebook.[33] Controversially, in 2021,

[26] https://data.consilium.europa.eu/doc/document/ST-14972-2019-INIT/en/pdf [last accessed 25.10.2022].

[27] https://ec.europa.eu/info/sites/default/files/communication-tackling-covid-19-disinformation-getting-facts-right_en.pdf [last accessed 25.10.2022].

[28] For discussion on the types of software commonly used by platforms for automatic take-down, see Lange and Lechterman (2021). For Facebook practice, see Wong and Floridi (2022).

[29] www.cjr.org/special_report/google-facebook-journalism.php [last accessed 25.10.2022].

[30] https://toolbox.google.com/factcheck/explorer [last accessed 25.10.2022].

[31] www.niemanlab.org/2021/01/google-is-giving-3-million-to-news-orgs-to-fact-check-vaccine-misinformation [last accessed 25.10.2022].

[32] https://pressgazette.co.uk/meta-facebook-another-5-9m-community-news-project [last accessed 25.10.2022].

[33] https://adobservatory.org [last accessed 25.10.2022].

Facebook subsequently blocked the accounts of team members of the project which was based at the Center for Cybersecurity at the NYU Tandon School of Engineering, thereby hampering public transparency of Facebook's advertising strategy.

Political advertising was addressed by the European Commission in its European Democracy Action Plan (EDAP) in December 2020.[34] It aimed at promoting fair elections, strengthening media freedom, and countering disinformation. The plan announced that there would be a revised Code of Practice on Disinformation. The EDAP expressed deep dissatisfaction with a lack of transparency in online political advertising. Twitter, TikTok, Pinterest, LinkedIn, and Amazon had banned political advertising in 2019.[35] Google limited targeting options for political advertising by affiliation or public voter record in 2019 in the run-up to the US 2020 presidential election and strengthened its ban on 'demonstrably false claims'. Apple has turned off its default tracking 'identifier for advertisers' (IDFA).

However, although Facebook and Instagram stopped advertisers targeting users based on their history of posting, reading, or liking related content from 2022, they have ruled out bans. Snapchat, Spotify, and Reddit also do not ban political advertising. Twitter may change its policy given the takeover by Elon Musk. It has already changed its policy on COVID-19 disinformation in its blog page on COVID-19 policy which states, 'Effective November 23, 2022, Twitter is no longer enforcing the COVID-19 misleading information policy'.[36] Věra Jourová, the EU Commissioner for Values and Transparency overseeing implementation of the EDAP and Code of Practice on Disinformation, has expressed concern about Twitter's 2022 laying off of 50 per cent of its 7,500 staff, 15 per cent of whom were content moderators (Espinoza et al., 2022). Although Twitter is meeting with national challenges under employment law over sudden staff lay-offs, it will also most likely reach the DSA thresholds to qualify as a very large online platform (VLOP). Meta also cut 13 per cent of staff from Facebook and Instagram and Snapchat 20 per cent of staff in 2022 due to economic slowdown.

The EDAP stipulated 'further restricting micro-targeting and psychological profiling in the political context'. It emphasised strengthening cooperation within the EU including RAS and the ECNE. Accordingly, the Commission published a Guidance to strengthen the Code of Practice on disinformation[37] in May 2021, a Vademecum on the organisation and functioning of the process,[38] and a call for interest to join the Code in July.[39] Following these actions, in November 2021

[34] https://ec.europa.eu/info/strategy/priorities-2019-2024/new-push-european-democracy/european-democracy-action-plan_en [last accessed 25.10.2022].
[35] https://privacyinternational.org/long-read/3703/apart-google-facebook-and-twitter-what-are-other-platforms-doing-about-political-ads [last accessed 25.10.2022].
[36] https://blog.twitter.com/en_us/topics/company/2020/covid-19 [last accessed 25.10.2022].
[37] https://ec.europa.eu/commission/presscorner/detail/en/ip_21_2585 [last accessed 25.10.2022].
[38] https://ec.europa.eu/newsroom/dae/redirection/document/78161 [last accessed 25.10.2022].
[39] https://digital-strategy.ec.europa.eu/en/news-redirect/716617 [last accessed 25.10.2022].

the EU proposed a Regulation on the transparency and targeting of political advertising.

At the time of writing, the current UK government has diverged from the EU in the approach to the regulation of online political advertising. Although the Department for Digital, Culture, Media and Sport (DCMS) criticised the negative effects of targeted political advertising in 2020 report, the UK government ruled out imposing measures in its Online Advertising Programme in 2022, stating that 'the government believes that having political advertising vetted or censored would have a chilling effect on free speech'.[40]

In October 2022, the DSA was adopted by the EU. Under the Act, limited legal liability is retained for intermediary services but it imposes obligations to act against infringements of illegal harmful content, terrorist content, and illegally copyrighted material. The DSA prevents targeting advertising based on the use of minors' personal data and the use of sensitive personal data such as that on gender, race, and religion. It also bans interfaces known as 'dark patterns', as defined in Chapter 5. Platforms are responsible for explaining to users the reasons for account blocking and providing users with the right to challenge decisions. Algorithmic transparency is required from platforms. Users must be offered feed not based on profiling and provide clear information on ad targeting and preferences.

Implementation will take place through a network composed of the European Commission, responsible for VLOPs and very large online search engines (VLOSEs), and national Digital Service Coordinators, independent regulators in charge of smaller platforms at the national level. Internally to the Commission, the European Centre for Algorithmic Transparency (ECAT) will 'support with assessments as to whether the functioning of algorithmic systems are in line with the risk management obligations that the DSA establishes for VLOPs and VLOSEs to ensure a safe, predictable and trusted online environment'.[41] Platforms are required to provide annual reports, including detail on the number of take-down orders received from member states or trusted flaggers. Additional rules exist for platforms reaching more than 10 per cent or 45 million consumers in Europe defined as VLOPs and VLOSEs, clearly aimed at platforms such as Amazon Store, Google, Facebook, Instagram, TikTok, and YouTube.[42] Failure to intervene in risks can result in large fines of up to 6 per cent of total turnover.

Four categories of risks relate to the dissemination of illegal content and the negative effects on fundamental rights, electoral processes, gender-based violence, or mental health. The first category deals with illegal content such as 'the dissemination of child sexual abuse material or illegal hate speech or other types of misuse

[40] www.gov.uk/government/consultations/online-advertising-programme-consultation/online-advertising-programme-consultation [last accessed 25.10.2022].

[41] https://ec.europa.eu/commission/presscorner/detail/en/ip_22_6906 [last accessed 25.10.2022].

[42] Cloud platforms such as Azure, Google Cloud Platform, and Amazon Web Services will be dealt with under the DMA.

of their services for criminal offences, and the conduct of illegal activities, such as the sale of products or services prohibited by Union or national law, including dangerous or counterfeit products, or illegally-traded animals'. Platforms are expected to report online child sexual abuse to national agencies.

The second category prohibits impact on fundamental rights as protected by the EU's 2000 Charter of Fundamental Rights of the European Union. This includes but is 'not limited to human dignity, freedom of expression and of information, including media freedom and pluralism, the right to private life, data protection, the right to non-discrimination, the rights of the child and consumer protection'. The third category requires platforms to assess the 'negative effects on democratic processes, civic discourse and electoral processes, as well as public security'.

The fourth category relates to the 'design, functioning or use, including through manipulation ... with an actual or foreseeable negative effect on the protection of public health, minors and serious negative consequences to a person's physical and mental well-being, or on gender-based violence'. This could originate from 'disinformation campaigns related to public health'. The Commission began designating online platforms to this very large category from 15 November 2022 when the DSA was enacted. The process for assignment is predicted to take four months. Online platforms have until 17 February 2023 to report the number of their active end users. It also established the European Centre for Algorithmic Transparency (ECTA)[43] to assess whether algorithms used by VLOPs and VLOSEs are in line with risk management obligations.

Third countries offering intermediary services within the EU, such as the UK, must appoint legal representatives in the EU on the basis of a 'significant number of recipients of the service in one or more Member States in relation to its or their population; or the targeting of activities towards one or more Member States'. This will be established by a number of factors including language, the use of a top-level domain, or the currency used for transactions. The member state where the legal representative is located will have jurisdiction for the service provider which will be regulated by a nominated national regulatory authority (NRA) 'Digital Services Coordinator'.

The Regulation is supported by the updated 2022 Code of Practice on Disinformation.[44] As summarised by Nenadić and Verza (2022: 181), the 2022 Code is:

> 1) reducing the monetisation of disinformation linked to sponsored content; (2) clearly label-ling all paid-for communication, with additional transparency provided around political advertising (defined as advertisements advocating

[43] https://algorithmic-transparency.ec.europa.eu/index_en [last accessed 25.10.2022].
[44] 2022 Code of Practice on Disinformation: https://digital-strategy.ec.europa.eu/en/policies/code-practice-disinformation [last accessed 25.10.2022].

for or against the election of a candidate or passage of referenda in national and European elections), and an attempt to also publicly disclose 'issue-based advertising'; (3) designing clear, accessible and effective policies regarding identity and misuse of automated bots on platform services, and developing appropriate measures to limit the artificial amplification of disinformation campaigns; (4) supporting 'adequate visibility of reliable information of public interest', while maintaining media pluralism; and (5) ensuring effective data disclosure for research on disinformation.

The Regulation is also flanked by the online safety framework as introduced in the 2018 Audiovisual Media Services Directive (AVMSD). Two other supporting pieces of legislation are the proposed child sexual abuse material (CSAM) Regulation and the Information Security Directive (NIS2). As Kolkman (2021) points out, the 2020 proposed NIS2 Directive, which covers domain name systems, replaces the phrase 'the entities providing domain name registration services' found in the 2016 NIS Directive with the words 'operators of root name servers with a significant footprint in the EU and that are of importance for the internal market'. This reflects the Commission's policy on digital sovereignty and the protection of national champions. The Commission has also published a proposal for a Cyber Resilience Act in 2022 based upon its European Agenda on Security (2015–20).

National measures

National legal bases for the regulation of online platforms differ across Europe (Richter, 2018; Heldt, 2019, Katsirea, 2019). Germany bases its legislation in hate speech and criminal law. The UK has taken an approach based upon the duty of care (Craufurd-Smith, 2019; Woods, 2019; Woods and Perrin, 2022). France grounds its approach on definitions of 'nouvelles fausses' (false information) according to Article 27 of the amended 1881 French Press Law and French Electoral Code.[45] Germany references 'unlawful content' ('Rechtswichige Inhalte') in its Netzwerkdurchsetzungsgesetz (NetzDG) based upon definitions in the German criminal code (Strafgesetzbuch).[46] The NetzDG requires social networks to define 'hate speech' within their terms of service. The UK 2022 Online Safety Bill uses the words 'harmful content'. In the original UK 2019 Online Harms proposal, disinformation was defined as being 'created or disseminated with the deliberate

[45] For an English translation of the Electoral Code, see http://europam.eu/data/mechanisms/PF/PF%20Laws/France/France_Electoral_Code_legislative_part_primary_leg_am2013_fr%20(1).pdf [last accessed 25.10.2022].

[46] Article 19 provides a translation of relevant parts of the Strafgesetzbuch (StGB) here: www.article19.org/wp-content/uploads/2018/07/Germany-Responding-to-%E2%80%98hate-speech%E2%80%99-v3-WEB.pdf [last accessed 25.10.2022].

intent to mislead; this could be to cause harm, or for personal, political or financial gain'.[47] At the time of writing, disinformation is not defined in the current UK Bill. Instead, powers are delegated to the regulatory body Ofcom to regulate against harmful content and activities covered by the duty of care.

Germany was the first state in Europe to regulate content on online platforms with its NetzDG (Law Improving Enforcement in Social Networks) in December 2017. It obliges online platforms with more than 2 million registered users in Germany, such as Meta, Twitter, and YouTube, to remove 'offensichtlich rechtswidrige Inhalte' ('obviously illegal content')[48] within 24 hours after notification by users or agencies or within 7 days if the content is not 'obviously' illegal. Take-down can take longer if users are consulted over the decision or the case is referred to an accredited co-regulatory body approved by the Ministry of Justice. Fines of between 5 and 50 million Euros can be issued to platforms by the Bundesministerium der Justiz und für Verbraucherschutz (Federal Ministry of Justice and Consumer Protection) if they do not comply. Facebook was the first online platform to be fined under the NetzDG with a fine of 2 million Euros in 2019.[49]

The NetzDG was proposed in the Bundestag by the German minister of justice, Heiki Maas, and is based on hate speech provisions in the German Constitution. To meet the criteria for take-down, the content must fall under one of the 21 conditions outlined in the Strafgesetzbuch (StGB) (German Criminal Code).[50] Each online platform is mandated to publish community guidelines[51] which delineate

[47] The 2019 proposal also referred to the DCMS Commons Select Committee definition of disinformation as: 'the deliberate creation and sharing of false and/or manipulated information that is intended to deceive and mislead audiences, either for the purposes of causing harm, or for political, personal or financial gain' in the publication 'Disinformation and "Fake News": Government Response to the Committee's Fifth Report of Session 2017–19', 23 October 2018, HC 1630 Government response to Interim Report, page 2.

[48] For an English translation, see: www.bmjv.de/SharedDocs/Gesetzgebungsverfahren/Dokumente/NetzDG_engl.pdf;jsessionid=D9F4B816F91A21413A3E95122O4ED293.1_cid334?__blob=publicationFile&v=2 [last accessed 25.10.2022].

[49] www.bundesjustizamt.de/DE/Presse/Archiv/2019/20190702_EN.html;jsessionid=AE3371DA35E5EEFEEB5A8BFF7F52AFCA.1_cid392?nn=3449818 [last accessed 25.10.2022].

[50] The 21 provisions are found under subsection 1 of the StGB and relate to: dissemination of propaganda material of unconstitutional organisations; using symbols of unconstitutional organisations; preparation of a serious violence offence endangering the state; encouraging the commission of a serious violence offence endangering the state; treasonous forgery; public incitement to crime; breach of the public peace by threatening to commit offences; forming criminal organisations; forming terrorist organisations; criminal and terrorist organisations abroad; incitement to hatred; dissemination of depictions of violence; rewarding and approving of offences; defamation of religions and religious and ideological associations; distribution, acquisition, and possession of child pornography; distribution of pornographic performances by broadcasting, media services, or telecommunications services; insult; defamation; intentional defamation; violation of intimate privacy by taking photographs; threatening the commission of a felony; and forgery of data intended to provide proof', as translated by www.article19.org/wp-content/uploads/2018/07/Germany-Responding-to-%E2%80%98hate-speech%E2%80%99-v3-WEB.pdf [last accessed 25.10.2022].

[51] See, for example, www.youtube.com/intl/de/yt/about/policies/#community-guidelines [last accessed 02.06.2022].

under which circumstances content is removed. Online platforms are obliged to publish transparency reports on how complaints are dealt with twice yearly.[52]

Because of the new requirements, there was a rapid and immediate increase in the hiring of content moderators by online platforms. Owing to the complexity and additional requirements under German law, German speakers accounted for one-sixth of Twitter's content team in 2018 (Theil, 2019: 49). Elon Musk laid off 50 employees in Germany in November 2022 reportedly largely responsible for content regulation. However, overall, the conditions under which content moderators are hired and paid across Europe have been a source of controversy. Facebook in particular has faced criticism for low pay and lack of mental health support for content moderators.[53]

In June 2021, Germany amended its NetzDG with the Gesetz zur Änderung des Netzwerkdurchsetzungsgesetzes (Act to Amend the Network Enforcement Act). The update increased requirements on online platforms and simultaneously implemented the 2018 AVMSD. The law obligates online platforms to pass on personal data of users to the German police if suspected of criminal activity. The 2021 NetzDG also created a new department within the Bundeskriminalamt (Federal Crime Office) dedicated to investigation of social media and online platforms. It is concentrating its activities on Facebook in particular and countering far-right extremist content online. The 2021 law also stipulates that platforms provide information on automated decision-making and adds an appeals process for the takedown of content.

The Amendment Act was part of a package of laws in 2021. This included an Act to Combat Right-Wing Extremism and Hate Crime (Gesetz zur Bekämpfung des Rechtsextremismus und der Hasskriminalität) which increases the list of criminal offences listed under the NetzDG. There were also amendments to Germany's StGB (Criminal Code), Bundeskriminalamtgesetz (BKAG), the Federal Constitutional Protection Act, the law on criminal procedure, Strafprozessordnung, Telemediengesetz (TMG), and the Telecommunication Act. Changes to the German laws were flanked by a court (Bundesverfassungsgericht, BVerfG) decision in February 2022 which outlined criteria courts need to apply when online criticism attacks the personality rights of politicians. The law underpinned the 2021 Reparaturgetz (Repair Act) enacted in March 2021 which addressed parliamentarians' concerns that the NetzDG contravened privacy protection in Germany, which specified in which cases German authorities could access user data. The changes to the laws and the court decision have, however, met

[52] See, for example, YouTube's transparency report for the period July to September 2022, https://transparencyreport.google.com/youtube-policy/removals?hl=en_GB [last accessed 25.10.2022].
[53] See www.bbc.co.uk/news/technology-61409556 and www.bbc.co.uk/news/technology-59819664 [last accessed 25.10.2022].

with harsh criticism from several digital rights groups and journalist organisations which view them as a counter to the freedom of speech and expression online.

One year following Germany's NetzDG, France passed its 2018 law on the manipulation of information. The French law focuses on disinformation during election periods after the 2017 French election was targeted by astroturfing and hacking. As an example, Couzigou explains, 'hacked e-mails from Macron's close collaborators, were posted on … Archiv.org and … Pastebin under the title "Emleaks" … The hackers had mixed falsified documents with genuine ones in order to sow doubt and disinformation … The hashtag #MacronLeaks was included in approximately 47,000 tweets in just three and a half hours'.

Different to German Act, the French law is based on Article 27 of the 1881 French Press Law which bans 'false news' or 'articles fabricated, falsified or falsely attributed to others' (Craufurd-Smith, 2019: 55). It also induces relevant clauses on genocide denial and crimes against humanity (Article 24), defamation (Articles 29–35 of the 1881 Press Law), and the Electoral Code,[54] under which (Article 97) 'false news, calumnies, or other fraudulent means' and commercial electoral advertising are prohibited (as cited in Craufurd-Smith, 2019: 55).

Unlike German laws which target hate speech, the French law is directed at political advertising and political party campaigning. The law requires transparency for sponsored content and political advertising. Three months prior to an election, online platforms are obliged to make public to users 'fair, clear, and transparent' information on the use of their personal data, the identity (natural persons or corporate name and registered office) of those paying money to sponsor political content, and the amount paid (over a given threshold). The information is provided to the public in an aggregated public register. Fines are substantially lower than in Germany, set at 75,000 Euros during the time of election, and target users or legal representatives of social media platforms who can face up to one year in prison if content is not removed within 48 hours. Fines are issued by the Autorité des Marchés Financiers (AMF).

Similar to the German law, the French law empowers users and regulatory bodies to report misinformation to online platforms along with an additional measure providing power to political parties to do the same. Accordingly, online platforms need to provide notification mechanisms for users so that they can flag false content. Under Article 14, platforms must make the algorithms which they use transparent, provide information on how content is accessed by users (how often and when, based on platform recommendations), explain how content related to 'a debate of national interest' is organised, promote authentic accounts, and

[54] Electoral law in France consists of several acts: the 1962 law relating to the election of the President of the Republic by universal suffrage; the 2017 Organic law for confidence in political life; and the Electoral Code. The 2018 Law on the fight against the manipulation of information is also regarded as electoral law, along with the Decision of the Constitutional Council no. 2018–773 DC of 20 December 2018.

take efforts to delete fake accounts. In conformity with French dirigiste policy,[55] the 2018 law mandates that platforms promote news publishers and news agencies which are seen to provide impartial, accurate information. Online platforms must provide the Autorité de régulation de la communication audiovisuelle et numérique (ARCOM)[56] with annual reports. ARCOM publishes regular reports on implementation on its website.

As in Germany, the law is part of a package of laws and as such represents an overhaul of French electoral and online platform law. It necessitates changes to the 1977 law on election to the European Parliament, the 1986 law on the freedom of communication (Léotard Law), the 2004 law on confidence in the digital economy, the Electoral Code, a decree from the Ministry of Culture on Article L111–7 of the Consumer Code,[57] the Education Code,[58] the 2018 law on filing candidacy for election, and the public order code overseas.[59] These were followed by a 2019 proposal for a law on audio-visual communication and cultural sovereignty in the digital age (Projet de loi elatif à la communication audiovisuelle et à la souveraineté culturelle à l'ère numérique) and a 2021 law 'consolidating respect for the principles of the Republic' ('loi confortant le respect des principes de la République') under which ARCOM can sanction online platforms up to 6 per cent of the operator's worldwide turnover (until the DSA comes into effect at the end of 2023). The 2021 law followed a failed attempt to regulate hate speech on online platforms in 2020 with the Avia Law which was declared unconstitutional.[60]

Under amendments to the 1986 law on the freedom of communication, ARCOM can reject licences for communication services (such as television, radio, or streaming) if they are considered to be controlled by a foreign state. ARCOM can also conditionally suspend licences for audio-visual channels which broadcast disinformation spread by foreign states. In this case, political party candidates may request that a judge sitting on urgent matters could halt the spread of false information online through closure of a public communications service (this could be online or through a traditional media channel). This measure was controversial given

55 See Godin and Chafer (2006) for definitions of French dirigisme.

56 ARCOM (the Regulatory Authority for Audiovisual and Digital Communication) is a French NRA resulting from a merger of the Conseil supérieur de l'audiovisuel (CSA) and Haute Autorité pour la Diffusion des Œuvres et la Protection des droits d'auteur sur Internet (Hadopi) in 2022.

57 2000 Ministry decree Consumer Code: www.csa.fr/Arbitrer/Espace-juridique/Les-textes-reglementaires-du-CSA/Les-deliberations-et-recommandations-du-CSA/Recommandations-et-deliberations-du-CSA-relatives-a-d-autres-sujets/Recommandation-n-2019-03-du-15-mai-2019-du-Conseil-superieur-de-l-audiovisuel-aux-operateurs-de-plateforme-en-ligne-dans-le-cadre-du-devoir-de-cooperation-en-matiere-de-lutte-contre-la-diffusion-de-fausses-informations [last accessed 25.10.2022]. For translation, see: http://ec.europa.eu/growth/tools-databases/tris/en/index.cfm/search/?trisaction=search.detail&year=2019&num=2&dLang=EN [last accessed 25.10.2022].

58 Articles 332–5, 771, 773, and 774 of the Code of Education were updated. www.legifrance.gouv.fr/affichCode.do?cidTexte=LEGITEXT000006071191 [last accessed 25.10.2022].

59 Overseas provisions, public order code: www.code-commande-publique.com/dispositions-relatives-a-loutre-mer [last accessed 25.10.2022].

60 www.conseil-constitutionnel.fr/decision/2020/2020801DC.htm [last accessed 25.10.2022].

that France has a long history of heavy-handed control of broadcasting (Kuhn, 1994). It is limited to the three months leading up to an election, however, and to media under the control of foreign influence.

The UK initiated its proposal to regulate online platforms following an Inquiry into Fake News[61] led by the UK DCMS Committee which took place between January and June 2017 preceding the June 2017 UK election. The DCMS committee launched a study into disinformation and 'fake news' in September 2017 which lasted two years.[62] The first part of the investigation focused on Facebook's business model which the Committee found to result in an insufficient response to the Cambridge Analytica scandal. Three oral evidence sessions were held and the committee received 23 written submissions. An 'international grand committee' took place in November 2018 with parliamentary representatives from nine different states.[63] An interim report was published on disinformation and 'fake news' in July 2018 and a final report published in February 2019.[64]

The key concern of the inquiry was inaccuracy and political bias in the news. The inquiry resembled investigations of fake news in France with a focus disinformation during election periods. The 2018 and 2019 reports found inadequacies in the legal liability of online platforms, data misuse, and targeting of political advertising, and that Facebook was knowledgeable about and participated in data sharing and political campaigning. The reports delve in depth into Russian influence in political campaigning and the influence of Strategic Communications Laboratories (SCL, of which Cambridge Analytica was a part) on foreign elections. The 2019 UK report found news to create a 'polarising effect and reduces the common ground on which reasoned debate, based on objective facts, can take place'. Similar to examinations conducted by the European Commission, a sizeable part of the final report dealt with security concerns with Russia referred to 78 times. The final section made some final recommendations surrounding digital literacy.

The DCMS together with the Home Office proposed the Online Harms White Bill in April 2019. The original Bill was very much focused on news provision. In this respect it concentrated on ensuring transparency of sources of news, the funding of news, and the way in which news is consumed by citizens, particularly through social media. The main recommended legal base for legislation, unlike in Germany and France, was the duty of care. As Woods (2019: 7–9) clarifies, the duty of care is based on common-law practice 'of negligence developed from Donoghue

[61] UK Digital, Culture, Media and Sport Committee (2017) 'Inquiry into Fake News': www.parliament.uk/business/committees/committees-a-z/commons-select/digital-culture-media-and-sport-committee/inquiries/parliament-2017/fake-news-17–19 [last accessed 25.10.2022].

[62] www.parliament.uk/business/committees/committees-a-z/commons-select/digital-culture-media-and-sport-committee/inquiries/parliament-2017/fake-news-17–19 [last accessed 25.10.2022].

[63] Argentina, Belgium, Brazil, Canada, France, Ireland, Latvia, Singapore, and the UK.

[64] https://publications.parliament.uk/pa/cm201719/cmselect/cmcumeds/1791/1791.pdf [last accessed 25.10.2022].

v Stephenson', initiated in the 1974 Health and Safety at Work Act. Similar to continental Europe proposals, the Bill initially recommended the adoption of technical measures and codes of practice.

In December 2019 the UK had a general election, resulting in a change in the lead in government. A Sub-Committee on Disinformation was set up by the Commons Select Committee in April 2020 and the Online Harms Bill underwent consultation.[65] After two years, the resulting 2021 Online Safety Bill is markedly changed from the original 2019 proposal. The 2021 and 2022 versions of the Bill are much more similar to the DSA and their continental European counterparts. It entrusts Ofcom to regulate online platforms to put in place systems to remove illegal and harmful content under the duty of care. Three categories (1, 2A, and 2B) are subject to different requirements and will be based upon platform size according to secondary legislation. Only user-to-user services will be included under category 1. Offences are categorised as harmful, false, and threatening.

A great deal of power has been given to the secretary of state. In particular, Ofcom needs to consult the secretary of state over codes of practice and approve exemptions. He/she can also modify codes and require Ofcom to review terrorism or child sexual exploitation and abuse codes and change the frequency of the transparency processes. The secretary of state must also be consulted over Ofcom guidance, review thresholds, and provide fee guidance. There are also exemptions for 'recognised news publishers' under Section 50.[66] The 2019 and December 2020 versions of the Online Harms Bill also excluded news publisher websites. Debate remains over whether newspaper website commentary sections should remain exempt.

Summarised, a 'recognised news publisher' includes the BBC, Sianel Pedwar Cymru, holders of licences under the Broadcasting Act 1990 and 1996 which publish licensed news-related content, and other entities which meet exemption conditions in the Bill. This encompasses newspapers 'subject to editorial control' that follow 'a code of standards that regulates the conduct of publishers, that is published by an independent regulator' or 'a code of standards that regulates the conduct of the entity in question, that is published by the entity itself'. It is unclear whether the latter requirement permitting newspapers to develop their own codes should simultaneously be overseen by an independent regulator, given the recommendations in the Leveson Inquiry.

The 2022 version of the Bill at the time of writing introduces some requirements for platforms on political advertising similar to the French law. Options for adult

[65] www.gov.uk/government/consultations/online-harms-white-paper/outcome/online-harms-white-paper-full-government-response [last accessed 25.10.2022].

[66] Exemptions to false communications offences are given to recognised news publishers as defined by Section 50; (b) the holder of a licence under the Broadcasting Act 1990 or 1996; (c) the holder of a licence under section 8 of the Wireless Telegraphy Act 2006; (d) the provider of an on-demand programme service.

users to verify their identify have been added. There is no mandatory disclosure requirement as under German law; however, users have the option to not interact with unverified users. Children will be prevented from seeing pornographic content on services. Notably, there is no definition of disinformation included in the Online Safety Bill. Instead, powers have been delegated to Ofcom to set up an advisory committee on disinformation and misinformation to identify how 'regulated services should deal with disinformation and misinformation on such services'.

Existing measures maintained from the original 2019 Bill include a recommendation to platforms to use algorithmic measures to locate and identify content ('content moderation technology'). The newer version of the Bill includes the option for Ofcom to recommend software. The 2022 Bill continues the mandate for platforms to implement Codes of Practice. The former 2019 version of the Bill stated that a code of practice would be established to 'minimise the spread of misleading and harmful disinformation and to increase the accessibility of trustworthy and varied news content'. This sentence has been removed. Instead, the 2022 Bill outlines instructions for a Code of Practice which will oversee: illegal content, children's online safety, adults' online safety, user empowerment, content of democratic importance, journalistic content, content reporting, and a complaints procedure.

The phrase 'legal but harmful' was dropped in November 2022 under lobbying from industry, particularly the News Media Association.[67] New provisions criminalising downblousing and deepfake pornography were introduced to the Bill in November as well as the criminalisation of encouraging self-harm or suicide and the abuse of intimate images. Platforms need to disclose rules on internal content moderation and age verification processes. Notably, all references to Europe and the European Commission have been removed. For example, the sentence 'close collaboration between government bodies, regulators and law enforcement overseas, in the EU and further afield, will be required' has been replaced with 'Co-operation and disclosure of information: overseas regulators'.

As in France and Germany, the UK Online Safety Bill is part of a package of changes to existing legislation. This includes updates to the Broadcasting Code[68] and the Advertising Standards Authority's (ASA's) Code of Non-Broadcast Advertising and Direct and Promotional Marketing (CAP code).[69] Ofcom is expected to coordinate with other regulatory bodies, namely the Competition and Markets Authority (CMA), Information Commissioner's Office (ICO), Financial

[67] www.ft.com/content/4c6ac9fa-bd52-4da2-bdf9-8a30d368d260 [last accessed 25.10.2022].

[68] www.ofcom.org.uk/tv-radio-and-on-demand/broadcast-codes/broadcast-code/section-two-harm-offence [last accessed 25.10.2022].

[69] www.asa.org.uk/static/47eb51e7-028d-4509-ab3c0f4822c9a3c4/4869041b-06d3-4745-b209d2a5c37500b3/The-Cap-code.pdf [last accessed 25.10.2022].

Conduct Authority (FCA), the Gambling Commission, the Electoral Commission, and the Equality and Human Rights Commission (EHRC).

Conclusion

Initiatives at both EU and national levels are self-regulatory in approach, but all have moved the responsibility for monitoring and policing content to online platforms and away from users. As gateway providers for communication, governments are increasingly dependent upon platforms for the removal of harmful content. Platforms are also the new mediators in elections and global conflict taking political choices such as the removal of politicians' Twitter accounts or removing Russian content covering the Ukraine war.

There are many similarities between the DSA and the UK Online Safety Bill, including transparency reporting requirements, legal representation, fines, and rules against fraudulent advertising transparency. The UK Bill is accompanied by codes of conduct on child sexual exploitation and abuse, terrorist content and activity online (enforceable by Ofcom), and traceability of traders (enforceable by the Digital Markets Unit). However, there are also many differences. For example, trusted flaggers will be appointed by 'Digital Services Coordinators' and the European Board for Digital Services (EBDS) at the EU level which can include rights holders, whereas there is no mention of trusted flaggers in the Online Safety Bill.

The UK proposal exempts content for news publisher websites, whereas the DSA covers disinformation published by traditional media. Article 17(2) states that intermediary services 'shall provide a clear and specific statement of reasons to any affected recipients of the service for any of the following restrictions imposed on the ground that the information provided by the recipient of the service is illegal content or incompatible with their terms and conditions'. But this could lead to a situation wherein content from, for example, UK online newspaper content might be subject to take-down of orders in the EU even though they are considered 'recognised news publishers' in the UK.

The UK's Bill covers content on online platforms which can be accessed by users in the UK. However, most online platforms targeting the UK are located in Ireland, which will be subject to the DSA. Representatives of online platforms at conferences have indicated that EU rather than UK law will take precedence. Ireland introduced its own Online Safety and Media Regulation Act in 2022 which established a new regulator, the Media Commission, which replaces the Broadcasting Authority of Ireland (BAI) and introduces an Online Safety Commissioner. It expands the remit for the regulator to on-demand services such as Amazon and Netflix. Similar to the UK and the EU, safety codes have been introduced for online platforms with potential fines of up to 20 million Euros or 10 per cent of turnover.

There is potential for memoranda of understanding (MoUs) with the UK and the European Commission. However, interviews have shown that the political environment in the UK, at the time of writing, is preventing closer cooperation. Otherwise, it is possible that bilateral engagements with other NRAs, such as the Media Commission (Ireland) and ARCOM (France), will be negotiated by the UK. Close cooperation between the Irish Media Commission and Ofcom in particular is expected. ERGA developed MoUs and guidelines on audio-visual media services over video-sharing platforms as a model for European Board for Digital Services cooperation.[70]

[70] https://erga-online.eu/wp-content/uploads/2021/06/2021.06.25-ERGA-DSA-Paper-final.pdf [last accessed 25.10.2022].

7
FinTech
The UK as a Global Model

Introduction

One week after the Brexit vote, the then chief executive of the Financial Conduct Authority (FCA) stated, 'This [Brexit] is not going to lead to a bonfire of regulation' (Hughs, 2019). The UK has since upheld most EU legislation relating to financial regulation and, at the time of writing, not yet made major changes to its domestic policy. However, increasing policy divergence between the EU and UK is expected, particularly in the pledge to remove all remaining EU legislation relating to financial services in the proposed 2022 Financial Services and Markets Bill. The transition period has not progressed as smoothly as the UK expected with it not receiving the equivalence decisions it had expected from the EU.

Office for National Statistics (ONS) data shows a 31 per cent fall in financial services exports to the EU and a 5 per cent rise to non-EU countries between 2019 and 2021.[1] Almost 500 UK-based companies relocated parts of their operations in the EU to continue access to EU markets.[2] A large number of companies have re-established in the EU, creating new FinTech hubs such as Lithuania and Malta. The *Financial Times* reported that 'insurance companies and asset managers have transferred more than £100bn in assets and funds from Britain to the EU in response to Brexit'. The Ernst & Young job tracker estimated that there had been 7,000 Brexit-related staff relocations due to Brexit by 2022.[3] These factors arguably have increased the UK's turn to trade with third countries and, in particular, emerging 'FinTech' (financial technology) markets. This chapter details the UK's growing focus on FinTech in the context of its relationship with the EU.

[1] www.ons.gov.uk/economy/nationalaccounts/balanceofpayments/articles/theimpactsofeuexitandcoronaviruscovid19onuktradeinservices/july2021#exports-and-imports-of-services [last accessed 25.10.2022].

[2] https://committees.parliament.uk/publications/22728/documents/167235/default [last accessed 25.10.2022].

[3] www.ey.com/en_uk/news/2022/03/ey-financial-services-brexit-tracker-movement-within-uk-financial-services-sector-stabilises-five-years-on-from-article-50-trigger [last accessed 25.10.2022].

Brexit and the Digital Single Market. Alison Harcourt, Oxford University Press. © Alison Harcourt 2023.
DOI: 10.1093/oso/9780192899378.003.0007

UK financial services regulation and EU equivalence

The Political Declaration setting out the framework for the future relationship between the European Union and the United Kingdom,[4] signed in October 2019, established the context for future equivalence decisions for financial services.[5] The European Commission has responsibility for determining whether a non-EU state is 'equivalent' to the 'corresponding EU framework' on a sector-by-sector basis. The deadline for equivalence assessments set out in the Political Declaration was June 2020. However, this deadline passed.

Subsequently, a Joint Declaration on Financial Services Regulatory Cooperation between the European Union and the United Kingdom[6] was signed in December 2020 under which the EU and UK planned to agree a Memorandum of Understanding (MoU) for Parties by March 2021.[7] However, this never came to fruition. A 2022 House of Lords inquiry concluded that 'most of the Committee's witnesses to the inquiry similarly identified the wider UK-EU relationship, and specifically the dispute over the implementation of the Protocol on Ireland/Northern Ireland, as the key obstacle to the conclusion of the MoU'.[8] Instead, a number of bilateral MoUs have been put into place between UK and continental European national regulatory authorities (NRAs).[9]

By 2022, the Commission had only taken two equivalence decisions in the area of banking and finance for the UK, one of which since expired. The UK is consequently lagging behind other EU trading partners such as Turkey and the US. The US by comparison has received 21 equivalence decisions from the European Commission.[10] As foreseen by James and Quaglia (2020: 150), this EU approach reflects 'a desire to defend the single market, but also Franco-German incentives to compete for post-Brexit business'. A report published by the House of Lords European Affairs Committee (2022: 3) similarly stated, 'this approach by the EU is political rather than technical and that the UK is being held to a higher standard

[4] https://assets.publishing.service.gov.uk/government/uploads/system/uploads/attachment_data/file/840656/Political_Declaration_setting_out_the_framework_for_the_future_relationship_between_the_European_Union_and_the_United_Kingdom.pdf [last accessed 25.10.2022].

[5] https://ec.europa.eu/info/business-economy-euro/banking-and-finance/international-relations/equivalence-non-eu-financial-frameworks_en [last accessed 25.10.2022].

[6] https://assets.publishing.service.gov.uk/government/uploads/system/uploads/attachment_data/file/948105/EU-UK_Declarations_24.12.2020.pdf [last accessed 25.10.2022].

[7] www.gov.uk/government/news/technical-negotiations-concluded-on-uk-eu-memorandum-of-understanding [last accessed 25.10.2022].

[8] https://committees.parliament.uk/publications/22728/documents/167235/default [last accessed 25.10.2022].

[9] www.fca.org.uk/news/statements/mous-european-authorities-securities-insurance-pensions-banking [last accessed 25.10.2022]. In addition, a UK–EU MoU was put in place for technical matters: www.gov.uk/government/news/technical-negotiations-concluded-on-uk-eu-memorandum-of-understanding and between the FCA and European Securities and Markets Authority (ESMA) for information exchange: www.fca.org.uk/publication/mou/mou-esma-fca.pdf [last accessed 25.10.2022].

[10] https://ec.europa.eu/info/sites/default/files/business_economy_euro/banking_and_finance/documents/overview-table-equivalence-decisions_en.pdf [last accessed 25.10.2022].

than other countries'. This approach of the EU has shaped the direction of UK financial policy going forward.

The main adequacy decision adopted by the European Commission was for UK equivalence for central counterparties (CCPs) under the European Market Infrastructure Regulation. The initial decision issued on 1 January 2021 expired on 30 June 2022 but was extended until 30 June 2025. The September 2020 Decision took place only two months before the end of the transition period on 31 December 2020. On Brexit day, UK CCPs had been delisted from the list of European Central Counterparties authorised to offer services in the EU[11] and became Recognised Third-Country CCPs until the adequacy decision came into effect.

The Decision was taken because, according to the Bank of England, 'there were £60 trillion of derivative contracts between UK CCPs and EU clearing members, £43 trillion of which was due to expire after December'.[12] The Decision was in avoidance of what Commissioner for Financial Services, Financial Stability and Capital Markets Union Mairead McGuinness termed a 'cliff-edge scenario'.[13] However, the adequacy decision providing a short period of just three years involves a high degree of market uncertainty for operators and there is every indication that the Commission plans to end temporary extensions to the UK. The European Market Infrastructure Regulation underwent revision in 2022 and is expected to bolster the EU share of the derivatives clearing market.

At the same time, the European Commission is actively seeking to reduce its overreliance on UK CCPs. Specifically, it is concerned about the 'heavy reliance of the EU financial system on services provided by UK-based CCPs' which present 'important issues related to financial stability'.[14] Accordingly, in 2021, the Commission established a Working Group with the European Central Bank, the European Supervisory Authorities, and the European Systemic Risk Board to find ways to achieve less reliance on UK CCPs for the transfer of derivatives from the UK to the EU.

The Commission plans to develop EU-based CCPs from 2022 to make 'the EU a more competitive and cost-efficient clearing hub and to enhance EU CCP's liquidity' and to better manage risk. The Commission plans to mandate that, on a progressive basis, the base for clearing houses to credit swaps and futures for Euro-denominated derivatives be moved to EU-based clearing houses. It set up a stakeholder dialogue between the Commission and national clearing house supervisors in December 2022.

[11] www.esma.europa.eu/sites/default/files/library/ccps_authorised_under_emir.pdf [last accessed 25.10.2022].
[12] www.bankofengland.co.uk/statement/2020/boe-statement-on-the-european-commission-equivalence-decision-on-the-future-uk-legal-and-supervisory [last accessed 25.10.2022].
[13] https://ec.europa.eu/commission/presscorner/detail/en/STATEMENT_21_5905 [last accessed 25.10.2022].
[14] https://ec.europa.eu/commission/presscorner/detail/en/IP_22_665 [last accessed 25.10.2022].

According to the *Financial Times*, the EU intends to put this system in place by summer 2023 because 'from next summer EU pension funds, which hold investments for thousands of EU citizens, will also be required to clear their derivatives trades'.[15] This, it stated, would benefit the Deutsche Börse in Germany and Euronext in Amsterdam, which was formed through a merger of the stock exchanges of Paris, Amsterdam, Brussels, and Lisbon, and put provide a significant role for the Parisian-based European Securities and Markets Authority. As van Kerckhoven (2021: 63) explains, 'the push from both France and Germany for creating a financial hub in the Eurozone is not new and has been on the back of the minds of European leaders and institutions for a while'.

London has lost business to Europe. The London Stock Exchange reported that most UK-based clearing of Euro-denominated repo and government bond trades relocated to Paris. London Clearing House (LCH), which is part of the London Stock Exchange Group and dominates the market, moved its Repoclear clearing operation to Paris in 2019, 'leaving only a "residual" amount at the London operation'.[16] That said, 115 trillion Euros in Euro-denominated derivatives is reportedly still cleared through LCH in London.[17] According to the European Research Centre for Economic and Financial Governance (2017), the UK's 'language, the legal system (many financial instruments are subject to English law), as well as the experienced regulatory environment are all part of the ecosystem', making London preferable to continental European located clearing houses. As further explained in a European Parliament report:

> France and Germany which are frequently cited as the most important OTC trading places in the EU are simply too small to match the margin pool benefits currently available in the UK. As long as they remain small, there is nothing to warranty that euro-denominated trades will be relocated in the EU instead of moving elsewhere as, for example, in New York, which has been granted equivalence in 2016 and it is already a big enough market.

In contrast to the EU, the UK has granted equivalence to European Economic Area (EEA) (including EU) states in 28 out of 32 financial service areas.[18] Initially, 16 equivalence decisions were made under the Equivalence Determinations for Financial Services and Miscellaneous Provisions[19] and one decision[20] under the Central Counterparties Regulations.[21] In November 2020, the then UK chancellor,

[15] www.ft.com/content/da41d878-2e60-42ca-9b34-945efbef8af4 [last accessed 25.10.2022].
[16] www.reuters.com/article/us-britain-eu-clearing-idUSKCN1QA2EY [last accessed 25.10.2022].
[17] www.ft.com/content/2d314a04-aa7c-42d3-b191-376d29cc98df [last accessed 25.10.2022].
[18] www.gov.uk/government/publications/hm-treasury-equivalence-decisions-for-the-eea-states-9-november-2020/hm-treasury-equivalence-decisions-for-the-eea-states-9-november-2020 [last accessed 25.10.2022].
[19] www.legislation.gov.uk/uksi/2019/541/contents/made [last accessed 25.10.2022].
[20] Central Counterparties (Equivalence) Regulations 2020 (SI 2020/1244).
[21] www.legislation.gov.uk/uksi/2018/1184/contents/made [last accessed 25.10.2022].

Rishi Sunak, published a further 11 UK equivalence assessments for EEA/EU states ahead of the end of the transition period in December 2020.[22] The imbalance between UK and EU equivalence decisions was noted as 'striking' by the House of Lords European Affairs Committee in 2022 which advised 'the Committee concludes that it would be unwise for the Government to base its strategy for financial services on a process that it cannot control, and which currently seems unlikely to bear fruit'.[23]

UK equivalence was granted to EU/EAA-based CCPs.[24] This took effect post-Brexit under Article 25(6) of the UK European Market Infrastructure Regulation (EMIR) which retains the EU 2012 Regulation on over-the-counter (OTC) derivatives, CCPs, and trade repositories in UK law. This means that UK companies can continue using European-based CCPs post-Brexit upon cooperation arrangements between the Bank of England (BoE) and national-level authorities in each European state. These are laid out in MoUs with NRAs which are required as part of the recognition process. Accordingly, the BoE has established classes of OTC derivatives subject to the UK clearing obligations in a public register.[25]

The UK Benchmarks Regulation Equivalence Directions 2020[26] permits European-based benchmarkers[27] to continue to access UK markets upon notification to the FCA. This takes place under the UK version of the 2016 EU Regulation on indices used as benchmarks in financial instruments and financial contracts or to measure the performance of investment funds. The equivalence decision permits benchmarks to supervised entities in the UK under the FCA's benchmark register set up post-Brexit to replace the European Securities and Markets Authority (ESMA) Register for UK supervised users and recognises third country-based benchmark administrators.[28] The 2022 Financial Services and Markets Bill proposed to extend the transition period for all overseas benchmarks to 2025.

The Capital Requirements Regulation Equivalence Directions 2020 retains EU regulations on prudential requirements for credit institutions and investment firms.[29] It provides guarantees to EEA banks and investment funds that

[22] www.gov.uk/government/publications/hm-treasury-equivalence-decisions-for-the-eea-states-9-november-2020/hm-treasury-equivalence-decisions-for-the-eea-states-9-november-2020 [last accessed 25.10.2022].

[23] https://committees.parliament.uk/publications/22728/documents/167235/default [last accessed 25.10.2022].

[24] www.esma.europa.eu/policy-rules/post-trading/central-counterparties [last accessed 25.10.2022].

[25] www.bankofengland.co.uk/-/media/boe/files/eu-withdrawal/clearing-obligation-public-register.pdf?la=en&hash=0AD1A4BCDD2EE2927694E79853B4263C2D9F1A33 [last accessed 25.10.2022].

[26] www.legislation.gov.uk/uksi/2019/541/pdfs/uksiod_20190541_en_009.pdf [last accessed 25.10.2022].

[27] www.handbook.fca.org.uk/handbook/glossary/G3508b.html [last accessed 25.10.2022].

[28] www.fca.org.uk/markets/benchmarks/new-uk-benchmarks-register [last accessed 25.10.2022].

[29] These were the 2013 Directive on access to the activity of credit institutions and the prudential supervision of credit institutions and the 2013 Regulation on prudential requirements for credit institutions and investment firms. Both were updated by the EU in 2022.

they will not risk increased capital requirements if operating in the UK. The EU has provided no such guarantee to the UK. Instead, when it proposed an update to the Regulation in 2021, the EU tightened CRR2 restrictions on third-country branches, providing a robust EU framework for third-country groups providing banking services in the EU, which have taken a new dimension after Brexit. The 2021 updates to the EU's Capital Requirements Regulation CRR2/CRD 5 were implemented in the UK with effect from 28 June 2021.[30]

Similarly, the Central Securities Depositories Regulation Equivalence Directions 2020[31] determines that European-based central securities depositories (CSDs) can continue to facilitate UK securities. The Credit Rating Agencies Regulation Equivalence Directions 2020[32] provides equivalence to EEA/EU-based credit rating agencies as long as they are registered with the ESMA and certified by the FCA. UK adequacy decisions were also granted to EEA/EU-based companies under the European Market Infrastructure Regulation (Article 2A) Equivalence Directions 2020,[33] the European Market Infrastructure Regulation (Article 13) Equivalence Directions 2020,[34] the Short Selling Regulation Equivalence Directions 2020,[35] and the Solvency 2 Regulation Equivalence Directions 2020.[36] These decisions exist in parallel to HM Treasury decisions taken in 2019 which granted equivalence under the retained EU 2017 Prospectus Regulation[37] and Transparency Directive.[38] HM Treasury also granted a number of exemptions to European central banks.[39]

The UK remains a member of the Single Euro Payments Area (SEPA) post-Brexit. SEPA was established by the European Payment Council (EPC) in 2008

[30] The CRR2 includes the Infrastructure Projects Supporting Factor brought in during the COVID-19 pandemic, which lowers capital requirements: https://ec.europa.eu/commission/presscorner/detail/el/qanda_20_757 [last accessed 25.10.2022].

[31] www.legislation.gov.uk/uksi/2019/541/pdfs/uksiod_20190541_en_010.pdf [last accessed 25.10.2022].

[32] www.legislation.gov.uk/uksi/2019/541/pdfs/uksiod_20190541_en_011.pdf [last accessed 25.10.2022].

[33] www.legislation.gov.uk/uksi/2019/541/pdfs/uksiod_20190541_en_013.pdf [last accessed 25.10.2022].

[34] www.legislation.gov.uk/uksi/2019/541/pdfs/uksiod_20190541_en_014.pdf [last accessed 25.10.2022].

[35] www.legislation.gov.uk/uksi/2019/541/pdfs/uksiod_20190541_en_012.pdf [last accessed 25.10.2022].

[36] www.legislation.gov.uk/uksi/2019/541/pdfs/uksiod_20190541_en_016.pdf [last accessed 25.10.2022].

[37] https://eur-lex.europa.eu/legal-content/EN/ALL/?uri=CELEX%3A32017R1129 [last accessed 25.10.2022].

[38] https://eur-lex.europa.eu/legal-content/EN/TXT/?uri=celex%3A32004L0109 [last accessed 25.10.2022].

[39] These were the Market Abuse Exemption Directions 2019 and the Market Abuse Exemption (No. 2) Directions 2019; the Markets in Financial Instruments Exemption Directions 2019; the OTC Derivatives, Central Counterparties and Trade Repositories Exemption Directions 2019 and the OTC Derivatives, Central Counterparties and Trade Repositories Exemption (No. 2) Directions 2019; and the Transparency of Securities Financing Transactions and of Reuse Exemption Directions 2019 and the Transparency of Securities Financing Transactions and of Reuse Exemption (No. 2) Directions 2019.

to facilitate EU-wide debit and credit payments. It eases cross-border payments, making them equivalent to domestic payments covering credit transfers, direct debits, and payment cards. Although it needs to comply with the Payment Services Directives and EU competition law, SEPA is a self-regulatory system. Accordingly, UK Finance, which is a trade association for the UK banking and financial services sector, applied to the EPC on behalf of UK payment services providers. The application was approved in March 2019.[40] However, Brexit has led to additional, and in some cases significant, fees in some states, refusal of payments, and supplementary requirements.[41]

The EU introduced its EU's Payment Services Directive II in 2019 which permits the provision of financial services for bank customers from non-financial companies. This has enabled new providers to propose new services which are on the increase, particularly with the growth in mobile phone use, voice interfaces, and social media platforms, which are easing the payment of online goods and services. However, non-European entrants such as Facebook's demised Deim proposal and the WhatsApp payment services (operative in Brazil and India) have not been viewed favourably by the EU. To flank this, the EU introduced a proposal for a European Digital Identity in 2021, updating its 2014 regulation for trust services (eIDAS).

The UK as a global FinTech hub

Historically, EU financial policy has been German-led (Dyson, 2009; Dyson and Quaglia, 2010; James and Quaglia, 2020). As Quaglia (2019) explains, the UK has supported EU harmonisation in the banking sector but maintained a hands-off approach to the regulation of capital markets. The UK opted out of the Eurozone and Treaty on Stability, Coordination and Governance in the Economic and Monetary Union,[42] which guarded against excessive government deficits. At the same time, the UK was 'a key driver of financial regulatory reforms at ... EU levels since the financial crisis, on account of the size of its financial sector and the renowned knowledge and expertise accumulated by its regulators' (James and Quaglia, 2020: 150). As explained by van Kerckhoven (2021: 64):

[40] www.europeanpaymentscouncil.eu/document-library/position-papers/epc-decision-paper-brexit-and-uk-psps-participation-sepa-schemes [last accessed 25.10.2022].

[41] Supplementary requirements mainly for third countries stipulate that credit and debit payments need to include full addresses of senders and Bank Identification Codes (BICs) of recipient banks: www.europeanpaymentscouncil.eu/news-insights/insight/payments-landscape-uk-after-brexit.[last accessed 25.10.2022].

[42] www.consilium.europa.eu/media/20399/st00tscg26_en12.pdf [last accessed 25.10.2022].

> the market-friendly approach promoted by the UK often stood in stark contrast with the preference of other EU member states for a stronger rules-based approach. This market-shaping coalition includes member states such as Germany, France, Belgium, Italy, and the other Mediterranean countries. Germany in particular has been seeking to establish a rule-based culture in the EU financial market and discourages flexibility out of fear that allowing suppleness might undermine the entire system.

The EU's unwillingness to provide the UK easy access to EU financial markets post-Brexit has triggered a rethink in the UK's approach to financial services markets. This began slowly with moderate changes beginning in 2022, which were aimed at red tape removal. The UK initially maintained the EU 2017 EU PRIIPs Regulation under the 2018 Withdrawal Act which outlines technical standards for documents related to packaged retail and insurance-based investment products (PRIIPs). In 2022, the UK changed PRIIP requirements to Key Information Documents (KIDs), which need to be produced when financial products are bought by retail investors. Performance information is no longer obligatory in a KID and changes were made to disclosure requirements for transaction costs. This change came ahead of EU proposals to change KID requirements, indicating expected divergence.[43]

The UK also proposed changes to its domestic Markets in Financial Instruments Directive (MiFID) legislation under its Wholesale Markets Review in March 2021.[44] The proposals included the removal of the best execution reporting in RTS 27 and RTS 28 and double volume cap requirements which were removed in November. The FCA extended the removal of double volume cap requirements on UK equities to all equities in 2022.[45] The EU is expected to do the same but on a different timetable. The UK changes were ahead of the EU's proposed changes to MiFID II published in November 2021[46] as announced in the Commission's 2020 Work Programme. The EU proposal plans better access to market data for small or medium-sized enterprises (SMEs) and retail for investment in shares and bonds.

The starkest UK reform in financial policy has been in its approach to FinTech. FinTech refers to technological solutions for electronic transactions such as blockchain, digital currencies, and peer-to-peer online lending. It also encompasses the analysis of large financial data sets via artificial intelligence and other

[43] www.eba.europa.eu/regulation-and-policy/consumer-protection-and-financial-innovation/regulatory-technical-standards-on-the-content-and-presentation-of-the-kids-for-priips [last accessed 25.10.2022].

[44] www.gov.uk/government/consultations/uk-wholesale-markets-review-a-consultation [last accessed 25.10.2022].

[45] www.fca.org.uk/news/statements/update-double-volume-cap [last accessed 25.10.2022].

[46] https://ec.europa.eu/info/topics/banking-and-finance_en [last accessed 25.10.2022].

software. London is a global hub for technologies applied to financial services (FinTech) (Arner et al., 2017; Quaglia, 2019; Nicoletti, 2017; Currie et al., 2018: 139).

The UK's FinTech market was worth £11 billion, representing 10 per cent of the global market according to the 2021 Kalifa Review of UK FinTech.[47] The greatest bulk of this income is from cryptocurrency transactions and peer-to-peer lending.[48] In 2021, FinTech made up 8.3 per cent of total UK economic output.[49] In 2021, the EU still comprised the UK's largest export market for financial services making up 20 per cent of all overall UK service exports to the EU.[50] There was, however, an overall decline in UK exports to the EU and a rise to non-EU states between 2019 and 2021.[51] By comparison, the EU made up 34.3 per cent of the UK's financial service exports in 2019.[52]

In the 2022 state of the sector annual review of UK financial services, the City of London and HM Treasury reported that 3,000 FinTechs were operating in the UK and that there had been 'consistent growth in the number of FinTechs based [in the UK] since 2017 ... The number of UK FinTechs is second to the US, but about four times more than Germany and France each, and 4.5 times more than Singapore' (2022: 36).[53] It reported that half of UK unicorns are FinTech companies. The most successful companies are those providing cloud-based digital-only banking applications such as Monzo, Revolut, and Starling Bank, which also provide financial services and products facilitated by artificial intelligence (Venkataramakrishnan, 2022).

UK employment in the FinTech sector was at 2.3 million in 2022, accounting for approximately 1 in 14 of all UK jobs.[54] It was predicted to double within 10 years according to the DIT 2020 UK FinTech State of the Nation report. However, it should be noted that much of the sector is London-centric, where 50 per cent of total output is generated.[55] Currently, cryptocurrencies are experiencing a crash with substantial job losses in the sector, highlighting the vulnerability of FinTech

[47] www.gov.uk/government/news/uks-global-fintech-leadership-bolstered-by-new-review [last accessed 25.10.2022].

[48] Peer-to-peer lending is facilitated by blockchains, cryptochains, and cryptocurrencies such as Bitcoins and Altcoins, including Ethereum, LiteCoin, PeerCoin, and Ripple.

[49] https://commonslibrary.parliament.uk/research-briefings/sn06193 [last accessed 25.10.2022].

[50] https://researchbriefings.files.parliament.uk/documents/CBP-7851/CBP-7851.pdf [last accessed 25.10.2022].

[51] www.ons.gov.uk/economy/nationalaccounts/balanceofpayments/articles/theimpactsofeuexitandcoronaviruscovid19onuktradeinservices/july2021#exports-and-imports-of-services [last accessed 25.10.2022].

[52] https://committees.parliament.uk/committee/516/european-affairs-committee/news/160809/new-ukeu-financial-services-inquiry-launched [last accessed 25.10.2022].

[53] https://assets.publishing.service.gov.uk/government/uploads/system/uploads/attachment_data/file/1092788/State_of_the_sector_annual_review_of_UK_financial_services_2022.pdf [last accessed 25.10.2022].

[54] https://committees.parliament.uk/publications/22728/documents/167235/default [last accessed 25.10.2022].

[55] https://commonslibrary.parliament.uk/research-briefings/sn06193 [last accessed 25.10.2022].

markets.[56] In November, FTX collapsed with a deficit of $32 billion, stopping customer withdrawals, and BlockFi also filed for bankruptcy, bringing into question the sustainability of the sector.

The UK has acted as a policy entrepreneur in its proactive approach to the formulation of FinTech regulation. This began in the UK when the FCA was looking for innovative ways to move the UK out of the 2008 financial crisis and at the same time to reform and regulate a changing financial sector. The UK introduced innovative ways to promote FinTech by lowering financial restrictions for selected companies. The FCA established Project Innovate, 'regulatory sandboxes', and its FinTech Initiative.

The sandbox schemes waiver some FCA rules for small numbers of FinTech start-ups chosen on an annual basis. This creates a 'safe space' for company innovation where companies can test new goods, services, and delivery mechanisms. The idea is not new but based upon 'Innovation Deals' such as the Green Deal programme of the Netherlands. Such deals 'do not support "normal" business activities but would be restricted to innovative initiatives that have only a recent and limited or even no access to the market with the potential of wide applicability' (European Commission, 2016).

Sandbox companies produce products and services ranging from virtual currencies to application programming interfaces (APIs) for the retail sector. The framework is also aimed at bringing new entrants and investment to the financial sector. The first FCA sandbox in 2016 fostered 24 companies.[57] In 2018, it had reached its fourth cohort with 29 firms.[58] In 2020, the FCA authorised 22 companies under Cohort 6.[59] In 2021, the regulatory sandbox cohort 7 approved 13 companies.[60] This attracted new start-ups such as Revolut to the UK[61] valued at £33 billion in 2022 and SETL which works in the retail sector as the first company to use a digital ledger.[62] The FCA also established 'Tech Sprints' to assist companies to modernise regulation around key themes such as women's empowerment and sustainability.

[56] www.ft.com/content/719cb1c6-1a12-4c7a-b845-3a08679cff4b [last accessed 25.10.2022].

[57] Billion, BitX, Blink Innovation Limited, Bud, Citizens Advice, Epephyte, Govcoin Limited, HSBC, Issufy, Lloyds Banking Group, Nextday Property Limited, Nivaura, Otonomos, Oval, SETL, Tradle, Tramonex, and Swave.

[58] BlockEx, Capexmove, Chasing Returns, Community First Credit Union, Creativity Software, CreditSCRIPT, Dashly, Ehterisc, Finequia, Fractal, Globacap, Hub85, London Media Exchange, Mettle, Mortgage Kart, Multiply, Natwest, NorthRow, Pluto, Salary Finance, TokenMarket, Tokencard, Universal Tokens, Veridu Labs, World Reserve Trust, and Zippen.

[59] AgeWage, AID:Tech, DLA Piper, Climate chain, CrediCar, Crowdz UK, Faizpay, Fronted, FundAdminChain, HipayUK, Hitachi Sustainable Finance Platform, HUB Financial Solutions, Huozhi, Mintago, Moneyfold, My Ahmed Ltd, Nest Insight, NestEgg, Project Pyctor, StudentFinance, Weather Solutions, and YourBlock.

[60] Bayfikr, Blockpass, Cardeo, Chekk, Hlthie, JO1N, Kontinuous, Project Endeavour, StarLiX, TrustElevate, VALK, CMS, and Willow Money.

[61] Post Brexit Revolut established a European company in Lithuania to which it transfered all non-UK customers. https://blog.revolut.com/transferring-our-lithuanian-customers-before-brexit/ [last accessed 25.10.2022].

[62] https://committees.parliament.uk/writtenevidence/901/pdf [last accessed 25.10.2022].

The 2021 Kalifa Review of UK FinTech made a number of new proposals. It announced the development of a Financial Market Infrastructure (FMI) 'scalebox', 'making permanent the digital sandbox pilot'[63] and the allocation of £5 million to the private sector led by the Centre for Finance, Innovation and Technology (CFIT).[64] The review recommended a new regulatory framework for crypto-assets and updating existing payments regulation. This proposal was backed by the then economic secretary John Glen.[65] The report also supported the development of a retail central bank digital currency (CBDC).

Accordingly, FinTech was a focus of the Financial Services and Markets (FSM) Bill in July 2022.[66] Schedule 1 proposes revocation of retained EU law relating to financial services and lists 30 EU Regulations retained in the Withdrawal Act and 25 EU Directives and their corresponding UK implementation laws still on the books in the UK, including the Markets in Financial Instruments Regulation (MiFIR). Removal, however, will not take place unless replaced by UK laws. As expected, it proposed that backed stablecoins be recognised as a future form of payment in the UK.[67] However, an HM Treasury and Bank of England taskforce to explore the potential of a UK CBDC is not in favour.[68]

Two days before the Bill was introduced, the UK chancellor of the exchequer Nadhim Zahawi discussed in a Mansion House speech how distributed ledger technology (DLT) could be used as a UK sovereign debt instrument. The Bill, like the Online Safety Bill, is controversial in relation to its 'call in' power which envisioned a greater power for ministers over the BoE. As explained by the Treasury Committee, the power would enable the Treasury to 'direct a regulator to make, amend or revoke rules' and has received backlash from the BoE over challenges to its independence.[69]

FinTech has been a key highlight of UK trade negotiations. This began in 2018 when the UK and India 'agreed to deepen bilateral collaboration on FinTech' and to establish a 'regulatory bridge' between respective regulatory authorities in 2018. This was supported by a joint statement by the finance minister of India and the chancellor of the exchequer at the 11th UK–India Economic and Financial

[63] www.gov.uk/government/news/ambitious-plans-to-boost-uk-fintech-and-financial-services-set-out-by-chancellor [last accessed 25.10.2022].

[64] www.gov.uk/government/publications/centre-for-finance-innovation-and-technology-steering-committee [last accessed 25.10.2022].

[65] www.reuters.com/business/finance/uk-says-it-will-regulate-stable-coin-payments-2022-04-04 [last accessed 25.10.2022].

[66] https://publications.parliament.uk/pa/bills/cbill/58-03/0146/220146.pdf [last accessed 25.10.2022].

[67] www.gov.uk/government/news/government-sets-out-plan-to-make-uk-a-global-cryptoasset-technology-hub [last accessed 25.10.2022].

[68] www.bankofengland.co.uk/research/digital-currencies/cbdc-taskforce-terms-of-reference [last accessed 25.10.2022].

[69] https://committees.parliament.uk/committee/158/treasury-committee/news/174072/government-confirms-regulatory-call-in-power-amendment-to-be-delayed [last accessed 25.10.2022].

Dialogue in September 2021.[70] The Department for International Trade (DIT) and HM Treasury have since established FinTech Bridge programmes with Australia China, Hong Kong, Singapore, and South Korea which were integrated into bilateral trade agreements.

The DIT has funded UK FinTech companies on trade missions to the Latin America and the Caribbean region in 2019 and Austria, Switzerland in 2020, and Canada in 2021. FinTech is a major component of the UK–India trade agreement which is predicted to be concluded in 2023. African states are also of key interest as over one-third of the population of East Africa use mobile money (Coulibaly, 2021: 3). Citizens in rural areas have limited access to banks and normally financial transactions are done via post offices and other local intermediaries which incur time and fees (European Investment Bank, 2016). Mobile phones are rapidly alleviating this problem with applications and online bank accounts which increase financial inclusion of citizens in the economy (GSMA, 2018). The DIT arranged the UK–Africa FinTech Partnership in 2019, establishing an Africa FinTech Investment Group as a sub-group of DIT's FinTech Steering Board, a DFID partnership with the FCA for support of regulatory efforts on FinTech in Africa, which has been piloted in Kenya and Nigeria, and establishing an initial £2 million for Nigerian FinTechs.

EU response to FinTech

The UK initiatives triggered interest from the European Commission and countries around the world (Parenti, 2020). A number of EU states began similar initiatives, particularly in the emerging FinTech hubs of Denmark, Germany, Ireland, the Netherlands, and Sweden. Other UK initiatives, including relaxing and introducing flexible rules for chosen new market entrants and the introduction of self-regulatory trust schemes, have also been imitated by other states. In 2016 European Commission document noted:

> Small firms in the EU rely too much on debt financing, but banks are often risk averse and the overall volume of risk capital invested in Europe is low. With the massive adoption of digital technologies, we are witnessing a new emergence of alternative financing options and the development of a new generation of technology-enabled financial innovations, 'FinTech'. An extended service portfolio emerging from FinTech's assets combining debt and equity could strongly impact the way small firms are funded at different stages, in different markets and with different ambitions. (Madelin and Ringrose, 2016)

[70] https://assets.publishing.service.gov.uk/government/uploads/system/uploads/attachment_data/file/1014712/Final_11th_UK-India_EFD_JS.pdf [last accessed 25.10.2022].

Accordingly, in 2018, the Commission announced its FinTech Action plan in which it asked the European Banking Authority (EBA) and ESMA to assess the application of the financial services regulatory framework to crypto-assets. The assessment concluded that most crypto-assets escaped EU requirements for consumer protection.[71] It pointed to a rise in EU member state efforts to close this gap which was creating market fragmentation, indicating a need for EU action. It also raised concerns that existing EU legislation may deter the use of DLT.

In September 2020, the European Commission published its EU digital finance package. The package introduced a new strategy on digital finance for the EU financial sector. The proposal introduced new rules for crypto-assets and a pilot project for DLT. It was accompanied by a proposal for a Regulation to build markets in crypto-assets, a proposal for a Directive to revise rules on EU financial services, and a Regulation for digital operational resilience. This culminated in agreements by the Council and the European Parliament in a pilot scheme for crypto-assets, a Regulation on markets in crypto-assets (MiCA), the Digital Operational Resilience Act (DORA),[72] and an electronic retail payments strategy in 2022.[73]

A pilot scheme for trade in crypto-assets was set out in a 2022 Regulation on a pilot regime for market infrastructures. It was based on DLT and will run from March 2023. It allows 'DLT market infrastructures to be temporarily exempted from some of the specific requirements of Union financial services legislation' similar to the sandbox approach introduced by the FCA. This takes place with permission from and cooperation between operators, national regulatory authorities, and ESMA. The Regulation outlines exemptions to six requirements under financial regulation,[74] a financial instrument limit of 6 billion Euros, and six years of operation granted throughout the EU. The pilot project essentially operates as a sandbox to allow market innovation and growth.

Crypto-assets such as e-money tokens and stablecoins are already regulated within the EU as they qualify as financial instruments under the 2014 Directive markets in financial instruments. The MiCA Regulation approved in 2022 extends the EU regulatory framework to crypto-assets which do not qualify as financial instruments under the 2014 Directive. MiCA covers issuers of unbacked crypto-assets and stablecoins,[75] bringing 'crypto-assets, crypto-assets issuers and

[71] ESMA, Advice on 'Initial Coin Offerings and Crypto-Assets', 2019; EBA report with advice on crypto-assets, 2019.

[72] www.consilium.europa.eu/en/press/press-releases/2022/05/11/digital-finance-provisional-agreement-reached-on-dora [last accessed 25.10.2022].

[73] www.ecb.europa.eu/paym/integration/retail/retail_payments_strategy/html/index.en.html [last accessed 25.10.2022].

[74] These are exemptions to Intermediation, Transaction reporting, 'book-entry forms' under Regulation (EU) No. 909/2014, rules on settlement discipline, the rules on rules on settlement finality, and requirements linked to cash settlement.

[75] www.consilium.europa.eu/en/press/press-releases/2022/06/30/digital-finance-agreement-reached-on-european-crypto-assets-regulation-mica [last accessed 25.10.2022].

crypto-asset service providers under a regulatory framework for the first time'.[76] It tightens restrictions for issuers of crypto-assets and third-country service providers (e.g. UK providers) authorised in the EU, including greater requirements for capital, complaints procedures, and increased investor rights. Asset-referenced tokens (ARTs) based on non-European currencies are restricted. ART issuers are required to register an office in the EU and adhere to EU rules on issuing. The Regulation takes effect in the latter half of 2024.

The proposed 2022 EU Digital Operational Resilience Act (DORA) and the DORA Amending Directive target harmonisation of security for financial companies which outsource to providers of software and cloud platforms and data analytics services. Building on the Network and Information Security (NIS) Directive, it is aimed at cyber threats in particular. There are detailed rules for sub-contacting to operators in third countries. In particular:

> Where contractual arrangements on the use of ICT services are concluded with an ICT third-party service provider established in a third-country, financial entities shall consider relevant, at least the following factors: (a) the respect of data protection; (b) the effective enforcement of the law; (c) insolvency law provisions that would apply in the event of the ICT-third party service provider's bankruptcy; (d) any constraints that may arise in respect to the urgent recovery of the financial entity's data.

The UK will most likely legislate for a UK equivalent of DORA with the aim of gaining EU adequacy and an agreement with the EU. However, the EU prefers that states agree bilateral agreements with third countries like the UK; namely, NRAs (the European Supervisory Authorities (ESAs)) 'should be encouraged to conclude cooperation arrangements with the relevant supervisory and regulatory third-country competent authorities to facilitate the development of best practices addressing ICT third-party risk'.

Lastly, the EU digital finance package introduced a new strategy for electronic retail payments in a 2022 Communication on a Retail Payments Strategy for the EU. The provision of payment services by non-financial companies in Europe was enabled by the EU's 2015 PSD2 Directive. Allowing third-party providers to access user account details has encouraged market concentration by large platforms in the sector (Ferrari, 2022). The EU's Strategy for electronic retail payments aims to address this.[77] It covers security and consumer protection for EU-wide instant payments with the key goal of 'lessening Europe's dependency on big global

[76] www.consilium.europa.eu/en/press/press-releases/2022/06/30/digital-finance-agreement-reached-on-european-crypto-assets-regulation-mica [last accessed 25.10.2022].

[77] https://eur-lex.europa.eu/legal-content/EN/TXT/?uri=CELEX:52020DC0592 [last accessed 25.10.2022].

players in this area'. Implementation entails a high degree of cooperation from the Euro Retail Payments Board (ERPB) and the European Forum for Innovation in Payments (EFIP) composed of stakeholders in the sector which liaise with the ECB and European Commission.

Conclusion

Although FinTech continues to be a growth area for the UK and provides potential for future trade partnerships, concerns have been expressed about the future trajectory of the sector. A 2022 House of Lords European Affairs Committee inquiry into the UK–EU relationship in financial services about the impact of Brexit on the financial services sector raised concerns about the absence of EU equivalence decisions and regulatory divergence.

The 2022 fall in the cryptocoin market saw Bitcoin halve within the first half of the year. In this respect, the 2022 proposals for the legalisation of stablecoins as a means of payment have been brought into question. In August 2022, two inquiries were established in the UK's FinTech sector, the first by the Treasury Committee,[78] which examines whether cryptocurrencies are likely to replace traditional currencies. The second was brought by the Crypto and Digital Assets All Party Parliamentary Group (APPG)[79] to discuss the proposals. Other problems are surfacing. The number of complaints relating to Fintech products has risen dramatically in 2021–22.[80] The UK also announced an intention to regulate buy now pay later (BNPL) companies to enhance consumer protection following concerns about mounting consumer debt (Jones, 2022).

There are also risks associated with trade deals. For example, the UK trade deal with Gulf Nations was called into question when the United Arab Emirates was put on a 'grey list' of jurisdictions subject to increased monitoring by the Financial Action Task Force (England, 2022). The UK trade agreement with the US is on temporary hold due to disagreement over the Northern Ireland protocol (Webber, 2022). Concerns have also been expressed about the loss of capital to the US in technology markets (Thomas et al., 2022a).

[78] https://committees.parliament.uk/committee/158/treasury-committee/news/172052/treasury-committee-launches-inquiry-into-cryptoassets [last accessed 25.10.2022].

[79] https://cryptouk.io/appg/#appg-crypto-inquiry-2022 [last accessed 25.10.2022].

[80] https://www.financial-ombudsman.org.uk/data-insight/quarterly-complaints-data [last accessed 25.10.2022].

8
Competition Law
Decision-Making in the Digital Sector

Introduction

The UK 2019 and 2020 Competition EU Exit Regulations removed most references to EU competition law. Post-Brexit, the UK is no longer a member of the EU's European Competition Network (ECN). UK courts and regulatory bodies are not bound by changes to future EU law and the UK is also no longer party to competition agreements between the EU and other states. Post-transition, jurisdiction for competition policy falls to the Competition and Market Authority (CMA).[1] However, UK courts and national regulatory authorities (NRAs) must continue to interpret UK competition law in line with EU legislation that was enacted up until the end of the transition period and EU competition law pertaining to block exemptions has been maintained in UK law.

While EU competition decisions may continue to affect UK markets, and UK companies operating within the EU are subject to EU competition law scrutiny, the UK market is no longer used in calculation of competition thresholds in EU competition law. At the same time, EU decision-making might give rise to differential address of markets than UK competition authorities. Investigations can be dealt with simultaneously, such as the separate investigations into Facebook Marketplace by the Directorate-General for Competition (DG Competition's) and the CMA in 2021, which may result in incompatible remedies.

At the time of writing, there has, however, been little divergence between the address of large digital services providers by the EU and UK. However, there has been a natural increase in the number of competition cases brought at the national level. This chapter analyses the development of EU competition law in relation to antitrust, mergers, and acquisitions. State aid will be addressed separately in Chapter 9 due to the need to address EU exemptions for public service broadcasting and content subsidies. This chapter firstly examines how the UK has been influential in shaping EU law, particularly in defining the public interest. It examines future UK and EU policy trajectories.

[1] www.gov.uk/government/publications/guidance-on-the-functions-of-the-cma-after-the-end-of-the-transition-period [last accessed 25.10.2022].

Brexit and the Digital Single Market. Alison Harcourt, Oxford University Press. © Alison Harcourt 2023.
DOI: 10.1093/oso/9780192899378.003.0008

EU competition policy

The EU's competition authority, DG Competition, working in conjunction with the European Competition Network, has the authority to make decisions which are not subject to approval by the Council of Ministers or the European Parliament, only to review by the European Court of Justice. Prior to 1990, all Commission competition decisions were made under Articles 85, 86, and 90 of the Treaty of Rome. Under these Articles, DG Competition could rule against mergers only after they had already taken place and required the divestiture of a merger or acquisition. With the introduction of the 1989 the Merger Regulation, prior notification was required, and joint venture decisions and thresholds were lowered from 5 to 2.5 billion European Currency Units. Intervention in digital markets began in earnest in the 1990s after the introduction of Merger Regulation, the Open Network Provision (ONP), and Television Without Frontiers Directive (TWF).[2] The Merger Regulation was amended in 1994, 1997, 2004, and 2013.

The renumbering of articles was brought in with the Lisbon Treaty, which entered into force on 1 December 2009. The antitrust Articles 81, 82, and 86 TEC became Articles 101, 102, and 106 of the Treaty on the Functioning of the European Union (TFEU), respectively, but they are identical. Competition law is applied in cases of anti-competitive practices (e.g. cartel formation and collusion) under Article 101 of the TFEU (ex-Article 81 TEC), the abuse of dominant position under Article 102 (formerly Article 82 TEC), state aid under Article 107 (ex-Article 87 TEC), and in the case of market dominance (mergers and acquisitions) under the Merger Regulation. In the digital sector, competition law has been applied to antitrust, the control of concentrations, access to distribution platforms, premium content collective rights management, and state aid.

At the time of writing, under the Merger Regulation, proposed mergers with a combined aggregate global turnover totalling over 5,000 million Euros and EU-wide turnover for each of a minimum of two of the firms over 250 million Euros are required to notify the Commission.[3] Alternatively, investigation can take place for merging firms with a worldwide turnover over 2,500 million Euros, a combined turnover of over 100 million Euros in each of at least three member states, a turnover of over 25 million Euros for each of a minimum of two of the firms in each of the three member states, and an EU-wide turnover of each of at least two firms of more than 100 million Euros. Notification allows firms to receive a quick decision from the Commission within 25 days under Phase I when 90 per cent of cases are decided, and 90 days under Phase II.

[2] Decision-making on mergers took place under the Merger Task Force which was a unit of DG Competition from 1989 until 2003 when it was disbanded after introduction of the Modernisation Regulation.

[3] https://competition-policy.ec.europa.eu/mergers/procedures_en [last accessed 25.10.2022].

Only a small percentage of cases are prohibited (Thatcher, 2014). From 2021, the European Commission changed its guidance for referrals in interpretation of Article 22 of the Merger Regulation.[4] Under the guidance, the Commission will accept referrals from member states which fall below national merger thresholds, even after the conclusion of a merger. It notes in the Guidance that 'these developments appear particularly significant in the digital economy, where services regularly launch with the aim of building up a significant user base and/or commercially valuable data inventories, before seeking to monetise the business'.

The main rationale behind European competition policy is to intervene in markets when agreements between firms are seen to come into conflict with the creation of a Single Market or there is generally a perceived threat to competition through cartels, monopolies, or mergers. However, McGowan and Cini (1999: 177) highlighted that a key objective of competition policy at national levels has been the protection of the consumer. Although there is no public interest test at the EU level, the European Commission has taken on board public interest considerations in competition decisions, taking a lead from the UK.

Under Article 21 of the 1990 and 2004 Merger Regulations, the Commission retains sole jurisdiction to examine concentrations with a Union dimension. There are, however, exemptions under the principle of subsidiarity. These can be found under Article 21(3) which states that 'Member States may take appropriate measures to protect legitimate interests other than those taken into consideration by the Merger Regulation and compatible with the general principles and other provisions of Community law'. As Morgan (2000: 161) explains, this is referred to as the 'English clause', reflecting UK preferences and championed by Leon Brittan who oversaw the initial implementation of the 1990 Merger Regulation.

In relation to the digital sector, Article 21(4) further states that 'public security, plurality of the media and prudential rules shall be regarded as legitimate interests'. Morgan (2000: 161) explains that 'plurality of the media, prudential rules and aspects of public security not dealt with under Article 223 are recognized as being legitimate interests. Any other public interest must be agreed by the Commission before it can be classed as a legitimate interest'. This was complemented by a 1990 Communication on Audio-visual Policy under which DG Competition recognised under paragraph 2.3, 'Pluralism and Mergers', that the sector had 'specific economic and cultural considerations'. This is evidence of the Commission's increasing recognition that the digital sector has the power to shape culture, education, information, and ultimately democratic outcome.

As the sector is considered by many member states to have public opinion formation powers, states have often required lower turnover thresholds in competition decisions, particular in broadcasting and newspaper markets. This approach

[4] https://ec.europa.eu/competition/consultations/2021_merger_control/guidance_article_22_referrals.pdf [last accessed 25.10.2022].

is justified under subsidiarity which permits states to apply lower thresholds and apply public interest tests in national competition decisions on media mergers and acquisitions. When a competition decision is taken at the EU level, member states can declare an additional legitimate interest and the European Commission has 25 days in which it can decide whether it qualifies.

Legitimate interests have rarely been invoked. In the 1994 Newspaper Publishing case, the European Commission allowed the UK to take additional measures under subsidiarity. Legitimate interests were invoked again by the UK when the European Commission approved News Corporation's bid to take full control of BSkyB[5] under grounds of 'media plurality' in 2010, but the acquisition never took place due to the UK 2011 News International hacking scandal. In 2017, the UK secretary of state for Culture, Media and Sport considered invoking legitimate interests to protect media plurality when Twenty-First Century Fox bid for Sky in 2017. However, the US communications group Comcast outbid Fox and Sky is currently owned by Comcast.[6]

In 2003, the EU agreed its Modernisation Regulation which came into force in May 2004. The Regulation changed EU competition law by removing the notification system and decentralising decision-making. The Regulation empowered NRAs to enforce Articles 101 and 102 (ex-Articles 81 and 82) and national courts to apply Article 101. Accordingly, cooperation between NRAs and the European Commission takes place under the European Competition Network (ECN) established in 2004. Up until 2004, only the European Commission held the power to grant exemptions under Article 101. Thereafter, exemptions could take place at the national level. The Regulation divides case allocation between the Commission and NRAs and enables information exchange. In 2018, the EU approved the ECN+ Directive. It updates enforcement instruments for NRAs, including independence 'from political and other external influence', 'adequate human and financial resources', and powers of investigation. It also enables NRAs to carry out inspections on behalf of other NRAs.

In 2019, DG Competition commissioned a report from three special advisors[7] on 'Competition Policy for the Digital Era'. The report identified: the goals of EU competition law in the digital era, the application of competition rules to digital platforms and data, and the role of merger control in preserving competition and innovation. It recommended sector-specific regulation for data access solutions. Significantly, the report highlighted that digital markets needed address

[5] Case COMP/M.5932 News Corporation/BskyB (IP/10/1767, 21.12.2010).

[6] Case M.8354 Fox/Sky, Commission decision of 7 April 2017: http://ec.europa.eu/competition/elojade/isef/case_details.cfm?proc_code=2_M_8354 [last accessed 25.10.2022].

[7] The special advisors were three academics, Heike Schweitzer, Jacques Crémer, and Yves-Alexandre de Montjoye. https://ec.europa.eu/commission/commissioners/2014-2019/ vestager/announcements/commission-appoints-professorsheike-schweitzer-jacques-cremer-and-assistant-professor-yves_ en and http://ec.europa.eu/competition/scp19 [last accessed 25.10.2022].

by theories of harm. It was followed with a public consultation which took place from 7 July to 30 September 2018, and a conference, 'Shaping Competition Policy in the Era of Digitisation', in Brussels in January 2019. This was followed by the 2020 Communication, 'Shaping Europe's Digital Future', which, among other declarations, announced a sector inquiry into competition. In 2021, the Commission published a Communication on a Competition Policy fit for New Challenges. It outlined 27 initiatives and plans to update the 1997 Market Definition Notice, state aid criteria, and Important Projects of Common European Interest (IPCEI).

In 2022, the EU approved the Digital Markets Act (DMA) as a strong competition instrument to apply ex-ante regulation to gatekeepers in the digital market which is expected to increase its intervention in online platform markets. As Cini and Czulno comment, when the Commission was seeking expert advice on reform of its competition regime, 'the majority of non-EU national reports originated in the UK (such as the 2019 Furman Report) and the US' (2022: 48) and the proposed New Competition Tool took 'inspiration from the UK Competition and Markets Authority's market investigation tool' (2022: 47). The NCT, which in the end was not adopted by the Commission, was promoted by the CMA (Vesterdorf and Fountoukakos, 2021).

The DMA sets out new criteria for online platforms to be identified as 'gatekeepers' which offer 'essential service platforms'. This includes not only search engines and online platforms but also web browser companies and digital voice assistance. The Act aims to prevent predatory acquisitions by large tech companies. Acquisitions and mergers are to be addressed by independent studies confirming that they will not 'impede competition or innovation'. The DMA promotes third-party access to platforms and regulates digital advertising, particularly in relation to transparency. It also permits publishers to verify advertisers, reflecting a core agenda of the European Commission in the promotion of European champions. The DMA is supported by the Observatory on the Online Platform Economy[8] which was established under the platform-to-business (P2B) Regulation. The DMA came into force on 1 November 2022.

At the time of writing, DG Competition is led by Commissioner Margrethe Vestager under the 2019–24 Commission, who is also executive vice-president (EVP) of the European Commission for 'A Europe Fit for the Digital Age'. The EVP role replaced the post of Commissioner for Digital Economy and Society previously held by Mariya Gabriel (2017 to 2019). In her role as Digital Commissioner, Vestager chairs the Commissioners' Group on 'A Europe Fit for the Digital Age', coordinating work on a European strategy on data and on the European approach to artificial intelligence. She also steers the Commission's work on upgrading liability and safety rules for digital platforms, services, and products as part of the

[8] https://platformobservatory.eu [last accessed 25.10.2022].

2022 Digital Services Act and coordinates the Commission's approach to digital taxation. This dual role is part of the Commission's focus on core priorities[9] and has marked a move to an ex-ante regulatory approach rather than ex-post approach to competition regulation in the digital sector (Cini and Czulno, 2022).

The EU has competition cooperation agreements with Canada, Japan, Mexico, Morocco, South Korea, Switzerland, and the United States[10] which relate to the exchange of information, coordination mechanisms, and reciprocal significant interests. The Commission is working on an agreement on data protection standards with the Canadian Competition Bureau in particular in line with the Opinion of the Court of Justice on the 2014 EU–Canada Passenger Name Record Agreement. The EU also has competition memoranda of understanding (MoUs) with Brazil, China, India, Russia, and South Africa and a number of bilateral agreements with further third states.[11] For example, it has cooperation agreements with the Korean Fair Trade Commission and the Japanese Fair Trade Commission and a 2019 cooperation agreement with China's State Administration for Market Regulation. These agreements, however, preclude the exchange of confidential information. In December 2021, the Commission established the EU–US Joint Technology Competition Policy with US competition authorities.

The UK is no longer party to EU competition agreements with third states but it can cooperate with competition authorities under a 2015 recommendation of the Organisation for Economic Co-operation and Development (OECD).[12] The OECD Recommendation covers notification and coordination mechanisms where one or more states are involved. The UK is also a member of the International Competition Network (ICN)[13] and the United Nations Conference on Trade and Development (UNCTAD),[14] which implements the UN set of principles on competition,[15] and the World Trade Organization (WTO).[16]

In addition, the CMA signed a mutual assistance and cooperation framework with competition authorities in the United States, Canada, New Zealand, and Australia. The CMA also agreed a 'common approach' to mergers with its German and Australian competition authorities.[17] As the CMA stated in 2021, 'we expect

[9] There are three EVPs which cover both Commissioner roles and VP oversight of three of the six core priorities: 'A Europe Fit for the Digital Age' (Vestager), 'A European Green Deal' (Timmermans), and 'An Economy That Works for People' (Dombrovskis).

[10] https://ec.europa.eu/competition/international/legislation/usa01.pdf [last accessed 25.10.2022].

[11] https://competition-policy.ec.europa.eu/international/bilateral-relations_en [last accessed 25.10.2022].

[12] www.oecd.org/daf/competition/2014-rec-internat-coop-competition.pdf [last accessed 25.10.2022].

[13] www.internationalcompetitionnetwork.org [last accessed 25.10.2022].

[14] https://unctad.org/topic/competition-and-consumer-protection/intergovernmental-group-of-experts-on-competition-law-and-policy [last accessed 25.10.2022].

[15] https://unctad.org/topic/competition-and-consumer-protection/the-united-nations-set-of-principles-on-competition [last accessed 25.10.2022].

[16] www.wto.org/english/tratop_e/comp_e/comp_e.htm [last accessed 25.10.2022].

[17] https://committees.parliament.uk/publications/30148/documents/174754/default [last accessed 25.10.2022].

to work closely with the European Commission in the same way as we have with other international competition authorities on previous cases'.[18] Although there is ongoing cooperation with Europe and other competition authorities on multi-jurisdictional mergers and acquisitions, there is a limitation to information exchange.[19]

European Commission competition policy decision-making, 1989–2022

Objectively, the EU's competition authority treats the digital sector like any other sector under the Single Market. However, it has been highly active in digital markets, particularly in mergers, breaking up state monopolies, state aid and exclusive rights agreements, and newly the operation of large platforms. As Piffaut (2021: 955) observes, competition decisions related to telecommunication, media, and internet services represented about 7 per cent of all cases notified to DG Competition since 1989, of which 13 per cent led to investigation. This is much higher than the average of 8 per cent. DG Competition is considered more progressive than the European Court of Justice (ECJ) in its decisions, taking on board public interest, particularly in digital markets where it has seen a number of its decisions overturned.

The bulk of decisions have been made under the 1998 and 2004 Merger Regulations and the 2013 Implementing Regulation with 7,784 decisions made in the 'information and communication'[20] sector between 1989 and 2022.[21] By comparison, there have been 3,038 antitrust cases and 1,992 state aid cases. As of August 2022, one-fifth of negative decisions taken by DG Competition have fallen into the 'information and communication' category, seven out of 31 prohibitions.[22] These have included a number of high-profile decisions, notably the e-Books decision (2013), antitrust decisions against Microsoft and browser lock in (2013),

[18] https://competitionandmarkets.blog.gov.uk/2021/01/06/how-the-end-of-the-transition-period-affects-uk-merger-control [last accessed 25.10.2022].

[19] www.gov.uk/government/publications/mergers-guidance-on-the-cmas-jurisdiction-and-procedure [last accessed 25.10.2022].

[20] The Information and Communication Code defined under the unified Statistical Classification of Economic Activities in the European Community (NACE code) includes: publishing activities (books, periodicals, directories, mailing lists, newspapers, journals and periodicals, software publishing, computer games), motion picture, video, and television programme production, sound recording and music publishing activities, programming and broadcasting activities (radio and television), telecommunications (wired, satellite, and other telecommunications activities), computer programming, consultancy and related activities, information service activities, data processing, hosting, and related activities, and web portals. Some cases can be assigned more than one code.

[21] https://competition-policy.ec.europa.eu/mergers/statistics_en [last accessed 25.10.2022].

[22] https://competition-policy.ec.europa.eu/mergers/statistics_en [last accessed 25.10.2022].

the Google Shopping decision (2017), Google and the Android operating system (2018), and abusive practices in online advertising (2019).

In the 1990s, the European Commission was successful in breaking up concentration in broadcasting, cable markets, and telecommunications markets. Even though the Commission's key aim was to increase competition, it often took into consideration cultural (and political) pluralism interest goals. This can be seen in a number of decisions, particularly under the direction of Commissioner Van Miert. The Commission took four negative decisions in the German market in 1994 breaking up alliances between Bertelsmann, Kirch, and Deutsche Bundespost Telekom (the public telecommunications group).[23]

In 1997, DG Competition's Merger Task Force decided against the proposed acquisition of the German pay-TV operator Premiere and BetaResearch by Bertelsmann and Kirch and against joint control of the D-Box decoder by Bertelsmann, Kirch, and Deutsche Telekom. This prevented concentration between Germany's largest media companies. In the UK, BSkyB was blocked from participating in British Digital Broadcasting (BDB, renamed ONdigital, which later became ITV Digital). DG Competition prevented British Telecom from taking a stake and forming a joint venture with Microwave Communications Inc. (MCI) in 1997. In the 1995 Holland Media Group (HMG) case, when DG Competition required the withdrawal of Endemol, thereby weakening its dominant position for independent Dutch-language television production, Van Miert stated:

> today's decision is a further example of the Commission's commitment to protect competitive market structures in media sector. It is also worth mentioning that the strict application of the competition rules can also contribute to maintaining plurality in this sensitive sector. (Lang, 1997: 42)

In cable markets, DG Competition prevented market concentrations in the Nordic states with its Nordic Satellite Distribution (NSD) in 1995, ensuring that there was no closure to third parties. In Spain, the Commission ruled against the acquisition of Cablevisión by Telefónica de España and Sogecable SA, a subsidiary of Canal Plus España in 1996. The telecommunications operator Telefónica and Sogecable SA (a subsidiary of Canal Plus España) were prohibited from jointly acquiring Cablevisión, necessitating the establishment of two satellite platforms in Spain, Telefónica and Canal Plus, rather than one.

In 1997, the joint acquisitions of Cable I Televisio de Catalunya by the electric company Endesa, the gas company Gas Natural, Stet (an Italian telecommunications group), and Caixa Catalunya bank were prohibited. General Electric and Bank of America successfully invested in Cable I Televisio de Catalunya later in the

[23] The 1994 MSG Media Service, 1998 Deutsche Telekom/Betaresearch, 1998 DF1/Premiere, and 1998 Betaresearch/Bertelsmann/Kirch cases.

year. The 1999 Cable Ownership Directive mandated that telecommunications operators separated their cable interests into structurally separate companies. Based upon this premise, the Commission was also able to require divestment by incumbent operators at national levels. For example, in the Telia/Sonera case, the parties divested in its cable company in Sweden.

Under the 1996 Full Competition Directive, the Commission brought a number of infringement proceedings in telecommunications markets. Five investigations were brought against into discriminatory behaviour in Belgium, Italy, Greece, Portugal, and Spain. In 1999, under Commissioner Mario Monti's direction, DG Competition opened a sector inquiry into leased lines. Leased lines are normally underground fibre-optic cables which are owned by one company but leased to another. Within a two-year period, leased line prices reduced within the EU by approximately 40 per cent.[24] In the Telia/Sonera case, the companies were required to legally separate their fixed and mobile networks. In Spain, an Opinion was sent concerning inconsistencies between full unbundled access tariffs set in 2000 and a price cap in 2001.

From 2000, there was an increased focus on sports broadcasting rights. In a 2001 decision on UEFA's broadcasting regulations,[25] UEFA simplified its rules for national associations to allow for only two and limited the blocked number of hours for broadcast. FIFA adopted new rules on international transfer of football players following a DG Competition investigation.[26] In the 2003 UEFA Champions League decision,[27] the Commission ruled against the collective selling of the broadcasting rights on an exclusive basis. All media rights were to be sold via tender in 14 separate packets for up to three years. Individual clubs were given the ability to exploit certain rights in parallel to UEFA and clubs were given the rights to produce new club-branded products. As a result, the number of broadcasters transmitting the UEFA Champions League doubled.

In similar cases at the national level, the Commission secured a new system for market broadcasting rights in first and second division Bundesliga matches under antitrust rules in Germany in 2002. Under the deal, broadcasting rights were unbundled so that live games could be shown over the internet and via mobile phones with first and second division Bundesliga clubs selling some of their own rights. In the UK, the FA Premier League (FAPL) asked for revision of the FAPL and BSkyB for live television rights in the same year. In France, the Commission pressured the

[24] https://ec.europa.eu/competition/sectors/telecommunications/archive/inquiries/leased_lines/exmemonovember2002.pdf [last accessed 25.10.2022].

[25] https://eur-lex.europa.eu/legal-content/EN/ALL/?uri=CELEX%3A32001D0478 [last accessed 25.10.2022].

[26] https://ec.europa.eu/commission/presscorner/detail/en/IP_02_824 [last accessed 25.10.2022].

[27] https://eur-lex.europa.eu/legal-content/EN/ALL/?uri=CELEX%3A32003D0778 [last accessed 25.10.2022].

French competition authority to modify rights provided by the Ligue du Football Professionnel in 2003.

The introduction of the regulation of electronic communications networks and services in 2002 allowed ex-ante application of competition law to telecommunications markets which dominated much of DG Competition's agenda for a number of years. Under the previous framework, ex-ante regulation could be applied to companies if they had a 25 per cent market share. The definition of 'significant market power' (SMP) was changed under the 2002 framework based on Article 82 of the Treaties in guidelines set out in a 2003 Recommendation pursuant to Article 15 of the Framework Directive.[28]

Under the new ex-ante rules brought in by the Directives on electronic communications, the Commission fined two telecommunications providers in 2002. Deutsche Telekom AG was fined 12.6 million Euros for local access to the fixed telephony network. The decision was confirmed in a CFI Deutsche Telekom v Commission case in 2008.[29] Wanadoo (72 per cent owned by France Télécom) was also fined 10.35 million Euros for predatory pricing in ADSL broadband services. France was sent a reasoned Opinion for having failed to comply with the Full Competition Directive and Cable Directive which stipulated that cable companies need to provide the same conditions as telecommunications operators.

Although the 2000s marked a convergence between broadcast, telecommunications, and pay television markets, the distinction between free and pay television markets was maintained. This could be seen in the 2002 Sogecable/Canalsatélite Digital/Vìa Digital, 2006 Providence/Carlyle/UPC Sweden, 2007 SFR/Télé 2, 2014 Liberty Global/Ziggo, 2015 Altice/PT Portugal (2015), and 2019 Telia Company/ Bonnier Broadcastings Holding cases (Piffaut, 2021: 1018). In the Telenor/Canal+ /Canal Digital and 2003 Newscorp/Telepiù[30] merger cases, conditions for third-party access to platforms and the duration and scope of licensing agreements for premium content were put in place.

In 2003, a new antitrust Regulation on the implementation of the rules on competition laid down in Articles 81 and 82 of the Treaty was introduced. Under the Regulation, companies were no longer required to notify agreements for clearance. Shared responsibility for implementation between the Commission and NRAs was introduced via the ECN. This lightened the regulatory burden for the Commission and freed it to investigate more serious cases. At the same time, the Merger Regulation was updated in 2004. It also changes the rules on procedures for allocating cases between the Commission and member states. Companies could

[28] Commission Recommendation 2003/311/EC of 11 February 2003 on relevant product and service markets within the electronic communications sector susceptible to ex ante regulation in accordance with Directive 2002/21/EC of the European Parliament and of the Council on a common regulatory framework for electronic communication networks and services (OJ L 114, 8.5.2003, p. 45).

[29] Case T-271/03 Deutsche Telekom AG v Commission.

[30] COMP/M.2876 Newscorp/Telepiù, 2.4.2003.

request referral of a case prior to notification to avoid multiple notifications in several member states. The Commission flanked the new Regulation with updated guidelines on horizontal mergers and best practice for investigations. It also introduced a block exemption Regulation for technology transfer agreements (last updated in 2014).

The introduction of the ECN in 2004 meant that NRAs needed to carry out analyses of relevant markets, identify SMP, and notify the Commission of any draft regulatory measures or remedies proposed. In 2004, the Commission received 89 notifications. In only three cases did the Commission object to national regulatory authority (NRA) assessments, all of which were related to telecommunications markets. Two were in relation to the Finnish NRA's decision not to identify TeliaSonera as having SMP in international telephone services due to low market entry and the Finnish market for access and call origination on public mobile telephone networks. In the third case, the Commission disagreed with the Austrian NRA decision that Telekom Austria did not hold SMP and intervened.

Similarly, in 2005, the Commission objected to Germany's NRA decision that 53 alternative fixed network operators did not have SMP, due to Deutsche Telekom's countervailing buyer power. There were also a number of investigations into NRAs enabling functional unbundling. Functional unbundling happens when incumbents run services separate to telephony; for example, separating their telephone networks and internet services into separate businesses. The Belgian, Italian, Maltese, and Polish NRAs[31] changed their market definitions under scrutiny from the European Commission.

The regulatory framework permitted the definition by NRAs of subnational geographic markets for ex-ante regulation. Ofcom in the UK was the first NRA to differentiate different geographic areas for broadband markets. A proposal for removing regulation in geographic areas where there was effective competition was put forward to and approved by the Commission. This led a number of further NRAs across Europe to do the same.

Because of the large number of cases in the sector, most of which centred on incumbent abuse of dominant position, the ECN established a subgroup on telecommunications and postal services in 2005. Subsequently, the mid-2000s marked a continued period of crackdown on incumbents. In 2007, the Commission imposed a fine of 151,875,000 Euros on the Spanish incumbent telecoms operator Telefónica for a five-year abuse of its dominant position in the Spanish broadband market. In 2010, in the Telekomunikacja Polska case,[32] the Commission sent a Statement of Objections to the Polish incumbent for infringement of Article 102 for abusing its dominant position in wholesale broadband services. In 2013, in the first cross-border case, the Commission fined Telefónica 66,984,000 Euros and

[31] BE/2007/0578; IT/2007/0575; MT/2007/0563; and PL/2007/0668.
[32] Case COMP/39525 Telekomunikacja Polska IP/10/213, 1.3.2010.

Portugal Telecom 12,290,000 Euros for agreeing not to compete with each other in telecommunications markets. Slovak Telekom and Deutsche Telekom were also fined 39 million Euros in 2014 for shutting out competitors to the Slovak broadband market.

By the mid-2000s, DG Competition had turned its attention to the internet and the big tech giants. A number of notable cases were decided against large US corporations. As explained in Chapter 5, this was coupled with a sector inquiry into e-commerce in the EU launched by DG Competition in 2016[33] as part of the 2015 Digital Single Market strategy. The inquiry was aimed at encouraging cross-border trade in electronics, clothing and shoes, and digital content, which were the most prevalent sectors for national online purchasing.

Accordingly, in 2010, the Commission began investigations into Google which was accused of abusing its dominant market position in online search, online advertising, and online advertising intermediation markets.[34] Google was inspected for lowering rankings for unpaid search results of competition services for specific content such as price comparison websites. Google was also scrutinised as to whether it preferentially placed its own results to preclude competition services. The corporation was also suspected of lowering the 'quality score' which determines the price advertisers pay to Google for sponsored links for competing search services. Lastly, the Commission considered whether Google was imposing exclusivity obligations on advertisers. A Statement of Objection was sent in 2015 concerning comparison shopping.[35]

In the Google Shopping case, the Commission fined Google 2.42 billion Euros in June 2017 for prioritising its own online shopping services in search results in 13 countries in the European Economic Area, including the UK. Google accordingly corrected its shopping box to permit third-party comparison websites. This case is still valid in the UK post-Brexit as the decision was taking before the end of the transition period. Google challenged the case in the General Court which upheld the Commission's decision in 2021. Google lost its appeal.[36] The Court found that the use of self-referencing amounted to abuse of dominant position under Article 102 of the TFEU.

[33] As explained in Chapter 5, the e-commerce inquiry focused on goods rather than services. It identified that the most goods sold online were: clothing; shoes; consumer electronics; electrical household appliances; computer games and software; toys and childcare articles; media (books, CDs, DVDs, and Blu-ray discs); cosmetics and healthcare products; sports and outdoor equipment; and house and garden products. Respondents could comment on any 'other' product categories.

[34] Cases COMP/39740 Foundem/Google, COMP/39775 E-Justice/Google and COMP/39768 Ciao/Google (IP/10/1624, 30.11.2010).

[35] Case AT.39740 Google search; see IP/15/4780 of 15 April 2015: http://europa.eu/rapid/press-release_IP-15-4780_en.htm [last accessed 25.10.2022].

[36] https://curia.europa.eu/jcms/upload/docs/application/pdf/2021-11/cp210197en.pdf [last accessed 25.10.2022].

In 2018, the Commission fined Google 4.34 billion Euros for the abuse of dominant position in the internet search market.[37] This constituted a record fine for the European Commission. The Commission found that Google had abused its dominant position by requiring Android operating system manufacturers to install the Google browser and search engine on mobile devices if they wanted to use the Google App Store. Google also paid manufacturers to make sure that Google was the only search application available on devices which prevented the development of competing mobile operating systems. Google was required to cease to abuse of its dominant position in the mobile device market within 90 days. Google challenged but lost the case in the General Court in 2022.[38]

In 2019, the Commission fined Google 1.49 billion Euros for preventing third-party competitors to Google (AdSense) from displaying search advertisements.[39] The Commission found that Google had abused its market dominance by imposing restrictive clauses in contracts with third-party website providers over a 10-year period. In 2020, the Commission imposed conditions on Google's acquisition of Fitbit that Fitbit data would not be used for Google ads, data collection would remain in separate data silos, and Google would permit third-party access to users' health and fitness data under consent.

In the 2021 Google Adtech case, the Commission similarly is investigating whether Google, which holds 90 per cent of the ad tech market, is favouring its own display advertising on devices using its Adtech software. Separate national cases were opened on Google Adtech practices in France, which fined Google 220 million Euros in 2021, the Netherlands, and the UK. In 2022, Google was also sued in Sweden for 2.1 billion Euros for lost profit in Denmark, Sweden, and the UK by the Swedish price comparison firm PriceRunner, which is undergoing acquisition by Klarna. An investigation into Google's Adtech has been running since 2019 in Ireland by Ireland's Data Protection Commission due to complaints by a number of market operators.

In parallel, the Commission began investigations into Apple, beginning with the iPhone in 2010.[40] Apple had only provided warranties that covered mobile phones in the states where they were bought. It also restricted independent developers to the use of Apple programming tools and software languages in the development of applications. The Commission investigations led to the introduction of cross-border iPhone warranties and relaxation of third-party development licences by Apple going forward.

[37] https://ec.europa.eu/competition/antitrust/cases/dec_docs/40099/40099_9993_3.pdf [last accessed 25.10.2022].

[38] https://curia.europa.eu/jcms/upload/docs/application/pdf/2022-09/cp220147en.pdf [last accessed 25.10.2022].

[39] https://ec.europa.eu/competition/elojade/isef/case_details.cfm?proc_code=1_40411 [last accessed 25.10.2022].

[40] IP/10/1175, 25.9.2010.

By the 2020s, DG Competition had opened a number of investigations into Apple. In the Apple Pay case, a Statement of Objections was sent to Apple about the integration of Apple Pay systems and limitation of access to near-field communication (NFC) tap and go to Apple devices.[41] In the Apple App Store Practices case,[42] DG Competition ruled that Apple abused the dominant position of its App Store in the music streaming app market following complaints lodged by Spotify. The platform was found to restrict iPhone and iPad users from accessing alternative platforms for music streaming. A Statement of Objections was sent to Apple in 2021[43] and found in 2022 that Apple had dominated its position.

Facebook was also investigated by DG Competition. In 2017, it was fined 110 million Euros for failing to declare that it had been aware of the technical possibility to automatically match Facebook and WhatsApp users' identities when it acquired WhatsApp in 2014. Witt (2022) argues that this has the potential for a landmark Court ruling. In 2021, the European Commission[44] opened an investigation into Facebook Marketplace at the same time as the CMA.[45] It stated at the time that 'the European Commission will seek to work closely with the CMA as the independent investigations develop'. In 2021, the EU, UK, and US also began parallel investigations into proposed acquisitions by Facebook, Illumina, and Nvidia. However, in summer 2022, the formal cooperation between DG Competition and the CMA was postponed due to political disagreement over the Northern Ireland protocol.

DG Competition also commenced a number of formal investigations into Amazon. In 2019, Amazon was investigated regarding whether it was illegally harvesting personal data gathered from independent retailers hosted on the Amazon marketplace platform to compete against its competitors.[46] In 2020, it delivered a Statement of Objections to Amazon, stating that Amazon had leveraged its dominant position to advantage its own position in the market in France and Germany.[47] DG Competition ruled in the case that Amazon had been feeding third-party seller data into algorithms to further its own retail business.

In a second formal antitrust investigation into Amazon's Buy Box,[48] the Commission examined whether Amazon was guilty of self-referencing and discriminatory practices, the criteria Amazon uses to offer products to Amazon Prime

[41] https://ec.europa.eu/commission/presscorner/detail/en/ip_22_2764 [last accessed 25.10.2022].
[42] Apple App Store Practices: https://ec.europa.eu/competition/elojade/isef/case_details.cfm?proc_code=1_40437 [last accessed 25.10.2022].
[43] https://ec.europa.eu/commission/presscorner/detail/en/speech_21_2093 [last accessed 25.10.2022].
[44] https://ec.europa.eu/competition/elojade/isef/case_details.cfm?proc_code=1_AT_40684 [last accessed 25.10.2022].
[45] www.gov.uk/cma-cases/investigation-into-facebooks-use-of-data [last accessed 25.10.2022].
[46] https://ec.europa.eu/commission/presscorner/detail/en/IP_19_4291 [last accessed 25.10.2022].
[47] https://ec.europa.eu/commission/presscorner/detail/en/ip_20_2077 [last accessed 25.10.2022].
[48] https://ec.europa.eu/competition/antitrust/cases/dec_docs/40703/40703_67_4.pdf [last accessed 25.10.2022].

users and the criteria for choosing the Buy Box winner. In July 2022, in joined cases AT.40462 and AT.40703, DG Competition found that that both Buy Box and Prime unjustifiably advantage Amazon's own retail business and proposed that Amazon 'refrain' from using non-public data gained from independent marketplace sellers and to treat all sellers equally in ranking offers for the Buy Box winner. The Commission consequently required Amazon Prime to set non-discriminatory conditions for sellers to allow Prime sellers to choose their own carriers for delivery and negotiate terms, and not to use information about terms and performance of third-party sellers for Amazon logistics services.[49]

The Commission also investigated the e-books sector under its sector inquiry. It adopted a decision against Apple and four e-book publishers in 2012: Simon & Schuster (CBS Corp.), Harper Collins (News Corp.), Hachette Livre (Lagardère Publishing), and Verlagsgruppe Georg von Holtzbrinck. They were found to have colluded on retail prices under the guise of retailer agency contracts. Amazon was also investigated in 2015 for its distribution practices in e-books. The Commission also looked into Amazon's distribution agreements with e-book publishers in 2017. It found that the agreement clauses prevented new entrants to the e-book platform market.

In the telecommunications sector, DG Competition made a number of decisions concerning national markets. In 2018, the Commission required Vivendi to divest in the television group Persidera (formerly Telecom Italia Media Broadcasting) in Italy when it took control of Telecom Italia in May 2017.[50] In Portugal, Altice was fined 124.5 million Euros in 2018 for acquiring the Portuguese telecommunications operator PT Portugal without notification or approval from the Commission. In the Czech Republic, the Commission investigated a mobile network sharing agreement between O2 CZ/CETIN and T-Mobile CZ in 2019 and the proposed acquisition by Vodafone of Liberty Global's interests in the Czech Republic, Germany, Hungary, and Romania.[51] In 2020, DG Competition fined Comcast 14.3 million Euros for restricting the selling of licensed merchandise to territories specified in contractual clauses. In the UK, DG Competition prohibited a merger between Hutchinson 3G and Telefonica UK due to a reduction in market choice in the UK mobile telephone market. The Hong Kong-based Hutchinson had planned to develop the UK's largest mobile telecoms network by merging Three UK with O2. The decision was, however, overturned in the General Court in 2020.

In the chipset market, the Commission made a number of high-profile decisions. It fined Qualcomm 997 million Euros for abuse of dominant position for

[49] https://eur-lex.europa.eu/legal-content/EN/TXT/PDF/?uri=CELEX:52022XC0720(01)&from=EN [last accessed 25.10.2022].

[50] Case M.8465 Vivendi/Telecom Italia, Commission decision of 30 May 2017: http://ec.europa. eu/competition/elojade/isef/case_details.cfm?proc_ code=2_M_8465 [last accessed 25.10.2022].

[51] https://ec.europa.eu/competition/elojade/isef/case_details.cfm?proc_code=1_40305 [last accessed 25.10.2022].

paying Apple to exclusively use its chipsets in iPhone and iPad devices between 2011 and 2016.[52] Then, in 2019, Qualcomm was fined 242 million Euros for predatory pricing and supplying 3G chipsets to Huawei and ZTE below cost to price its UK start-up competitor Icera out of the market.[53] In 2019, Broadcom was found to be abusing its dominant position in systems-on-chip, fibre modems, and xDSL modems for setting up exclusivity contracts with television set-top box manufacturers.[54] The Commission made the commitments legally binding in 2020.[55]

DG Competition made several rulings on geo-blocking. In 2019, Sky UK and the film studios Disney, NBC Universal, Sony, and Warner Bros. were required to remove contractual restrictions in European pay television licensing agreements for five years, in a case initially opened in 2014.[56] The case concerned geo-blocking. This decision still stands post-Brexit as it was made before the end of the transition period. In 2021, it fined the videogame platform Valve and five publishers, Bandai Namco, Capcom, Focus Home, Koch Media, and ZeniMax, 7.8 million Euros for geo-blocking cross-border by geographical location within the European Economic Area in combined cases.[57]

In the late 2000s, the Commission also turned its attention to the corporation taxation practices of online platforms. In 2016, DG Competition concluded under state aid rules that Ireland had applied different corporate taxation rules to Apple than other companies between 2003 and 2014 and ruled that Ireland should recover the 13 billion Euros in unpaid tax. The General Court overturned the decision in 2020.[58] The European Commission has appealed the court's decision in the ECJ, which at the time of writing is still to be heard. In a similar ruling, the Commission made a state aid ruling against Amazon in Luxembourg in 2017.[59] It found that Amazon's cost-sharing arrangement breached state aid law and that it needed to pay back 250 million Euros in taxes. Amazon had restructured

[52] http:// ec.europa.eu/competition/elojade/isef/case_details. cfm?proc_code=1_40220 [last accessed 25.10.2022].

[53] https://ec.europa.eu/competition/elojade/isef/case_details.cfm?proc_code=1_39711 [last accessed 25.10.2022].

[54] https:// ec.europa.eu/competition/elojade/isef/case_details. cfm?proc_code=1_40608 [last accessed 25.10.2022].

[55] https://ec.europa.eu/competition/antitrust/cases/dec_docs/40608/40608_2794_3.pdf [last accessed 25.10.2022].

[56] DG Competition initially sent a Statement of Objections to Sky UK and six US film studios in 2014: Disney, NBC Universal, Paramount Pictures, Sony, Twentieth Century Fox, and Warner Bros. It concerned licensing agreements under Sky UK. The Commission drew attention to the fact that the studios were limiting their licensing agreements with broadcasters other than Sky which needed remedy: https://ec.europa.eu/competition/elojade/isef/case_details.cfm?proc_code=1_40023 [last accessed 25.10.2022].

[57] https://ec.europa.eu/commission/presscorner/detail/es/ip_21_170 [last accessed 25.10.2022].

[58] https://curia.europa.eu/juris/document/document.jsf?text=&docid=228621&pageIndex=0&doclang=EN&mode=lst&dir=&occ=first&part=1&cid=9634515 [last accessed 25.10.2022].

[59] https://ec.europa.eu/competition/state_aid/cases/254685/254685_1966170_891_2.pdfhttps://curia.europa.eu/juris/document/document.jsf?text=&docid=241188&pageIndex=0&doclang=EN&mode=lst&dir=&occ=first&part=1&cid=2060898 [last accessed 25.10.2022].

its European operations through Amazon EU Sàrl, a Luxembourg-based subsidiary, an office base which had no employees or activities. From 2003, the subsidiary received royalty payments from an exclusive intellectual property (IP) licence to Amazon EU. The European Commission claimed that the costs for IP development, which were paid to Amazon US, were inflated. The General Court annulled the decision in 2021, finding that there was 'no selective advantage' in the choice of basing the subsidiary in Luxembourg. These sorts of investigations may be mitigated by a future agreement on the taxation of digital services as discussed in Chapter 5.

United Kingdom competition policy post-Brexit

Chapter 2 of the 2020 EU–UK Trade and Co-operation Agreement (TCA), entitled 'Competition Policy', requires the UK to maintain an operative competition regime tackling anti-competitive behaviour and mergers and abuses of dominant position administered by an independent body. It outlines prohibited subsidies and subsidies subject to conditions. The chapter also specifies arrangements for future cooperation between the UK and the EU and EU member state competition authorities. Before the end of the transition period, December 2020, where a case met the threshold tests, the European Commission retained the right to review mergers. If a case was formally notified before the end of the transition period, it remained with the EU.

The UK 2019 Competition Regulations removed Articles 101 and 102 of the TFEU and the Merger Regulations from the Competition Act 1998 and the Enterprise Act 2002.[60] The UK will only undertake investigations under chapters I and II prohibitions after 31 December 2020. The CMA has been provided power to implement UK competition policy[61] and a role under the 2020 Internal Market Act.[62] Accordingly, the Office for the Internal Market (OIM) has been established within the CMA.[63] A Section 60A amendment to the 1998 Competition Act stipulates that UK courts and regulatory authorities must continue to interpret UK competition law in line with EU legislation and case law implemented prior to the end of the transition period.[64] For example, the prohibition of data sharing between Facebook and WhatsApp made by the European Commission 2014 still

[60] www.legislation.gov.uk/ukdsi/2019/9780111173930/contents [last accessed 25.10.2022].
[61] www.gov.uk/government/publications/guidance-on-the-functions-of-the-cma-after-the-end-of-the-transition-period [last accessed 25.10.2022].
[62] www.legislation.gov.uk/ukpga/2020/27/contents/enacted [last accessed 25.10.2022].
[63] www.gov.uk/government/organisations/office-for-the-internal-market [last accessed 25.10.2022].
[64] S. 60A inserted (31.12.2020) by The Competition (Amendment etc.) (EU Exit) Regulations 2019 (S.I. 2019/93), regs. 1(1), 23 (as amended by S.I. 2020/1343, reg. 5); 2020 *c.* 1, Sch. 5 para. 1(1) www.legislation.gov.uk/uksi/2020/1343/contents/made [last accessed 25.10.2022].

applies in the UK.[65] The Competition (Amendment etc.) (EU Exit) Regulations 2020[66] made arrangements for the transfer of monitoring compliance of EU remedies to UK competition authorities.

EU block exemption regulations have been retained under section 10 of the UK Competition Act.[67] This pertains to a number of Regulations in the rail, road, water, vehicle, shipping, R&D, specialisation, and technology transfer agreements.[68] Decisions made to date remain valid and future decisions can continue to be made under the block exemptions. The power to revoke block exemption decisions lies with the secretary of state in consultation with the CMA. When EU implemented block exemptions expire, the CMA will decide whether to set in place new regulations.[69]

The first block exemption to expire post-Brexit was on vertical agreements. The EU updated this with its 2022 Vertical Block Exemption Regulation (VBER). The Commission took the opportunity to narrow the scope of safe harbours for online platforms, specifically for dual distribution, where sellers sell through independent distributors, and also to end customers and parity obligations, where sellers are required to offer the same conditions across all platforms. Significantly, 'certain aspects of dual distribution and certain types of parity obligations will no longer be exempted under the new VBER but must instead be assessed individually under Article 101 TFEU'.[70] In the UK, the corresponding 2022 Vertical Agreements Block Exemption Order does not single out online platforms which will still be able to benefit from block exemptions as before, representing regulatory divergence between the UK and EU.

Historically, UK competition law differed from EU member states in that the application of competition law was balanced for decades by the use of the public interest tests. Until 2002, UK mergers were assessed by public interest tests under the Monopolies and Restrictive Practices (Inquiry and Control) Act 1948 and Fair Trading Act 1973.[71] The latter considered the public interest to be 'all matters which appear to them in the particular circumstances to be relevant', including 'maintaining and promoting the balanced distribution of industry and employment in the United Kingdom'.

Over time, concerns were raised in the UK that public interest test decisions were made on political rather than economic grounds (Wilks, 1999). Accordingly,

[65] https://ec.europa.eu/competition/elojade/isef/case_details.cfm?proc_code=2_M_7217 [last accessed 25.10.2022].

[66] www.legislation.gov.uk/uksi/2020/1343/contents/made [last accessed 25.10.2022].

[67] www.legislation.gov.uk/ukpga/1998/41/section/10 [last accessed 25.10.2022].

[68] Namely, Council Regulation (EC) 169/2009; Regulation (EC) 906/2009, Regulation (EU) 461/2010, Regulation (EU) 1217/2010, Regulation (EU) 330/2010, Regulation (EU) 1218/2010.

[69] www.gov.uk/government/publications/retained-block-exemptions/retained-block-exemptions [last accessed 25.10.2022].

[70] https://ec.europa.eu/commission/presscorner/detail/en/IP_22_2844 [last accessed 25.10.2022].

[71] www.legislation.gov.uk/ukpga/1973/41 [last accessed 25.10.2022].

the Enterprise Act 2002 removed the public interest test except for in cases of national and public security, media plurality and broadcasting standards, and financial services.[72] This was most recently updated to national security (including public security), financial stability, media plurality, and public health emergency in 2020.[73] UK competition decisions are today primarily made on competition grounds by the CMA. Appeal can be made to the Competition Appeal Tribunal (CAT). However, government intervention is gradually creeping back in under 'national security' grounds wherein the secretary of state can issue a Public Interest Intervention Notice (PIIN).[74] For example, an additional test, for businesses with a role in public health emergencies, was added in 2020 in light of the COVID-19 pandemic. This intervention was flanked by the National Security and Investment Act (NSI) 2022 which gives the government powers to intervene in mergers and acquisitions to protect national security.

Post-Brexit, the CMA proposed a code of conduct for online platforms with Strategic Market Status (SMS). The Code of Conduct stipulates that users can choose between competitive services. Other requirements include the stipulation that companies are able to operate on 'fair and reasonable' terms on online platforms and transparency measures regarding data use. It also includes support for the sustainability of the news publishing industry, helping to rebalance the relationship between publishers and online platforms. These proposals went hand in hand with the new digital services tax introduced in April 2020 which imposed a 2 per cent tax on the income of search engines, social media services, and online marketplaces operating within the UK.

A newly established Digital Markets Unit (DMU) within the CMA oversees online platforms and digital advertising in cooperation with Ofcom and the Information Commissioner's Office (ICO). The DMU was established in April 2021 but it does not yet have statutory backing. The government proposed plans for a Digital Markets, Competition and Consumers Bill in the 2022 Queen's Speech[75] based upon the 2021 consultation on Reforming Competition and Consumer Policy.[76] This included powers for the DMU with penalties proposed up to £50 million and maximum fines of 10 per cent of global annual income. It aims to increase investigatory powers for the CMA into anti-competition behaviour, particularly for 'killer acquisitions' whereby large corporations buy up rival players before

[72] www.legislation.gov.uk/ukpga/2002/40/contents [last accessed 25.10.2022].

[73] https://assets.publishing.service.gov.uk/government/uploads/system/uploads/attachment_data/file/902531/Enterprise_Act_2002_guidance_on_changes_to_the_turnover_and_share_of_supply_tests_for_mergers__Orders_2020_.pdf [last accessed 25.10.2022].

[74] This includes the lowering of turnover and share of supply tests for mergers in the areas of the military, computing hardware, quantum technologies, artificial intelligence, cryptographic authentication technology, and advanced materials.

[75] https://assets.publishing.service.gov.uk/government/uploads/system/uploads/attachment_data/file/1074113/Lobby_Pack_10_May_2022.pdf#page=34 [last accessed 25.10.2022].

[76] www.gov.uk/government/consultations/reforming-competition-and-consumer-policy/outcome/reforming-competition-and-consumer-policy-government-response [last accessed 25.10.2022].

they enter services and products on the market. However, smaller mergers (under £10 million) will not be caught by the Bill 'to reduce bureaucracy and keep the burden on smaller businesses to a minimum'. The Bill has not yet been proposed at the time of writing and the government has consequently drawn criticism from the House of Commons Business Energy and Industrial Strategy Committee but is expected in April 2023.[77]

The government also recommended strengthening CMA powers to investigate online advertising violations under the Digital Markets Competition and Consumer Bill. This was in response to a report by the Department for Digital, Culture, Media and Sport Committee which drew attention to the fact that influencers have low levels of compliance with advertising legislation.[78] However, generally the government has preferred a self-regulatory approach through the Advertising Standards Authority Code of Conduct for the Influencer Marketing Trade Body and Society of British Advertisers' (ISBA's) Influencer Code of Conduct under its Online Advertising Programme.[79]

The UK is increasing its address of large online platform and technology companies under competition law. The UK opened a number of cases into Google post-Brexit. In 2021, the UK Competition Appeal Tribunal transferred a case from the High Court against Kelkoo and 10 other companies against Google, claiming that Google illegally is favouring its own shopping comparison website to that of other companies in search results. A second case is taking place at the CAT, which is pursuing compensation for banner advertising websites. In a third case, a group of publishers are requesting compensation from Google in a joint UK/Dutch case, in the Netherlands representing EU publishers, and, in the UK CAT, UK publishers.

Separately, Google was also the subject of a class action brought by a former director of the consumer organisation Which over Safari privacy settings in iPhone which allegedly gathered data on the health, race, ethnicity, sexuality, and finance of users, but Google's appeal against the claim for compensation was upheld in the UK Supreme Court in 2021.[80] TikTok is also being challenged by the former Children's Commissioner for alleged collection of children's data without consent.

Meta was challenged on a number of fronts in the UK post-Brexit. In 2021, the UK's CMA ruled that the merger between Meta and GIPHY gave rise to substantial competition concerns. GIPHY is a US company which contains the world's largest online database of Graphic Interchange Formats (GIFs), emojis, and stickers as well as text and arcade games. Facebook challenged the CMA ruling in the CAT

[77] https://committees.parliament.uk/committee/365/business-energy-and-industrial-strategy-committee/news/173840/report-consumers-at-risk-if-digital-markets-unit-not-given-teeth-say-mps [last accessed 25.10.2022].

[78] Influencer Culture: Lights, camera, inaction? https://publications.parliament.uk/pa/cm5802/cmselect/cmcumeds/258/report.html [last accessed 25.10.2022].

[79] www.gov.uk/government/consultations/online-advertising-programme-consultation [last accessed 25.10.2022].

[80] www.bbc.co.uk/news/technology-59221037 [last accessed 25.10.2022].

in 2022 and lost. At the same time, Meta is being sued for its demand of personal data as a condition of access to the platform in 2022. A collective action case[81] was taken to the CAT in January 2022. A certification hearing took place in January 2023. In September 2022, the CMA opened an investigation into the dominance of cloud markets by Amazon, Microsoft, and Google. It also raised alarm over Microsoft's acquisition of Activision Blizzard which was subsequently taken up by DG Competition.

The CMA established a Behavioural Hub under its Data, Technology, and Analytics unit in 2022. As outlined in its paper, 'How Digital Design Can Harm Competition and Consumers', it identified the practice of 'online choice architecture' (OCA) which dealt with the design of applications, devices, and websites which could cause harm. The paper, which draws extensively on EU decision-making, explained that 'not only the choice structure facing consumers, but also the information they use and the pressure they can face in their decision making'. It identifies 21 types of OCAs under three categories including dark nudging and the use of virtual currencies in gaming to force outcomes. The CMA indicated that it will take action if competition is distorted.

Conclusion

At the time of writing, the government is supportive of a light-touch regulatory environment in relation to digital markets.[82] However, there are questions as to the capacity of regulators to cope with increased workload, staff shortages, and the loss of information exchange with their European counterparts. In September 2022, a House of Commons Committee of Public Accounts report entitled 'Regulating after EU Exit' identified the CMA as one of three regulators which is experiencing increased difficulties.[83] It reported that, even though the CMA needed additional staff to cope with its increased workload post-Brexit, it has been asked to cut staff up to 40 per cent under the spending review. The CMA is also finding it difficult to compete with the private sector to recruit and retain competition lawyers and economists, particularly given the fact that it has taken on global-level competition cases which would previously have been handled by the European Commission. The Business, Energy and Industrial Strategy Committee reported that the CMA had a vacancy rate of 25 per cent for legal roles in March 2022.[84]

[81] www.facebookclaim.co.uk/wp-content/uploads/2022/08/2022-08-23-CPO-Application-and-Hearing-Notice-L-L-G-v-Meta.pdf [last accessed 25.10.2022].

[82] www.gov.uk/government/consultations/a-new-pro-competition-regime-for-digital-markets/outcome/a-new-pro-competition-regime-for-digital-markets-government-response-to-consultation [last accessed 25.10.2022].

[83] https://committees.parliament.uk/publications/30148/documents/174754/default [last accessed 25.10.2022].

[84] https://committees.parliament.uk/publications/30458/documents/175742/default [last accessed 25.10.2022].

The CMA is now fully responsible for investigations, but it has suffered from a loss of access to EU sharing and cooperation agreements. In particular, it can no longer pass confidential information on cases to the Commission or EU member states. Under the TCA's chapter 2, Competition Policy, it is possible for the UK to set up confidential sharing agreements with the Commission and third states. Specifically, it states that:

> To implement the objectives of this Article, the Parties may enter into a separate agreement on cooperation and coordination between the European Commission, the competition authorities of the Member States and the United Kingdom's competition authority or authorities, which may include conditions for the exchange and use of confidential information.

The Committee of Public Accounts report stated that 'the CMA told us this agreement has not yet been agreed, and progress on this would be welcome as it would remove a significant barrier to effective competition enforcement'. It was indicated that there are political objections to cooperation, namely 'there is tight control from the centre of government over when and how they talk to co-regulators in the EU'. This reflects similar views from Ofcom civil servants who, in interviews for this book, stated that there was political reluctance for Ofcom to take a greater role in EU NRA fora.

A further Brexit outcome is that the risk of regulatory divergence may mean greater costs for business. Uncertainty is a factor given that UK legislation is predicted to change, but there is no indication yet as to how or when. Related to this are the different timetables taken by the UK and EU into investigations into the same companies. Divergence in approaches to consumer policy internally to the UK in the devolved regions is also expected post-Brexit.

9

State Aid and Exclusive Rights Agreements

Introduction

Post-Brexit, the UK is no longer subject to Directorate-General for Competition (DG Competition) scrutiny of state aid and exclusive rights agreements. This may provide opportunities to expand funding to the production of UK digital content in a number of sectors ranging from the provision of public service broadcasting, film, and television programming to subsidy of online newspapers and gaming. However, the Trade and Cooperation Agreement (TCA) continues to commit the UK to some agreements surrounding state aid. Under Article 363 of the TCA, the UK is required to adhere to a subsidy control agreement and, under Article 373, an effective mechanism of recovery. The UK must also publicly publish subsidy information within six months of aid awards and provide information to interested parties upon request. The TCA also requires oversight by an independent regulatory body, which is the Competition and Market Authority (CMA), and enforceability in the courts. Lastly, the EU reserves the right to impose countervailing measures in the form of quotas or tariffs or retaliate if UK subsidies affect EU trade and investments.

World Trade Organization (WTO) rules serve as an additional layer of scrutiny concerning UK state aid. Services not 'provided on a commercial basis' could be subject to retaliation by WTO members, including the EU, under the 1995 WTO Agreement on Subsidies and Countervailing Measures. The EU has not shied away from using this measure against the UK. In a 2022 case in the energy market the EU has already challenged the UK over subsidisation of low-carbon energy generation projects.[1] Importantly, the funding of public service broadcasting has been protected by Most Favoured Nation exemptions to the WTO's 1995 Agreement on Subsidies and Countervailing Measures. This determines whether or not a subsidy can be used by a WTO member. These exemptions were negotiated on behalf of the EU for its member states and need now to be negotiated separately by the UK.

This chapter details the development of the EU competition law approach to state aid and exclusive rights agreements in digital markets beginning with public service broadcasting, then moving to the rollout of broadband and cultural subsidies. Attention will be paid to past decisions where lessons might be drawn about

[1] www.wto.org/english/news_e/news22_e/ds612rfc_30mar22_e.htm [last accessed 25.10.2022].

Brexit and the Digital Single Market. Alison Harcourt, Oxford University Press. © Alison Harcourt 2023.
DOI: 10.1093/oso/9780192899378.003.0009

the EU's future approach to the sector. The chapter also considers the effect the UK has had on EU policy to date in relation to the public interest. It then considers the UK's approach to state aid in the digital sector post-Brexit.

Public service broadcasting

Subsidies to public service broadcasters (PSBs), film production, gaming, the heritage sector, and online newspapers[2] fall subject to state aid rules. Additionally, exclusive rights agreements (such as those approved by the European Broadcasting Union (EBU), which is the umbrella association for public service broadcasters in Europe) are also prohibited under EU competition law. Over time, exemptions were established which are considered to be compatible with market competition. This has proven challenging for the Commission as historically it possessed few tools with which to grant exemptions, and nothing existed in the Treaties to provide public service broadcasting with special status until 1996. The EU did not distinguish between commercial and state broadcasting until the mid-1990s as only the broader definition of broadcasting, which had been defined as a 'service' by the European Court of Justice (ECJ), was available.

Throughout the 1990s, the European Commission competition authority was faced with numerous complaints from commercial broadcasters about the activities of public service broadcasters. This led it to develop a distinct policy towards public service broadcasting through the application of competition law. This began with its 1993 'exemption' decision for Eurovision. Subsequent decisions on exclusive rights and state aid in the General Court (formerly the European Court of First Instance) and ECJ led to the adoption of a PSB protocol and Article 7d in the 1997 Amsterdam Treaty. These decisions laid the foundations for the 2000 Communication on Services of General Interest (SGEI) in Europe and 2001 Communication on the Application of State Aid Rules to Public Service Broadcasting. The 2003 ECJ Altmark case interpreted Article 7d on general services with regard to state aid. This was later incorporated into the 2009 Communication on the application of state aid rules to public service broadcasting.

Under the 1993 decision, the European Commission exempted Eurovision's exclusive rights agreement. Established by the EBU in 1954, Eurovision was an agreement set up by public service broadcasters to share news and sports broadcasting between them. From 1988, the EBU Marino Charter was agreed, which ended restriction to future EBU membership to public service broadcasters only. Accordingly, the EBU was able to maintain membership of broadcasters which had joined the EBU before the Marino Charter, namely the commercial broadcasters

[2] https://ec.europa.eu/competition/sectors/media/sa_decisions_to_media.pdf [last accessed 25.10.2022].

Canal Plus, RTL, and TF1, which had joined in 1984 and in 1986. The French former public service broadcaster TF1 did not leave the EBU when it was privatised in 1987. All of these groups had continued access to Eurovision exclusive rights agreements.

In 1988, the private satellite television service Sky established a Eurosport sports channel together with the EBU. Under the Eurosport Consortium Agreement, public service broadcasters and Sky were sharing rights to sports programming between them. The rival UK-based satellite sports channel, Screensport, filed a complaint with the European Commission. The agreement did not include third-party access, precluding Screensport from bidding for sports rights. The Commission ruled in 1993 that non-EBU members should be able to bid for Eurovision sports programming. In parallel, the European Commission granted Eurovision a five-year exemption from competition rules. This 'exemption' decision of 1993 recognised the EBU members' special public service role.

However, when commercial groups applied to join the EBU, they were refused membership even though the private channels Canal Plus, TF1, and RTL remained members. Following the exemption decision in 1994, applications from La Cinq, M6, and Antena 3 for EBU membership were rejected. Indeed, M6 had been refused membership six times between 1987 and 1994. This provoked a challenge to the exemption decision in the European Court of First Instance from La Cinq and M6 from France together with RTI from Italy and Antena and Telecinco from Spain. The court, in a joint ruling in joined cases T-528/93, T-542/93, T-543/93, and T-546/93 in 1996, overturned the European Commission's 1993 exemption decision.

The court's 1996 exemption decision indicated that public service broadcasting needed special recognition under EU competition law (Herold, 2002). It was flanked by a number of other developments. The WTO was established and began investigation of state aid cases under its 1995 Agreement on Subsidies and Countervailing Measures. At the EU level, PSBs were identified as presenting obstacles to market growth in the European Commission's 1998 Convergence green paper.

The European Parliament consequently pushed for special recognition of public service broadcasting in the Amsterdam Treaty in its 1996 Resolution on the role of public service television in the multi-media society. This was supported by a 1996 Council of Europe Recommendation on the Guarantee of the Independence of Public Service Broadcasting. Subsequently, a protocol was inserted into the 1997 Amsterdam Treaty, which states that 'the system of public broadcasting in the Member States is directly related to the democratic, social and cultural needs of each society and to the need to preserve media pluralism'.

Public interest services were also granted recognition in Article 7d of the Amsterdam treaty relating to services of general economic interest which states:

> without prejudice to Articles 77, 90 and 92 and given the place occupied by services of general economic interest in the shared values of the Union as well as their role in promoting social and territorial cohesion, the Community and the Member States, each within their respective powers and within the scope of application of this Treaty, shall take care that such services operate on the basis of principles and conditions which enable them to fulfil their missions.

Following these developments, the European Commission reapproved the Eurovision system in 1999 based on the Amsterdam Treaty protocol with an exemption from competition law from 2000 to 2005. The exemption was challenged for a second time in court by private broadcasters. The EBU appealed but the ECJ dismissed the case, finding that the Commission had not sufficiently defined the market. Therefore, it was impossible to determine whether third-party access to Eurovision met the conditions for exemption under Article 81 (Herold, 2002).

From the 1990s, the Commission also faced complaints from commercial broadcasters over the state financing of public service broadcasters. Objections originated in France, Spain, and Portugal in the early 1990s. In 1997 and 1998, challenges came from Germany, Italy, Portugal, and the UK. The German association of commercial broadcasters (Verband Privater Rundfunk und Telekommunikation) complained about competition from the digital PSB channels Kinderkanal and Phoenix. Fininvest objected to the underwriting of RAI's debts by the Italian government. BSkyB accused challenged the illegal application of state aid in the creation of the BBC News 24. In the German and UK cases, the Commission ruled in 1999 that state funding of digital channels was permissible under Article 87 of the Treaty. In the UK case, an allowance for emergent services as News 24 was only available to 10 per cent of the UK population at that time.

Six Commission decisions concerning state aid to PSBs were challenged in the ECJ. Commercial broadcasters contested both the licence fee and use of advertising. The Court ruled that the Commission must formulate a more formal policy on PSBs. The Commission's Directorate for Competition therefore published two Communications in 2000 and 2001. The 2000 Communication on Services of General Interest in Europe interpreted Article 7D of the Treaty. It stated:

> the choice of the financing scheme falls within the competence of the Member State, and there can be no objection in principle to the choice of a dual financing scheme (combining public funds and advertising revenues) rather than a single funding scheme (solely public funds) as long as competition in the relevant markets (e.g. advertising, acquisition and/or sale of programmes) is not affected to an extent which is contrary to the Community interest.

The 2001 Communication on the application of state aid rules to public service broadcasting was based upon rationales for public service broadcasting outlined in the protocol of the 1997 Amsterdam Treaty. It articulated:

> the broadcast media play a central role in the functioning of modern democratic societies, in particular in the development and transmission of social values. Therefore, the broadcasting sector has, since its inception, been subject to specific regulation in the general interest. This regulation has been based on common values, such as freedom of expression and the right of reply, pluralism, protection of copyright, promotion of cultural and linguistic diversity, protection of minors and of human dignity, consumer protection.

It also quoted Commissioner Oreja as stating:

> public service broadcasting has an important role to play in promoting cultural diversity in each country, in providing educational programming, in objectively informing public opinion, in guaranteeing pluralism and in supplying, democratically and free-of-charge, quality entertainment.

The 2001 Communication outlined four conditions under which public service broadcasters could be exempt from state aid provisions. Firstly, it demanded that member states formally define public service broadcasting. Up until this point many member states had never formally defined public service broadcasting in a legal act. Under entrustment, it required broadcasters to be controlled by a clear regulatory body. The third criterion demanded greater transparency of PSB accounts if licence fee- or state-funded, and to determine whether grants were being used to cross-subsidise new market services. The fourth criterion required that state aid did not exceed the PSB's public service mission. The 2001 Communication led to a serious re-assessment of public service broadcasting at national levels. It also led to greater European cooperation in the definition of public service broadcasting (Donders, 2015).

From this time onwards, PSB funding was notified to the Commission for approval prior to implementation. This began in 2002 with two decisions approving PSB funding by the Commission under the four criteria. In Belgium, the Commission approved aid to local television stations.[3] In the UK, the establishment of nine new thematic digital radio and television channels by the BBC was approved.[4] The funding was found not to constitute state aid within the meaning of Article 87(1). The Commission concluded that 'public service broadcasters can develop and diversify their activities in the digital age, as long as they are addressing

[3] Case N 548/01) (369).
[4] Case N 631/2001.

the same democratic, social and cultural needs of the society', reconfirming the special status of PSBs.

In 2003, the Court of Justice interpreted Article 7d in its landmark Altmark Decision. The case determined that funding does not constitute state aid within the meaning of Article 87(1) of the Treaty (Article 107(1) TFEU) if undertakings have 'public service obligations'. The court case related to transport but was significant for subsequent state aid assessments of public service broadcasting. The Court ruling formulated the Altmark test which determined whether or not the public service in question constitutes state aid according to four criteria:[5]

(a) the recipient undertaking must actually have public service obligations to discharge, and the obligations must be clearly defined;
(b) the parameters on the basis of which the compensation is calculated must be established in advance in an objective and transparent manner;
(c) the compensation cannot exceed what is necessary to cover all or some of the costs incurred in the discharge of public service obligations, taking into account the relevant receipts and a reasonable profit for discharging those obligations;
(d) when the company is not chosen pursuant to a public procurement procedure, the level of compensation needed must be determined on the basis of an analysis of the costs which a typical undertaking, well run and adequately equipped, would have incurred in discharging those obligations.

The European Commission applied the Altmark test to decisions on the public service channels Portugal's RTP,[6] Italy's RAI,[7] and France 2 and France 3 from 2003.[8] Although they did not pass the Altmark test, the Commission ruled that state aid was permissible because they met the principles outlined in its 2001 Communication, namely definition, entrustment, effective monitoring, and proportionality. DG Competition found in all three cases that the funding constituted existing aid as recurrent funding mechanisms. However, it required some amendments to the licence fees to maintain safeguards against excessive compensation. A similar decision was made regarding Spain's licence fee in the same year.

In some cases, PSBs did not meet the 2001 criteria. The first of these was decided against the Danish public service broadcaster TVDanmark's channel TV2 in 2003. The Commission found that TV2 had been over-compensated between 1995 and 2002 and was fined 87.8 million Euros (84.4 million Euros plus interest). This is because TV2 was dual-funded by both the state and commercial advertising and was

5 https://ec.europa.eu/competition/publications/cpn/2004_1_17.pdf.
6 Financiamento de RTP pelo Estado, Decision C(2003)3526.
7 Misure in favore della RAI, Decision C(2003)3528.
8 Aid to France 2 and France 3, Decision C(2003)4497.

thereby distorting competition in the Danish advertising market. The case was held up in the CFI in joined cases TV 2 v Commission. The Danish case was initiated by complaints from private broadcasters, but the Commission subsequently began to open its own cases from then on. In 2005, France, Ireland, Germany, Ireland, Italy, the Netherlands, and Spain were asked to revise their public service broadcasting funding schemes.[9]

In 2005, DG Competition approved state aid for a new French international news channel, 'Chaîne française d'information internationale' (since 2006 renamed France24) under the ECJ's Altmark judgment decision. However, as the new channel was financed by both the public broadcaster, France Télévision, and the commercial broadcaster, TF1, the Commission required safeguards against profit making and the function of advertising. Although approved by the Commission, TF1 withdrew its share mainly due to complaints by commercial operators and France24 is currently wholly state-owned.

Post-2005, state aid came under reform under the Lisbon strategy. DG Competition launched its state aid action plan (SAAP) which lasted from 2005 to 2009.[10] It targeted European competitiveness and job creation, noting 'with the development of new digital technologies and of Internet-based services, new issues have arisen regarding the scope of public service broadcasting activities'. One of these areas was the transition from analogue to digital broadcasting ('digital switchover'). The 2006 Commission Communication on accelerating the transition from analogue to digital broadcasting stipulated a deadline for the switch from analogue to digital broadcasting by the beginning of 2012.[11]

However, the Commission sanctioned a number of states for providing state aid to commercial broadcasters for digital switchover. In the digital decoders decision, the Commission sanctioned the Italian state 200 million Euros for aid to digital decoders granted between 2004 and 2005.[12] In the sanctioned cases, the Italian state did not provide aid for decoders using satellite broadcasting so it was not technologically neutral. Subsequent Italian subsidies for digital switchover were approved in 2007.[13] In Germany, in the DVB-T Germany case,[14] the Berlin-Brandenburg media authority was scrutinised for subsidising the digital switchover costs of commercial broadcasters, e.g. RTL and ProSiebenSat.1, to the sum of 4 million Euros in exchange for choosing DVB-T as a platform. DVB-T was a terrestrial

[9] Case E 0/2005 (France) Licence fee, Commission decision of 20.4.2005. Case E 9/2005 (Italy) Capital and other measures—RAI, Commission decision of 20.4.2005. Case E 8/2005 (Spain) Spanish national public broadcaster RTVE, Commission decision of 20.4.2005; SA.18957 (E3/2005) Aid to the German public broadcasters.

[10] https://ec.europa.eu/competition/state_aid/reform/saap_en.pdf.

[11] COM(2005) 204 final (OJ C 49, 28.2.2006, p. 24).

[12] Case C 52/2005 (ex NN 88/2005), Subsidy to digital decoders in Italy (OJ L 147 8.6.2007).

[13] Cases N 270/2006 Subsidy to digital decoders with open API (OJ C 80, 13.4.2007) and N 107/2007 Subsidies to idTV—Italy (OJ C 246, 20.10.2007).

[14] Case C 25/2004 (ex NN 36/04) Digital terrestrial TV (DVB-T) in Berlin-Brandenburg.

digital television network, a subsidiary of Deutsche Telekom AG. After the DVB-T decision, the Commission opened investigations into Bavaria and North Rhine-Westphalia. In North Rhine-Westphalia, the Commission took a negative decision.[15]

The Commission approved state aid for digital switchover in the Austrian Digitalisierungsfonds[16] and Spanish Soria cases in 2007.[17] But it opened an inquiry into UK state aid to fund Channel 4's digital switchover in 2008 based on a complaint from ITV. The Commission expressed 'serious doubts' that the aid met the criteria of the Commission's 2001 Broadcasting Communication.[18] As Wheeler (2010: 57–59) details, after some correspondence between the Commissioner Neelie Kroes and British Foreign Secretary David Miliband, the UK secretary of state for the Department for Digital, Culture, Media and Sport (DCMS) Andy Burnham withdrew the £14 million state aid for Channel 4's digital transmission costs.

In 2009, the European Commission issued a press release which stated that public broadcasters were receiving over 22 billion Euros annually from licence fees or direct government grants, placing them third, after agriculture and transport companies, among recipients of state aid in Europe.[19] Based upon the 2003 Altmark decision, the Amsterdam Protocol, and outcomes of relevant competition decisions,[20] it announced an updated Communication on the Application of State Aid Rules to Public Service Broadcasting in 2009.[21]

Overall, the Communication provided greater flexibility in financing but tightened the definition of the public service mission. The Communication updated the rules around SGEI under which aid to small, local, or regional PSBs was compatible under Article 86(2) EC and did not need to submit prior notification to the Commission for approval. The 2009 Communication incorporated criteria from Germany's 3 Stufen test. The German 3 Stufen test to assess public service funding, adopted in 2009, had in turn been based on the UK's 2007 UK 'public value test', although, as many authors point out, there have been difficulties in defining 'public value' (Humphreys, 2010; Cañedo et al., 2022).

[15] Case C/2006 Introduction of digital terrestrial television (DVB-T) in Bavaria; Case C 34/2006 (ex N 29/2005), Introduction of digital terrestrial television (DVB-T) in North RhineWestphalia, Commission decision of 23.10.2007.

[16] Case N 622/2003 Digitalisierungsfonds, Commission decision of 6.3.2005.

[17] Case N 103/2007, Support for the acquisition of digital decoders and for the adaptation of antennas in Soria, Commission decision of 25.9.2007 (OJ C 262, 1.11.2007).

[18] https://ec.europa.eu/commission/presscorner/detail/en/IP_08_490 [last accessed 25.10.2022].

[19] 2009 European Commission IP/09/1072: https://ec.europa.eu/commission/presscorner/detail/en/IP_09_1072 [last accessed 25.10.2022].

[20] These were the German IP/07/543 and MEMO/07/150 cases, Irish IP/08/317, and Belgian IP/08/316 cases, which related to the Commission's approach to public service broadcasting remits in the new media era.

[21] https://eur-lex.europa.eu/legal-content/EN/ALL/?uri=CELEX%3A52009XC1027%2801%29.

Based on the Amsterdam Protocol No 29[22] on the system of public service broadcasting in the member states, which was annexed to the Treaty on the European Union (TEU) and the Treaty on the Functioning of the European Union (TFEU), the Commission acknowledged that member states had jurisdiction for the functioning and funding of public service broadcasting. However, the Commission stipulated that that public funding should not exceed what is necessary for public broadcasters to achieve their public service mission and should not lead to a distortion of market competition. Regarding the relevant cases cited in its 2009 press release on PSB funding, two cases were related to general funding systems, the Belgian case Flemish public service broadcaster VRT case and the Irish public service broadcasters RTÉ and TG4 cases. Commitments were had been required in the cases from Belgium and Ireland relating to revisions of public service missions regarding new media services and safeguards to counter overcompensation, cross-subsidisation, and commercial activities.

The first case the Commission scrutinised under the 2009 Communication was state funding to Austria's ORF, which was required to revise its aid scheme accordingly. In its second case, the Commission opened an investigation into France Télévisions' new funding system which involved the removal of advertising funding. In the same year, the Commission opened an investigation into the new financing of Spain's PSB RTVE which was based on the same model. Both cases were approved in 2010.[23] However, in France, President Sarkozy had proposed that the phasing out of advertising would be compensated by a tax on telecommunications companies of 1.3 per cent of all turnover over 5 million Euros to cross-subsidise PSBs.[24] The battle over the new tax was fought for five years until the French funding model was finally approved by European Commission,[25] only for the decision to be overturned by the ECJ in 2013.

In May 2012, the Commission approved a major reform of state aid rules, the State Aid Modernisation. It permitted member states to approve state aid more quickly at the national level, freeing up the Commission to focus on more serious cases which were likely to distort competition. The State Aid Modernisation brought in a number of rules, some of which had an expiry date of 2020. Procedural rules were outlined in the 2015 Regulation on the application of state aid rules and its implementation Regulation. These were followed by, in 2016, a Notice on the notion of aid which provided further guidance on definitions of state aid. In 2018, the Commission developed a Transparency Award Module for submission and

[22] https://eur-lex.europa.eu/legal-content/EN/TXT/?uri=CELEX%3A12012E%2FPRO%2F29 [last accessed 25.10.2022].

[23] Case C 27/09 Subvention pluriannuelle pour France Télévisions; C 38/09 New tax-based funding system for public broadcasting in Spain (OJ L 1, 4.1.2011, pp. 9–19).

[24] Aide d'état C 27/2009 (ex N 34/A/2009 & N 34/B/2009)—France Subvention budgétaire pour France Télévisions. LOI n° 2009-258 du 5 mars 2009 relative à la communication audiovisuelle et au nouveau service public de la télévision.

[25] http://europa.eu/rapid/press-release_MEMO-13-904_fr.htm [last accessed 25.10.2022].

publication of data on state aid which eased the workload of the Commission and provided greater independence to member states. By the end of 2018, 25 member states had joined the Transparency Award Module and over 43,000 state aid grants had been in 25 member states and Iceland, including state aid to public service broadcasting.

To mitigate the expiration of state aid rules, the Commission applied its Better Regulation Guidelines to evaluation of the rules under the State Aid Modernisation package, accordingly extending their validity beyond 2020. These rules were extended[26] again due to the COVID-19 outbreak with a Regulation (2020/972) and a Communication (C/2020/4355) under the Temporary Framework for State aid measures to support the economy in the current COVID-19 outbreak, and the Recovery and Resilience Facility[27] until the end of 2023. A large number of grants were approved at the European level under the framework to support the media sector ranging from lost revenue from cultural events, gaming, and broadcasting to newspaper markets.[28]

The 2014 Risk Finance Guidelines also expired at the end of 2021 and were replaced with Guidelines on State aid to promote risk finance investments. The Commission continues to make EU-level decisions as demonstrated by its investigation into Czechia's subsidisation of DTT in 2021[29] and into the spending plans of YLE in Finland in 2022 based upon private company complaints. However, between 2009 and 2020, the European Commission had only made 40 PSB decisions at the European level under the 2009 Communication. Notably, it has refrained from taking more political decisions such as intervention into the financing of public service broadcasting in Hungary and Poland as brought by complaints by civil society groups.[30]

Cinema and content production

Subsidies to cinema and audio-visual production have also been scrutinised under EU competition rules. Similar to PSBs, the Commission received a number of complaints about the anti-competitive effects of film subsidies. In 1998, the Commission made a decision on France's scheme of automatic aid for film

[26] https://ec.europa.eu/commission/presscorner/detail/en/ip_20_1247 [last accessed 25.10.2022].
[27] https://competition-policy.ec.europa.eu/state-aid/coronavirus/rrf-guiding-templates_en [last accessed 25.10.2022].
[28] Cases SA.100006, SA.100825, SA.103565, SA.57051, SA.57106, SA.57132, SA.57246, SA.57399, SA.57453, SA.57530, SA.57646, SA.58206, SA.58522, SA.58690, SA.58984, SA.60323, SA.62191, SA.62231, SA.62801, SA.63029, SA.63031, SA.63098, and SA.63172.
[29] https://ec.europa.eu/commission/presscorner/detail/en/IP_22_3462 [last accessed 25.10.2022].
[30] www.ecpmf.eu/european-commission-must-urgently-address-media-market-distortion-in-hungary [last accessed 25.10.2022].

production. As Bellucci (2010) explains, this decision lay the groundwork for the Commission policy on national film support schemes going forward.

Following a sector inquiry, EU member states were required to request prior notification to DG Competition under a set of criteria in a 2001 Communication on certain legal aspects relating to cinematographic and other audio-visual works (the 'Cinema Communication'). Firstly, aid must be directed to a cultural product as defined nationally. Secondly, a producer must be permitted to spend at least 20 per cent of the film budget in other member states. Thirdly, aid was limited to 50 per cent of a production budget. Fourthly, aid for further services such as post-production services was not permitted.

In 2004, two decisions were made under the 2001 Cinema Communication. The Commission approved state aid to film and television production in the German Länder and a Belgium tax shelter. In 2006, a French film fund, a UK film tax incentive scheme,[31] and a German Film Fund were approved by the Commission under the Communication. The film funds differed substantially as demonstrated by the UK tax incentive schemes, as explained in Chapter 3. The French film support scheme covered the development, production, and distribution of films as well as aid to cinemas and the video industry. The German Film Fund provided direct aid for the production of animation films, feature films, and documentaries based upon a culture test. Additionally, the Commission approved film funds in Ireland and Poland and music recordings by new talent in France under Article 87(3)(d)[32] and newspaper distribution in Denmark under Article 87(3)(c).[33]

In 2006, the European Commission extended its 2001 Cinema Communication until 31 December 2009. The Commission also adopted the 2006 Risk Capital Guidelines in the same year. Arguably the most significant decision under the 2001 Communication was the 2007 Dutch film support scheme which the Commission approved upon agreement that the national regulatory authority (NRA) would monitor the scheme for any changes relating to state aid going forward. By 2008, the Commission had approved numerous film support schemes across Europe. The UK's National Endowment for Science, Technology and the Arts' (NESTA's)[34] 35.3-million-Euro funding scheme to support small or medium-sized enterprises was the first state aid package to be approved by the Commission under the Risk Capital Guidelines in 2006.

[31] https://ec.europa.eu/competition/state_aid/cases/201489/201489_629015_97_2.pdf [last accessed 25.10.2022].

[32] Article 87(3)(d) states that 'aid to promote culture and heritage conservation where such aid does not affect trading conditions and competition in the Community to an extent that is contrary to the common interest' shall be considered to be compatible with the common market.

[33] Article 87(3)(c) states that 'aid to facilitate the development of certain economic activities or of certain economic areas, where such aid does not adversely affect trading conditions to an extent contrary to the common interest' shall be compatible with the common market.

[34] Case NN 8/2005 Nesta invention and innovation programme.

In 2009, the Cinema Communication was extended to 31 December 2012 following consultation which, similar to the parallel Communication on public service broadcasting, focused on new media services. The Commission also prolonged its Guidelines on State Aid for Rescuing and Restructuring Firms in Difficulty until October 2012. In 2009, the European Audiovisual Observatory estimated that 1.6 billion Euros were spent on film support schemes annually within the EU and that most aid focused on production in the form of direct grants or tax incentives.[35]

However, the Commission recognised a number of developments in notifications for film state aid towards increased support of film distribution, the digitisation of cinemas, and regional film support schemes. There was also increased aid directed at attracting foreign investment. Accordingly, the 2010 Communication on State aid for films and other audio-visual works extended the scope of the Cinema Communication to permit a broader number of cultural activities and the promotion of cultural heritage.

The Cinema Communication was last revised in 2013.[36] It has not been updated since this time given that projects promoting culture and heritage conservation were included in the 2014 General Block Exemption Regulation (GBER). Accordingly, state aid projects were approved at the national level by member states under the GBER from this time onwards. Indeed, the Commission now permits authorisation of state aid for both commercial and non-commercial broadcasters as long as productions qualified as a cultural product. Post-Brexit, the UK retained the CMA's right to approve aid to promote culture and heritage conservation.[37] Following the UK's lead, in 2017 the Commission turned to the importance of videogames. It approved state aid in the development of videogames in Denmark and Germany[38] based upon cultural significance.[39] Accordingly, in 2018, it approved aid to game development in Belgium, France, and Sweden.[40]

[35] European Audiovisual Observatory, Focus 2009: World film market trends, p. 14.

[36] https://eur-lex.europa.eu/LexUriServ/LexUriServ.do?uri=OJ:C:2013:332:0001:0011:EN:PDF [last accessed 25.10.2022].

[37] www.legislation.gov.uk/ukdsi/2019/9780111178768/data.xht?view=snippet&wrap=true [last accessed 25.10.2022].

[38] State Aid case A.51820—Germany—Video games support—North Rhine Westphalia, Commission decision of 10 December 2018: http://ec.europa.eu/competition/elojade/isef/case_details.cfm?proc_code=3_SA_51820 [last accessed 25.10.2022].

[39] SA.46572—Germany—Bavarian games support measure, Commission decision of 4 September 2017: http://ec.europa.eu/competition/elojade/isef/index.cfm?fuseaction=dsp_result&policy_area_id=3 [last accessed 25.10.2022]; SA.45735—Denmark—Scheme for the development, production and promotion of cultural and educational digital games, Commission decision of 12 May 2017: http://ec.europa.eu/competition/elojade/isef/index.cfm?fuseaction=dsp_result&policy_area_id=3 [last accessed 25.10.2022].

[40] SA.49947—Belgium—Funds for videogames—Flanders, Commission decision of 28 May 2018: http://ec.europa.eu/competition/elojade/isef/index.cfm?fuseaction=dsp_result&policy_area_id=3 [last accessed 25.10.2022]; State aid case SA.50512—France—Fonds d'aide aux jeux video, Commission decision of 21 August 2018: http://ec.europa.eu/competition/elojade/isef/index.cfm?fuseaction=dsp_result&policy_area_id=3 [last accessed 25.10.2022]; SA.49405—Sweden—Media Aid, Commission decision of 22 October 2018: http://ec.europa.eu/competition/elojade/isef/case_details.cfm?proc_code=3_SA_49405 [last accessed 25.10.2022].

Broadband and mobile phone infrastructure

In 2003, the Commission published 'Guidelines on criteria and modalities of implementation of structural funds in support of electronic communications', outlining conditions for the subsidisation of broadband under state aid rules. Based upon the guidelines, the Commission approved a series of subsides for broadband rollout beginning in 2004.[41] Under the guidelines, state-owned broadband was not considered state aid under Article 97(1). Commercial provision needed to comply with public procurement rules. If subsidised, the undertaking could not make a profit. If market provision was already available, state funding should be provided through open call for tender and kept to a minimum to allow the project to proceed.

For example, in 2007, the Commission began investigation into the 'Wireless Prague' project. Prague accordingly significantly downsized the project to the public sector only and access to public sector and e-government websites only to prevent competition with private markets.[42] Under the guidelines, the Commission also assessed aid to mobile phone markets. In 2003, the Commission authorised a rescue package for MobilCom AG in Germany. The company had attempted to set up its own 3G network but ran into financial difficulty. France Télécom assumed 7.1 billion Euros in debt and Germany granted 50 million Euros in state financial aid and guaranteed a loan of 112 million Euros.[43]

The Commission took into consideration that broadband rollout was necessary in geographic areas where there was either no broadband or unsatisfactory coverage. In the Pyrenées-Atlantiques case it was deemed that the project met the criteria set out in the Altmark judgment and therefore it did not constitute aid. In Scotland, the East Midlands, and Lincolnshire the Commission decided state aid did not distort competition and was compatible with Article 87(3)(c). The Commission further approved broadband rollout subsidy schemes in Alto Adige,[44] Baden-Württemberg,[45] Ireland,[46] North Yorkshire,[47] the Sicoval,[48] the Veneto,[49] and Wales.[50]

[41] N213/2003 Project Atlas Broadband infrastructure scheme for business parks, 9.9.2004; N307/2004 Broadband in Scotland Remote and rural areas; N199/2004 Broadband business fund; N381/04 High-speed network project in the Pyrenées-Atlantiques, 16.11.2004; Broadband for SMEs in Lincolnshire—Connecting rural businesses, 15.12.2004.

[42] Case NN 24/2007 Prague Municipal Wireless Network Commission decision, 30.5.2007.

[43] OJ C 80 of 3.4.2003, NN 115, 3.4.2002.

[44] N 473/2007, Broadband connections for Alto Adige, Commission decision of 11.10.2007.

[45] N 570/2007, Broadband in rural areas of Baden-Württemberg, Commission decision of 23.10.2007; N 442/2007.

[46] Cases N 475/2007, National Broadband Scheme Ireland, Commission decision of 25.9.2007.

[47] Cases N 746/2006, North Yorkshire NYNET Project United Kingdom, Commission decision of 21.2.2007.

[48] N 890/2006, Aide du Sicoval pour un réseau de très haut debit, Commission decision of 10.7.2007.

[49] Aid in favour of broadband in remote areas of Veneto, Commission decision of 23.10.2007.

[50] Case N 46/2007 Welsh Public Sector Network Scheme Commission decision, 30.5.2007.

By 2008, the Commission's focus moved to assessing support for very high-speed broadband networks ('next-generation' networks). This resulted in 2009 Guidelines on the application of state aid rules to public funding for the rapid deployment of broadband networks, which emphasised the importance of customer affordability in next-generation broadband deployment. The Commission expanded its assessment of projects beyond basic networks (ADSL, cable, mobile, wireless, or satellite broadband services) to very high-speed next-generation access (NGA) networks (fibre-based or advanced upgraded cable networks). Under the new guidelines the first case to be approved was the French NGA project in Hauts-de-Seine for 59 million Euros.

In 2010, when the European Commission published its Digital Agenda for Europe under the Europe 2020 strategy, it identified the goal of achieving access for all Europeans to internet speeds of above 30 Mbps and for at least 50 per cent of European households to subscribe to internet connections above 100 Mbps. Accordingly, DG Competition revised its assessment of state aid schemes to broadband to acknowledge that private operators might not have sufficient market incentives to provide broadband services. Broadband networks were therefore recognised as SGEI. National incumbents still dominated markets in most states but, under its 2010 Guidelines, the Commission acknowledged that broadband upgrading might encompass a mix of public and private investment. In 2010, the Commission approved 20 state aid schemes for the development of broadband networks worth 1.8 billion Euros.

In 2012, as mentioned above, the Commission approved its State Aid Modernisation package. Under the package it introduced its 2013 Broadband Guidelines, which brought state aid for broadband into line with the objectives of the Digital Agenda. In 2013, it also approved the Enabling Regulation encompassing six new categories of state aid to be included under the 2014 GBER. The six areas were identified, namely innovation aid to large enterprises, broadband infrastructures, aid for culture and heritage (including audio-visual works), aid for sport, aid for natural disasters, and social aid for transport in remote areas. By 2018, the Commission had approved 39 billion Euros in state aid funding and member states had approved 126 broadband state aid projects under the GBER.[51]

The GBER addressed underserved areas and permitted member states to approve state aid to broadband networks without Commission notification. The thresholds for notification to the Commission were also raised. Under the 2013 Community Guidelines for the application of state aid rules in relation to rapid deployment of broadband networks, the Commission exempted categories of aid for broadband infrastructure from notification. These were 'white' areas for basic

[51] European Commission, Directorate-General for Competition, Report on competition policy 2018: including Commission staff working document, Publications Office, 2019: https://data.europa.eu/doi/10.2763/296993.

broadband in regions where there was no infrastructure, small aid packages for NGA rollout in white areas, and aid related to civil engineering works.

In 2016, the Commission published its Communication 'Connectivity for a Competitive Digital Single Market: Towards a European Gigabit Society', which identified very high-capacity network rollout as a strategic priority. State aid was recognised as a means to achieving this. The Communication set further targets for internet connections for schools, transport hubs, and providers of public services for download/upload speeds of 1 Gigabit of data per second by 2025. It aimed for European households to have access to speeds of at least 100 Mbps, to be upgraded to 1 Gigabit by 2025. Urban areas and major terrestrial transport paths were to have uninterrupted 5G coverage by 2025.

A number of gigabit schemes were accordingly approved under state aid. In 2016, the Commission approved the French broadband scheme 'Plan Très Haut Débit', the Italian ultra-broadband plan for 2016–22, and the UK National Broadband Scheme for 2016–20. In 2017, plans were approved for Croatia, Germany, and Poland. In 2018, state aid was approved for Austria,[52] six Bavarian municipalities,[53] Germany,[54] Lithuania,[55] and the Netherlands.[56] A European network of Broadband Competence Offices and the Toolkit for Rural Broadband were established in 2017 to assist with the exchange of knowledge and best practice. In 2019, the Commission approved 2.6 billion Euros in state aid for the Irish National Broadband Plan, a 50-million-Euro voucher scheme in Greece for faster broadband services, and 400 million Euros in state aid for very high-speed broadband networks in Spain[57] and the UK.[58]

[52] State aid case SA.50844—Austria—Broadband Styria, Commission decision of 8 November 2018 and State aid case SA.48325—Austria—NGA-Broadband project in Upper Austria, Commission decision of 26 July 2018: http://ec.europa.eu/competition/elojade/isef/index.cfm?fuseaction=dsp_result&policy_area_id=3 [last accessed 25.10.2022].

[53] State aid case SA.48418—Germany-Bayerisches Gigabit Pilotprojekt (Bavarian gigabit pilot project), Commission decision of 18 December 2018: http://ec.europa.eu/competition/elojade/isef/case_details. cfm?proc_code=3_SA_48418 [last accessed 25.10.2022].

[54] State aid case SA.50847—Germany—Prolongation of NGA Bayern Abänderung (SA.38690), Commission decision of 4 June 2018: http://ec.europa.eu/competition/elojade/isef/index.cfm?fuseaction=dsp_result&policy_area_id=3 [last accessed 25.10.2022].

[55] State aid case SA.49614—Lithuania—Development of Next Generation Access Infrastructure—RAIN 3, Commission decision of 12 October 2018: http://ec.europa.eu/competition/elojade/isef/index.cfm?fuseaction=dsp_result&policy_area_id=3 [last accessed 25.10.2022].

[56] State aid case SA.46613—The Netherlands—Broadband Rivierenland Region, Commission decision of 10 April 2018: http://ec.europa.eu/competition/elojade/isef/index.cfm?fuseaction=dsp_result&policy_area_id=3 [last accessed 25.10.2022].

[57] Case SA.49935 Superfast Broadband (SFBB) Project—Greece, Commission decision of 7 January 2019; Case SA.54472 National Broadband Plan—IE, Commission decision of 15 November 2019.

[58] State aid case SA.49445—UK—Modification of the National Broadband Scheme for the UK for 2016–2020 (BDUK—SA 40720), Commission decision of 15 January 2018: http://ec.europa.eu/competition/elojade/isef/index.cfm?fuseaction=dsp_result&policy_area_id=3 [last accessed 25.10.2022].

In 2017, a Decision[59] was taken by the European Parliament and the Council which enabled the 700 MHz band for the deployment of wireless broadband services by June 2020 to promote 5G introduction. This meant that any prior users needed to leave the band. The Decision allowed remaining terrestrial television services to utilise the band until 2030 and enabled member states to compensate them for spectrum migration. The Commission therefore approved German compensation for migration under state aid in 2018.

A number of further projects were approved between 2018 and 2021. A joint project between France, Germany, Italy, and the UK for research into microelectronics was approved under state aid rules in 2018. In 2020, an Italian scheme for low-income family access to high-speed broadband services and a Greek scheme for students learning online were agreed. In 2021, the 2.1 million Euro deployment of high-performance 5G terrestrial public mobile electronic communications networks ('mobile networks') by the German state and the provision of 4G mobile communications services by the Spanish state[60] were deemed appropriate under state aid rules. Based on these decisions, the Commission widened the scope of the GBER again to include fixed-broadband networks, 4G and 5G mobile networks, and trans-European digital connectivity infrastructure projects in 2021. In 2021, its Communication on State Aid Rules for Important Projects of Common European Interest was approved with application from January 2022. It targets innovation in technology and infrastructure in particular.

Conclusion

Release from EU state aid rules was extolled as a Brexit benefit by the UK government[61] in an effort to provide the UK with greater flexibility and quicker application of aid without undergoing lengthy and complex EU approval.[62] In 2022, the government passed the Subsidy Control Act 2022 which took effect in January 2023. Under the new system, larger subsidies awarded to public authorities and businesses up to £10 million need to be scrutinised by the Subsidy Advice Unit at the CMA.[63] Smaller subsidies under £315,000 are approved under the Minimal

[59] Decision (EU) 2017/899 of the European Parliament and of the Council of 17 May 2017 on the use of the 470–790 MHz frequency band in the Union: https://eur-lex.europa.eu/legal-content/en/ TXT/?uri=CELEX%3A32017D0899 [last accessed 25.10.2022].

[60] https://ec.europa.eu/competition/state_aid/cases1/202203/SA_64394_80CE437E-0000-CD69-844E-F3D5ACFD602C_66_1.pdf [last accessed 25.10.2022].

[61] www.gov.uk/government/news/new-subsidy-control-system-will-support-uk-jobs-boost-the-economy-and-strengthen-the-union [last accessed 25.10.2022].

[62] www.gov.uk/government/news/big-boost-for-uk-economy-as-subsidy-control-system-comes-into-force-from-january [last accessed 25.10.2022].

[63] www.gov.uk/government/publications/guidance-on-the-operation-of-the-subsidy-control-functions-of-the-subsidy-advice-unit/operation-of-the-subsidy-control-functions-of-the-subsidy-advice-unit [last accessed 25.10.2022].

Financial Assistance fund. All grants over £100,000 must be published in a transparency register. Funding must be assessed according to seven Subsidy Control Principles, six or which were outlined in the TCA, unless they are listed in the three streamlined routes: energy usage, R&D, and local growth.

Cultural subsidies fall outside the subsidy definition if they are not commercial. However, the UK prefers tax incentives to direct subsidies for film, as demonstrated in Chapter 3. Funding for broadband has been maintained under the 2022 Autumn budget.[64] There was subsequently continued commitment to the UK's £1 billion Shared Rural Network project which aims to roll out mobile broadband coverage to 95 per cent of the UK and the £5 billion Project Gigabit programme to make gigabit-capable broadband available to 85 per cent of the UK premises by 2025 and 99 per cent nationwide by 2030. However, there have been substantial cuts to PSBs.[65] The BBC licence fee, which accounted for 74 per cent of £5.06 billion of income,[66] was frozen from 2022 to 2024, then will be abolished in 2027. A number of proposals for alternative funding have been put in place, including a direct grant, subscription, and cross-subsidisation from broadband markets. Channel 4 may be sold and lose its PSB remit.[67]

[64] www.ispreview.co.uk/index.php/2022/11/uk-chancellor-protects-gigabit-broadband-and-mobile-funding.html [last accessed 25.10.2022].

[65] https://committees.parliament.uk/publications/5243/documents/52552/default [last accessed 25.10.2022].

[66] https://researchbriefings.files.parliament.uk/documents/CBP-8101/CBP-8101.pdf [last accessed 25.10.2022].

[67] www.gov.uk/government/consultations/consultation-on-a-change-of-ownership-of-channel-4-television-corporation/outcome/government-response-to-the-consultation-on-a-potential-change-of-ownership-of-channel-4-television-corporation [last accessed 25.10.2022].

10
Data Protection and Privacy Post-Brexit

Introduction

Prior to the General Data Protection Regulation (GDPR), considerable variation existed across Europe on regulatory requirements for data protection and privacy. During GDPR negotiations, the UK was able to push through flexible policy solutions to EU legislative reform with the support of key private actors. Since this time, the UK has represented an attractive and stable regulatory environment for data handling in the EU as the Information Commissioner's Office (ICO) is recognised as well resourced in terms of regulatory expertise. This can be seen as a claiming authority strategy (Princen, 2011). However, the UK's new role as a third state removes its influence and status in Europe. Current regulatory proposals risk the UK's adequacy status. This chapter will detail the UK's positions on privacy and data protection, assess the effect of Brexit on the UK, and make some predictions about future UK and EU policy directions.

The history of EU data protection policy and UK entrepreneurship

Historically, there has been substantial divergence between the UK and continental EU states on approaches to regulation of privacy and data protection (Hildén, 2019: 42). This came to the fore in 2012 when the European Commission proposed the revision of the EU's 1995 Data Protection Directive.[1] Article 1(2) of the 1995 Directive ensured the free flow of personal data. But the basis for the GDPR came with Article 16 of the Treaty on the Functioning of the European Union which, post-Lisbon, provided a legal basis for the EU to legislate for 'rules relating to the right to the protection of personal data and the rules relating to the free movement of such data'.[2] This was in recognition of the way in which the internet was increasing cross-border data handling which the EU needed to address.

A number of core issues emerged during negotiation for the GDPR, namely: whether identifiers should be considered 'personal data' (Edwards,

[1] When the 1995 Directive was agreed, the UK abstained from its adoption.

[2] https://eur-lex.europa.eu/legal-content/EN/TXT/HTML/?uri=CELEX:52019DC0250&rid=2 [last accessed 25.10.2022].

Brexit and the Digital Single Market. Alison Harcourt, Oxford University Press. © Alison Harcourt 2023.
DOI: 10.1093/oso/9780192899378.003.0010

2019: 150); whether there should be a single regulatory authority responsible for data protection (based upon the country of origin principle); whether provisions for data profiling should be statutory or self-regulatory; what provisions should be in place for 'Big Data' mining; the time allowed for breach notification; whether there should be a 'right to be forgotten'; rules for data portability; and standards of consent.

National differences in approach could be most clearly seen within the Article 29 Data Protection Working Party (DP WP). The Article 29 DP WP operated as a national regulatory authority (NRA) network under the 1995 Data Protection Directive. It was established as a committee to agree common approaches to personal data issues and consisted of government representatives, regulatory authority representatives, representation from the European Commission, and, from 2004, the European Data Protection Supervisor.[3] It was active until 2018 when it was until it was replaced by the European Data Protection Board (EDPB). Here discrepancy between the UK and other states could be easily observed.

There were national differences in data handling and data processing. For example, prior to the GDPR, northern EU states (Scandinavian states, Finland, Ireland, and the UK) required greater transparency with no barrier fees in the handling of subject access requests wherein individuals could request a copy of information an organisation held on them. For example, companies operating in the UK and Ireland needed only provide data protection agencies with summaries of activities. Other member states, particularly Austria and France, were required to provide highly detailed reports. There was also a long period of ambiguity as to whether the 'right to be forgotten' was an absolute right.

Member states diverged in restraints on the time allowed for breach notification. The 2009 Directive on Privacy and Electronic Communications (e-Privacy Directive) required breach notification periods for telecommunications companies and internet service providers but not for other organisations (Edwards, 2019: 113). According to the 2009 Directive, breach notifications were not required for some communications services if 'the provider has demonstrated to the satisfaction of the competent authority that it has implemented appropriate technological protection measures, and that those measures were applied to the data concerned by the security breach'. Consequently, many member states also differed in their requirements for private and public organisations. As Hildén writes (2019: 150):

> the notification procedure emanated from the French tradition and was not applied elsewhere prior to the Data Protection Directive .... Some of the DPAs were already opposed of the procedure (like the Swedish Datainspektionen), virtually all companies regarded it as useless, and even some civil society organisations did

[3] The European Data Protection Supervisor was established in a 2004 EU Decision.

> not see it as contributing to the privacy of individuals. However, it did have some supporters. The UK Ministry of Justice was against abolishing the notification procedure because the fees helped fund the Information Commissioner's Interest representative's input and policy output Office (ICO). Removing the notification procedure would, in the view of the Ministry of Justice, challenge the independence of the ICO.

Two consultation rounds,[4] including workshops, seminars, and a high-level conference, preceded a proposal for a General Data Protection Regulation in 2012. Consultation over the legal framework for the fundamental right to the protection of personal data took place from 9 July to 31 December 2009 with 168 responses.[5] Consultation on the Commission's comprehensive approach on personal data protection in the EU took place from 4 November 2010 to 15 January 2011[6] with 305 responses, 220 from private organisations, a sizeable proportion of which were located in the UK (Hildén, 2019: 103).

In development of the GDPR, the UK showed a preference for consent by affirmation, whereas many civil society groups and also the European Parliament, as well as key large member states (notably France and Germany), put forward proposals for 'explicit consent' which was eventually adopted under the GDPR. Notwithstanding this outcome, the UK managed to bring about a more self-regulatory approach despite the initial opposition by key member states and the European Parliament. The UK's official response came from the Ministry of Justice and the ICO. This was preceded by a consultation with UK stakeholders by the Ministry for Justice.[7]

The 2015 European Court of Justice (ECJ) decision in Case C-362/14 Maximillian Schrems v Data Protection Commissioner, in which Safe Harbor was declared invalid,[8] paved the way for final agreement on the Regulation which had stagnated for years, particularly as a solution needed to be found for transferring data outside of the EU. Safe Harbor was replaced by Privacy Shield in 2016 which allowed continued data transfer to the US as long as there was adherence to the GDPR. The 2015 ruling was flanked by the 2014 ECJ case, Google Spain SL, Google Inc. v Agencia Española de Protección de Datos, Mario Costeja González over

[4] COM(2010)171 final.

[5] Non-confidential contributions are available here: http://ec.europa.eu/justice/newsroom/data-protection/opinion/090709_en.htm [last accessed 25.10.2022].

[6] Non-confidential contributions are available here: http://ec.europa.eu/justice/newsroom/data-protection/opinion/101104_en.htm [last accessed 25.10.2022].

[7] https://consult.justice.gov.uk/digital-communications/data-protection-proposals-cfe/results/summary-responses-proposed-data-protection-legislation.pdf [last accessed 25.10.2022].

[8] The 2000 Safe Harbor agreement between the US and the EU permitted US self-regulated codes of conduct ('opt out' of data tracking rather than 'opt in') to prevail over EU statutory protection (under Article 12(b) of the 1995 Data Protection Directive) initially for a 20-year period (Zinser, 2004; Swire, 2007; Leathers, 2009; EC, 2010) until struck down by the ECJ in 2015.

ambiguity on the 'right to be forgotten'. A number of remaining issues that were undergoing heated debate were solved more quickly directly following the court's rulings.

Under the resulting 2016 GDPR,[9] subject access requests were updated to include the right to knowledge about storage periods, rights to rectification (to rectify inaccurate personal data) and to erasure, and rights to lodge complaints. Information as to how data protection authorities handle complaints was outlined. Article 17 in the GDPR determined that an individual can request to remove personal data if it is no longer relevant under the 'right to be forgotten and erasure' principle based upon the ECJ ruling.[10] Under Article 18, the right to data portability 'is based on consent or on a contract'. Breach notification was agreed at 24 hours Europe-wide under Article 67.[11] Data protection impact assessments need to be carried out by public authorities (Article 73).

It was under Article 93 that the UK's 'one-stop-shop' approach was adopted. UK stakeholders were overwhelmingly proponents of the 'one-stop-shop' proposal which allows companies to go to one national regulatory authority only for operation across Europe based upon the country of origin principle (ICO, 2013). Accordingly, each state is required to establish a Data Protection Authority (DPA) under the GDPR. The Article 29 Data Protection Working Party was replaced with a European Data Protection Board (EDPB) in 2018 which is made up of national DPAs. For data processing, the Regulation does not require reporting to data protection agencies but obliges companies and organisations to maintain detailed internal records.

The UK was most isolated in its approach to the definition of identifiers. This concerned whether or not an IP address should be seen as an identifier (personal data) and whether this data can be marketed. Article 29 WP viewed IP addresses as identifiers[12] as it recognised that IP addresses can be linked to specific persons (Article 29 WP, 2013). This premise was initially agreed upon by member states in the Article 29 WP which stated in 2008 that 'unless the Internet Service Provider is in a position to distinguish with absolute certainty that the data correspond to users that cannot be identified, it will have to treat all IP information as personal data, to be on the safe side. These considerations will apply equally to search engine operators'.

The UK, however, argued consistently against this view. Instead, it maintained that IP addresses are not be used by data handlers for identification, hence IP

[9] https://eur-lex.europa.eu/legal-content/EN/TXT/?uri=consil:ST_5419_2016_INIT [last accessed 25.10.2022].

[10] However, the court also determined that 'the right to the protection of personal data is not an absolute right'.

[11] https://ico.org.uk/for-organisations/guide-to-data-protection/guide-to-the-general-data-protection-regulation-gdpr/personal-data-breaches [last accessed 09.05.2022].

[12] http://ec.europa.eu/justice/data-protection/article-29/index_en.htm [last accessed 25.10.2022].

addresses are generally not 'personal data'. This is based upon the 'context-based approach' (also called the 'relative approach') wherein data should be considered 'personal' relative to its use (McCullagh, 2007). Under the UK's context-based approach it does not customarily view IP addresses as personal data. The UK was isolated on this position not only within the Article 29 WP but also during GDPR development where most other EU member states maintained that IP addresses should always be considered 'personal data' and therefore could not be passed to third parties without consent.

Notably, France and Germany had adopted lengthy provisions for data profiling and factors used in the mining of 'Big and Smart Data' due to stricter national rules on privacy (Spiecker Döhmann et al., 2018). This approach was adopted by the EU in two ECJ cases. In the 2011 Scarlet Extended case, the ECJ ruled that static IP addresses 'are protected personal data because they allow those users to be precisely identified'. In the 2016 ECJ Patrick Breyer v Bundesrepublik Deutschland case, the EU decided that dynamic IP addresses can also be considered personal data. However, the court shied away from taking an 'absolute approach' (Finck and Pallas, 2020: 17–18).

However, at the same time, the 2013 František Ryneš ECJ case provided an exemption to notification in the processing of personal data under the 1995 Data Protection Directive.[13] Based upon this premise, the UK's ICO argued during GDPR consultation that a 'simple "all or nothing" approach to data protection coverage no longer suffices, given the breadth of information now falling within the definition of personal data'.[14] Private sector associations flanked the UK approach. For example, the Interactive Advertising Bureau Europe representing 5,000 companies in Europe argued that data linked to IP addresses should be considered personal for some companies, e.g. by internet service providers who can link data to identified individuals but not by data-handling companies.[15]

Eventually, member states agreed to flexibility with respect to the definition of 'data controller' in agreement of the GDPR. Compromise was found in that the definition of personal data ('online identifiers') was widened to include Cookie IDs, device IDs, and IP addresses[16] and stringent requirements were introduced for automatic processing for data-handling companies. But, if companies can prove that data is being collected for 'legitimate purpose', they can retain it if they sufficiently secure the data. In this way, the UK's more flexible approach was accommodated.

[13] C-212/13—Ryneš František Ryneš v Úřad pro ochranu osobních údajů.

[14] http://ec.europa.eu/justice/news/consulting_public/0003/contributions/public_authorities/ico_uk_en.pdf [last accessed 25.10.2022].

[15] http://ec.europa.eu/justice/news/consulting_public/0003/contributions/organisations/iab_europe_en.pdf [last accessed 25.10.2022].

[16] https://ico.org.uk/for-organisations/guide-to-data-protection/guide-to-the-general-data-protection-regulation-gdpr/what-is-personal-data/what-are-identifiers-and-related-factors [last accessed 25.10.2022].

The Proposal for a Regulation of the European Parliament and of the Council concerning the respect for private life and the protection of personal data in electronic communications (Regulation on Privacy and Electronic Communications or e-Privacy Regulation) is undergoing trilogue at the time of writing in 2022. It covers electronic communications content which crosses services and networks and its corresponding metadata.[17] The Regulation was proposed by the Commission in January 2017 and at the time of writing the last version was agreed in February 2021.[18] It applies Article 83 of the GDPR to Regulation infringements, namely 'fines up to EUR 10,000,000, or in the case of an undertaking, up to 2 per cent of the total worldwide annual turnover of the preceding financial year, whichever is higher'.

The Regulation targets direct cross-border marketing, Big Data, telemarketing, and business-to-business sharing (B2B). Data capture is used in marketing, which raises questions about: definitions of explicit consent for cookie use, harmonisation on conditions governing electronic communications use, use of electronic communications for marketing, and B2B. Stakeholders were consulted on periods for confidentiality of communications, rules on data traffic and location, unsolicited online marketing, bill itemisation, call restrictions, subscriber directories, and automatic call forwarding. The UK's position on tracking, self-regulated 'codes of conduct', and what constitutes a breach of confidentiality differed markedly from that of key member states, particularly Germany and France.

The Regulation deals with unsolicited marketing communications such as spam emails and texts and telephone calls. Marketing communications should be clearly labelled and consumers should be able to opt out and/or block such communications. However, exemptions are allowed for direct marketing if end users have given prior consent and not initially refused contact and also if a customer has bought products or services from a supplier previously. The European Commission also proposed that the GDPR's provisions relating to confidentiality be extended to over-the-top (OTT) services including Voice over Internet Protocol (VoIP) (such as Skype), web mail, instant messaging (such as WhatsApp), and instant messaging via social networks (such as Facebook) in revision of e-Privacy. This would extend current rules that protect confidentiality over telephones, emails, and SMSs to OTT services. This includes confidentiality of metadata such as time, location, and sender information. The UK was not in favour of this extension as voiced in the 2016 Department for Digital, Culture, Media and Sport (DCMS) Review of the EU's Electronic Communications Regulatory Framework.

[17] www.consilium.europa.eu/en/press/press-releases/2021/02/10/confidentiality-of-electronic-communications-council-agrees-its-position-on-eprivacy-rules [last accessed 25.10.2022].

[18] https://data.consilium.europa.eu/doc/document/ST-6087-2021-INIT/en/pdf [last accessed 25.10.2022].

Regarding metadata, the proposal permits processing in four cases: the provision of service requirements,[19] for billing purposes, for security protection during a connection, or when 'providers of electronic communications services ... obtain end-users' consent to process electronic communications metadata'. Metadata needed for service provision must be anonymised if no consent is obtained. Trilogue debate has surrounded whether this anonymised data can be used for purposes other than the original collection. A salient part of the debate concerns whether states can derogate from rules on metadata retention for the purpose of specific public interests, namely 'criminal detection or prosecution of criminal offences, or the execution of criminal penalties'. There has been disagreement between France, which wishes to retain metadata information, and Germany, which is opposed to possible mass data retention. The European Data Protection Board (EDPB) also expressed concerns regarding 'processing and retention of electronic communication data for the purposes of law enforcement and safeguarding national security'[20] and that they remain compatible with ECJ case law which mandates targeted measures only.

The proposal importantly reopened the debate on cookie and device ID use. The e-Privacy Regulation is aimed at simplifying consent for cookies in order that cookie request banners and notices will no longer be constantly popping up on users' screens. However, the proposal notes that 'it may become more difficult for online targeted advertisers to obtain consent if a large proportion of users opt for "reject third party cookies" settings'. The proposal recommendations is for operators to obtain consent via 'individual requests' to end users.

There have been a number of ECJ cases on the use of cookies. In 2022, in case C-319/20 brought by the Federation of German Consumer Organisations (Verbraucherzentrale Bundesverband—VZBV) against Meta (formerly Facebook), the ECJ decided that consumer protection organisations should be able to prosecute data protection violations in addition to DPAs. The query from the German national court dealt with whether Article 80 precluded the consumer organisations' role if intervention was not requested by the data subject. The case dealt with Facebook's hosting of third-party game websites. The VZBV claimed that Meta was not complying with requirements for 'effective consent' under the GDPR. Indeed, Germany has in many ways pre-empted the e-Privacy Regulation with introduction of its 2021 data protection act, the Telekommunikation-Telemedien-Datenschutz-Gesetz (TTDSG), which provides a high level of consumer data protection.

The e-Privacy proposal does not, as in the GDPR, provide a one-stop shop for regulation. Instead, under Article 18, each member state needs to provide a

[19] Requirements are outlined in the 2018 Directive (EU) 2018/1972 OF of the European Parliament and of the Council of 11 December 2018 establishing the European Electronic Communications Code.

[20] https://edpb.europa.eu/system/files/2021-03/edpb_statement_032021_eprivacy_regulation_en_0.pdf [last accessed 25.10.2022].

national regulatory authority for oversight of the regulation. The supervisory authority should meet GDPR requirements. It does not need to be the same NRA that implements the GDPR, despite this provision having been recommended by the EDPB, but cooperation between the two authorities is required.

The Regulation on the free flow of non-personal data was approved in 2018 which prevents states from installing data localisation restrictions, unless for national security. As explained by Perarnaud (2021), the request for the legislation came from the UK and Northern European states with support from Central and Eastern European states in a letter to Donald Tusk, president of the European Council, in 2016. Opposition came from France and Germany. Support from the Regulatory Scrutiny Board (RSB) and the Commission in coalition with supportive states was able to push through the initiative.

The 2018 Regulation only applies to EU states and permits organisations to store and process data within and across the EU. This is mainly targeted at cloud storage and also public authorities to enable access when data is located in another EU state. Access by the private sector embeds a substantial amount of self-regulation with the development of codes of conduct overseeing conditions under which users can move data between cloud service providers. This is outlined in the 2019 Communication Guidance on the Regulation on a framework for the free flow of non-personal data. The Communication requires agreement between member states and sector stakeholders in the form of workshops and monitoring exercises executed by 'self-regulatory cloud stakeholder groups' developing codes of conduct and cloud security certification schemes.[21]

Related to the GDPR and e-Privacy Regulations, in 2022 the European Commission approved its European Strategy for Data. It provides for neutral spaces where organisations can voluntarily trade data which will not be subject to privacy breaches or data misuse regulations. Organisations which meet the criteria will be listed in a public register. Included are rules for the use of public sector data and the 'sharing of data among businesses, against remuneration in any form'. Chapter IV of the agreement includes facilitation of 'data altruism' which permits organisations to register as 'Data Altruism Organisation(s) recognised in the EU', which can release data on a not-for-profit basis, 'allowing data use on altruistic grounds'. A Data Innovation Board will be set up. There is a mechanism for the exchange of public sector data with third-country organisations, but not industrial data, with adequacy decisions in place for individual non-EU countries. As with the GDPR, the European Commission will adopt model contractual clauses and publish examples of private contracts which meet compliance.

A key component of the European Strategy for Data is a Regulation on harmonised rules on fair access to and use of data ('Data Act') which was proposed in 2022.

[21] https://digital-strategy.ec.europa.eu/en/news/cloud-stakeholder-working-groups-start-their-work-cloud-switching-and-cloud-security-certification [last accessed 25.10.2022].

Its main aim is to promote data sharing in public and private sectors. It builds on the 2019 Open Data Directive which facilitated data sharing in the public sector and publicly funded research. It aims to address legal certainty for the generation of data outlining under which conditions data can be used and shared. The 2019 Directive addressed fairness in contractual terms in an aim to empower small or medium-sized enterprise (SMEs) when entering into agreements to access data held by large corporations. The Commission plans to develop model contract clauses ('smart contracts') for fair data sharing.

Under the proposed Act, cloud service providers will need to permit customers (including companies) to switch from one service to another more easily. This is to close a legal gap in data portability rights as the GDPR only covers personal data. Currently, 'vendor lock-in' is dealt with on a self-regulatory basis only within the 2018 Free Flow of Non-Personal Data Regulation. The most controversial part of the proposal is that private companies will be compelled to share data to public sector organisations in the case of the public interest ('exceptional data need') which has been criticised in a joint statement by the EDPB and European Data Protection Supervisor (EDPS).[22]

Nine initial Common European data spaces have been created for data sharing under the European Data Strategy.[23] A key issue is interoperability for which the Commission is recommending harmonisation based upon European Standards Organisation (ESO) standards. The initial Data Act draft also contained a data localisation requirement for 'data sharing services' to be EU based only. This flanked the geolocation requirements within the 2018 Free Flow of Non-Personal Data Regulation. However, this was changed in the published proposal which includes rules for third-country data transfer. In March 2022, the European Commission and United States also announced a Trans-Atlantic Data Privacy Framework.[24] The Data Act also proposal recommends the establishment of a European Data Innovation Board to be composed of NRAs for the promotion of best practice. Lastly, it clarifies that sui generis protection of data rights does not apply to data generated by machine learning and other technologies.

The Data Act also builds on the 2019 EU Regulation on platform-to-business (P2B) regulations, which regulate conditions for sellers which provide products to consumers through online platforms, e.g. shops located on Etsy. Under the accompanying 2020 Guidelines on ranking transparency, platforms are required to adhere to the transparency of 'the use of algorithmic sequencing, rating or review

[22] https://edpb.europa.eu/system/files/2022-05/edpb-edps_joint_opinion_22022_on_data_act_proposal_en.pdf [last accessed 25.10.2022].

[23] http://dataspaces.info/common-european-data-spaces/#page-content [last accessed 25.10.2022].

[24] https://ec.europa.eu/commission/presscorner/api/files/attachment/872132/Trans- Atlantic%20Data%20Privacy%20Framework.pdf.pdf and www.whitehouse.gov/briefing-room/statements-releases/2022/03/25/fact-sheet-united-states-and-european-commission-announce-trans-atlantic-data-privacy-framework [both last accessed 25.10.2022].

mechanisms, visual highlights, or other saliency tools, or combinations thereof'. This will be strengthened by the Digital Markets Act which requires gatekeeper platforms to share data models with consumers. The 2022 Data Act extends this requirement to end users which collect product-generated data. This is overseen by the Observatory on the Online Platform Economy.[25]

Despite substantial revision to EU legislation, it is estimated that 92 per cent of the world's data is still processed within the United States.[26] Academics have articulated concern about global market concentration with Amazon Web Services (AWS) and Google Cloud Platform dominating the market (Floridi, 2020). A market response to this has been Microsoft's 'EU Data Boundary for the Microsoft Cloud' service which processes and stores company data solely within the EU.[27] However, this has come under challenge from European groups due to market dominance and customer lock in (Chee, 2022). The EU's response to the dominance by US groups has been to support the France–Germany initiative GAIA-X to harmonise standards and practices within the EU and to introduce a Cloud Code of Conduct in 2021.[28] Cloud storage provides remote computing service access not available on local services such as AI, 5G, and IoT and is viewed as cost efficient. Under the Code, which was developed by the Cloud Infrastructure Services Providers in Europe (CISPE), 'independent monitoring bodies' will oversee operators approved by national DPAs.

Policy divergence post-Brexit

Post-Brexit, the GDPR was maintained in the UK through amendment of the Data Protection Act 2018,[29] referred to as the 'UK GDPR'. National debate remains, however, on whether cookies can be considered 'personal data' within the UK. As Spiecker Döhmann et al. (2018) note, 'As the UK considers its future approach to data protection in the light of Brexit ... [w]hether cookies are considered personal data is contextual: the ICO notes that though the PECR apply to all cookies, the DPA applies only to cookies that "process personal data", implying that "anonymised" cookie data do not constitute personal data while whether IP addresses constitute personal data under UK law remains uncertain'.

Until 30 June 2021, data flowed between the EU/European Economic Area and UK continued under the EU–UK Trade and Cooperation Agreement. In June 2021, the European Commission decided that the UK would remain adequate under EU data protection rules for cross-border data transfer post-Brexit.[30] The

25 https://platformobservatory.eu [last accessed 25.10.2022].
26 www.weforum.org/agenda/2021/03/europe-digital-sovereignty [last accessed 25.10.2022].
27 https://blogs.microsoft.com/eupolicy/2021/05/06/eu-data-boundary [last accessed 25.10.2022].
28 https://eucoc.cloud/en/about/about-eu-cloud-coc [last accessed 25.10.2022].
29 www.legislation.gov.uk/ukpga/2018/12/contents/enacted [last accessed 25.10.2022].
30 https://ec.europa.eu/commission/presscorner/detail/en/ip_21_3183 [last accessed 25.10.2022].

adequacy decision was granted by EU member states under the comitology procedure.[31] In its decision, the European Commission took into consideration the opinion of the EDPB and the 2020 Max Schrems II judgment under which the ECJ reassessed standard contractual clauses (SCCs). SCCs establish a contract between data exporters within EU states and data importers in third countries such as the UK under approval by the European Commission. The ruling noted that SCCs do not bind organisations who are not party to agreements, including NRAs such as the ICO. The decision therefore arguably curbed the ICO's power to guarantee GDPR-standard protection within the UK. The decisions were updated in October 2022 with two adequacy decisions, one under the GDPR[32] and the other for the Law Enforcement Directive.[33]

From March 2022, following Schrems II, a Transfer Impact Assessment (TIA) is needed to judge the impact personal data transfers to third states may have on privacy which is written by a controller or a processor. The data controller or a processor must make an assessment as to whether the laws of the state to which the data is being transferred present surveillance risks, i.e. whether they can be accessed by those states' governments. This is based upon the Schrems II decision which stated that 'above all, for that controller or processor to verify, on a case-by-case basis and, where appropriate, in collaboration with the recipient of the data, whether the law of the third country of destination ensures adequate protection, under EU law, of personal data transferred pursuant to standard data protection clauses, by providing, where necessary, additional safeguard to those offered by those clauses'.

The European Commission subsequently took a decision in June 2021 which established updated standard contractual clauses based upon the Schrems II case. Clause 19 states 'the transfer and processing of personal data under standard contractual clauses should not take place if the laws and practices of the third country of destination prevent the data importer from complying with the clauses'.[34] Under Module Four, transfer processor to controller ('where the EU processor combines the personal data received from the third country-controller with personal data collected by the processor in the EU'), the following is required:

[31] The European Commission has provided adequacy decisions to Andorra, Argentina, Canada (commercial organisations only), the Faroe Islands, Guernsey, Israel, the Isle of Man, Japan, Jersey, New Zealand, the Republic of Korea, Switzerland, the United Kingdom, and Uruguay. These are referred to as 'white-listed' countries. The United Kingdom is also permitted to exchange data with EU states for law enforcement purposes under the EU's Law Enforcement Directive ((EU) 2016/680).

[32] https://ec.europa.eu/info/files/draft-decision-adequate-protection-personal-data-united-kingdom-general-data-protection-regulation_en [last accessed 25.10.2022].

[33] https://ec.europa.eu/info/files/draft-decision-adequate-protection-personal-data-united-kingdom-law-enforcement-directive_en [last accessed 25.10.2022].

[34] https://eur-lex.europa.eu/legal-content/EN/TXT/?uri=CELEX:32021D0914 [last accessed 25.10.2022].

> (a) The Parties warrant that they have no reason to believe that the laws and practices in the third country of destination applicable to the processing of the personal data by the data importer, including any requirements to disclose personal data or measures authorising access by public authorities, prevent the data importer from fulfilling its obligations under these Clauses. This is based on the understanding that laws and practices that respect the essence of the fundamental rights and freedoms and do not exceed what is necessary and proportionate in a democratic society to safeguard one of the objectives listed in Article 23(1) of Regulation (EU) 2016/679, are not in contradiction with these Clauses. (b) The Parties declare that in providing the warranty in paragraph (a), they have taken due account in particular of the following elements: (i) the specific circumstances of the transfer, including the length of the processing chain, the number of actors involved and the transmission channels used; intended onward transfers; the type of recipient; the purpose of processing; the categories and format of the transferred personal data; the economic sector in which the transfer occurs; the storage location of the data transferred and format of the transferred personal data; the economic sector in which the transfer occurs; the storage location of the data transferred; (ii) the laws and practices of the third country of destination—including those requiring the disclosure of data to public authorities or authorising access by such authorities—relevant in light of the specific circumstances of the transfer, and the applicable limitations and safeguards (12); (iii) any relevant contractual, technical or organisational safeguards put in place to supplement the safeguards under these Clauses, including measures applied during transmission and to the processing of the personal data in the country of destination.

Schrems was interpreted by the EDPB in June 2021.[35] According to the EDPB Recommendations, if data is transferred to a third country without an adequacy decision from the European Commission, the data controller must determine whether 'anything in the law and/or practices in force in the third country that may impinge on the effectiveness of the appropriate safeguards of the transfer tools you are relying on, in the context of your specific transfer. Your assessment should be focused first and foremost on third country legislation that is relevant to your transfer and the Article 46 GDPR transfer tool you are relying on'. Interviews showed that this is the most difficult requirement of Schrems to implement as company data controllers do often not feel qualified to make these assessments and need to hire outside legal counsel. The extra cost plus the risk of fines has constrained the willingness to transfer data to third states.

The UK announced a National Data Strategy in 2020.[36] In 2021, a National Data Strategy Forum was set up alongside publication of a National Data Strategy

[35] https://edpb.europa.eu/system/files/2021-06/edpb_recommendations_202001vo.2.0_supplementarymeasurestransferstools_en.pdf [last accessed 25.10.2022].
[36] www.gov.uk/government/publications/uk-national-data-strategy [last accessed 25.10.2022].

Mission. The DCMS ran a consultation in 2021 entitled 'Data: A New Direction' with the aim of updating the UK's Data Protection Act 2018 which implemented the GDPR. This will take the form of a Data Reform Bill which was announced in the Queen's Speech, which was proposed as the Data Protection and Digital Information Bill (DPDI) in July 2022.[37] The Queen's Speech declared that the UK intended to create a 'less burdensome data rights regime compared to the EU's GDPR', signalling changes at the national level. The ICO is also undergoing substantial reform at the time of writing. It is also updating guidance on a range of issues.[38] At the same time, the UK is attempting to foster greater data exchange agreements through international fora such as the Global Privacy Assembly and the Commonwealth Common Thread Network.

The DPDI was proposed in 2022. Part I of the Bill deals with changes to the general framework on data protection, subject access requests, automatic data processing, obligations of controllers and processors, international transfer, research, and national security exemptions. Part II stipulates the framework for the sharing of data with the private sector and digital identities. Under Part III, BEIS deals with the use of customer and business data, including smart data services. Part IV changes the use of personal data at the domestic level in public services, particularly in relation to digital verification services, health, security, and social care. There is expected to be much greater data sharing between existing civil service department databases and the home office. Part V abolishes the ICO and replaces it with the Information Commission.

The Act also abolishes the office of Surveillance Camera Commissioner and the Office of Commissioner for the Retention and Use of Biometric Material. The requirement for the retention of Records of Processing Activities (ROPAs) had been removed and replaced with reduced Records of Processing of Personal Data (RPPDs). Data Protection Impact Assessments (DPIAs) are updated with less detailed Assessments of High-Risk Processing. Data controllers are no longer required to consult the ICO on high-risk DPIAs. International transfer requirements have been loosened with the introduction of a 'data protection test' to determine whether 'the country or by the organisation is not materially lower than the standard of the protection' in the UK.

The DPDI was accompanied by a proposal for a 'Bill of Rights'.[39] Stakeholders to the 2022 consultation were overwhelmingly opposed to the Bill of Rights reform.[40] The Law Society commented, 'We're concerned the Bill of Rights Bills would

[37] https://bills.parliament.uk/bills/3322 [last accessed 25.10.2022].

[38] See, for example, the draft guidance on anonymisation of data: https://ico.org.uk/about-the-ico/ico-and-stakeholder-consultations/ico-call-for-views-anonymisation-pseudonymisation-and-privacy-enhancing-technologies-guidance [last accessed 25.10.2022].

[39] https://bills.parliament.uk/bills/3227 [last accessed 25.10.2022].

[40] www.gov.uk/government/consultations/human-rights-act-reform-a-modern-bill-of-rights [last accessed 25.10.2022].

damage the rule of law and make it harder for people to protect their rights'.[41] In particular, the Society took issue with the fact that the law would require persons to provide evidence that they have 'suffered (or would suffer) a significant disadvantage in relation to the act (or proposed act)' in order to take a claim to court; that deportation orders made by the secretary of state for offenders would face higher thresholds based on the rights to private and family life; the removal of courts' jurisdiction to interpret legislation for compatibility with the European Convention on Human Rights; and restricting human rights claims from overseas military operations.

Both the DPDI and the Bill of Rights reform arguably threaten the UK's adequacy under the GDPR. The Information Commissioner's response to the Ministry of Justice consultation on Human Rights Act Reform[42] warns:

> The government will be aware that the European Commission considered that the UK's domestic and international commitments to human rights were particularly important elements for its adequacy decisions in respect of the UK. The Human Rights Act 1998 and the European Convention on Human Rights (ECHR) are referenced extensively throughout both decisions .... Cooperation on law enforcement and criminal justice between the UK and the EU under the Trade and Cooperation Agreement is also underpinned by the UK's human rights commitments ... the Government should be aware that failure to adhere to the UK's commitments under the ECHR may affect compliance with those instruments and represent a risk to adequacy. In order to maintain EU adequacy decisions, the Government should ensure its proposals continue to effectively implement the ECHR in British law. A November 2020 report estimated the impact on the British economy of not having such decisions in place as a cost of £1–1.6 billion.

Human rights were also a key consideration in the 2021 European Parliament resolution of on the adequate protection of personal data by the United Kingdom.[43]

Conclusion

As detailed in the government paper 'The Benefits of Brexit', under the data component of trade negotiations, the government intends to establish 'new data adequacy partnerships' with new partners 'such as Australia, the United States, Singapore

[41] www.lawsociety.org.uk/topics/human-rights/human-rights-act-reforms [last accessed 25.10.2022].
[42] https://ico.org.uk/media/about-the-ico/consultation-responses/4018588/dcms-consultation-response-20211006.pdf [last accessed 25.10.2022].
[43] https://eur-lex.europa.eu/legal-content/EN/TXT/HTML/?uri=CELEX:52021IP0262 [last accessed 25.10.2022].

and the Republic of Korea, and free zones in the UAE'.[44] Areas targeted are 'finance, technology and professional and business services' which are areas where trade in services is increasing between these states. However, the 2022 UK GDPR rules have created additional costs for companies trading with these states. In particular, financial service companies are reporting falling short of GDPR rules in audits by large accountancy firms.

The UK GDPR, which came into force in March 2022, introduced DPIAs which require companies to implement risk assessments under Schrems for transfer outside the EU. Exporters can utilise either the international data transfer agreement (IDTA) or the UK addendum when making restricted transfers. Under IDTA contracts, the ICO has stipulated that UK-based companies and organisations can transfer personal data to third countries without the new EU's 2021 SCCs, whereas the UK addendum implements the 2021 EU SCCs. The new SCCs refer to Article 35 of the GDPR which states that a DPIA must consider 'risks to the rights and freedoms of natural persons', which comprises both risks to privacy and data protection, but also wider fundamental rights and interests implementing the 2021 EC Decision and EDPB Recommendations on Schrems II. Interviews indicate that companies mainly rely on the six principles from the EDPB Recommendations in assessing risk.

If data is transferred to a country without an adequacy decision, which encompasses trading partners important to the UK such as the US, India, and Singapore,[45] the data controller must complete a Transfer Impact Assessment (TIA) which performs a risk assessment as to whether the laws of the states to which the data is being transferred present surveillance risks. Interviews have shown that the surveillance risk assessment in particular has greatly increased workloads for companies. Companies report lack of expertise and often reliance on the Democracy Index by the Economist Intelligence Unit (EIU) to form methodologies. Oftentimes assessments result in increases in internal staff costs and the necessity to hire external lawyers to provide counsel on security risks of third states. As a consequence of the additional costs, companies often take decisions not to trade with third countries. There are additional constraints put on UK companies from partners in Nordic states and Germany in particular. Clients are also requesting detailed TIA amendments. Amazon or Google use has also been flagged as an issue of concern with continental European clients.

The DPDI Bill aims to loosen third-country risk assessment as outlined above. However, the Bill is coming under substantial criticism from digital rights groups. In particular, as with the Online Safety Bill and changes to public interest

[44] https://assets.publishing.service.gov.uk/government/uploads/system/uploads/attachment_data/file/1054643/benefits-of-brexit.pdf [last accessed 25.10.2022].

[45] www.gov.uk/government/publications/uk-singapore-digital-economy-agreement-explainer/uk-singapore-digital-economy-agreement-final-agreement-explainer [last accessed 25.10.2022].

definitions under competition law, the DPDI provides much greater power to the secretary of state. Indeed, the DPDI draft Bill mentions the secretary of state 192 times. Secretary of state powers relate to definitions of 'legitimate use', automatic decision-making, and approval of a new Code of practice about the disclosure of information. The secretary of state powers would weaken the independence of the ICO, which is a requirement of the GDPR, but also decrease regulatory (and hence market) certainty given that governments, and secretaries of state, change and their opinions with them. There are also more exemptions under the Act relating to national security. The Bill is undergoing scrutiny at the time of writing. Ministerial decisions are expected to be discussed with the European Commission.

Lastly, as Bradford (2020: 149–153) writes, most countries are mimicking EU GDPR legislation in regulatory reform on data protection in recognition of its importance for trade, including Japan, the Republic of Korea, and Latin American and African states,[46] but also states within the US. Canada's new privacy law the 2022 Canadian Consumer Privacy Protection Act also incorporates many of the GDPR's provisions. Corporations globally too have adapted to EU regulation in what Bradford (2020) terms the 'Brussels Effect'. The EU has also not shied away from fining large US corporations over data breaches, as demonstrated in 2022 when the Irish DPA fined Meta 405 million Euros for the release of children's data between Instagram and Meta. Companies have consequently sunk considerable costs in implementing the GDPR, often applying EU rules globally. As with online platform regulation, this indicates that global corporations will most likely prefer EU data protection law to UK law.

[46] Argentina, Brazil, Chile, Colombia, Costa Rica, Mexico, Peru, and Uruguay; and Senegal and South Africa.

11
Brexit and Copyright

Introduction

The UK continues to be governed by international copyright treaties. It is signature to the 1886 Berne Convention, 1961 International Convention for the Protection of Performers, Producers of Phonograms and Broadcasting Organizations (1961 Rome Convention), 1971 Geneva Convention for the Protection of Producers of Phonograms Against Unauthorized Duplication of their Phonograms, 1974 Convention Relating to the Distribution of Programme-Carrying Signals Transmitted by Satellite, 1995 TRIPS agreement, 1996 Copyright Treaty (WCT), and 1996 Performances and Phonograms Treaty (WPPT), all of which are implemented by the World Intellectual Property Organization (WIPO).

However, the UK is no longer following EU copyright legislation and is treated as a third country post-Brexit. This chapter analyses the UK's historical position on EU copyright legislation, then assesses divergence post-Brexit and consequences for the sector. It is organised as follows: firstly, the chapter tracks the history of EU copyright legislation while analysing the UK's position therein. It then assesses changes to UK copyright rules post-Brexit. The conclusion discusses the future trajectory of UK and EU copyright legislation.

The history of EU copyright legislation

There is a historical dissimilarity between continental European moral rights and UK economic rights approaches to copyright. As Rosati (2021: 56) writes, 'EU copyright law harmonization has been hampered by the iconic divide between the civil law ("droit d'auteur") tradition and the common law vision of copyright, whose most prominent representative has been the UK'. Under the 1988 Copyright, Designs and Patents Act which is the key piece of legislation for copyright in the UK, moral rights are granted to authors under chapter IV. However, unlike most continental European states, the UK permits authors to sign away their moral rights by legal contract. As Porter (1989) explains, this was a key stumbling block to greater European harmonisation in copyright. The UK did not have a rental right for individual authors and performers as proposed in the European Commission green paper on copyright in its 1988 Green Paper on Copyright and

Brexit and the Digital Single Market. Alison Harcourt, Oxford University Press. © Alison Harcourt 2023.
DOI: 10.1093/oso/9780192899378.003.0011

the Challenge of Technology. The UK also did not impose levies on recordings but supported commercial provision to the public.

Authors' rights permit an author an exclusive right of authorising the reproduction of his or her works as protected in Article 9 of the 1886 international Berne Convention. Related rights make copyright available for use for a specified period of time for commercial advantage. Normally, related rights duration is shorter than authors' rights duration. Altogether, EU legislation has harmonised the length of authors' rights, related rights, the purpose of licensing of content, and the management of collective licensing, under which creators transfer their rights to agencies.

As with much internal market legislation, the European Court of Justice (ECJ) has been a key actor in copyright legislation. This began with harmonisation of authors' rights and related rights. Two ECJ cases laid the basis for the initial 1992 Council Directive on rental right and lending right and on certain rights related to copyright in the field of intellectual property (the Rental Directive) (Mazziotti, 2021: 210). In the 1988 Warner Brothers and Metronome Video v Erik Viuff Christiansen case, the court recognised the right of Denmark to restrict video-cassette distribution in the UK based upon rights holders' copyright restrictions. Similarly, in the EMI Electrola v Patricia and others case, the ECJ agreed with blocking of the sale of vinyl records in Germany based upon national Danish copyright expiration. The Directive ensured that authors of literary, musical, dramatic, and artistic works were granted exclusive rental and lending rights. Performers were granted exclusive rights to recordings of performances. Authors who transfer exclusive rights retained the right to 'equitable remuneration' for the rental of the sound recording or film.

One year later, the 1993 Directive on the coordination of certain rules concerning copyright and rights related to copyright applicable to satellite broadcasting and cable retransmission (SatCab Directive) was agreed. The SatCab Directive allowed linear content (satellite channels, cable, and digital terrestrial packages) to be broadcast from one member state to another without restrictions. It also addressed copyright issues, namely the protection of copyright for the original owners (performers and record producers), in cross-border broadcasting.

As Renda et al. (2015: 7) explain, precedence for the Directive can be found in the 1982 Coditel SA, Compagnie générale pour la diffusion de la télévision, and others v Ciné-Vog Films SA and others case wherein the ECJ 'made it clear that the principle of Community-wide exhaustion applied only to the physical dissemination of copyrighted goods, without extending it to intangible forms of commercial exploitation such as a cross border re-transmission of a film'. In the case, the court ruled that a film broadcast (classified as a service) from Belgium to Germany needed copyright permission from the rights holders. This upheld the exclusive rights of authors and ensured that broadcasting rights for satellite needed to be agreed on contractual basis. However, rights cleared in one state could be recognised as cleared in other member states, which greatly simplified requirements for cross-border broadcasting.

SatCab was flanked by the 1993 Directive harmonising the term of protection of copyright and certain related rights (the Duration Directive). The Directive harmonised the copyright of authors of literary or artistic work to 70 years after death; cinematographic or audio-visual works to 70 years after the death of the last of principal director, the author of the screenplay, or the author of the dialogue and the composer of music used in the work. The rights of producers of phonograms were set at 50 years after the fixation is made. Copyright for films at and the rights of broadcasting organisations were also set at 50 years after the first transmission. The Directive also required a publication right protection of 25 years for works in which copyright has expired but has not yet been published. It expanded on provisions in the Rental Directive and SatCab Directives, allocating copyright to film directors of their works.

Accordingly, the UK 1988 Act was amended by the 1995 Duration of Copyright and Rights in Performances Regulations and the 1996 Copyright and Related Rights Regulations which implemented the European Directives. The 1996 Regulations implemented the 1992 Rental Directive, the 1993 Satellite and Cable Directive, and remaining parts of the 1993 Duration Directive not covered under the 1995 Regulations, namely the 25-year publication right provision. The Rental Directive established that exclusive 'rental and lending rights' were granted to authors and provides that an 'unwaivable equitable remuneration is obtained by authors and performers who must remain able to entrust the administration of this right to collecting societies representing them'.

As stated above, the 1993 Directive harmonised the term of protection of copyright and certain related rights within the EU. The copyright of a literary or artistic work is protected for the lifetime of the author plus 70 years after the author's death. However, the UK long asserted an exemption to copyright protection to 25 years to promote the commercial exploitation of industrial design, for example in the manufacture of jewellery or furniture. This exemption was based on the 1988 Copyright, Designs and Patents Act (CDPA) which contained an exemption to copyright protection for industrially manufactured artistic works.[1] This exemption was overturned in the 2011 ECJ case Flos v Semeraro, which forced a repeal of Section 52 of the CDPA.[2] In the ruling, the ECJ interpreted Article 17 of the 1998 Directive on the legal protection of designs, which related to copyright, to prohibit such exemptions in national law. The UK accordingly repealed the CDPA exemption in its 2013 Enterprise and Regulatory Reform Act.

[1] 'Artistic work' is defined under Section 4 of the CDPA as '(a) A graphic work, photograph, sculpture or collage irrespective of artistic quality (b) A work of architecture (c) A work of artistic craftmanship'.

[2] https://assets.publishing.service.gov.uk/government/uploads/system/uploads/attachment_data/file/606207/160408_guidance_s52_final_web_accessible.pdf [last accessed 25.10.2022].

Since this time, the EU has agreed a vast number of copyright measures to facilitate cross-border commerce. As many authors have pointed out, most of this legislation is aimed at the promotion of the creative industries sector. The initial Directives were followed by a 1996 Database Directive; 2001 Directive on the harmonisation of certain aspects of copyright and related rights in the Information Society; 2004 Directive on the enforcement of intellectual property rights ('IPR Enforcement Directive' or 'IPRED'); 2012 Orphan Works Directive; 2014 Directive Collective management of copyright and related rights and multi-territorial licensing of rights in musical works for online use in the internal market ('Collective Rights Management Directive'); 2017 Regulation on cross-border portability of online content services; and 2017 Marrakesh Directive and Regulation.

The 2001 Directive on the harmonisation of certain aspects of copyright and related rights in the information society (the Information Society) Directive was a landmark agreement implementing the 1996 WIPO Copyright Treaty and 1996 WIPO Performances and Phonograms Treaty. It is the first European act to prohibit member states from protecting circumvention of 'effective technological measures' in defence of digital rights management. It distinguishes exclusive rights for reproduction under Article 2 and the 'right of communication to the public of works and right of making available to the public other subject-matter' under Article 3. Article 2 ensured reproduction rights for 50 years for producers for first fixations of films and for broadcasting organisations for fixations of broadcasts. Article 3 was developed to encompass copyright issues on the internet and to link works communicated to the public (via the internet) to exhaustion rights.

Article 4(2) of the 2001 Information Society Directive states 'the distribution right shall not be exhausted within the Community in respect of the original or copies of the work, except where the first sale or other transfer of ownership in the Community of that object is made by the right holder or with his consent'. This is the principle of exhaustion. It means that rights holders can control distribution by the terms of their first sale of their creations. Rights holders can prevent the import of their creations into the EU even if they had been placed on the market in a third country where resale to the EU had not been prohibited.[3] The Directive was implemented in the UK Copyright and Related Rights Regulations 2003 modifying the 1995 and 1996 Regulations.

In 2011, the 1993 and 1996 copyright Directives were repealed and replaced by the Directive on the term of protection of copyright and certain related rights. The 2011 Directive extended the copyright for recordings from 50 to 70 years. UK-based actors played a substantial role in this extension. In 2006, the performing artist Cliff Richard had lobbied for the UK to extend copyright for performers from

[3] This is explained in a report from the Taskforce on Innovation Growth and Regulatory Reform: https://assets.publishing.service.gov.uk/government/uploads/system/uploads/attachment_data/file/994125/FINAL_TIGRR_REPORT__1_.pdf [last accessed 25.10.2022].

50 to 95 years, a battle which was lost. He, along with other artists, notably Paul McCartney, consequently lobbied the European Commission which proposed harmonisation at 95 years for sound recordings in 2008 (Smartt, 2020: 458). Labelled 'Cliff's law', the 2011 Directive harmonised copyright and related performance rights for music performers and sound recordings at 70 years across the EU. The 70-year rule remains in place post-Brexit as implemented at the national level into the 2013 Copyright and Duration of Rights in Performances Regulations.

The 2012 Orphan Works Directive was largely the EU's reaction to the Google Library Project. Orphaned works are copyrighted material for which the owner cannot be determined or contacted. A number of US Google cases[4] promoted concern within the EU that Google was moving towards a monopoly position on the provision of orphaned works. The 2012 Directive permitted member states to register orphaned works with the EU Intellectual Property Office, allowing access for use across the EU. Under the Directive, European Economic Area (EEA)-based cultural institutions (such as museums, libraries, and archives) can digitise orphaned works without permission of the rights holders.[5] The Directive also provided for the mutual recognition of orphan works. The UK's 2014 Copyright and Rights in Performances (Certain Permitted Uses of Orphan Works) Regulations implemented the Directive by amending the Copyright, Designs and Patents Act 1988 with a new Section 44B which protected relevant bodies from copyright infringement set out in Schedule ZA1 to the Act.

The 2014 Directive on collective management of copyright and related rights and multi-territorial licensing of rights in musical works for online use in the internal market (CMO Directive) enabled cross-border Collective Management Organisations (CMOs), organisations that manage licences of copyright works on the behalf of rights holders, to offer multi-territorial licensing of online rights of musical works. The Directive importantly injected much more transparency in CMO standards of governance and financial management (Street et al., 2018). Member states are required to notify the European Commission of the competent monitoring bodies at national levels under Articles 36–39.

There is a provision within the Directive which requires that CMOs provide multi-territorial licensing of their online rights upon request. On average, there are about 30 separate copyright licences for online music per member state (EC, 2021: 7). Half of these are multi-territorial licences issued by CMOs or their subsidiaries. These cover both mechanical and performance rights. The 2014 CMO Directive was implemented in the UK by the 2016 Collective Management of Copyright (EU Directive) Regulations.

[4] The 2008 Google Books settlement with US publishers; 2011 US District Judge Denny Chin decision; the 2012 Association of American Publishers (AAP) and the Google Library Project agreement.

[5] The 2012 Directive only covered printed and audio-visual work and not videogames or unpublished manuscripts.

The groundwork for the 2014 Directive had its beginnings in soft law (Schwemer, 2019: 123). The EU foresaw the development of online music markets as a key objective of its Lisbon Strategy. As detailed by Schwemer (2019), the soft law approach began in 2005 with the Commission's 'Online Music Recommendation'. The Recommendation recommended the introduction of multi-territorial licences and that rights holders should be able to choose a CMO. It outlined principles on equal treatment of categories of rights holders in the distribution of royalties.

The Recommendation had followed a 2004 exemption decision by the Directorate-General for Competition (DG Competition) on the Santiago Agreement. The Santiago Agreement, which had been agreed in October 2000 between five collecting societies, including the Performing Rights Society (PRS) from the UK and Broadcast Music Inc. from the US, aimed at creating a 'one-stop shop' for international licences for broadcasting and public performance rights for producer companies. It eased the purchasing of rights for radio and television broadcasters engaged in simulcasting on the internet. The agreement meant that broadcasters only needed to purchase one international licence from one EEA-based collecting society. The agreement met with complaints to DG Competition initially by collecting societies in the UK, France (SACEM), Germany (GEMA), the Netherlands, and, eventually, all of the EEA (except SPA in Portugal and SUISA in Switzerland). The Commission initially sent a Statement of Objections that the Santiago Agreement could be in breach of EU competition rules. Eventually, DG Competition agreed an exemption decision in 2004 which included conditions for the licensing imposed by collecting societies on copyright users.

In 2006, DG Competition subsequently adopted the Cannes Extension Agreement decision under Article 9 of the Modernisation Regulation.[6] The Cannes Extension Agreement was an arrangement between 13 European collecting societies and 5 major music publishers. It aimed to manage 'mechanical copyright' which was the right devolved from the production of physical products of sounds recordings, e.g. CDs. DG Competition became involved when collecting societies were excluded from granting rebates to record producers in central licensing agreements. Rebates are granted to collecting societies from administration fees collected from royalties collected on behalf of their members. Firstly, under the Decision, in the context of rights management, record producers could continue to receive rebates from collecting societies from copyright licence fees paid. Secondly, collecting societies could not be prevented from entering music publishing or record production markets.

In the same year, DG Competition issued a Statement of Objections against the International Confederation of Societies of Authors and Composers (CISAC) and

[6] Council Regulation (EC) No 1/2003 of 16 December 2002 on the implementation of the rules on competition laid down in Articles 81 and 82 of the Treaty: https://eur-lex.europa.eu/legal-content/en/ALL/?uri=CELEX%3A32003R0001 [last accessed 25.10.2022].

collecting societies in member states. The Statement of Objections related only to music broadcasting via satellite, cable retransmission, and internet transmission. DG Competition had concerns about the CISAC model contract under which rights holders could not select the EEA of their choice. It also found that purchasers could also not obtain multi-repertoire, multi-territorial licences. In 2007, CISAC and 18 EEA collecting societies made commitments under Article 9.

In 2008 DG Competition took a decision against 24 EEA collecting societies regarding the management of music right on behalf of authors (composers and lyricists). The CISAC prohibited membership and held exclusivity clauses in reciprocal representation agreements between collecting societies and rights holders based upon territoriality. This prevented rights holders from choosing an EEA collecting society of their choice as their rights manager and restricted the development of multi-territorial licences. This was flanked by a 2008 ECJ case brought by Kanal 5 and TV 4 AB against STIM, the Swedish collecting society, for abuse of dominant position.[7]

The decision prompted discussion at the European level over the increase in online distribution of music in Europe under the steer of DG Competition. A number of meetings were organised between consumer and industry representatives in 2009. This was followed by two Online Roundtables on Music, the first attended by iTunes, EMI, and the French collecting society SACEM and the second adding further market players, Nokia, Amazon, the UK's PRS for Music, Sweden's STIM collecting societies, Universal Music Publishing, and the consumer association BEUC. Post the roundtables, two joint statements were issued on General Principles for the Online Distribution of Music and a Common Framework for Rights Ownership Information. This lay the groundwork for later agreement on the 2014 CMO Directive.

In 2019, the EU agreed three copyright Directives: the 2019 Online Broadcasting Directive, the 2019 exercise of copyright and related rights applicable to certain online transmissions of broadcasting organisations and retransmissions of television and radio programmes (the television and radio programmes Directive), and the 2019 Directive on copyright and related rights in the Digital Single Market. The Online Broadcasting Directive states 'in order to facilitate the clearance of rights for the provision of ancillary online services across borders, it is necessary to provide for the establishment of the country of origin principle as regards the exercise of copyright and related rights'. This is found under Article 3(1) which outlines that 'an online service by or under the control and responsibility of a broadcasting organisation, as well as the acts of reproduction of such works ... shall, for the purposes of exercising copyright and related rights relevant for those acts, be deemed to occur solely in the Member State in which the broadcasting organisation has

[7] Case C-52/07 Kanal 5 Ltd TV 4 AB v Föreningen Svenska Tonsättares Internationella Musikbyra (STIM) upa, not yet reported in the ECR.

its principal establishment'. This aims at making copyright easier to clear in one state only under the country of origin principle. However, as Mylly and Herrero (2022: 1060) point out, the country of origin principle only applies to specific types of content, namely news and current affairs and the broadcaster's own productions.

The EU 2019 television and radio programmes Directive extended the principle of origin to non-linear services allowing video-on-demand services, online games, and music streaming based in one EU member state to be received without restrictions in another. The 2019 Copyright in the Digital Single Market Directive includes a mechanism to facilitate negotiations of licensing agreements for European-produced films and television and radio programmes to promote their availability across borders on, e.g., video-on-demand platforms. This is coupled with an extension to online services for European content quotas under the Audiovisual Media Services Directive (AVMSD) which also has requirements for visibility of European content in film/programming catalogues.

The 2019 Copyright in the Digital Single Market Directive updated the 2000 Directive on certain legal aspects of information society services and the 2000 e-Commerce and 2001 InfoSoc Directives. It targets online content-sharing service providers such as YouTube and Twitter[8] which are obliged to seek licensing agreements with rights holders for use of their content. Article 16 provides rights holders with the right to be 'entitled to a share of the compensation for the use of the work'. Article 17 moves liability for content use to online platforms, marking a change from the 2000 Directive (McDonagh, 2022: 326). The deadline for implementation of the Directive was July 2021.

A number of high-profile UK-based performing artists were considerably vocal during the formation of the 2019 Copyright Directive, including James Blunt, Paul McCartney, and Annie Lennox. As Bechtel (2020: 247) details, Paul McCartney lobbied the European Parliament to 'address the value gap and help assure a sustainable future for the music ecosystem and its creators, fans and digital music services alike'. The original proposal included a provision mandating that hosting services use filtering technologies. This was also heavily lobbied for by rights holders and their supporting associations at the EU level, including the European Magazine Media Association, the European Newspaper Publishers' Association, New Media Europe, the European Publishers' Council, Nightlife Music, and Australia's Independent Record Labels Association (Bechtel, 2020: 247). Although this condition was removed in the final version, Article 17 obliges that content hosting services make 'best efforts' to obtain authorisation for copyright.

The main objection to automatic take-down software is the concern that it would potentially block legal uses of exempted copyrighted material defined in the Directive as 'the specific purposes of quotation, criticism, review, caricature, parody

[8] Content platforms which have more than three years of existence in the EU, a turnover of more than 10 million Euros, and more than 5 million monthly users.

or pastiche', thereby curtailing free speech. In Republic of Poland v European Parliament and Council of the European Union case, decided in 2022, the ECJ upheld Article 17 provided it 'has been accompanied by appropriate safeguards by the EU legislature in order to ensure respect for the right to freedom of expression and information of the users of those services'.

Online platforms adapted their copyright policies accordingly. For example, in 2019 YouTube updated its licensing requirement with the software 'Content ID' (or 'YouTube Audio ID') and 'YouTube Video ID'. Copyright owners upload videos to a database and stipulate how Google should respond to uploaded copyrighted content with a choice of blocking videos, monetising videos by running ads or sharing revenue with the uploader or tracking the videos viewing statistics. This is done through a clickwrap licence. If a match occurs in the 'Content Verification Program', the video is entitled to a claim. Claims can be geographically specific, i.e. videos might be monetised in one state but blocked in another. It is claimed that this creates a balance between 'the economic incentives furthered through copyright protection of original works … [and] the ability of creators to make and share such transformative works on the Internet' (Bechtel, 2020: 251).

Under its terms of service,[9] YouTube grants 'a worldwide, non-exclusive, royalty-free, sublicensable and transferable license to use that Content (including to reproduce, distribute, prepare derivative works, display and perform it) in connection with the Service and YouTube's (and its successors' and Affiliates') business, including for the purpose of promoting and redistributing part or all of the Service' once creators upload their content. Here, YouTube has decided to apply an EU policy on a worldwide basis (Bradford, 2020).

At the same time, however, ECJ rulings have not yet held YouTube responsible for its illegal content. This was confirmed in the joined cases Frank Peterson v Google LLC, YouTube Inc., YouTube LLC, and Google Germany GmbH; and Elsevier Inc. v Cyando AG. In the first case, a music producer, Frank Peterson, brought a case against YouTube for unauthorised uploads of tracks from the album *A Winter Symphony*. In Cyando, the publisher Elsevier bought a case against the hosting platform Uploaded for a number of copyrighted works including 'Gray's Anatomy for Students' and 'Atlas of Human Anatomy'. The court ruled in both cases that the sharing platforms were not making a 'communication to the public' and were not aware of the illegally uploaded content. The decisions were made in June 2021.

A similar case brought against TikTok has been ongoing since 2019. Similar to YouTube, TikTok's licensing policy entitles it to an

[9] www.youtube.com/static?gl=CA&template=terms#54e2c59bb9 [last accessed 05.05.2022].

> unconditional irrevocable, non-exclusive, royalty-free, fully transferable, perpetual worldwide licence to use, modify, adapt, reproduce, make derivative works of, publish and/or transmit, and/or distribute and to authorise other users of the Services and other third-parties to view, access, use, download, modify, adapt, reproduce, make derivative works of, publish and/or transmit your User Content in any format and on any platform, either now known or hereinafter invented.

This led International Copyright Enterprise (ICE) to bring a case to the UK's Copyright Tribunal in 2019. The dispute was withdrawn by the end of the year and ICE and TikTok entered into arbitration and brokered a Europe-wide licensing deal. TikTok then went on to sign deals with other collecting societies, Believe and its subsidiary TuneCore, and the US National Music Publishers Association (NMPA) in 2020. As Bosher (2021: 118) explains, this agreement was different as it provides users 'permission for other users to re-use their content. This is significantly different from other social media platforms, such as Instagram ... which commonly state that users either upload their own original content or content that they have sought permission to use'. This is being done on a royalty-free basis.

UK policy divergence post-Brexit

There has been substantial UK divergence from EU copyright law post-Brexit. The Orphan Works Directive, which provided for the mutual recognition of orphaned works across Europe, no longer applies to the UK post-Brexit. Orphaned works are those where the rights holders cannot be identified or located so copyright cannot be obtained. The Directive importantly authorised cultural heritage institutions, defined in the UK as including 'publicly accessible libraries, education establishments and museums as well as archives, film or audio heritage institutions and public service broadcasters',[10] to reproduce and make publicly available orphan works. Importantly, this included the digitisation of orphaned works in their collections without permission of the rights holders.[11]

In reference to the orphan works copyright exception, the Department for Business, Energy and Industrial Strategy (BEIS) and the Intellectual Property Office (IPO) indicated that 'UK-based Cultural Heritage Institutions that make works available online in the EEA under the exception may be infringing copyright' post-Brexit.[12] For example, the British Library needed to remove access to

[10] www.legislation.gov.uk/uksi/2014/2861/pdfs/uksiem_20142861_en.pdf [last accessed 25.10.2022].

[11] https://cdn.nationalarchives.gov.uk/documents/archives/orphan-works-guidance.pdf [last accessed 25.10.2022].

[12] www.gov.uk/guidance/orphan-works-and-cultural-heritage-institutions [last accessed 25.10.2022].

the Spare Rib digital archive in January 2021.[13] Section 44B of the CDPA, Sec. 44B and Schedule ZA1 of the UK's 2014 Copyright and Rights in Performances were repealed with Brexit[14] and cultural institutions now need to obtain a licence from the UK IPO which lasts seven years.[15] If UK cultural institutions want to make content available in EU states, separate licences need to be attained to provide digital online copies in each member state the content is made available in, and vice versa. This is reportedly costly to do.

From January 2021, EU-based CMOs are no longer mandated to represent UK-based organisations for the multi-territory licensing of online rights for musical works under the 2014 CMO Directive.[16] Under Article 232 of the UK EU Trade and Cooperation Agreement (TCA), the UK and EU are encouraged to 'promote cooperation between their respective collective management organisations for the purpose of fostering the availability of works and other protected subject matter in their respective territories and the transfer of rights revenue between the respective collective management organisations'.[17] There is also a call for transparency of revenue collected and deductions applied on the use of rights and distribution policies. Although UK rights holders and CMOs can request representation by EU CMOs, there is no longer any obligation for them to represent UK rights holders or catalogues of UK CMOs for the online licensing of musical rights. By contrast, UK CMOs continue to represent catalogues of EU CMOs for multi-territorial licensing upon request.

The European Commission distinguishes between CMOs which are not-for-profit and independent management entities (IMEs) which are for-profit commercial entities but not owned or controlled by rights holders.[18] The UK CMOs operating in the EU prior to Brexit were ACS, ALCS, DACS, NLA Media Access, PRS for Music Ltd, and RadioPro Ltd. The UK CMOs specifically for music are the Mechanical Copyright Protection Society (MCPS) and PRS, allied under the PRS for Music Ltd. They collect royalties for circa 160,000 members.[19] There are only two IMEs for music located in the UK, Soundreef and CreaCollect, which were both established in 2018.

[13] www.researchprofessionalnews.com/rr-news-uk-open-access-2021-1-concern-as-post-brexit-copyright-rules-restrict-access-to-materials [last accessed 25.10.2022].

[14] www.legislation.gov.uk/ukpga/1988/48/section/44B [last accessed 25.10.2022].

[15] www.gov.uk/guidance/copyright-orphan-works [last accessed 25.10.2022].

[16] www.gov.uk/guidance/collective-rights-management-in-the-eu [last accessed 29.04.2022].

[17] Under the TCA section on copyright: www.gov.uk/government/publications/ukeu-and-eaec-trade-and-cooperation-agreement-ts-no82021 [last accessed 25.10.2022].

[18] In a 2021 study, DG Connect identified 69 CMOs operating exclusively in the music sector, 21 operating exclusively in the visual arts sector, 46 operating exclusively in the audiovisual sector, 33 operating exclusively in the literary and publishing sector, six operating exclusively in the dramatic arts sector, and 79 operating in multiple sectors (EC, 2021: 17).

[19] www.prsformusic.com/-/media/files/prs-for-music/corporate/financials/the-big-numbers/the-big-numbers-infographic-2021.pdf [last accessed 29.04.2022].

MCPS covers mechanical rights for reproduction[20] and PRS covers liver performance rights. The Phonographic Performance Limited (PPL) organises rights for the recording industry (related rights). Authors rights are transferred to PPL which organises collective rights management for sound recordings for over 130,000 performers and recording rights holders.[21] In 2018, PRS For Music formed a joint venture, PPL PRS Ltd.,[22] to issue TheMusicLicence licences.

Cross-border cooperation between CMOs include ICE which is a joint venture between PRS For Music, STIM in Sweden, and GEMA in Germany. It handles multi-territory online licensing, the processing of copyright data, and online processing. ICE is registered in Germany with offices in Sweden and the UK. PRS For Music also has a joint venture with Nordisk Copyright Bureau (NCB) called Network Music Partners (NMP) for the Nordic States which mainly concentrates on digital service providers (e.g. Spotify, iTunes, and YouTube). However, from January 2021, UK patent attorneys and lawyers can no longer represent their clients vis-à-vis regulatory bodies overseeing CMOs in most EU states as representation requires domestic qualifications. EEA-qualified legal representatives therefore must be assigned in disputes.

Most profit in the music industry goes to Sony Music Entertainment, Universal Music Group, and Warner Music Group, which combined held 74 per cent of the digital market share globally in 2021.[23] The House of Commons Digital, Culture, Media and Sport Committee called for the CMA to investigate 'the economic impact of the dominance by major music companies Universal, Sony and Warner of the UK's music recording industry'[24] and to ensure that the UK legal system is not enabling market dominance. The report also requested the CMA to investigate dominance in direct licensing negotiations with streaming services. The parliamentary committee also probed business models for Spotify, Apple Music, Amazon Music, SoundCloud, and Tidal.[25] Following the report, the UK Competition and Markets Authority launched an investigation into the online streaming market in 2022.[26] Streaming accounted for 83 per cent of UK music consumption in 2021 with iTunes, Spotify, and Google Play dominating sales.[27] These groups are based in Ireland.

[20] www.prsformusic.com/-/media/files/prs-for-music/membership/mcps/0-mcps-distribution-policy.pdf [last accessed 29.04.2022].

[21] www.ppluk.com [last accessed 25.10.2022].

[22] https://pplprs.co.uk/about-pplprs [last accessed 25.10.2022].

[23] https://musicandcopyright.wordpress.com/2022/04/05/sme-and-wmg-the-biggest-market-share-winners-in-2021 [last accessed 05.05.2022].

[24] https://committees.parliament.uk/work/646/economics-of-music-streaming/news/156593/mps-call-for-a-complete-reset-of-music-streaming-to-fairly-reward-performers-and-creators [last accessed 25.10.2022].

[25] https://committees.parliament.uk/publications/6739/documents/72525/default [last accessed 25.10.2022].

[26] www.gov.uk/cma-cases/music-and-streaming-market-study [last accessed 27.01.2022].

[27] www.bpi.co.uk/news-analysis/2021-in-music-more-artists-succeed-as-streaming-drives-music-growth-fuelled-by-record-label-investment [last accessed 25.10.2022].

EU copyright Directives are flanked by the 2017 Regulation on cross-border portability permits, 2018 Geo-blocking Regulation, and 2018 Digital Content and Digital Services Directive governing online contracts. The Geo-blocking Regulation was applicable in the UK from 2018, but no longer applies post-Brexit. The Geo-blocking Regulation does not apply to audio-visual content (Mylly and Herrero, 2022: 1044). Interestingly, public service broadcasting is exempt from the Regulation because it is classified as a 'service(s) of general economic interest that [is] subject to specific public service obligations' (Mazziotti, 2021: 225). Similarly, audio-visual services have an exemption under the 2006 Directive on services in the Internal Market (the 'Services Directive').

The 2017 Portability Regulation on cross-border portability permits consumers to view packages such as Sky Cinema or Spotify subscribed to in one country while travelling abroad. Although the 2017 Portability Regulation was operative in the UK, post-Brexit the Regulation 'will cease to apply to UK nationals when they travel to the EU. This means online content service providers will not be required or able to offer cross-border access to UK consumers under the EU Regulation. UK consumers may see restrictions to their online content services when they temporarily visit the EU'.[28] In practice, this means that UK residents might not be able to access UK subscriptions to subscription streaming services such as Netflix or Disney+ when travelling abroad in the EU. This is dependent upon whether the programmes are also offered within the state they are travelling to, in which case the rights will have been cleared for that state.

In 2017, the EU implemented the Marrakesh Treaty in its Directive for the benefit of persons who are blind, visually impaired, or otherwise print-disabled. The international Treaty entered into force in a national capacity on 1 January 2021.[29] Notably, in its amendment, the UK removed the compensation mechanism. The Directive ensures that 'accessible format copies made by authorised entities in any Member State can be circulated and accessed by beneficiary persons and authorised entities throughout the Union'. UK-based persons will no longer be able to access accessible format copies of works from the EU. Instead, the UK is treated as a third country under the 2017 Regulation. The Directive was implemented by the UK in 2018 but updated in 2021 after a two-year review.

Books and journal exports continue to have zero tariffs post-Brexit. Prior to Brexit, in 2018, of £3.5 billion, roughly 60 per cent of UK export publishing sales were in the physical book market, 35 per cent of which was made up of European sales.[30] Customs declarations and the requirement for Economic Operators Registration and Identification (EORI) numbers to move books between the UK

[28] www.gov.uk/government/publications/copyright-if-theres-no-brexit-deal/copyright-if-theres-no-brexit-deal [last accessed 26.05.2022].

[29] www.gov.uk/guidance/the-marrakesh-treaty [last accessed 25.10.2022].

[30] www.publishers.org.uk/wp-content/uploads/2020/03/A-Blueprint-for-UK-Publishing-2018.pdf [last accessed 25.10.2022].

and EU have created additional bureaucracy for sellers post-Brexit. Rules governing exports are outlined in the EU 1987 Common Transit Convention which UK became a member of in January 2021. As a result, exports to Europe have declined and there has been an increase in exports to the US and Australia.[31]

The Publishers Association had a seat on the Expert Advisory Group negotiating the 2020 EU–UK TCA. It lobbied for the UK to continue to apply the Brussels Regime[32] and Lugano Convention post-Brexit. As detailed in Chapter 5, this would have guaranteed the enforcement of parties' contractual choice of jurisdiction and mutual recognition of court decisions between the UK and EU states. However, both Brussels and Lugano ceased to apply to the UK for proceedings after January 2021. The UK applied to join the Lugano Convention in April 2020. The European Free Trade Association (EFTA) states supported the UK application, but the European Commission opposed UK membership.[33] The Publishers Association continues to represent publishers on the Department for International Trade's Creative Industries' Trade Advisory Group, and presented written submissions regarding free-trade agreements (FTAs) with Canada, Singapore, Canada, and other states.[34] It wants to ensure that publishing receives the same tax and regulatory treatment as domestically produced goods and services in FTA agreements.

The UK decided not to implement the 2019 Copyright Directive. The 2019 Intellectual Property (Copyright and Related Rights) (Amendment) (EU Exit) Regulations make amendments to relevant UK regulation.[35] Under the UK's Withdrawal Act, four notices covering intellectual property relate to copyright directives and regulations. The notices state that operators when 'broadcasting into the EEA may need to clear copyright in each member state to which they broadcast' post-Brexit, in addition to which the AVMSD has supplementary requirements.[36] In practice, post-Brexit, UK-based broadcasters need to clear rights in each state

[31] www.publishers.org.uk/wp-content/uploads/2022/04/Publishing-in-2021-FINAL.pdf.

[32] 2001 Brussels Regulation (for disputes up until 2015) and Brussels Regulation (the 'Brussels Recast Regulation') (for disputes occurring after 10 January 2015).

[33] https://ec.europa.eu/info/sites/default/files/1_en_act_en.pdf; www.eda.admin.ch/dam/eda/fr/documents/aussenpolitik/voelkerrecht/autres-conventions/Lugano2/20210701-LUG-ann-EU.pdf; and www.eda.admin.ch/dam/eda/fr/documents/aussenpolitik/voelkerrecht/autres-conventions/Lugano2/20210701-LUG_en.pdf [all last accessed 25.10.2022].

[34] www.publishers.org.uk/wp-content/uploads/2022/04/Publishers-Association-Annual-Report-2021.pdf [last accessed 25.10.2022].

[35] Amendments to the Copyright, Designs and Patents Act 1988; Amendments to the Duration of Copyright and Rights in Performances Regulations 1995; Amendments to the Copyright and Related Rights Regulations 1996; Amendments to the Copyright and Rights in Databases Regulations 1997; Amendments to the Artist's Resale Right Regulations 2006; Amendments to the Copyright and Rights in Performances (Extended Collective Licensing) Regulations 2014; Amendments to the Copyright and Rights in Performances (Licensing of Orphan Works) Regulations 2014; Amendments to the Collective Management of Copyright (EU Directive) Regulations 2016; Amendments to the Copyright and Performances (Application to Other Countries) Order 2016; Revocation of the Portability of Online Content Services Regulations 2018; Amendments to the Copyright and Related Rights (Marrakesh Treaty etc.) (Amendment) Regulations 2018.

[36] http://data.parliament.uk/DepositedPapers/Files/DEP2018-0944/Copyright_UPDATE_Jan_2019.docx [last accessed 25.10.2022].

they are broadcasting to. This does not work in reverse. Operators broadcasting to the UK 'will not need specific right holder permission for the UK, except where: the broadcast is commissioned or uplinked to a satellite in the UK, or it originates from a country that provides lower levels of copyright protection'.[37]

Although the UK did not implement the Directive, it showed support for and voted in favour of its ratification in the Council of Ministers. France was the first to implement the Directive, resulting in a framework agreement between L'Alliance de la Presse d'Information Générale (APIG) and Google for reuse of news content. This relates to the press publication right under Article 15 or 'link tax' under which search engines and news aggregation services should obtain licenses from publishers for news snippets and links to original content. Newspapers retain copyright for reproduction and online use for two years (from 1 January) after publication and are ensured a share of online revenue. Similar agreements are not expected in the UK (Ganter, 2022).

The UK's 2019 Intellectual Property (Exhaustion of Rights) (EU Exit) Regulations retained the principle of exhaustion for the distribution of goods (e.g. physical books) from the EU and EEA in the UK. The government launched a consultation to address this in 2021[38] to which the creative industries which were the most represented stakeholders in the consultation gave 54 responses.[39] Key industry actors, notably the Publishers Association, the Society of Authors, the Association of Authors' Agents, and the Authors' Licensing and Collecting Society, lobbied against any changes to the existing copyright rules in a Launching a Save Our Books joint campaign in 2021. The biggest fear was a change which would allow the import of copies of authors' books published for other markets into the UK without permission from the rights holders, thereby threatening author royalties. In its conclusion, the government decided in January 2022 that there was not enough data on the economic impact of the changes for it to take a position.

Another campaign took place in 2022 when the government supported a proposed exemption to copyright and patent legislation in its response to an IPO consultation on Artificial Intelligence and Intellectual Property: copyright and patents.[40] The IPO proposed 'For text and data mining, we plan to introduce a new copyright and database exception which allows TDM (text and data mining) for any purpose'. The government responded, 'The Government has decided to

[37] www.gov.uk/guidance/copyright-clearance-for-uk-satellite-broadcasting [last accessed 25.10.2022].

[38] www.gov.uk/government/consultations/uks-future-exhaustion-of-intellectual-property-rights-regime [last accessed 25.10.2022].

[39] www.gov.uk/government/consultations/uks-future-exhaustion-of-intellectual-property-rights-regime/uks-future-exhaustion-of-intellectual-property-rights-regime-summary-of-responses-to-the-consultation#refannex-a [last accessed 25.10.2022].

[40] www.gov.uk/government/consultations/artificial-intelligence-and-ip-copyright-and-patents/outcome/artificial-intelligence-and-intellectual-property-copyright-and-patents-government-response-to-consultation [last accessed 25.10.2022].

introduce a new copyright and database exception which allows TDM for any purpose'. This would include commercial purposes. It added: 'These changes make the most of the greater flexibilities following Brexit. They will help make the UK more competitive as a location for firms doing data mining'.

The Publishers Content responded that 'a broad copyright exception will seriously undermine the United Kingdom's intellectual property framework, conflict with international law, and unintentionally provide international rights holders and non-UK-based research organizations with a competitive advantage'.[41] It went on to state that 'certain businesses will have no choice but to exit the UK market or apply paywalls where access to content is currently free'. The debate is not yet closed at the time of writing. In summary, the industry is arguing that the UK's current copyright framework is necessary to maintain its global reputation for copyright security.[42] Its main concern, however, is allowing an exemption for commercial as well as public or research use. UK copyright already contains an exemption for researchers to make copies of works 'for text and data analysis', including carrying out computational analysis, but this 'must be for the purpose of non-commercial research'. But it does not include an exemption for machine learning or commercial use.

In 2022, the UK government also ran a public consultation[43] querying whether an exemption for industrially manufactured artistic works under Section 52 of the CDPA should be reinstated. The copyright term for industrially manufactured artistic works was reduced to 25 years up until 2011 when the ECJ ruled that Section 52 CDPA should be repealed so that all types of artistic work be equally protected. As stated above, Section 52 was repealed in the Enterprise and Regulatory Reform Act 2013. The CREATe research centre has argued that Section 52 should be reinstated post-Brexit (Porangaba, 2022). The consultation is still under review. In the scope of the type of work most affected are 'furniture, jewellery, ceramics, lighting and other homewares. This would be both the 3D manufacture and retail and the 2D representation in publishing'.

Divergence from the EU copyright law can be seen in national court decisions. In 2020, the UK's Intellectual Property Enterprise Court ruled in the Response Clothing Ltd v Edinburgh Woollen Mill (EWM) Ltd that a jacquard fabric used by EWM was infringing Response Clothing's copyright. A swatch of Response's fabric had been utilised by another company to produce a new design. The ruling

[41] www.publishers.org.uk/wp-content/uploads/2022/08/PCF-TDM-Letter-as-of-080822.pdf [last accessed 25.10.2022].

[42] The signatories of the letter are the Association of Learned and Professional Society Publishers, Independent Publishers Guild, News Media Association, NLA Media Access, Press Database and Licensing Network, Professional Publishers Association, Publishers Association, and the Publishers' Licensing Services.

[43] www.gov.uk/government/consultations/repeal-of-section-52-cdpa-and-related-amendments-call-for-views/post-implementation-review-of-the-repeal-of-section-52-of-the-cdpa-1988-and-associated-amendments-call-for-views [last accessed 25.10.2022].

was based upon the aesthetic value of the work and was incompatible with the 2019 ECJ Cofemel-Sociedade de Vesturário SA v G-Star Raw CV case wherein 'aesthetic effect' was ruled to be incompatible with Article 2(a) of the 2001 Directive on the harmonisation of certain aspects of copyright and related rights in the Information Society (InfoSoc Directive).

UK database users' rights are no longer enforceable in the EU post-Brexit. There is no obligation for EU database owners to provide rights to UK-based users. The owners of UK databases created post-Brexit need to consider further protections such as restrictive licensing agreements or attaining copyright for databases. The EU 1996 Database Directive harmonised national treatment of databases and provides rights to database creators where they do not attain copyright based upon original intellectual creation. This is what is called a sui generis protection of databases for their creators. It was implemented in the 1997 Copyright and Rights in Databases Regulations in the UK. Copyright harmonisation is based upon originality criteria and protecting authors' rights. Database rights are considered separately to copyright. The 2022 EU proposal for a Data Act excludes machine-generated data (essentially from the Internet of Things) from owning database rights. The 1997 regulation is expected to be updated to make clear the same exclusion in the UK.

Conclusion

On 1 January 2021, the UK was no longer participant to a number of agreements enabling cross-border copyright recognition. This included copyright clearance for satellite and cable and broadcasting and online streaming. This means that rights holders need to clear copyright in each state to which they are broadcasting. UK-based organisations no longer benefit from the orphan works copyright exception. Publishers are wary of cheap copies of book imports to the domestic market. UK-based researchers and users have lost EU database access rights.

As EU copyright law no longer applies to the UK post-Brexit, there is potential for UK divergence. It is unclear at the time of writing which way this will fall. Lawyers have also commented on the UK's 'closed list' approach to copyright which was consistently challenged by the ECJ (Rosati, 2021). Copyright lawyers have also pointed out that the UK could post-Brexit adopt a fair use exception for copyright in these instances which was prevented by Article 5 of Directive 2001/29/EC (Aplin, 2019: 981). However, this is an unlikely scenario. At the time of writing, the UK does not look like it will veer substantially in legislation given domestic pressure to maintain the status quo. Divergence will most likely come in the form of UK case law which could trigger substantial change.

Additionally, 'the interpretations of parody and quotation and the role of the three-step test are not as embedded within UK case law' (Aplin, 2019: 980). There is also potential from departure from EU legislation in future UK court rulings. However, as Aplin adds, 'it would be preferable, in this author's view, to interpret EU-derived domestic (copyright) legislation consistently with the EU acquis unless and until there is parliamentary intervention' in order not to interfere with potential trade loss (Aplin, 2019: 981).

12

Conclusion

The UK's New Place in the Global Digital World

Introduction

This book has established how the UK played a historical role in steering EU policy agendas during EU membership. The multiple streams (MS) framework is a useful analytical lens to observe this process as it investigates which policy issues receive attention and which actors are mobilised when a policy window opens (Kingdon, 2011). Under the MS framework, problem streams identify societal problems requiring policy action. In the context of the book, problem streams constituted the policy sectors under study. The policy streams were represented by the solutions (policy proposals) lobbied for by different stakeholders.

The politics stream is constituted by the governance architecture, the backdrop against which decision-making is made. Key EU governance architectures identified in the book are the Lisbon Agenda, the Convergence Initiative, the Better Regulation Agenda, and the Digital Single Market (DSM) Agenda, which enabled the success of many UK policy solutions at the European level. Focusing events such as court decisions and competition decisions triggered the opening of policy windows under which UK policy solutions were brought to the fore. The explanatory cause in this respect is temporal, with decisions opening up windows of opportunity through which the UK was able to push through its policy preferences and couple streams at key moments in the legislative timeline.

Examples of focusing events detailed in the book were the European Court of Justice (ECJ) cases. The 1982 case Coditel made copyright harmonisation possible. The 1982 British Telecommunications and 1988 Telecommunications Terminal Equipment cases enabled EU telecommunications sector liberalisation. The 1996 Commission v the UK and 1997 Denuit cases confirming the country of origin principle enabled the UK to push for a change to the definition of the principle of origin in the 1997 Television Without Frontiers (TWF) Regulation. The RTI case enabled actors to push for teleshopping liberalisation. The Max Schrems and Google Spain cases paved the way for General Data Protection Regulation (GDPR) agreement. The 2008 Directorate-General for Competition (DG Competition) decision on the International Confederation of Societies of Authors and Composers (CISAC) facilitated the development of multi-territorial licences for online copyright.

Brexit and the Digital Single Market. Alison Harcourt, Oxford University Press. © Alison Harcourt 2023.
DOI: 10.1093/oso/9780192899378.003.0012

These focusing events provided windows of opportunity for the UK to lobby for its interests in a wide number of DSM policy areas. It accomplished this often in tandem with the European Commission which utilised the UK's liberalising agenda to forward greater harmonisation in digital markets regulation, and therewith, ultimately, European integration. In this respect, the Commission and the ECJ were conducive to the opening up of policy windows, creating governance architectures which were favourable for policy change. This validates Ackrill and Kay's (2011: 874) argument that the separation of policy entrepreneurs and decision-makers is not so clear cut.

Each chapter assessed policy framing and the manipulation of frames by the UK. The UK, as a policy entrepreneur in this process, enabled the coupling of the problem, policy, and politics steams during opened policy windows. As a state actor, the UK was often able to effectively mobilise support or opposition under successive EU governance architectures bringing about policy change. This endorses academic work by Ackrill and Kay (2011: 878) who argued that policy entrepreneurs could construct policies from changes in the policy environment. The EU is viewed in the academic literature as more susceptible to the UK's pluralist lobbying style than continental style corporatist lobbying (Mazey and Richardson, 1993; Greenwood, 2003). Arguably, the UK's pluralistic policy style gave it a competitive advantage in the DSM strategy.

UK policy entrepreneurship

Princen (2011) argued that agenda setters forwarded preferences through four strategies: mobilising support, arousing interest, claiming authority, and building capacity. The UK was shown to proactively mobilise support in a number of DSM policy areas. It enabled a major advance in Single Market policy-making with the seminal white paper, 'Completing the Internal Market', authored by the UK Commissioner Arthur Cockfield. In audio-visual services policy the UK mobilised alliances between national government representatives, companies, and national regulatory bodies to support a change in definition to the country of origin principle. In telecommunications policy, the UK's model of market liberalisation was exported to the EU level with the European Commission adopting the sectoral approach from the 1980s onwards. This was supported by ECJ rulings which challenged the dominant positions of domestic incumbents and introduced proportionality and transparency in the rollout of universal service.

The UK successfully opposed statutory legislation for online platforms in coalition with other states in Northern (Denmark, Finland, Luxembourg, Sweden) and Central and Eastern Europe (Bulgaria, the Czech Republic, Estonia, Latvia, Lithuania). Instead, it pushed through soft governance and self-regulatory measures to regulate the sector. These were enabled through the EU's Better Regulation

Agenda which was based on UK domestic policy. The European Commission in turn adapted the soft governance model to further its European integration agenda as it was able to forward initiatives in areas with weak treaty basis. The EU's adoption of the Better Regulation Agenda with the use of codes of conduct, transparency measures, and regulatory sandboxes was used in audio-visual, telecommunications, e-Commerce, and FinTech policies based upon UK models.

The UK was instrumental in influencing EU competition policy, firstly through the appointment of Leon Brittan to competition Commissioner who championed liberalisation in utilities markets. The UK successfully also supported exemptions under the 1990 and 2004 Merger Regulations under the principle of subsidiarity (referred to as the 'English clause') to protect the legitimate interests of public security, plurality of the media, and prudential rules. The UK's public value test came to be adapted to EU state aid exemptions for public service broadcasting. More recently, the EU considered a New Competition Tool influenced by the Competition and Market Authority's (CMA's) cross-sector market investigation tool.

The UK innovated ways to promote the development of FinTech markets, a model which was largely imitated by the European Commission. The UK was able to push through flexible policy solutions to data protection policy, preserving data-handling exemptions for legitimate purposes under EU law. This was done in coalition with private sector actors. Lastly, the UK copyright model slowed EU copyright policy harmonisation.

UK regulatory bodies acted as claiming authorities, building capacity in proficiency and forging lasting partnerships with stakeholders over time. In audio-visual and telecoms policy, the Independent Television Commission (ITC), OFTEL, and subsequently Ofcom established themselves as reliable and trusted national regulatory authorities (NRAs) which were well resourced in terms of regulatory expertise. Similarly, the Information Commissioner's Office made the UK an attractive and stable regulatory environment for data handling in Europe. The Financial Conduct Authority (FCA), CMA, Office of Fair Trading, and Bank of England established the UK as an attractive location for companies providing financial services across Europe. The FCA is viewed as having 'renowned knowledge and expertise' in the financial sector (James and Quaglia, 2020: 150). The BFI and UK cultural arts networks are viewed by stakeholders as efficient and transparent in the allocation of funding compared with many European counterparts. These organisations were instrumental in establishing the UK as an appealing regulatory environment for investment.

Capacity loss

However, as the book has shown, much of this capacity was lost with Brexit. The loss of the country of origin has been a disincentive for pan companies operating in Europe to continue to headquarter in the UK. UK-based companies are now dealing with both UK regulatory bodies and NRAs in each European state they operate in. This means significant added costs. For example, clearance rights holders need to clear copyright in for each European country to which they are broadcasting. Under data protection policy, companies face the threat of fines from multiple states. UK cultural institutions need to attain licences for digitalised orphan works from multiple European states.

For this reason, many digital companies have relocated headquarters to an EU state. The starkest areas for company flight were shown to be broadcasters, with most pan-European companies having left London for continental Europe, including AMC Networks, Discovery, Disney, the Modern Times Group, 21st Century Fox, Time Warner, Sony, Universal Studios, and Viacom. A substantial number of FinTech companies have also relocated headquarters or obtained additional licences in the European Economic Area (EEA). KPMG reported that the most FinTech flight was to Ireland followed by the Netherlands and Lithuania.[1] In 2022, the UK lost its position to France as Europe's most-valued stock market.[2] It also lost its position as the most popular country for cross-border online shoppers from Europe to Germany in the same year.[3]

Access to European services by UK citizens is also complicated post-Brexit. Musicians, theatre performers, and artists are encountering problems in getting visas to tour across Europe. UK customers no longer benefit from a ban on roaming charges when travelling to the EU or the portability of steaming services. UK researchers have lost EU database rights. EU-level dispute mechanisms are no longer accessible to UK consumers. They have lost access to cross-border dispute mechanisms such as the European Consumer Centres Network, the European Interoperability Framework, the Online Dispute Resolution network, One Stop Shop, and Your Europe. This is notwithstanding the fact that the EU remains the UK's largest trading partner for e-commerce.

UK citizens are receiving a large amount of unregulated content from streaming and platforms based in EU states. This includes Amazon Prime Video, Netflix, and Disney+ in streaming markets and Apple Music, Amazon Music, SoundCloud, Spotify, and Tidal in music markets. This has prompted parliament to request changes to domestic legislation to remedy this. However, interviews have shown that platforms are more likely to conform to European-level rules than UK rules. This approach is also expected from online platforms and social media networks in reaction to the Digital Services Act (DSA). Platforms implementing the DSA may

[1] https://home.kpmg/nl/en/home/insights/2022/10/popular-brexit-relocation-spots-for-FinTechs.html [last accessed 25.10.2022].

[2] www.bbc.co.uk/news/business-63623502 [last accessed 25.10.2022].

[3] www.cbcommerce.eu/press-releases/fourth-edition-of-the-top-16-countries-cross-border-europe-an-annual-ranking-of-the-best-16-european-countries-in-cross-border-online-shopping [last accessed 25.10.2022].

automatically take down 'recognised news publishers' as protected under the UK's Online Safety Bill. In audio-visual markets, EU-based streaming providers may be subject to EU pressure to discontinue recognition of British content as counting towards European works quotas.

The loss of data sharing and networking with European has had a great effect on NRAs' operational capacity. The UK no longer has access to EU-level information exchange platforms such as the EU Observatory on the Online Platform Economy and the Single Digital Gateway. At the same time, UK customers receive a large number of services from online platforms based abroad, particularly from Facebook, Google, Twitter (operating from Ireland), Netflix (the Netherlands), Amazon, and PayPal (Luxembourg). Ofcom, the CMA, and the Information Commissioner's Office (ICO), in particular, face difficulties dealing with out-of-jurisdiction corporations. They cannot request data from EU states in investigations or run inspections.

Brexit has seen increasing domestic political intervention in the operation of national regulatory authorities. The Online Safety Bill proposes much greater government steer in policy-making. Ofcom needs to consult the secretary of state over guidance, review thresholds, and fees. The secretary of state can also modify existing codes of practice and require Ofcom to review terrorism or child sexual exploitation and abuse codes. He/she can also change the frequency of transparency requests from companies. Similarly, the Data Protection and Digital Information Bill provides substantial powers to the secretary of state, thereby reducing the regulatory independence of the ICO, the independence of which was a key requirement of the GDPR. The secretary of state, who is referred to 192 times in Bill, can steer definitions of legitimate use, automatic decision-making, and codes of practice. Indeed, the DPDI and Bill of Rights proposals, along with reform of the ICO, threaten the UK with loss of adequacy under the GDPR.

Concern was expressed by the Bank of England over its future independence under proposals under the 2022 Financial Services and Markets (FSM) Bill. The Bill envisions greater power for ministers over the Bank of England. The UK also risks losing its adequacy status for central counterparties now it is no longer an EU member. Greater government intervention in competition policy can be seen post-Brexit with changes to public interest definitions and many more exemptions added for national security. The secretary of state can issue a greater number of Public Interest Intervention Notices on 'national security' grounds under competition law and intervene in mergers and acquisitions under the National Security and Investment Act 2022. 'National security' grounds were invoked, for example, by the secretary of state in on a competition decision on Nexperia in 2022.

The weakening of independent regulatory authorities makes the UK a less stable regulatory environment for companies as government opinions can change quickly and with each successive government, thereby diminishing market certainty. This also affects NRA regulatory capacity. Regulators are facing funding cuts, increased workloads, and staff shortages, as well as the loss of information exchange with their European counterparts. The CMA was identified as experiencing the most difficulties, particularly as it has been requested to cut staff up to 40 per cent under the 2022 spending review. The newly established Digital Markets Unit does not yet have statutory backing. Ofcom is facing increasing pressure from the internet service provider lobby to deregulate the net-neutrality requirement.

Although there is potential for the UK to join aspects of the Single Market under future bilateral agreements, and UK regulatory authorities could participate in NRA networks under memoranda of understanding or association status, both of these options have met with resistance under the current UK political climate. The government has also not yet set up confidential sharing agreements with the Commission and third states for the CMA's use in competition decisions, with the Committee of Public Accounts reporting political objections to cooperation and 'tight control from the centre of government over when and how they talk to co-regulators in the EU'. Ofcom has experienced similar constraints for participation in the Body of European Regulators for Electronic Communications (BEREC) and European Regulators Group (ERGA) for Audiovisual Media Service. Indeed, even bilateral sectoral agreements (the 'Swiss' model) have been objected to from factions within the UK Conservative Party, making many forms of political agreement with the EU difficult.

This political thinking gained momentum in 2022 with the introduction of the Retained EU Law (Revocation and Reform) (REUL) Bill and the Northern Ireland Protocol Bill. The REUL, which proposed the removal of all EU attained legislation by the end of 2023, has met with substantial political backlash from a wide range of industry associations and unions (Thomas et al., 2022b). Although the current prime minister Rishi Sunak initially aimed to move the deadline forward, it is clear that the government now recognises that this is unrealistic and indeed the aim to review all legislation is not remotely sensible. The aims of the Bill are expected to be amended if it passes in parliament.

Political support for the Northern Ireland Protocol Bill is reportedly weakening (Parker, 2022). The EU has prevented or delayed collaboration with the UK over the Northern Ireland Protocol dispute in many digital market policy areas. The EU has not yet signed a Memorandum of Understanding with the UK on Financial Services Regulatory Cooperation due to the dispute. The Northern Ireland dispute also led the EU to temporarily block UK membership of the EU Horizon Europe science programme. Formal cooperation between DG Competition and the CMA was also halted in 2022 due to political disagreement over the protocol. The US delayed its UK trade agreement negotiations on the same grounds (Parker and Schwartz, 2022).

Future policy trajectories

Although the EU remains the UK's largest trading partner, the EU very much views the UK as a competitor on its doorstep. The UK has maintained pre-Brexit EU legislation in most digital market policy areas. However, there is little reciprocity from the EU. The UK has only been granted a limited number of adequacy decisions. This can be seen most starkly in finance markets. The Commission only granted two adequacy decisions to the UK in financial services, one of which, for UK equivalence for central counterparties, is expected to be withdrawn in 2025. By contrast, the UK granted equivalence to EU states in 28 out of 32 financial service areas.

An uneven balance in reciprocity can be seen in many areas. Even though UK citizens might not have access to home streaming services when travelling to the EU, EU citizens will have access to streaming services when travelling to the UK. UK citizens and residents can no longer register .eu domain names but EU residents can register .uk addresses post-Brexit. EU-based CMOs are no longer obliged to represent UK-based organisations for multi-territory licensing of online rights for musical works, but UK CMOs continue to represent EU CMOs.

Companies are experiencing great difficulties with more red tape post-Brexit. The delivery of goods faces adherence to EU requirements on conformity assessment, taxation, and rules of origin and at the same time a growing amount of new UK legislation such as the UK Conformity Assessed (UKCA) mark. Staff costs, transport, and storage have increased. UK goods imported to the EU need to conform to the 2018 Directive concerning contracts for the sale of goods. Books and journal exports also face customs declarations and requirements for Economic Operators Registration and Identification (EORI) numbers.

UK service exporters must comply with the 2018 Directive concerning contracts for the supply of digital content and digital services which addresses business-to-consumer (B2C) consumer contract laws including requirements for security updates. UK-based companies offering digital services within the EU are also required to appoint an EU legal representative under the DSA. The Markets in Crypto-Assets Regulation has tightened restrictions for UK service issuers of crypto-assets with greater requirements for capital, complaints procedures, and investor rights. Firms face greater costs associated with risk assessments for data transfer outside the EU. The EU's 2021 standard contractual clauses require assessment of 'risks to the rights and freedoms of natural persons', meaning data controllers must complete a Transfer Impact Assessment (TIA) for countries without EU adequacy decisions. This has resulted in mounting costs and workloads for companies and often the necessity to hire external expertise. Many companies report internal decisions not to increase trade with third countries as a result.

In 2022, the Office for Budget Responsibility (OBR) reported that there was a 9 per cent fall in goods exports to the EU from 2019 levels; 'however, there is little sign to date of UK goods exports to non-EU countries making up for lower exports to the EU, with the former down 18 % on 2019 levels'.[4] Services trade has fallen to 5 per cent lower than 2019 levels and 10 per cent lower to non-EU states. EU service imports to the UK were down by 30 per cent from 2019 levels. One study confirmed that 17 per cent of German companies have ceased to export to the UK. Although some of this can be contributed to the pandemic, the OBR observes that, although other advanced economies' trade volumes had rebounded to 3 per cent above their pre-pandemic levels, UK exports remained 12 per cent below pre-pandemic levels with an accompanying 12 per cent fall in GDP, twice that of other G7 states. Meanwhile, the UK remains London-centric with responsibility for a quarter of the UK's GDP, with income highly dependent on digital markets.

Creative industries can no longer apply for Creative Europe funding and UK cities can no longer apply to be European Capitals of Culture under EU structural funding. Replacement funding is uneven, with funding for film and gaming not having changed considerably post-Brexit, but the UK is making substantial cuts to public service broadcasting and the creative arts sector. There is a government push for a more global focus on British content with greater dependence on the market and tax relief for funding. This has resulted in an influx of funding from the US large platforms for content production in particular, but less funding for independent UK producers.

Brexit is affecting the policy trajectories of the UK and the EU in the area of digital market regulation. EU integration is advancing faster with the internal market approach applied to areas only addressed to date with soft governance instruments. The DSA and also the European Media Freedom Act are sound examples of this, under which the EU is harmonising national approaches to content regulation, the protection of editorial independence, media pluralism tests, and the transparency of state advertising. The UK was historically opposed to this level of European integration.

EU digital market legislation has increasingly incorporated the EU's recent policy on digital sovereignty. The policy was launched by the Von der Leyen Commission, which identified digital markets as key political priorities which 'would require the Union to update and adapt a number of its current legal, regulatory and financial instruments, and to promote more actively European values and principles'.[5] This can be seen in decision-making around supercomputers and cloud computing in particular, which closes off markets to the UK. The EU is also expected to bring in tougher rules on the Internet of Things (Espinoza, 2022). It is even proposing to build an EU domain name system infrastructure with its Domain Name System for

[4] https://obr.uk/box/the-latest-evidence-on-the-impact-of-brexit-on-uk-trade [last accessed 25.10.2022].

[5] www.europarl.europa.eu/RegData/etudes/BRIE/2020/651992/EPRS_BRI(2020)651992_EN.pdf [last accessed 25.10.2022].

the European Union (DNS4EU) initiative under the EU Cybersecurity Package. Much of the digital sovereignty policy is aimed at strengthening European companies and maintaining infrastructure and data on European soil.

This is flanked by stricter rules on data protection, as shown by the 2022 ECJ decision in joined Cases C-37/20 and C-601/20, Luxembourg Business Registers and the Sovim Anti-money-laundering Directive. The court struck down a provision within the EU's 5th Anti-Money Laundering Directive requiring provide public access to beneficial ownership registers based upon data protection grounds. The EU is clearly placing here requirements of personal data protection enshrined in the GDPR above the transparency of company beneficial owners. This level of transparency was long lobbied for by the UK. It is not clear yet what effect this will have on the UK's Companies House given that the UK is bound by GDPR rules. This is consistent with the European Commission's mandate that Internet Corporation for Assigned Names and Numbers permit domain name registries to redact registrant contact information from public display under the GDPR. The EU's turn to statutory instruments makes it more difficult for the UK to participate under EU-level soft initiatives post-Brexit. As detailed in this book, the UK continues to participate, for example, in the European Advertising Standards Alliance agreement for cross-border advertising complaints and the EU Code of Practice on Disinformation. It also has potential to participate in NRA fora such as BEREC and ERGA under association status. However, the EU legislative train is increasingly closing the UK out of future initiatives as it turns away from soft solutions to regulatory problems towards harder measures.

Indeed, the acceleration of EU legislation is causing problems for the UK in that domestic legislation is 'frozen' in many areas as the EU moves forward. Since the end of the transition period, the EU has moved ahead with a large number of significant regulations for the digital sector, particularly the AI Act, Data Act, DSA, DORA, DMA, European Chips Act, MiCA, NIS II, and the Omnibus Directive. Although the UK has proposed its own initiatives in many of these areas, it is lagging behind the EU legislation agenda and reliant on former versions of EU legislation enacted before the end of the transition period.

As shown in Chapters 5 and 11, the EU prefers to liaise with the UK through international treaty platforms rather than bilateral agreements. This was shown by its preference to deal with the UK via the Hague Convention, the Organisation for Economic Co-operation and Development (OECD), and the World Trade Organization (WTO) rather than through bilateral sector agreements or approving the UK's application to the Lugano Convention in a clear rejection of the 'Swiss model'. Instead, UK NRAs have been establishing agreements between the UK and key member states, for example in the oversight of FinTech and online platforms, where bilateral memoranda of understanding have been put into place with European NRAs.

This has pushed the UK to international-level solutions. This can be seen most starkly in the area of data protection. During its presidency of the G7 in 2021, it established the Global Pandemic Data Alliance and common principles for trusted government access to personal data under the G7 Trade Ministers' Digital Trade Principles.[6] It has sought agreement within the OECD's Working Party on Data Governance and Privacy in the Digital Economy. The UK is also playing a significant role in the negotiation of the revised WTO E-Commerce Joint Initiative.

The UK is also focusing on digital trade in free-trade agreements (FTAs) with non-EU states. As detailed in the chapters, it has commenced FTAs with Australia, Comoros, EFTA (Iceland, Liechtenstein, and Norway), ESA (Mauritius, Seychelles, and Zimbabwe), Madagascar, Turkey, and New Zealand and economic partnership agreements with Japan and Singapore. In 2022, it initiated FTAs with Jordan, Chile, and a new agreement with Canada. As FTAs are subject to scrutiny by the WTO, the latter are currently undergoing approval at the international level.[7] Further states have been considered for agreements.[8]

The role of the state

Lastly, the book's findings add to wider conclusions regarding the important role of the state as a policy entrepreneur. A question arises as to whether the UK is unique in this role. The time, energy, and resources spent by UK stakeholders on lobbying are generally much higher than other member states. This could be attributed to key features of the UK political system and its pluralist style of interest representation. Extensive open consultation over legislative proposals is much more common in the UK than in continental Europe. This is due to the centralisation of power in the UK which is not shared between large numbers of actors with veto powers, as would be the case in many continental European states.[9]

As noted by many authors, policy networks characterise British policy-making areas, wherein the private sector, government departments, professional organisations, civil society, and other key interests engage in complex bargaining processes. This encourages a higher level of lobbying activity which historically spilled over from the UK to the EU level with a large number of UK-based interest groups represented in consultations. German and French organisations by contrast, are represented in the EU by large umbrella associations. To date, the EU institutional consultation style has mimicked the UK pluralist style of lobbying (Richardson, 2013).

[6] www.gov.uk/government/news/g7-trade-ministers-digital-trade-principles [last accessed 25.10.2022].

[7] www.wto.org/english/news_e/news22_e/rta_27jun22_e.htm [last accessed 25.10.2022].

[8] https://commonslibrary.parliament.uk/research-briefings/cbp-9314 [last accessed 25.10.2022].

[9] For example, when the French government launched public consultations on the right to be forgotten, response rates were much lower than in the UK and the survey limited the number of respondents.

Historically, this enabled UK-based stakeholders to drown out competing voices in DSM policy formation. Brexit may signal an end to pluralist lobbying in the EU and a return to more neo-corporatist models of representation within the sector. As Menz (2003: 549) explains, 'strongly neo-corporatist and statist systems produce self-preserving protectionist responses'. In addition to the loss of UK state representation in the EU, this would greatly change the opportunity structure for UK-based stakeholders. It is predicted that, as the UK liberal model wanes, the EU will take a much more hands-on approach to regulation of the digital sector, following an older path of industrial policy favouring the growth of European champions and the curtailing of large US groups in European markets.

References

Ackrill, R, and Kay, A (2011) 'Multiple streams in EU policy-making: The case of the 2005 sugar reform' *Journal of European Public Policy* 18(1): 72–89.

Ackrill, R, Kay, A, and Zahariadis, N (2013) 'Ambiguity, multiple streams, and EU policy' *Journal of European Public Policy* 20(6): 871–87.

Apa, E and Gangemi, G (2021) 'The promotion of European works by audiovisual media service providers'. In P Parcu and E Brogi (eds.) *Research Handbook on EU Media Law and Policy*. Northampton, MA: Edward Elgar Publishing, pages 326–51.

Aplin, T (2019) 'United Kingdom'. In B Lindner and T Shapiro (eds.) *Copyright in the Information Society: A Guide to National Implementation of the European Directive*. Northampton, MA: Edward Elgar Publishing, pages 952–81.

Arner, D, Barberis, J, and Buckey, R (2017) 'FinTech, RegTech, and the reconceptualization of financial regulation' *Northwestern Journal of International Law & Business* 37(3): 371–414.

Article 29 Working Party (2013) Advice Paper on Essential Elements of a Definition and a Provision on Profiling within the EU General Data Protection Regulation. 13 May 2013.

Association of Licensed Multiple Retailers (2019) Written evidence to the House of Lords EU Internal Market Sub-Committee Inquiry into trade in non-financial services after Brexit.

Bastos, M and Mercea, D (2019) 'The Brexit botnet and user-generated hyperpartisan news' *Social Science Computer Review* 37(1): 38–54.

Bechtel, M (2020) 'Algorithmic notification and monetization: Using YouTube's content ID system as a model for European Union copyright reform' *Michigan State International Law Review* 28(2): 237–72.

Bellucci, L (2010) 'National support for film production in the EU: An analysis of the Commission decision-making practice' *European Law Journal* 16(2): 211–32.

BFI (2022) An Economic Review of UK's Independent Film. www.bfi.org.uk/industry-data-insights/reports/economic-review-uk-independent-film.

Bickel, F (2021) *Customs Unions in the WTO: Problems with Anti-Dumping*. Cham, Switzerland: Springer International Publishing.

Blázquez, F, Cappello, M, Fontaine, M, Talavera Milla, J, and Valais, S (2018) 'Brexit: The impact on the audiovisual sector' European Audiovisual Observatory. https://rm.coe.int/09000016808f064f.

Bosher, H (2021) *Copyright in the Music Industry: A Practical Guide to Exploiting and Enforcing Rights*. Northampton, MA: Edward Elgar Publishing.

Bradford, A (2020) *The Brussels Effect: How the European Union Rules the World*. Oxford: Oxford University Press.

Bradshaw, S and Howard, P (2019) 'The global disinformation order: 2019 Global Inventory of Organised Social Media Manipulation'. Working Paper 2019.3. Oxford: Project on Computational Propaganda. comprop.oii.ox.ac.uk.

Brittan, L (1995) 'Why Europe needs competition' *Intermedia* 23(4): 8.

Brittan, L (2000) 'The early days of EC merger control'. *EC Merger Control: Ten Years On*. 10th Anniversary Conference Held in Brussels in September 2000. European Commission Directorate General for Competition and the International Bar Association.

Cabrera Blázquez F, Cappello M, Enrich E, Talavera Milla J, and Valais S (2018) 'The legal framework for international co-productions'. *IRIS Plus*, Strasbourg: European Audiovisual Observatory. https://rm.coe.int/iris-plus-2018-3-the-legal-framework-forinternational-co-productions/168090369b.

Cañedo, A, Rodríguez-Castro, M, and López-Cepeda, A (2022) 'Distilling the value of public service media: Towards a tenable conceptualisation in the European framework' *European Journal of Communication* 37(6) 586–605.

Carlini, R (2021) 'Digital taxation and media policy'. In P Parcu and E Brogi (eds.) *Research Handbook on EU Media Law and Policy*. Northampton, MA: Edward Elgar Publishing, pages 249–62.

Cini, M and Czulno, P (2022) 'Digital single market and the EU competition regime: An explanation of policy change' *Journal of European Integration* 44(1): 41–57.

City of London and HM Treasury (2022) State of the sector: Annual review of UK financial services. https://assets.publishing.service.gov.uk/government/uploads/system/uploads/attachment_data/file/1092788/State_of_the_sector_annual_review_of_UK_financial_services_2022.pdf.

Claveloux, D (1993) 'EC splits over telecom policy' *Electronics* 66(3): 3.

Council of Europe (2017) 'Information disorder: Toward an interdisciplinary framework for research and policy making', commissioned report authored by Claire Wardle and Hossein Derakhshan, DGI(2017)09. https://edoc.coe.int/en/media/7495-information-disorder-toward-an-interdisciplinary-framework-for-research-and-policy-making.html.

Coulibaly, S (2021) 'A study of the factors affecting mobile money penetration rates in the West African Economic and Monetary Union (WAEMU) compared with East Africa' *Financial Innovation* 7(1): 1–26.

Couzigou, I (2021) 'The French legislation against digital information manipulation in electoral campaigns: A scope limited by freedom of expression' *Election Law Journal: Rules, Politics, and Policy* 21(1): 98–115.

Craufurd-Smith, R (2003) 'European community audiovisual policy and review of the Television without Frontiers Directive' *European Current Law* xi–xvi.

Craufurd-Smith, R (2019) 'Fake news, French law and democratic legitimacy: Lessons for the United Kingdom?' *Journal of Media Law* 11(1): 52–81.

Creative Industries Council (2021) *Games: Why the UK*. 9 January 2021.

Cross-Border Commerce Europe (2022) *TOP 16 Cross-Border EU Countries*. Brussels, 23 June 2022.

Cuan-Baltazar, J, Muñoz-Perez, M, Robledo-Vega, C, Pérez-Zepeda, M, and Soto-Vega, E (2020) 'Misinformation of COVID-19 on the internet: Infodemiology study' *JMIR Public Health and Surveillance* 6(2): e18444.

Currie, W, Gozman, D, Seddon, J, and Jonathan, J (2018) 'Dialectic tensions in the financial markets: A longitudinal study of pre- and post-crisis regulatory technology' *Journal of Information Technology London* 33(4): 304–25.

De la Porte, C (2002) 'Is the open method of coordination appropriate for organising activities at European level in sensitive policy areas?' *European Law Journal* 8(1): 38–58.

de Streel, A and Hocepied, C (2021) 'The EU regulation of electronic communications networks and services'. In P Parcu and E Brogi (eds.) *Research Handbook on EU Media Law and Policy*. Northampton, MA: Edward Elgar Publishing, pages 111–40.

Department for Culture, Media and Sport (DCMS) (2014) Creative Industries Economic Estimates. www.gov.uk/government/uploads/system/uploads/attachment_data/file/271008/Creative_Industries_Economic_Estimates_-_January_2014.pdf.

Department for Culture, Media and Sport (DCMS) (2018a) Digital Sector Economic Estimates. www.gov.uk/government/statistics/dcms-sectors-economic-estimates-2017-gva.

Department for Digital, Culture, Media and Sport (2018b) Disinformation and 'fake news': Interim Report (HC 363), 29 July 2018. https://publications.parliament.uk/pa/cm201719/cmselect/cmcumeds/363/36302.htm.

Department for Culture, Media and Sport (DCMS) (2021a) DCMS Sectors Economic Estimates 2019: Trade in services. 11 February.

Department for Culture, Media and Sport (DCMS) (2021b) DCMS Sectors Economic Estimates 2019: Trade in services. June 2021.

Department for Digital, Culture, Media and Sport (DCMA) and the Home Office (2019) 'Online Harms White Paper'. April. Command Paper 57. https://assets.publishing.service.gov.uk/government/uploads/system/uploads/attachment_data/file/793360/Online_Harms_White_Paper.pdf.

Digital Catapult (2019) Written evidence (TAS0013) House of Lords EU Internal Market Sub-Committee Inquiry into trade in non-financial services after Brexit. https://committees.parliament.uk/writtenevidence/73664/html/.

Digital, Culture, Media, and Sport (2019) Committee of the British House of Commons Final Report into Disinformation and 'Fake News'. https://committees.parliament.uk/committee/378/digital-culture-media-and-sport-committee/news/103668/disinformation-and-fake-news-final-report-published/.

Dobber, T, Ó Fathaigh, R, and Zuiderveen Borgesius, F (2019) 'The regulation of online political micro-targeting in Europe' *Internet Policy Review* 8(4): 1–20.

Donders, K (2015) 'State aid to public service media' *European State Aid Law Quarterly* 14(1): 68–87.

Dongchul, K and Kimm, M (2020) 'Trade negotiations in the digital era: The case of OTT video streaming services' *Global Policy* 11(2): 14–22.

Dyson, K (2009) 'The evolving timscapes of European economic governance: Contesting and using time' *Journal of European Pubilc Policy* 16(2): 286–306.

Dyson, K and Humphreys, P (1990) *The Political Economy of Communications: International and European Dimensions*. London: Routledge.

Dyson, K and Quaglia, L (2010) *European Economic Governance and Policies: Volume II: Commentary on Key Policy Documents*. Oxford: Oxford University Press.

Edwards, L (2019) *Law, Policy and the Internet*. Oxford: Hart Publishing.

Edwards, L, Schafer, B, and Harbinja, E (2020) *Future Law: Emerging Technology, Regulation and Ethics*. Edinburgh: Edinburgh University Press.

Esping-Andersen, G (1990) *The Three Worlds of Welfare Capitalism*. Princeton, NJ: Princeton University Press.

European Audiovisual Observatory (EAO) (2018) 'Brexit in Context: The UK in the EU28 Audiovisual Market'. https://rm.coe.int/brexit-in-context/16808b868c.

European Audiovisual Observatory (EAO) (2022) 'Investing in European works: The obligations on VOD providers'. https://rm.coe.int/iris-plus-2022en2-financial-obligations-for-vod-services/1680a6889c.

European Commission (1997) 'Building the European information society for us all'. High Level Group of Experts. Final version, April. (Convergence report)

European Commission (2010) 'A comprehensive approach on personal data protection in the European Union'. COM(2010) 609 final.

European Commission (2015) 'Public consultation on Directive 2010/13/EU on Audiovisual Media Services (AVMSD): A media framework for the 21st century'. 06.07.2015. http://

ec.europa.eu/digital-agenda/en/news/public-consultation-directive-201013eu-audiovisual-media-services-avmsd-media-framework-21st.

European Commission (2016) 'Better regulations for innovation-driven investment at EU level'. Directorate-General for Research and Innovation. https://ec.europa.eu/info/law/law-making-process/planning-and-proposing-law/better-regulation-why-and-how/better-regulation-guidelines-and-toolbox_en.

European Commission (2018a) 'Study on emerging issues on collective licensing practices in the digital environment'. Final Report for the Directorate-General for Communications Networks, Content and Technology (DG CNECT) of the European Commission, SMART 2018/0069. https://data.europa.eu/doi/10.2759/611658.

European Commission (2018) 'Final report of the High Level Expert Group on fake news and online disinformation'. https://ec.europa.eu/digital-single-market/en/news/final-report-high-level-expert-group-fake-news-and-online-disinformation.

European Commission, Directorate-General for Communications Networks, Content and Technology (2017) 'An economic analysis of the impact of some online intermediaries on the distribution of copyright protected content'. Final report, Publications Office. https://data.europa.eu/doi/10.2759/75012.

European Commission, Directorate-General for Communications Networks, Content and Technology (2021) 'Study on selected issues relating to the application of the CRM Directive'. Final report, Publications Office. https://data.europa.eu/doi/10.2759/91877.

European Investment Bank (2016) Banking in sub-Saharan Africa: Recent Trends and Digital Financial Inclusion. November. https://www.eib.org/attachments/efs/economic_report_banking_africa_digital_financial_inclusion_en.pdf.

European Research Centre for Economic and Financial Governance (2017) 'Implications of Brexit on EU financial Services'. www.europarl.europa.eu/RegData/etudes/STUD/2017/602058/IPOL_STU(2017)602058_EN.pdf.

Eurostat (2021) 'E-commerce statistics for individuals 27/01/2021'. https://ec.europa.eu/eurostat/statistics-explained/pdfscache/46776.pdf.

Fanta, A and Dachwitz, I (2020) 'Google, the media patron: How the digital giant ensnares journalism'. A project of the Otto Brenner Foundation (OBS) Frankfurt am Main. www.otto-brenner-stiftung.de/fileadmin/user_data/stiftung/02_Wissenschaftsportal/03_Publikationen/AH103_Google_EN.pdf.

Faucher, C (2022) 'Resilience and adaptation of the UK's arts sector during the process of the UK's withdrawal from the EU' *International Journal of Cultural Policy*. December.

Ferrari, V (2022) 'The platformisation of digital payments: The fabrication of consumer interest in the EU FinTech agenda' *Computer Law & Security Review* 45: 1–20.

Finck, M and Pallas, F (2020) 'They who must not be identified—distinguishing personal from non-personal data under the GDPR' *International Data Privacy Law* 10(1): 11–36.

Floridi, L (2020) 'The fight for digital sovereignty: What it is, and why it matters, especially for the EU' *Philosophy & Technology* 33: 369–78.

Ganter, S (2022) 'Governance of news aggregators' practices across five emblematic cases: Policy regimes between normative acceptance and resistance' *The Information Society* 38(4): 290–306.

García-Orosa, B, Gamallo, P, Martín-Rodilla, P, and Rodrigo M (2021) 'Hybrid intelligence strategies for identifying, classifying and analyzing political bots' *Social Sciences* 10(10): 1–18.

Gibbons, T and Humphreys, P (2011) *Audiovisual Regulation under Pressure: Comparative Cases from North America and Europe*. London: Routledge.

Godin, E and Chafer, T (2006) *The French Exception*. Oxford: Berghahn Books.

Golberg, E (2018) 'Better regulation: European Union STYLE'. September 2018. M-RCBG Associate Working Paper Series, No. 98, Mossavar-Rahmani Center for Business & Government Weil Hall. Harvard Kennedy School. www.hks.harvard.edu/mrcbg.

González-Tosat, C and Sádaba-Chalezquer, C (2021) 'DNI's DNA: Where is Google's money in European media?' *Sustainability* 13(20): 11457.

Greenwood, J (2003) *The Challenge of Change in EU Business Associations*. London: Palgrave Macmillan.

GSMA (2018) State of the Industry Report on Mobile Money. www.gsma.com/r/wp-content/uploads/2019/05/GSMA-State-of-the-Industry-Report-on-Mobile-Money-2018-1.pdf.

Hahn, W (1982) Report drawn up on behalf of the Committee on Youth, Culture, Education, Information and Sport on radio and television broadcasting in the European Community. Working Documents 1981-82, Document 1-1013/81, 23 February 1982. [EU European Parliament Document].

Harcourt, A (2003) 'Europeanisation as convergence: The regulation of media markets in the European Union'. In K Featherstone and C Radaelli (eds.) *The Politics of Europeanization*. Oxford: Oxford University Press, pages 179–203.

Harcourt, A (2012) '"Cultural coalitions" and international regulatory co-operation' *Journal of Common Market Studies* 50(5): 709–725.

Haskins, C (1999) 'Regulation and risk: Striking the right balance' *European Business Journal* 11(1): 2.

Heldt, A (2019) 'Reading between the lines and the numbers: An analysis of the first NetzDG reports' *Internet Policy Review* 8(2): 1–18.

Herold, A (2002) 'Rules governing the acquisition by third parties of television rights for sporting events under Eurovision in breach of the European competition law' *International Journal of Communications Law and Policy* 7.

Hildén, J (2019) 'The politics of datafication: The influence of lobbyists on the EU's data protection reform and its consequences for the legitimacy of the General Data Protection Regulation'. Doctoral thesis (Monograph). University of Helsinki.

Hildén, J (2021) 'Lobby in/policy out? Assessing lobbyist influence on the GDPR' *European Data Protection Law Review* 7(4): 520–38.

HM Treasury (2020) 'News story review launched to boost UK Fintech sector'. www.gov.uk/government/news/review-launched-to-boost-uk-fintech-sector.

HMRC (2018) 'Corporate tax and the digital economy: Position paper update'. Position paper. March. https://assets.publishing.service.gov.uk/government/uploads/system/uploads/attachment_data/file/689240/corporate_tax_and_the_digital_economy_update_web.pdf.

Hörnle, J (2021) *Internet Jurisdiction Law and Practice*. Oxford: Oxford University Press.

House of Lords (2007) European Union Committee 3rd Report of Session 2006–07: Television without Frontiers?. 23 January.

House of Lords (2013a) 3rd Report—Supporting the creative economy: Volume I. HC 674. 26 September.

House of Lords (2013b) *European Union Committee 3rd Report of Session 2006–7: Television Without Frontiers?* London: House of Lords.

House of Lords European Affairs Committee (2022) 'The UK-EU relationship in financial services', HL Paper 21 of session June 2022–23.

Howells, G, Twigg-Flesner, C, and Wilhelmsson, T (2017) *Rethinking EU Consumer Law*. London: Routledge.

Humphreys, P (2005) 'The EU: An Agency for De-Regulation or Re-Regulation? A Case Study of Audiovisual Regulation' 3rd General Conference of the European Consortium for Political Research (ECPR), 8–10 September. Budapest, Hungary.

Humphreys, P (2010) 'EU state aid rules, public service broadcasters' online media engagement and Public Value Tests: The German and UK cases compared' *Interactions: Studies in Communication & Culture* 1(2): 171–84.

IMRG (2021) Cross-border index. www.imrg.org.

Incorporated Society of Musicians (2019) Written evidence submitted to the Culture, Media and Sport Committee inquiry into the impact of Brexit on the creative industries, tourism, and the Digital Single Market.

Indepen, Ovum and Gathom (2005) 'Extension of the Television Without Frontiers Directive: An impact assessment'. Final report for Ofcom, September. www.ofcom.org.uk/__data/assets/pdf_file/0024/16179/twf.pdf.

Information Commissioner's Office (ICO) (2013) Implications of the European Commission's proposal for a general data protection regulation for business Final report to the Information Commissioner's Office by London Economics. https://ico.org.uk/media/about-the-ico/documents/1042341/implications-european-commissions-proposal-general-data-protection-regulation-for-business.pdf.

Ingram, M (2018) 'The platform patrons: How Facebook and Google became two of the biggest funders of journalism in the world' *Columbia Journalism Review* 16 May.

Internal Revenue Services (2018) Internal Revenue Bulletin. Notice 2014-21. 25 March. www.irs.gov/pub/irs-drop/n-14-21.pdf.

James, S and Quaglia, L (2020) *The UK and Multi-Level Financial Regulation: From Post-Crisis Reform to Brexit*. Oxford: Oxford University Press.

Jaursch, J (2020) 'Defining Online Political Advertising. How Difficulties in Delineating Paid Political Communication Can Be Addressed'. Report for the Stiftung Neue Vergantwortung. www.stiftung-nv.de/sites/default/files/snv_definingpoliticalads.pdf.

Joint statement by the Chancellor of the Exchequer and the Finance Minister of India at the 9th UK–India Economic and Financial Dialogue held in Delhi on 4 April 2017.

Katsirea, I (2014) 'The Television Without Frontiers Directive'. In K Donders, C Pauwels, and J Loisen (eds.) *The Palgrave Handbook of European Media Policy*. London: Palgrave Macmillan, pages 297–31.

Katsirea, I (2017) 'Newspaper websites as audiovisual media services: The new media online GmbH preliminary ruling' *European Law Review* 42(1): 92–100.

Katsirea, I (2019) '"Fake news": Reconsidering the value of untruthful expression in the face of regulatory uncertainty' *Journal of Media Law* 10(2): 159–88.

Kingdon, JW (1994) 'Agendas, ideas, and policy change'. In *New Perspectives on American Politics*. Washington, DC: CQ Press, pages 215–29.

Kingdon, JW (1995) *Agendas, Alternatives, and Public Policies* (2nd ed.). Longman, MI: The University of Michigan.

Kingdon, J (2011) *Agendas, Alternatives, and Public Policies*. London: HarperCollins.

Kohl, U (2017) *The Net and the Nation State: Multidisciplinary Perspectives on Internet Governance*. Cambridge: Cambridge University Press.

Kolkman, O (2021) 'NIS2 Inconsistency—A DNS Supply Chain Perspective' *Internet Society Blog*. December 2021. www.internetsociety.org/blog/2021/12/nis2-inconsistency-a-dns-supply-chain-perspective/.

Kostovskak, I, Raats, T, and Donders, K (2020) 'The rise of the "Netflix tax" and what it means for sustaining European audiovisual markets' *The European Journal of Social Science Research* 33(1): 1–19.

KPMG (2021) 'Taxation of the digitalized economy: Developments summary'. https://tax.kpmg.us/content/dam/tax/en/pdfs/2021/digitalized-economy-taxation-developments-summary.pdf.

Kramler, T (2017) 'The European Commission's e-commerce sector inquiry' *Journal of European Competition Law & Practice* 8(2): 81.

Krebber, D (2001) *Europeanisation of Regulatory Television Policy*. Baden-Baden: Nomos.

Kuhn, R (1994) *The Media in France*. London: Routledge.

Lang, JT (1997) 'Media, Multimedia and European Community Antitrust Law', Directorate-General for Competition (IV), European Commission.

Lange, B and Lechterman, T (2021) 'Combating disinformation with AI: Epistemic and ethical challenges' *IEEE International Symposium on Technology and Society* (ISTAS) October: 28–31.

Leathers, D (2009) 'Giving bite to the EU–US data privacy safe harbor: Model solutions for effective enforcement' *Case Western Reserve Journal of International Law* 41: 193.

Leiva, MTG and Albornoz, LA (2021) 'VOD service providers and regulation in the European Union: An audiovisual diversity approach' *International Journal of Cultural Policy* 7(3): 267–81.

Lips, W (2020) 'The EU Commission's digital tax proposals and its cross-platform impact in the EU and the OECD' *Journal of European Integration* 42(7): 975–90.

Mac Sithigh, D (2017) '"TV-like": Aesthetics, quality and genre in the regulation of video-on-demand services' *Journal of British Cinema and Television* 14(4): 464–84.

Madelin, R and Ringrose, D (2016) *Opportunity Now: Europe's Mission to Innovate*. Luxembourg: Publications Office of the European Union. https://www.oecd.org/education/ceri/GEIS2016-MadelinReport-Full.pdf.

Marchal, N, Kollanyi, B, Neudert, L, and Howard, P (2019) 'Junk news during the EU parliamentary elections: Lessons from a seven-language study of Twitter and Facebook'. *Data Memo*, https://comprop.oii.ox.ac.uk/wp-content/uploads/sites/93/2019/05/EU-Data-Memo.pdf.

Marsden, C (2010) *Net Neutrality: Towards a Co-regulatory Solution*. London: Bloomsbury Academic.

Marsden, C (2013) 'Network neutrality: A research guide'. In I Brown (ed.) *Research Handbook on Governance of the Internet*. Cheltenham: Edward Elgar Publications, pages 419–44.

Marsden, C and Meyer, T (2019) 'How can the law regulate removal of fake news?' *Society for Computers and Law*. www.scl.org/articles/10425-how-can-the-law-regulate-removal-of-fake-news.

Marsden, C, Meyer, T, and Brown, I (2020) 'How can the law regulate digital disinformation?' *Computer Law & Security Review* 36.

Martens, B, Aguiar, L, Gomez-Herrera, E, and Mueller-Langer, F (2018) 'The digital transformation of news media and the rise of disinformation and fake news', *JRC Technical Reports*. ec.europa.eu/jrc/communities/sites/jrccties/files/dewp_201802_digital_transformation_of_news_media_and_the_rise_of_fake_news_final_180418.pdf.

Mazey, S and Richardson, J (1993) *Lobbying in the European Community*. Oxford: Oxford University Press.

Mazziotti, G (2010) 'New licensing models for online music services in the European Union: From collective to customized management' *Columbia Journal of Law & the Arts* 34: 757.

Mazziotti, G (2021) 'The intersection of EU media policy and copyright: Protecting the value of cultural creation in television and online content services'. In P Parcu and E Brogi (eds.) *Research Handbook on EU Media Law and Policy*. Northampton, MA: Edward Elgar Publishing, pages 208–34.

McCullagh, K (2007) 'Data sensitivity: Proposals for resolving the conundrum' *Journal of International Commercial Law and Technology* 2(4): 190–201.

McDonagh, L (2022) 'Directive 2019/790/EU (Directive on copyright and related rights in the digital single market). In AR Lodder and AD Murray (eds.) *EU Regulation of E-commerce: A Commentary*. London: Edward Elgar Publishing, pages 308–33.

McGowan, L and Cini, M (1999) 'Governance discretion and politicization in EU competition policy: The case of merger control' *Governance* 12(2): 175–200.

Menz, G (2003) 'Re-regulating the Single Market: National varieties of capitalism and their responses to europeanization' *Journal of European Public Policy* 10(4): 532–55.

Merdi, T (2017) 'The 2018 new deal on better enforcement and modernisation of EU consumer law: An actually good digital deal?' In TE Synodinou, P Jougleux, C Markou, and T Prastitou (eds.) *EU Internet Law in the Digital Era: Regulation and Enforcement*. Cham, Switzerland: Springer, pages 347–65.

Michalis, M (2007) *Governing European Communications: From Unification to Coordination*. Lanham: Lexington Books.

Michalis, M (2014) 'Focal points of European media policy from inception till present: Plus ça change?' In K Donders, C Pauwels, and J Loisen (eds.) *The Palgrave Handbook of European Media Policy*. London: Palgrave Macmillan, pages 128–42.

Micklitz, H and Villanueva, A (2019) 'REFIT or Rethink. The Politics of EU Research: A Grand Misunderstanding?' In E van Schagen and A Weatherill (eds.) *Better Regulation in EU Contract Law: The Fitness Check and the New Deal for Consumers*. London: Hart Publishing, pages 37–60.

Morgan, EJ (2000) 'Subsidiarity and the division of jurisdiction in EU merger control' *The Antitrust Bulletin* 45(1): 153–93.

Mutu, A (2021) 'The determinants of independence of audiovisual media regulators: The scope of Article 30'. In P Parcu and E Brogi (eds.) *Research Handbook on EU Media Law and Policy*. Northampton, MA: Edward Elgar Publishing, pages 352–64.

Mylly, U and Herrero, M (2022) 'Free movement of audiovisual content for benefit of European consumers of culture' *IIC: International Review of Intellectual Property and Competition Law* 53: 1038–70.

Natalicchi, G (2001) *Wiring Europe: Reshaping the European Telecommunications Regime*. Lanham, MD: Rowman & Littlefield Publishers.

Nelson, M and Jaursch, J (2020) 'Germany's new media treaty demands that platforms explain algorithms and stop discriminating. Can it deliver?' *Algorithm Watch*. 9 March 2020. https://algorithmwatch.org/en/new-media-treaty-germany/.

Nenadić, I and Verza, S (2022) 'European policymaking on disinformation and the standards of the ECtHR'. In E Psychogiopoulou and S de la Sierra (eds.) *Digital Media Governance and Supranational Courts*. Northampton, MA: Edward Elgar Publishing, pages 175–98.

Nicoletti, B (2017) *The Future of FinTech: Integrating Finance and Technology in Financial Services*. London: Palgrave Macmillan.

Nikoltchev, S. (2015) 'Territoriality and its impact on the financing of audiovisual works', IRIS Plus. Strassbourg: European Audiovisual Observatory.

Ofcom (2012) Ofcom Guidelines for dealing with regulators of other EU Member States in Relation to UK Licensed Television Channels and UK Based On-Demand Services. http://stakeholders.ofcom.org.uk/binaries/broadcast/international/Procedural_Guidelines.pdf.

Ofcom (2014) UK communications deals cheaper than in other major countries. The Communications Market Report: International. http://stakeholders.ofcom.org.uk/market-data-research/market-data/communications-market-reports/cmr14/international.

Ofcom (2022) Media nations UK 2022. www.ofcom.org.uk/__data/assets/pdf_file/0016/242701/media-nations-report-2022.pdf.

OSCE (2017) Joint Declaration on Freedom of Expression and 'Fake News', Disinformation and Propaganda. www.osce.org/fom/302796.

Oxford Economics (2007) 'The Economic Impact of the UK Film Industry'. Supported by the UK Film Council and Pinewood Shepperton plc. www2.bfi.org.uk/sites/bfi.org.uk/files/downloads/uk-film-council-economic-impact-of-the-uk-film-industry.pdf.

Palmer, M and Tunstall, J (1991) *Media Moguls*. London: Taylor & Francis Group.

Papis-Almansa, M (2019) 'VAT and electronic commerce: The new rules as a means for simplification, combatting fraud and creating a more level playing field?' *ERA Forum* 20: 201–23.

Parenti, R. (2020) *Regulatory Sandboxes and Innovation Hubs for FinTech: Impact on Innovation, Financial Stability and Supervisory Convergence*. Study Requested by the ECON Committee. Luxembourg: Policy Department for Economic, Scientific, and Quality of Life, pages 60–61.

Pauwels, C (2014) 'Genesis and rationales for European intervention in media'. In *The Palgrave Handbook of European Media Policy*. London: Palgrave Macmillan, pages 113–27.

Perarnaud, C (2021) 'A step back to look ahead: Mapping coalitions on dataflows and platform regulation in the Council of the EU (2016–2019)' *Internet PolicyReview* 10(2).

Petley, J (2014) 'The regulation of pornography on video-on-demand in the United Kingdom' *Porn Studies* 1(3): 260–84.

Piffaut, H (2021) 'Chapter 2: Telecommunications, media and internet services'. In C Jones and L Weinert (eds.) *EU Competition Law Volume II: Mergers and Acquisitions*. London: Edward Elgar, pages 939–1160.

Plank, M, Ogunyemi, A, and Blok, J (2020) 'Improving the user experience with audiovisual content: The Project "Europeana Media"' *Bibliothek Forschung und Praxis* 44(3): 445–53.

Porangaba, L (2022) 'Copyright (in design) post-Brexit: Should section 52 of the CDPA 1988 be reinstated?' *European Intellectual Property Review* 44(1): 1–4.

Porter, F (1989) 'The Copyright Designs and Patents Act 1988: The triumph of expediency over principle' *Journal of Law and Society* 16(3): 340–51.

Princen, S (2011) 'Agenda-setting strategies in EU policy processes' *Journal of European Public Policy* 18(7): 927–43.

Publishers Association (2019) Written evidence (TAS0039) Submission to the Lords EU Internal Market Sub-Committee on the inquiry Brexit: Future trade between the UK and the EU. https://committees.parliament.uk/writtenevidence/73998/pdf/.

Quaglia, L (2019) 'The politics of an "incomplete" Banking Union and its "asymmetric" effects' *Journal of European Integration* 41(8): 955–69.

Ramalho, A and Gomez Garcia, M (2017) 'Copyright after Brexit' *Journal of Intellectual Property Law & Practice* 12(8): 669–72.

Ramella, F and Manzo, C (2020) *The Economy of Collaboration: The New Digital Platforms of Production and Consumption*. London: Routledge.

Renda, A, Simonelli, F, Mazziotti, G Bolognini, A, and Luchetta, G (2015) 'The implementation, application and effects of the EU Directive on Copyright in the Information Society'. *CEPS Special Report* No. 120, November. www.ceps.eu/wp-content/uploads/2015/11/SR120_0.pdf.

Richardson, J (2013) 'New governance or old governance? A policy style perspective'. In D Levi-Faur (eds.) *The Oxford Handbook of Governance*. Oxford: Oxford University Press.

Richter, A (2018) 'Fake news and freedom of the media' *Journal of International Media & Entertainment Law* 8(1): 1–34.

Rosati, E (2021) *Routledge Handbook of EU Copyright Law*. London: Routledge.

RWAP Services (2019) Written evidence submitted to the Culture, Media and Sport Committee inquiry into the impact of Brexit on the creative industries, tourism, and the Digital Single Market.

Sandholtz, W (1993) 'Institutions and collective action: The new telecommunications in western Europe' *World Politics* 45(2): 242–70.

Schneeberger, A (2021) 'Audiovisual media services in Europe'. European Audiovisual Observatory (Council of Europe) https://rm.coe.int/audiovisual-media-services-in-europe-2020/1680a2fc29.

Schwemer, S (2019) *Licensing and Access to Content in the European Union: Regulation between Copyright and Competition*. Cambridge: Cambridge University Press.

Senden, L (2005) 'Soft law, self-regulation and co-regulation in European law: Where do they meet?' *Electronic Journal of Comparative Law* 9(1): 1–29.

Smartt, U (2020) *Media & Entertainment Law Media and Entertainment Law* (4th ed.). London: Routledge.

Smith, G (2007) *Internet Law and Regulation*. London: Sweet and Maxwell.

Spiecker Döhmann, I, Tambou, O, Bernal, P, Hu, M, Molinaro, C, Negre, E, Sarlet, I, Mendes, L, Witzleb, N, and Yger, F (2018) 'Multi-country: The Regulation of commercial profiling—A comparative analysis' *European Data Protection Law Review* 2(4): 535–54.

Stokes, S (2019) *Digital Copyright: Law and Practice*. Oxford: Hart Publishing.

Street, J, Laing, D, and Schroff, S (2018) 'Regulating for creativity and cultural diversity: The case of collective management organisations and the music industry' *International Journal of Cultural Policy* 24(3): 368–86.

Swire, P (2007) 'Google and Privacy: Merger with DoubleClick Prompts New Privacy Guidelines' *Center for American Progress*. 20 December.

Tambini, D (2022) 'The democratic fightback has begun: The European Commission's new European Media Freedom Act'. LSE blog. 16 September. https://blogs.lse.ac.uk/europpblog/2022/09/16/the-democratic-fightback-has-begun-the-european-commissions-new-european-media-freedom-act.

Thatcher, M (2001) 'The Commission and national governments as partners: EC regulatory expansion in telecommunications 1979–2000' *Journal of European Public Policy* 8(4): 558–84.

Thatcher, M (2014) 'European Commission merger control: Combining competition and the creation of larger European firms' *European Journal of Political Research* 53(3): 443–60.

Theil, S (2019) 'The Online Harms White Paper: Comparing the UK and German approaches to regulation' *Journal of Media Law* 11(2): 41–51.

Thomas, L (2018) 'The case for a federal regulatory sandbox for fintech companies' *North Carolina Banking Institute* 22: 257–82.

Trade and Cooperation Agreement (TCA) (2020) Between the European Union and the European Atomic Energy Community, of the one part, and the United Kingdom of Great Britain and Northern Ireland, for the other part, 24 December. https://eur-lex.europa.eu/legal-content/EN/TXT/?uri=uriserv%3AOJ.L_.2020.444.01.0014.01.ENG.

UK Digital, Culture, Media and Sport Committee (2017) 'Inquiry into fake news'. www.parliament.uk/business/committees/committees-a-z/commons-select/digital-culture-media-and-sport-committee/inquiries/parliament-2017/fake-news-17-19.

UK Interactive Entertainment (2019) Written evidence (TAS0016) Ukie response to the House of Lords EU Internal Market Sub-Committee's inquiry into the trade in services after Brexit. https://committees.parliament.uk/writtenevidence/73708/pdf/.

Valcke, P and Ausloos, J (2014) 'Audiovisual Media Services 3.0: (Re)defining the scope of European broadcasting law in a converging and connected media environment'. In K Donders, C Pauwels, and J Loisen (eds.) *The Palgrave Handbook of European Media Policy*. Basingstoke: Palgrave Macmillan.

Van Kerckhoven, S (2021) 'Post-Brexit leadership in European finance' *Politics and Governance* 9(1): 59–68.

Veale, M, and Zuiderveen Borgesius, F (2021) 'Demystifying the draft EU Artificial Intelligence Act' *Computers and Society* 22: 97–112.

Vesterdorf, B and Fountoukakos, K (2021) 'A new competition tool into old bottles? Considerations on the legal design of the European Commission's proposed NCT' *Journal of European Competition Law & Practice* 12(4): 284–300.

Vlassis, A (2016) 'European Commission, trade agreements and diversity of cultural expressions: Between autonomy and influence' *European Journal of Communication* 31(4): 446–61.

Walden, I (2018) *Telecommunications Law and Regulation an Introduction*. Oxford: Oxford University Press.

Walden, I, Kemmit, H, and Angel, J (2018) 'The telecommunications regime in the United Kingdom'. In *Telecommunications Law and Regulation: An Introduction*. Oxford: Oxford University Press, pages 101–45.

Wei, D, Nehf, J, and Marques, C (2020) *Innovation and the Transformation of Consumer Law*. Singapore: Springer.

Wheeler, M (2010) 'The European Union's Competition Directorate: State aids and public service broadcasting'. In P Iosifides (ed.) *Reinventing Public Service Communication: European Broadcasters and Beyond*. London: Sage, pages 49–61.

Wilks, S (1999) *In the Public Interest: Competition Policy and the Monopolies and Mergers Commission*. Manchester: Manchester University Press.

Williams, G (2007) 'Behind the screens: Corporate lobbying and the EU audiovisual policy'. In D Miller and W. Dinan (eds.) *Thinker, Faker, Spinner, Spy*. London: Pluto Press.

Williams, G (2017) 'From isolation to consensus: The UK's role in the revision process of the Television Without Frontiers Directive' *Westminster Papers in Communication and Culture* 4(3). https://doi.org/10.16997/wpcc.96.

Witt, A (2022) 'Facebook v. Bundeskartellamt: May European competition agencies apply the GDPR?' *Competition Policy International* TechREG Chronicle, April.

Wong, D and Floridi, L (2022) 'Meta's oversight board: A review and critical assessment' *Minds and Machines* October: 1–19.

Woods, L (2019) 'The duty of care in the Online Harms White Paper' *Journal of Media Law* 11(1): 6–17.

Woods, L and Perrin, W (2022) 'Obliging platforms to accept a duty of care'. In M Moore and D Tambini (eds.) *Regulating Big Tech*. Oxford: Oxford University Press, pages 93–109.

Yar, M (2018) 'A failure to regulate? The demands and dilemmas of tackling illegal content and behavior on social media' *International Journal of Cybersecurity Intelligence & Cybercrime* 1(1): 5–20.

Zahariadis, N (2003) *Ambiguity and Choice in Public Policy: Political Decision Making in Modern Democracies*. Washington, DC: Georgetown University Press.

Zahariadis, N (2007) 'The multiple streams framework: Structure, limitations, prospects'. In P Sabatier (ed.) *Theories of the Policy Process*. Boulder, CO: Westview Press, pages 65–92.

Zinser, A (2004) 'International Data Transfers between the US and EU: Are the procedural provisions of the Safe Harbor solution adequate?' *Computer Law and Security Report* 20(3): 182–84.

Newspaper articles

Barker, Alex and Leila Abboud (2022) 'US streaming giants feel squeeze of regulation in Europe' *Financial Times*. 8 February.

Boffey, Daniel (2021) 'EU prepares to cut amount of British TV and film shown post-Brexit' *The Guardian*. 21 June.

Cain, Sian (2022) 'Netflix is introducing a new subscription with ads. Here's what you need to know' *The Guardian*. 14 October.

Chee, Foo Yun (2022) 'Microsoft faces new EU antitrust complaint on cloud computing practices' *Reuters*. 9 November.

Dziadul, Chris (2021) 'Brexit brings huge channel licence migration' *Broadband News*. 17 June.

Edgecliffe-Johnson, A (2006) 'Media groups blast Brussels over directive' *Financial Times*. 17 April.

England, Andrew (2022) 'Middle East Financial crimes watchdog puts UAE on "grey list"' *Financial Times*. 4 March.

Espinoza, Javier (2022) 'EU to impose tough rules on "internet of things" product makers' *Financial Times*. 27 September.

Espinoza, Javier, Ian Johnston, and Cristina Criddle (2022) 'Closure of Twitter Brussels office prompts online safety fears' *Financial Times*. 24 November.

Garrahan, Matthew (2018) 'Tax relief fuels boom in Britain's film and creative industries' *Financial Times*. 8 October.

Gray, Alistair (2022) 'UK indie production companies battle streamers in talent war' *Financial Times*. 17 October.

Hughs, Emily Anne (2019) 'Why Brexit could be good news for advisors' *Financial Times*. 18 January.

Jones, Rupert (2022) 'A third of UK "buy now, pay later" users say they can't handle payments' *The Guardian*. 23 June.

Killeen, Molly (2022) 'The European Media Freedom Act' *Euroactiv*, podcast, 23 September.

McDonald, Karl (2019) 'UK Netflix, regulated only in the Netherlands, has never faced a complaint despite removing content after misinformation claims' *Inews*. 23 May.

Parker, George and Felicia Schwartz (2022) 'Liz Truss admits UK trade deal with US is not on the agenda' *Financial Times*. 27 September.

Parker, George and Peter Foster in London and Sam Fleming (2022) 'The Brexit standoff: Boris Johnson's Christmas truce in Brussels' *Financial Times*. 18 November.

Thomas, Daniel et al. (2022a) 'Liz Truss plans last-ditch bid to persuade SoftBank to list Arm in London in London and Leo Lewis in Tokyo' *Financial Times*. 15 September.

Thomas, Daniel et al. (2022b) 'UK business and unions demand scrapping of planned bonfire of EU rules in London' *Financial Times*. 23 November.

Venkataramakrishnan, Siddharth (2022) 'Revolut receives green light to run UK cryptocurrency business' *Financial Times*. 27 September.

Webber, Esther (2022) 'UK's Liz Truss admits US trade deal out of reach' *Politico*. 20 September.

Index

For the benefit of digital users, indexed terms that span two pages (e.g., 52–53) may, on occasion, appear on only one of those pages.